THE POWER
OF DISCOURSE

AN INTRODUCTION TO
DISCOURSE ANALYSIS

THE POWER OF DISCOURSE

AN INTRODUCTION TO DISCOURSE ANALYSIS

Moira Chimombo
University of Malawi

Robert L. Roseberry
University of Brunei Darussalam

 LAWRENCE ERLBAUM ASSOCIATES, PUBLISHERS
1998 Mahwah, New Jersey   London

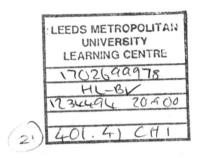

Copyright © 1998 by Lawrence Erlbaum Associates, Inc.
All rights reserved. No part of this book may be reproduced in
any form, by photostat, microfilm, retrieval system, or any other
means, without the prior written permission of the publisher.

Lawrence Erlbaum Associates, Inc., Publishers
10 Industrial Avenue
Mahwah, New Jersey 07430

Cover design by Kathryn Houghtaling Lacey

Cartoon Art by Leah Taylor (p. 65, 69,
107, 153, 171, 185, 247, 290, 349), and
Christopher Chimombo (p. 207).

Library of Congress Cataloging-in-Publication Data

The power of discourse : an introduction to discourse analysis /
    Moira Chimombo and Robert L. Roseberry.
        p.   cm.
    Includes bibliographical references and index.
    ISBN 0-8058-2635-1 (alk. paper). —ISBN 0-8058-2636-X (pbk. :
alk. paper).
    1. Discourse analysis. I. Chimombo, Moira,
II. Roseberry, Robert L., 1945–   . III. Title.
P302.C46 1997
401'.41—dc21   97-14162
                                                                    CIP

Books published by Lawrence Erlbaum Associates are printed on acid-free paper,
and their bindings are chosen for strength and durability.

Printed in the United States of America
10 9 8 7 6 5 4 3 2 1

CONTENTS

PREFACE

The Power of Discourse: An Introduction to Discourse Analysis is intended for students at the high school and university levels who desire a practical introduction to the use of language in daily and professional life. The text is designed for use either as part of a course or as an aid to independent study. Although some familiarity with the basic principles of general linguistics would be helpful, no previous linguistic knowledge is required; and, readers will find that concepts relating to language and discourse are in boldface in the text, explained clearly, illustrated in examples and practice exercises, and defined in the Subect Index With Glosses at the back of the book.

The book has two parts: an introduction to the elements and practice of discourse analysis in general, and an introduction to the actual kinds of discourse crucial to personal and professional life. In Part I, the student is led to an understanding of what discourse and text are, with particular focus on the process of text production and the roles of those involved in this process. Language and context are shown to be the dimensions of discourse, with context determining the form, or *genre*, appropriate for a particular use, and with language describing the *register*, or language choices, that are appropriately used with a given genre. Both the context and the language are analyzable into a number of elements in ways that make them easily accessible to students of discourse.

Chapters 1 and 2 begin with a general introduction explaining the elements in that section. Each element contains explanation, examples, practices, guidelines for analysis, a sample analysis, an application exercise, and suggested readings. The practice and application exercises attempt to involve the student in a personal discovery of different aspects of discourse. For this reason, many of the practices do not have fixed or unique answers. Answers that can be clearly suggested are given in a special section near the end of the book.

To stress the practical purpose of the book, examples and practice exercises frequently make use of a variety of genres many common in daily and professional life. These include advertisement, biography, travel guide, news clipping, prose fiction, students' writing, telephone conversation, poetry, police–suspect interview, face-to-face conversation, war cry, political speech, medical text, legislation, textbook, discourse of the mentally disturbed, detective fiction, and others. Wherever feasible, authentic examples are used.

Part II applies the principles and techniques of Part I to an investigation of discourse in daily use. There are chapters on discourse in education, medicine, law, the media, and literature. These will be of particular interest to students planning to enter any of these professions. But they are also of general interest, because everyone encounters them in daily life. A common theme uniting both parts of the book and playing a major role in part II is the power relationship that exists between producers of discourse and the intended audience. A deeper understanding of this power relationship will not only enable future (and current) professionals to communicate more effectively in their work, but will also give clients a greater sense of control and security in their dealings with these professionals.

GENERAL INTRODUCTION

This book is for individuals who like to talk and listen, read letters or poems, squeeze the "hot air" out of the speeches of politicians, and make sure that advertisers are not able to pull the wool over consumers' eyes. It is a book on discourse and how to analyze it. But more than that, it is a book designed to demonstrate how people—as masters of the language they speak—are already experts in this field and require only some communicative "fine tuning" and some added awareness of what it is that people do when they attempt to communicate through words, gestures, or signs.

First consider **discourse** and what it is. Discourse is a process resulting in a communicative act. The communicative act itself takes the form of a **text**. A text is commonly thought of as consisting of written or printed words on a page; but a text may also consist of sign language or spoken words, or it may comprise only the thoughts of a writer, or speaker, on the one hand, or a reader or listener, on the other. In addition to words, a text may consist of other symbols, sounds, gestures, or silences, in any combination that is intended to communicate information such as ideas, emotional states, and attitudes. It may fail to communicate, but if the intention to communicate is clearly there, it must be regarded as a text. Figure GI.1 shows schematically this relation between discourse and text.

Analysis of discourse is a methodology for examining texts and the communicative process that gives rise to them. Its primary purpose is to enable discourse analysts to gain a deeper understanding and appreciation of texts. Because most texts are goal oriented, part of the

DISCOURSE: A COMMUNICATIVE PROCESS

resulting in a

COMMUNICATIVE ACT

realized as a

TEXT

FIG. GI.1. Discourse: A text-creating process.

purpose of discourse analysis is to enable people to recognize the intended goal of the writer or speaker and thus achieve some measure of control over the discourse. The term *control* implies a power relationship between those who produce texts and those for whom these texts are intended. For example, politicians, lawyers, doctors, advertisers, business executives, teachers, and many others exercise power over their clients through the discourse that is characteristic of these professionals. Analysis of professional discourse can reveal these power relationships and the goals that may be hidden in them. The understanding that may be gained in this way helps to equalize the power relationship and enables an escape from the role of victim such that individuals may assume a greater degree of control over their lives. This book demonstrates that discourse is typically used to a greater or lesser degree for exploitation. Different types of discourse are intended to exploit consumers, voters, employees, children, women, minorities, and many other groups within society. An ability to analyze discourse offers such groups a means of protection.

Goal-oriented power relationships, however, are not the only uses of discourse. Discourse has instructive, descriptive, and narrative uses that help people to understand, appreciate, and create their world. In this sense, discourse provides individuals with a sense of belonging and continuity by passing down the history, folk wisdom, and values of the cultures and groups to which they belong. As art, the discourse of literature provides pleasurable ways of discovering who people are in relation to the world and to the various social and cultural groups it contains. As conversation and correspondence, discourse cements ties among people and helps individuals maintain connections within networks of family and friends.

Discourse is an extremely complex process, comprised of many interacting components or elements. It arises out of mental constructs that interact with, for example, the psychological, social, cultural, situational, political, and personal aspects of life. A model of discourse must, therefore, be some kind of workable simplification of reality. The model presented here has the advantage of being comprehensible and manageable without losing the important complexities and subtleties that are needed for a deeper understanding of discourse.

The model presented here views discourse as consisting of two interacting dimensions: *Context* and *Language*. Each of these is subdivided into its main components or elements, and each component enables individuals, as analysts, to focus specifically on one aspect of discourse. What is important to bear in mind is that every element of the discourse interacts simultaneously with every other element. In complex ways, then, context and language interact with each other. The resulting product is a text. Figure GI.2 shows a simplified model of this interaction. Here, both language and context are shown to consist of elements labeled L1, L2, and so on for language, and C1, C2, and so on for context. These elements feed into each other in many ways. The process of interaction is discourse, and text is the product resulting from that process.

Chapter 1, The Context of Discourse, consists of eight elements or components: culture, participants, relationships between participants, setting, channel, attitudes toward the text, purpose, and topic.

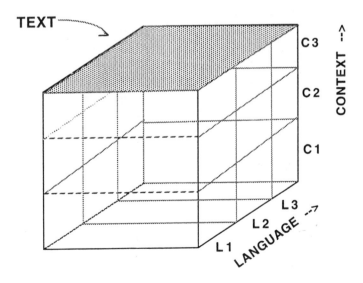

FIG. GI.2. The elements of discourse.

Taken together, these elements determine the appropriate genre, or form, of the text. Some familiar genres are the letter of application, a telephone conversation, a product advertisement, a poem, a sermon, and so on.

Chapter 2, The Language of Discourse, also contains eight elements: reference and coreference, words and lexical units, substitution and ellipsis, conjunction and clause relations, linguistic features, literal and nonliteral meaning, implicature, and nonverbal meaning. These show the ways in which language patterns can be extended from sentence grammar, that is, beyond a single clause or sentence, to tie together larger stretches of text. Taken together, these elements determine the appropriate register, or language description, of the text. The register must be matched grammatically and appropriately with the genre in order for a text to be considered acceptable by a listener or reader. A piece of legislation, for instance, cannot appropriately use the language of a personal telephone conversation. And nobody, not even a lawyer, would speak casually to a close friend in the language in which laws are written.

Part II turns to an examination of how discourse analysis can be applied to better understand the numerous ways in which people communicate in different situations. First is a look at the kinds of communications used in the classroom. Then the discourse of doctor and patient are considered. Next both the written discourse of law, as in a will, and the oral discourse of lawyer and client are examined. The discussion then turns to the discourse of journalism, considering both radio and TV journalism and written news reports. Finally, there is an examination of the discourse of literature.

It is our express wish that students will find this book to be both useful and interesting. Hopefully, the journey mapped out in the following pages will lead to a greater understanding of the world and of yourself, of the ways in which you relate through language to your own groups and communities, and of the pleasure you derive through the power and finesse of your own discourse. Any suggestions or comments that might improve this book are welcome.

Moira Chimombo
Robert L. Roseberry

I

THE PROCESS
OF DISCOURSE

Introduction to Part I:
The Elements of Discourse

The process of discourse draws on context and language to create text. Part I is concerned with that process. More specifically, however, it is concerned with the **acceptability** of text, because a text cannot be said to exist for the person who reads or hears it unless that person accepts it as such. Within every culture certain standards of text, whether spoken or written, are considered by the majority of hearers or readers to be "acceptable," whereas other standards, by contrast, are considered "unacceptable." What constitutes acceptable or unacceptable text to an interpreter is, to a large extent, controlled by the language of the text as well as by the context in which the text appears.

Acceptability is a function of **appropriateness** and **grammaticality**. The first of these, appropriateness, is determined primarily by cultural and situational factors. It might be called "context acceptability." As de Beaugrande and Dressler (1981, p. 11) put it, "The appropriateness of a text is the agreement between its setting and the ways in which the standards of textuality are upheld." For a text to be judged appropriate, it must reflect basic values of the culture without violating any such values. It must also reflect the situation that gives rise to it. These are the contextual issues of discourse, and they are dealt with in various ways in chapter 1.

The other ingredient of acceptability, grammaticality, is a measure of language usage. It might be called "language acceptability." If a text is judged grammatical, this is the same as saying that most readers or listeners accept the language of the text and find no serious fault in it. Just as there is a grammar of the sentence, there is also a grammar of discourse, governing discourse language. Chapter 2 examines discourse language and discourse grammaticality.

3

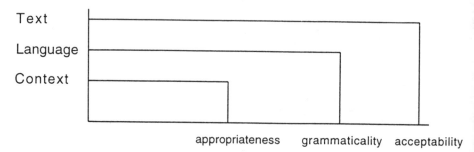

FIG. I.1. Relationship between acceptability and discourse.

Different degrees of acceptability or unacceptability result from combining different degrees of appropriateness or inappropriateness with different degrees of grammaticality or ungrammaticality. When perceived by the reader or hearer of a text, these varying combinations translate into judgments of relative acceptability or lack of acceptability. The relation between the concepts of acceptability and text may be diagramed as in Fig. I.1. Figure I.1 shows that text is a product of context and language in much the same way as acceptability is a product of grammaticality and appropriateness.

The context of the discourse results in specifications for an appropriate form of the text. This form is known as the **genre**; chapter 1 is concerned with the elements that specify the genre. The genre, in turn, specifies a certain kind of language acceptability, or grammaticality. This is the **register** of the text. When the genre and register are matched in a way that is most effective for the intended purpose, the resulting text is likely to be considered highly acceptable. Chapter 2 is concerned with the elements of discourse language and with the way in which acceptable language can be matched with acceptable form to produce acceptable and effective texts.

1

THE CONTEXT
OF DISCOURSE

What is the source of meaning of a text? How do people know how to interpret the words and nonverbal elements of a text? The answer is that every text comes along with another text that contains the key to its interpretation. This accompanying text—the **CONtext**—has its roots in the culture and the situation, including the interpersonal and intertextual relationships that gave rise to it.

At its most general level, the context is the culture. How people in their societies view the world and their place in it is a crucial part of understanding the texts they create. Unfortunately, very little is known about the relationship of language to culture. It is not possible to make accurate predictions about language based on knowledge of a specific culture. However, people's attention can be drawn to connections between language and culture, and guidelines for understanding **cultural context** and the effect it has on the form and content of texts can be given.

Within any culture, it is possible to describe situations that give rise to texts. It is easier to see the role of language within **situational contexts** than within cultural ones. For example, language may reflect location through prepositional phrases. Also, certain types of functional language may be appropriate to a given situation. The elements of the situational context discussed in this chapter closely follow the analytical framework devised by Biber (1994). Although there have been many descriptions of situation, Biber's is the only one that allows a true classification by restricting the variations in each element.

It is, therefore, the only situational framework that can uniquely specify a genre.

Within its contexts, a text is simultaneously process and product. It is created out of the mutual interaction of producer and interpreter(s). At each stage in its production and interpretation, unspoken reference is made to the contexts that provide the environment for its development. Text and context continually feed each other. No text—written, spoken, signed, or otherwise communicated—is ever devoid of context.

The different components of context relate in predictable ways to discourse and text. Specifically, they give rise to the genre, which is the form of the text appropriate to its particular purpose within the situation.

CULTURE

In any society, culture, in its most general sense, is concerned with individuals in a group. It has four main functions: It determines the various ways open to the individual within the group to develop the self, and hence the group as well. It specifies means for self-preservation. It determines the individual's place within the group. And, it determines the individual's and the group's perception of the world. The specific culture of the group restricts each of these cultural attributes to a range of values or possibilities deemed acceptable to the members of that culture. Thus, the ways in which an individual can achieve self-fulfillment or perceive the world within a given society are limited by that society's cultural norms and practices.

The relation between culture and discourse may be shown diagrammatically as in Fig. 1.1. Place in the world, perceptions of the world, self-development, and self-preservation combine to provide the cultural context of discourse. Out of the cultural context arise, among others, discourses concerned with ethnicity and solidarity, power and exploitation, prejudice, sexism, ideology, and territory and time. Every text is based in a context of culture.

To function as members of a culture, speakers must have a high degree of **communicative competence**. They must know how to speak appropriately in given situations: what degree of respect is appropriate, what markers of politeness are required, what rules governing turn-taking are in force, and much more. In some cultures, qualities of voice (such as breathy or clear), volume, contour, tempo, and pitch may carry important cultural meanings such as degree of

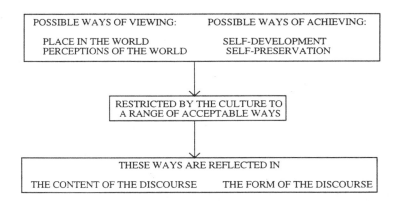

FIG. 1.1. The relationship between culture and discourse.

status, whether a person is acting as a petitioner or a patron, and which role in the situation the speaker is assuming. **Gestures**, postures, and **facial expressions** (to be discussed in detail later) may also play an important role in cultural communication. All of these comprise a culture's styles of speaking, and these styles of speaking may be so important in a given culture that they may continue to exist long after the language itself has died out. An example of this is the Ngoni of southern Africa, who continue to use Ngoni styles of speaking even though they have lost their original Ngoni language.

The individual's linguistic and cultural development, while making intracultural communication possible, can severely impede cross-cultural communication. Problems in cross-cultural communication have become an increasingly important concern in a world where economic and political decisions have international consequences. Wierzbicka (1991), summarizing a number of recent investigations into cross-cultural communication, listed the following four points as the main ideas emerging from these studies:

1. In different societies, and different communities, people speak differently.
2. These differences in ways of speaking are profound and systematic.
3. These differences reflect different cultural values, or at least different hierarchies of values.
4. Different ways of speaking, different communicative styles, can be explained and made sense of, in terms of independently established different cultural values and cultural priorities.

To take one example of different cultural attitudes toward speaking, consider Wierzbicka's analysis of "self-assertion" as expressed in Black American culture, White Anglo-American culture, and Japanese culture:

> *Black American culture*
> I want/think/feel something now
> I want to say it ("self-assertion," "self-expression")
> I want to say it now ("spontaneity")
>
> *White Anglo-American culture*
> I want/think/feel something
> I want to say it ("self-assertion," "self-expression")
> I cannot say it now
> because someone else is saying something now ("autonomy," "turn-taking")
>
> *Japanese culture*
> I can't say: I want/I think/I feel something
> someone could feel something bad because of this
> if I want to say something
> I have to think about it before I say it

In these descriptions, spontaneity, an important value in Black American culture, is in conflict with autonomy and turn-taking, crucial to White Anglo-American culture. Both of these values conflict with the value the Japanese place on not saying anything that would embarrass or hurt the feelings of another person. Imagine individuals from these three cultures attempting to hold a conversation, in which the Black American would spontaneously interrupt the White Anglo-American, and the Japanese would continue to remain silent.

In a study of the cross-cultural miscommunication of British and Asian speakers of English, Gumperz, and Roberts (1980) found that each group had its own list of irritants that impeded the communication. For the English, these included what they perceived in the Asians' speech to be inappropriately high or low pitch, wrong stress, wrong use of **turn-taking**, misleading use of "yes" and "no," lack of features binding the text together, lack of specifics, and redundant words. The Asians, on the other hand, found the following English speech habits irritating or confusing: stressing particular words for emphasis (seems

impolite or emotional), interrupting, apparently not listening or changing the subject, using derogatory words such as "silly," indefinite
commitments (mistaken for definite ones, e.g., "I'll see what I can do"),
and using explanations and apologies when giving a refusal (appears
not to be a refusal after all). It is worth noting that miscommunication
of the type described here is not restricted to differences between vastly
dissimilar cultures. It can exist as well between members of subgroups
or subcultures within a single society.

One's cultural place in the world can take the form of **solidarity**
and group membership and can be shown linguistically in a number
of ways. One of the most common is the choice of second-person
pronoun of address. Throughout the world, many languages make a
pronoun distinction similar to that of the French *tu* and *vous*. Here,

---

Practice 1:
Read each of the following examples of cross-cultural miscommunication and
try to explain (a) what went wrong and why, and (b) how the problem might
have been prevented.

(i) Passengers crowd into a London bus, and ignore the regulation that they
should have exact change at hand. The Asian bus driver repeats firmly,
"Exact change, *please.*" The passengers find this behavior rude, although
it was not intended to be.
(From Gumperz, 1982, pp. 168–171. Paraphrased from Coupland, Giles, &
Wiemann, 1991, p. 113)

(ii) An American walks into the lobby of a hotel in Lagos, Nigeria. The woman
at the front desk looks up from a newspaper and, without smiling, says,
"May I help you?" with falling intonation. The American feels like turning
around and walking out. (When the American later mentions this episode
to several Nigerian friends, they all confirm that the desk clerk's behavior
was perfectly acceptable by local cultural standards.)
(Authors' notes, 1976)

(iii) The cultural anthropologist Price, working among Brazil's Nambiquara In-
dians, wants to orient himself using a map of the region. He asks his
Nambiquara friend Americo the names of several major rivers on the map.
His friend invariably replies, "Big water." Price becomes discouraged as
Americo agrees that the rivers have names, but refuses to divulge them.
When Price finally gives Americo the reason for his inquiry, Americo re-
sponds by giving the names of the rivers.
(Price, D. (1989). *Before the bulldozer: The Nambiquara Indians and the
World Bank.* Cabin John, MD: Seven Locks. Paraphrased from Coupland,
et al., 1991, p. 107)

the singular form *tu* is used to demonstrate camaraderie with colleagues, fellow students, workmates, and the like, as well as with close relatives. *Vous* is used to address strangers, officials, elders, teachers, and persons to whom one should, in general, show a heightened respect. Other languages that make this distinction divide their pronouns along similar, though not precisely exact lines. For example, among the Chewa of south central Africa, the pronoun *iwe*, corresponding roughly to the French *toi*, is often used by children to address each other in situations where European children would be more likely to use names.

In addition to pronouns of address, languages employ different kinds of terms of address to indicate status, relationship, and group membership. Thus, at work individuals may be addressed by first names; at home by a term of endearment, such as "dear," or a term of relationship, such as "Mom"; at the dentist's office as "Ms. Gonzales"; at a faculty board meeting as "Professor Gonzales"; and so on. Each of these shows membership in a different network of relationships, each having its own degree of attachments.

In many languages, address terminology is a much more complex matter than it is in English. Among the Nuer of Sudan, for example, each person has a personal name given by the parents when the child is born. Often, a second personal name is given by the maternal grandparents. Thus, different relations may use different names in addressing the person. As males reach adulthood, their personal names are replaced by *Gwa*, meaning "father" when they are addressed by younger males. Each Nuer also has a clan name, used on ceremonial occasions, and an "ox name," derived from a favorite ox and used by age-mates of the same sex.

Pronouns of address and other address terminology are among the devices that a society uses to show **politeness** (a topic discussed further later). But politeness can be shown linguistically in other ways as well. In some societies, politeness is integrated so completely into the language that it is impossible to make an utterance without at the same time indicating a position on a scale of politeness. Geertz (1960) showed that an example of such a language is Javanese, which forces the speaker to choose a high, middle, or low style of speech, and to combine this style with high **honorifics** (terms that show a high degree of deference to the addressee), low honorifics (showing a lesser degree of deference), or no honorifics at all. In all, there are six possible speech levels resulting from the combinations of style with honorifics. High style with high honorifics may be used by people at the highest levels of society. People in the towns often use middle style with each other, especially if they are not intimates. Low style is used by children and by persons of high status when speaking to inferiors, and so on. In general, a variety of complex rules for usage govern the choice of speech level in Javanese.

The cultural opposite of solidarity occurs when there is a **power** relationship in which one discourse participant uses language to dominate one or more others. Within any society, language is constantly used in this way. Most of these uses, however, are subtle; the element of power often escapes the notice of those to whom the discourse is directed. When a young, unmarried woman goes to a male doctor, for instance, the doctor may use discourse to guide her in very subtle ways toward a birth control decision with which she is uncomfortable. Nevertheless, she may take the doctor's advice on the grounds that he is the expert and therefore knows what is best. Another common example is the discourse relationship between pupil and teacher. Here, teachers maintain control through discourse and even use discourse in pragmatically unusual ways, such as asking questions whose answers they already know. Furthermore, there is no choice but to attempt to answer these questions. The pupil does not have the option to reply, "I'd rather not answer that question," or "I think I'll turn that one over to Sammy; it's more in his line." Such replies would be considered impertinent in a classroom because of the power relationships that exist there, even though they would be perfectly acceptable in many real-life situations.

Societal institutions (e.g., the judiciary, the educational system, the media, and the church) function to create social reality. The most powerful way of doing this is through discourse. Sermons, textbooks, newspapers, advertising, and legislation are among the sources of discourse that give legitimacy to the existing social structure. They construct an **ideology** favorable to those in power and give the impression that those who wield power in a society are justified in their behavior and that, in fact, no other form of social reality is conceivable. In this sense, according to Fowler (1985, p. 62), "Language is a reality-creating social practice." He further pointed out that the language of power is either *directive* or *constitutive*. It is directive when it takes a form that is deliberately constructed to manipulate others, such as an order given by a military officer. It is constitutive in most of the examples already provided, where its function is subtly to reinforce cultural stereotypes and create social reality.

When language is used constitutively, different categories of language use and form provide means of recreating the social power structure. One such category is the set of available words in a language. Concepts that have particular significance in a culture will command a large set of terms to describe them. In a democracy, for example, there will be more words related to democratic processes than there will be in a dictatorship. In a dictatorship, a person wishing to discuss concepts of democracy may find it necessary to engage in circumlocutions and definitions to replace terms that are unavailable. The lack of such terms may contribute to a belief that the concepts themselves are not part of reality. As an example, when Malawi achieved independence in 1964, the official language, Chichewa, had no term for "politics." The meaning of the term *ndale* (trickery) was extended to include the concept of "politics" as well.

In general, all societies create groups that are the holders of power. In most societies, the so-called professions are among those groups. As respected subcultures within society, the professions offer their members substantial in-group power. This power enables the members not only to exploit clientele for personal (if not always mutual) benefit, but also to support, enhance, and even redefine the values of the culture. It derives from the deep-seated beliefs of the culture. If those beliefs place power in the hands of the gods, for example, then priests and witchdoctors are the owners of power. Conversely, in technologically advanced societies, people believe themselves capable of controlling a large part of nature, and hence scientists and doctors are among the professionals vested with the power to construct cultural reality.

Fowler (1985) noted that in addition to the availability or lack of words to express a concept, power in language usually attaches to words that are abstract, general, foreign, or complex, rather than concrete, specific, native, or simple. Thus, words like "democracy," "empowerment," "neoliberalism," "solidarity," "disenfranchised," and so on, are more likely to be ideologically self-defining and power-laden than are "school," "home," "niece," and "changed."

Among the other tools of the constitutive use of language, according to Fowler, are syntax, structuring of information, deletion, complexity, modality, the sound system, and the use of personal reference and turn-taking. The following extracts from an interview with Margaret Thatcher, then prime minister of England, serve to illustrate some of these:

(1) Yes you HAVE got to be strong on law and order and do the things that only governments can do but there it's part government and part people because you CAN'T have law and order observed unless it's in partnership with people . . .
(Fairclough, 1989, p. 174)

(2) But of course it showed that we were reliable in the defence of freedom and when part of Britain we: was invaded of course we went we believed in defence of freedom we were reliable . . .
(Fairclough, 1989, p. 175)

Both these examples clearly exhibit power-loaded words, such as "law and order," "freedom," and "defence." However, syntactic choices, such as "we were reliable in the defence of freedom," constitute the political reality in a different way from, say, "I (or the Members of Parliament) were reliable. We defended freedom. Our soldiers defended freedom." By using a noun (defence) instead of a verb (defend), the utterance "we were reliable in the defence of freedom" obfuscates the subject. It is unknown who was reliable or who defended freedom. It is impossible to be sure what is meant by "freedom." The choice of "we" perhaps intentionally suggests a collusion between the government, or Mrs. Thatcher herself, and the English people without actually claiming such cooperation.

The utterance "you CAN'T have law and order observed" demonstrates not only an emphasis on the modality "can't" (definiteness, impossibility), but raises the status of "law and order" to a subtheme by moving it forward in comparison with the more common sequencing, "you can't insure that X will observe law and order." The missing agent, "X," is neatly deleted by this construction as well. In general, these utterances avoid direct address or personal reference and thus imply, rather than state, that the English people agree with and support Mrs. Thatcher's views.

Discourse is an important tool in describing, defining, and even creating power bases within a culture. It is no wonder then that the literate and articulate members of a society often attempt to find ways to use the power of discourse in their service. This exploitative use of discourse characterizes professions such as medicine, law, and advertising, for example, and is clearly an important part of political discourse. In various ways, discourse may function at one time or

---

Practice 2:
Explain how the following texts from newspaper advertisements intend to exploit readers. Identify the target group in each case and suggest how members of that group can increase their power in the discourse situation.

(i)   **ELIMINATE BALDNESS**
Enjoy a full head of hair in only 3 hours!

(ii)   **STRENGTHEN YOUR CAREER!!!**
Yes, W. . . can help you strengthen your career
through computer training.

(iii)   **QUALIFY for promotion through XXX**
In the convenience of your home, at your own time,
you can study an XXX course from the U.K. or the U.S.A.

---

another to exploit children, women, minorities, workers, students, and political, social, and ethnic groups. Such exploitation is often accomplished through threats, advertisements, editorials, manifestos, propaganda, selective reporting of news, and laws that benefit the powerful and privileged. Exploitation can easily arise from the power relationships that exist between participants in discourse.

Discourse can also be used by a cultural in-group to separate itself from one or more out-groups in the society. Such discourse is an expression of **prejudice** and may be the result of economic uncertainty, fear of change, misunderstood cultural practices, and cross-cultural miscommunication. Psychological and social forces interact to produce a shared, stereotypical image of members of the out-group. This stereotype may have little or no basis in reality, but those who share it will selectively use observation, rumor, and innuendo

---

Practice 3:
An important example of power differential in discourse occurs in the discourse of education. Examine sections of this book to find examples of power discourse. How does your attitude toward education change when you become aware of instances of the power differential between yourself as a student and members of the educational establishment: teachers, textbook writers, scholarly authorities, and so on?

---

to support and maintain the negative image. In other words, evidence or reports of desirable traits and actions on the part of the out-group will be ignored in favor of news about undesirable traits. In this way, a small amount of negative evidence, real or imagined, can be used to build a complex negative stereotype, shared by members of the in-group. Van Dijk (1984, p. 137) suggested that such stereotypes are built on the following hierarchy of cultural categories:

(a) National origin and/or appearance;
(b) Socioeconomic position;
(c) Sociocultural norms, values, religion, beliefs, language;
(d) (Typical) actions or interactions; and
(e) Assigned personal properties (intelligence, etc.).

Prejudice begins with the higher categories in this hierarchy. If the higher categories turn out to be irrelevant in a specific case, then the lower categories begin to come into play. Thus, discrimination by Whites against Blacks is triggered at (a), but discrimination by men against women is more likely to begin at level (b), (c), or (d).

The discourse of prejudice reflects the stereotypes that derive from this prejudice-building hierarchy. Like all specialized discourses, it has its own contexts, topics, semantic strategies, and styles. For example, prejudiced topics, according to van Dijk, group themselves largely into the following four major categories: (a) They are different (culture, mentality); (b) They do not adapt themselves; (c) They are involved in negative acts (nuisance, crime); and (d) They threaten our (social, economic) interests. Some of the most prevalent stylistic devices in prejudicial discourse include contrasting the in-group and the out-group, generalizing, exaggerating, understating extremely negative views, using terms of sincerity, repeating, enumerating, and comparing. Some of these topics and stylistic devices are shown in the following extract from an interview:

(3) Interviewee: ... Because of the foreigners it is really run down. Because if you say nowadays well uh, then they are already behind your back they are already with a knife, right? I have been through it myself on the market and uh I have seen it myself in the store, so that you uh uh think that, a black one is coming, "hally hop," look out because one of them is coming ... (Van Dijk, 1984, p. 136)

Here, topics (c) and (d) figure predominantly. Stylistically, there is much generalizing, exaggeration, and repetition.

It is not surprising that prejudice, like other power relationships, makes use of the same discourse devices described earlier in the section on power in discourse. In the following extract from a 1968 speech by the English politician Enoch Powell, power clearly rests with the state, and particularly with the Conservative government. Note the way in which word choices, use of the passive voice, and subject deletion in particular contribute to the dehumanizing of "coloured immigrants" in this discourse. Note especially such phrases as "rate of net inflow," "falls at a steady rate," "yield more family units," and so on. Such phrasing, which is normally associated with economics, agriculture, or marketing to refer to production, here describes human beings and their families:

> (4) Let us take as our starting point the calculation of the General Register Office that by 1985 there would be in this country 3½ million coloured immigrants and their offspring—in other words that the present number would have increased between two and three-fold in the next 17 years— on two assumptions, current rate of intake and current birthrate.
>
> The first assumption is that the rate of net inflow continues at present. It has not indeed diminished since the estimate was made, but I am willing to suppose that, especially with the substantially greater limitations which a Conservative government has undertaken to apply, the rate would be markedly reduced during the period in question. For the purposes of argument I will suppose that it falls at a steady rate from 60,000 in 1968 to nil by 1985. In that case the total in the latter year would be reduced by about half-a-million, that is to 3 million.
>
> I now turn to the second and more crucial assumption, the birthrate. . . . There are grounds for arguing that the immigrant birthrate is likely to rise during the next two or three decades: for instance the proportion of females must increase as dependents join male workers, so that a given total of immigrant population will yield more family units.
> (Quoted in Sykes, 1985, pp. 96–97)

A very important, cultural determiner of an individual's place in the world is sex. Different cultures may attach very different values to the roles assigned to the two sexes. These differences may be more blatant in some languages than in others, although there may be little correlation between **sexism** as reflected in a language and the actual degree of sexism in the society. Just as there are language communities and other groupings within a culture, there are sex-defined communities, including homosexual communities. Within each of these sex-based communities, there are different patterns of linguistic interaction and, hence, specific types of discourse. One of the most significant ways in which the traditional male–female power structure in society is described and perhaps even recreated is through sexist discourse. This is a special case of power discourse, which was examined earlier. In this case, however, discourse is used in subtle ways to subjugate a major part of the society or, in other words, to "keep women in their place."

In most societies, men and women have clearly differentiated roles. As a typical example, men may function as breadwinners and soldiers and take an active role in the reproductive cycle. Women, on the other hand, may look after domestic chores and childrearing and take a more passive role in reproduction. In recent years, women's groups, particularly in the technologically advanced societies of North America and Europe, have begun to change such stereotypes by spearheading a movement toward greater equality of the sexes. Nevertheless, there is considerable evidence that sexism, or arbitrary role differentiation based on sex, continues to pervade even the most enlightened societies.

Sexist discourse may be examined from two cultural points of view: how members of a society talk about men and women, and how men and women talk. The first of these is related to prejudicial discourse. The second is related to power structures and how these are reflected in discourse. The two strands are closely related and work together to define women and men differently.

To see how a society might structure discourse about men and women, consider the case of English, which reflects familiar cultural values. When individuals talk about men or women in English, they are restricted in various ways by choices available in the language. Women are routinely described in terms of men. They are addressed by surnames that derive from their fathers or husbands, and they are frequently classified by terms that derive from a male standard. For example, there are many pairs of words in English similar in contrast to "actor–actress," "steward–stewardess," "lion–lioness," and so on. The first member of each of these pairs is not merely a masculine term; it is the generic term as well. For instance, both a male "lion" and a female "lioness" belong to the species "lion." Both an "actor" and an "actress" may belong to the "actors' guild," and so forth. In this connection, one of the most famous "actresses" in the United States once said that she preferred to be called an "actor" because of the implication that an "actress" is merely a special, and perhaps inferior, kind of "actor."

A number of words in common use in English contain the word "man" (Fig. 1.2). "Chairman," "postman," and "deliveryman" are a few examples. Most such compounds can be altered by replacing "man" with "woman" whenever this is appropriate. However, if this is done, then the same problem of inferior connotation arises as in the "-ess" words discussed earlier. In other words, people are conditioned to think of a "chairman" as a person who chairs a meeting. If a woman chairs the meeting and is referred to as a "chairwoman," the implication is that she is a special, and perhaps inferior, kind of "chairman." Attempts to abolish both terms and replace them with "chair" have met with little success. Perhaps it is better to be thought of as an inferior kind of

"It's always men, men, men!"

FIG. 1.2. It is usually desirable to avoid sexist terms, such as words containing "man." Drawing by Ross; © 1990. The New Yorker Magazine, Inc.

"chairman" than as a piece of furniture! A more desirable alternative is the coinage "chairperson." However, such coinages will be regarded as neutral with respect to sex only if the original terms, such as "chairman," disappear completely from common use.

Another problem with male–female word pairs is that they are not always parallel. That is, the female item in the pair often has a connotation unlike any that are contained in the male item. Examples of such nonparallel pairs in English include "bachelor–spinster," "widow–widower," and "master–mistress," to name a few. Although a bachelor is merely an unmarried man, "spinster" contains the connotation that the woman ought to have married but did not. With regard to "widow" and "widower," it is possible to be "John's widow" but not "Joan's widower." There is a built-in implication that the woman is dependent on the man, but not vice versa. The same distinction applies to "master" and "mistress," with the additional connotation that a "mistress" is the dependent and perhaps more illicit part of a sexual relationship. There is, not surprisingly, no corresponding term for the power-bearing male partner in the relationship. Other words may take on different meanings when applied to men and women. For example, "he is a handsome man" as opposed to "she is a handsome woman" and "he's a professional" as opposed to "she's a professional."

Sexism may be carried in the grammar as well as in the vocabulary. A particularly annoying problem of this kind in English is the lack of a sex-neutral pronoun to replace "he" and "she." There is an increasing tendency to fill the gap with "they," as in "if anyone wants the job, they should apply at the head office." The rather common use of "he" to represent either "he" or "she" results in the same problem discussed earlier in connection with masculine and feminine word forms. This problem is much more pronounced in gender-based languages such as Russian and German, where every noun is marked as masculine, feminine, or neuter. In addition, adjectives and demonstratives must match the modified noun in gender. Thus, in German, "a small table" (masculine) is *ein kleiner Tisch*, whereas "a small cat" (feminine) is *eine kleine Katze*. Similar distinctions pertain in Russian where, in addition, past-tense verbs must also be marked for gender. Thus, a man saying "I saw him" in Russian would say *Ya videl yego*, whereas a woman would say *Ya videla yego*. Furthermore, professional designations in both languages are marked for gender. A male and female teacher, respectively, would be *Lehrer* and *Lehrerin* in

---

Practice 4:
Locate as many examples of discourse sexism as you can in the following text. Also try to look beyond the language to some of the cultural assumptions underlying the text. Can you suggest ways to make the text less demeaning to women?

A good fire must have good firewood if it is to burn well. So must a person be stoked with good food if he is to be healthy and strong and happy. This book, which is written especially for use in Malawi using ingredients which are locally available, is designed to give the house-wife some ideas and suggestions to improve her "firewood." It is hoped that the recipes given in this book will enable her to add variety to the diet and thereby improve the family nutrition as well as earn her a good reputation amongst her neighbours.
(Cole-King, S. M., from the Foreword to Shaxson, A., Dickson, P., & Walker, J. (1985). *The Malawi cookbook*. Zomba: Government Printer)

German, and *uchitel* and *uchitel'nitsa* in Russian. Clearly, as in the English "waiter–waitress," the feminine forms are the marked members of the pairs, and the "normal" or "typical" (unmarked) forms are the masculine ones.

Complementing the issue of discourse about women is the equally important question of women's discourse itself. In recent years, a number of studies have focused on how women talk and structure discourse. Many of these studies point to significant perceived differences between men's and women's speech. Although some of the studies in this area are inconclusive, a number of important tendencies have been noted.

At the word level, women are said to use certain words and expressions with significantly greater frequency than men. These include "adorable," "oh dear," and "my goodness." Also, women are supposed to use more adjectives of approximation (e.g., "about"), more intensifiers (e.g., "very"), and more reduplicated forms (e.g., "teeny-weeny") than men. Politeness terms and euphemisms are thought to be more indicative of women's speech, whereas slang and swearing are said to occur more often in the speech of men.

At the level of grammar, Lakoff (1975) in particular found that women use tag questions (e.g., ". . . isn't it?") more frequently than men in certain speech situations. Women are also said to use more hedges (e.g., modals and expressions such as "I suppose"). Complex differences in the directness of men's and women's discourse have also been noted, but not yet conclusively proved. Sentence length and completeness appear to differ between the sexes as well, with women using shorter sentences and leaving more sentences incomplete. However, this may be explained by the fact that men interrupt women more often than women interrupt men in conversation.

In pronunciation, women are said to be more conservative than men, tending toward prestige forms rather than, for example, forms associated with the working classes. Thus, women have been found to use "-ing" more often than men, who show a preference for "-in'," as in "going" versus "goin'." With regard to intonation, McConnell-Ginet (1978) showed that women's intonation patterns are more dynamic than men's and that women's tone groups end more frequently with a nonfalling final tone than those of men. Such a pattern might be interpreted as tentativeness or a desire to avoid commitment.

Finally, at the level of discourse itself, men use more commands in discourse than women. Women's discourse is characterized by attempts at greater cooperation and politeness. For example, women attempt more often than men to initiate conversations. They often fail at this, however, because men frequently do not permit the discourse to be maintained. Related to this lack of male cooperation is the fact that men, as mentioned earlier, interrupt women far more often. Similarly, men show a tendency to reject topics raised by women, whereas women tend to support topics raised by men. Finally, women frequently use such backchannel signals as "mm-hmm" to indicate that they are continuing to listen. When men use this signal, it often carries the very different meaning, "I agree." Hence, men often accuse women of giving contradictory signals regarding agreement.

Differences in men's and women's speech are commonly found throughout various cultures. One of the most famous examples involves the Carib Indians in the Lesser Antilles. The differences in word choice and grammar between the speech of men and women are so extreme among the Caribs that some investigators have come to the erroneous conclusion that Carib men and women speak two unrelated languages.

A similar, but less extreme example exists in Japanese, where women use a characteristically female speech, consisting of special vocabulary items. Japanese women exclusively use the sentence-final particle "ne" to indicate women's speech. They also use "watashi" or "atashi" to refer to "I," whereas men use "washi" or "ore." Japanese

Practice 5:
Read and contrast the following two conversations:

(a) Explain what has gone wrong in conversation (i). To what extent is the cultural view of women's place in the world responsible? If you were the woman, how could you gain greater control over the situation?

(b) Why is conversation (ii) more successful than (i)? What work is being done to aid the conversation and keep it flowing smoothly? Pay special attention to timing and indicators of appreciation. What cultural reasons related to women's place in the world are at work here?

(# indicates a short pause; = indicates lack of a pause; :: indicates that the syllable is prolonged; (indicates an overlap; numbers in parentheses show elapsed time in seconds.)

(i) Woman: Both really (#) it just strikes me as too 1984ish y'know to sow your seed or whatever (#) an' then have like it develop miles away not caring (i f   )

Man: (Now::) it may be something uh quite different (#) you can't make judgments like that without all the facts being at your disposal

(West, C., & Zimmerman, D. (1977). Women's place in everyday talk: Reflections on parent–child interaction. *Social Problems, 24,* 521–529, p. 527; quoted in West & Zimmerman, 1985, p. 118)

(ii) Man: I saw in the paper where Olga Korbut
Korbut=

Woman: =Yeah=

Man: =went to see Dickie.
(#)

Woman: You're kidding! What for?
(#)

Man: I don't know.
(2.0)

Woman: I can just imagine what she would go see Dick Dick Nixon for. I don't get it.
(7.0)

Man: I think she's on a tour of the United States
(3.0)

Woman: Has he sat down and talked to her?
(#)

Man: (Shows the picture in the paper)
(1.0)

Woman: Today's paper? (2.0) You're kidding me.

(Fishman, P. (1978). What do couples talk about when they're alone? In D. Butturff & E. Epstein (Eds.), *Women's language and style.* Akron, OH: L & S Books, pp. 11–22. Page 16A, quoted in West & Zimmerman, 1985, p. 112) women also use very high pitch and considerable nasalization to differentiate their speech from that of men.

One final example of differentiated men's and women's speech is the "mother-in-law language" used by the Dyirbal of Australia. A Dyirbal switches from the standard dialect into "mother-in-law" speech whenever a parent-in-law of the opposite sex is present. The "mother-in-law" speech has essentially the same phonology and syntax as the standard variety, but an entirely different vocabulary.

Cultural groups, subgroups, and individuals within the culture have their own belief systems, called **ideologies**. Discourse produced within the culture often shows the ideological bias of the group or individual. This bias may be transparent to other members of the group, who will regard it as truth or reality, for reasons already discussed. The two earlier extracts from the Thatcher interview express a definite ideology, namely, a conservative political position within a parliamentary democracy. Terms such as "conservative" and "democracy," of course, are themselves loaded with biases of power and ideology. However, it is safe to say that most citizens of Britain, regardless of their political ideologies, would have been able to relate Mrs. Thatcher's discourse to the political reality as it then existed. In particular, those who shared Mrs. Thatcher's ideology would have seen nothing unusual in such keywords as "law and order," "defence of freedom," and so on. The terms of power would have been transparent to them. Those of a different ideological base, however, would soon find themselves questioning the specific meanings and contexts of such terms.

In general, all discourses of power support or oppose elements of the prevailing ideology. Often, a given text will take simultaneously contradictory positions regarding the ideology. For example, a text that attempts to define a societal power term, such as "freedom" or "law and order," will almost inevitably fall into this error because the power terms refer to concepts that lie at the foundation of the ideology. They are not definable, except by reference to a contrasting ideology. If "freedom" is defined, for example, as the right of individuals to do whatever they wish, short of anarchy, there is still the problem of defining "anarchy."

An important indicator of a culture's perception of the world is its attitude toward territory and time. In most Western democracies, both time and territory are sharply defined and have monetary value. People speak of "owning" land and "having" time. They think of time, in

Practice 6:
This text is from a school geography textbook. What does the book teach in addition to geography? What ideology pervades the text? Think of a radically different ideology. What kinds of changes would you expect if the writer followed this different ideology?

> The environmental conditions of this region mean that it is poorly suited to most forms of agriculture. It receives most of its rainfall during the summer monsoons, and then experiences a winter drought. Furthermore, the natural savanna woodlands vegetation and grasslands have few nutrients for intensive grazing, the soils are poor, the region is a long distance from markets, and transport facilities are poorly developed. Thus the land is used for little else except extensive beef cattle grazing on farms which sometimes exceed 15,000 square kilometres in size. The large size of the farms is needed because of the land's poor carrying capacity, which may mean one beast needs 20 to 30 hectares to survive.
> (Codrington, S., & Codrington, D. (1982). *World of contrasts: Case studies in world development for secondary geography*. Sydney: William Brooks, p. 193; quoted in Kress, 1989, p. 68)

particular, as a commodity that can, at least in English, be "spent," "wasted," "lost," "made up," and even "borrowed," "bought," and "sold." In this sense, an entire discourse of time has arisen.

That many other societies have attitudes toward time that differ greatly from the Western is graphically illustrated by Barley's (1983, pp. 78–79) description of the major adjustments he had to make when working among the Dowayo of Cameroon, West Africa:

> The timing of events in Dowayoland is a nightmare to anyone seeking to plan more than 10 minutes in the future. . . . Dowayos . . . do things in their own good time. This took me a long while to get used to; I hated wasting time, resented losing it and expected return for spending it. I felt that I must hold the world record for hearing "It is not the right time for that," whenever I sought to pin down Dowayos to show me a particular thing at a particular time. Arrangements to meet at a fixed time or place never worked. People were astonished that I should be offended when they turned up a day or even a week late, or when I walked 10 miles to find they were not at home. Time was simply not something that could be allocated.

A similar example is the Nuer, likewise of Africa, who have no word for time. Both Dowayo and Nuer cultures conceive of time as something quite different from the Euro-American conception of it, and their languages allow no description of the passing, wasting, or saving of time, for example (Taylor, 1980, p. 86).

It is expected not only that the content of discourse, but also the norms of discourse, would reflect the culture's perception of time and territory. So, for example, actual times and places might be set aside for particular discourses, as with religious discourse, legal discourse, academic discourse, and the like. In many societies, news articles may appear in print in newspapers and magazines published periodically, or may be broadcast over the radio or television at set times. In many other societies, such articles might appear at irregular intervals, posted on bulletin boards in public places or, nowadays, on the Internet.

The place in which a specific text appears may carry a great deal of cultural significance, which may determine the meaning of the text. Thus, the sentence, "Sharks have teeth," written in a book on marine biology, clearly has a different significance from that of the same sentence spray painted on the wall of a building by members of a youth gang known as "The Sharks." By contributing cultural meaning to a text, place and time form part of a text's situational context, which is examined in detail later.

In addition to the meaning and situation of a text, the actual appearance of a text may reflect cultural attitudes toward time and space. For example, in a fast-paced, highly mobile society, road signs must be easy to read and understand quickly. Similar requirements placed on advertisements in printed texts dictate such matters as layout, type size, borders, color, and so on. Concerns such as these figure to some extent in the publication of all kinds of printed and written texts.

Regarding spoken discourse, different persons might be allocated different amounts of time in conversation, for example, based on such factors as status, age, and sex. Classrooms, churches, and business meetings are among the settings where these factors may play a significant role. And within different cultures, there may be different lengths of pauses between turns in conversations and different meanings attached to such pauses and to the lengths of silences. Similarly, conversation, like other types of text, will typically occur in different places, depending on such factors as association, sex, and purpose.

Finally, culture affects choices of written and spoken language in many ways. Obviously, if the culture is primarily an oral one, then most of the society's discourse will be oral. For example, the society's history will be memorized and passed down from generation to generation orally through specially appointed *griots*, as in many West African societies.

In an evolved, technological society, on the other hand, written discourse provides ways of storing permanent records of its history for posterity. In addition, it provides the basis for economics, politics, science, and all advanced human thought and experience. Writing captures the current state of human knowledge and presents it as a product to be used as a foundation for further advancement. At the same time, oral discourse in such societies serves mainly to forge interpersonal ties necessary to the individual's ongoing survival within the culture.

In any culture, the individual's self-development begins in early childhood and is effected through oral discourse. In literate societies, written discourse plays an increasingly important role in education as the child matures. Still, talk continues to be a major force in self-development as well. Clearly this would be the case in nonliterate societies. However, it is also the case in advanced, technological societies, where nonprint media such as radio and television are so pervasive.

Individual and group self-preservation within a culture is very much a matter of a choice between oral and written language. In a technologically advanced society, there are few opportunities for the illiterate. Here, status attaches to literacy; professions such as medicine, law, teaching, and so on place great value on the ability to produce and interpret sophisticated written discourse.

A culture's perception of the world, especially regarding time and space, dictates when and where written and oral discourse are appropriate. Furthermore, it assigns meanings to such discourse depending on when and where it appears. As an example, in a Christian society, a marriage ceremony, to be valid, must be performed orally and in a church or other authorized premises. The amount of time allocated to particular persons in a conversation may also be dictated by cultural norms. Other time and space matters affecting oral language include how often turns change in a conversation, how close people stand when talking, whether different people talk at the same time, whether listeners look at the speaker, and so on. A person's sex, age, and status within the society are among the factors that allocate power to the individual and help to determine time and space allocations in oral discourse.

The individual's place in the world depends on a complex network of ties to other individuals and groups, so much of the discourse concerning this aspect of culture is expected to be oral. Individuals function as family members, friends, colleagues, and service providers. Family discussions, teaching, resolving disputes, planning events, contributing to work groups and meetings, requesting services, and so on are among the many kinds of speech events that typically use large amounts of oral discourse even if writing is also involved. Even at the professional level, where there is much written discourse, the importance of oral discourse cannot be neglected. Court trials depend on oral testimony of witnesses; medical diagnoses depend on verbal responses to doctors' questions, and so on.

An important concern in oral professional discourse is the way power is distributed among the participants. The doctor's relationship to the patient, for example, may determine who does most of the talking, who asks and who answers, how turn-taking is carried out, who has the right to interrupt, and so on. These phenomena are not restricted to professional discourse, but are found in any cultural setting where power is distributed unequally among discourse participants. Power relationships involving women versus men, the elderly versus the young, professionals versus lay people, and so on will greatly affect all matters of conversation structure.

Nothing has contributed more to the history of cultural advancement than the development of writing. Even such diverse matters as taking action (e.g., through politics), making social contact (through clubs, religious institutions, etc.), informing (through newspapers, magazines, and letters), and entertaining (through novels, movie reviews, sports write-ups, etc.) depend on writing. A society without writing is denied much of what inhabitants of technologically advanced societies take for granted as the essentials of daily life.

Guidelines for Analyzing Culture

Examine the discourse for orientation. Determine whether or not it is oriented toward self-development, self-preservation, perception of the world, place in the world, or a combination of these. Note that orientation may be shown both through content and through form, and that each may have a different orientation.

Within the orientation of the discourse, determine whether or not it is affected by ethnicity, solidarity, power relationships, exploitation, ideologies, attitudes toward territory and time, prejudice, attitudes toward men and women, professional grouping, or a combination of these. Again note that these may be shown both through content and through form, and each may have a different purpose and/or message.

Sample Analysis: Culture

Study the CODE advertisement in Fig. 1.3 (from *Time*, 27 July 1992). With regard to the cultural context, this text may be analyzed as follows:

> The content of the discourse is oriented toward self-preservation and self-development through literacy education. This orientation results from a perception of the world that contains a belief in the power of education to change society.
> The form of the discourse is largely based on self-preservation. As a soliciting advertisement, it attempts to exploit potential benefactors. To do this, it derives power from Christian (and other) cultural values that prevail in the society that produced it. In order for the advertisement to achieve its purpose, these values must compete successfully against the strong capitalist self-help values that dominate the same society.

Application

Find or collect an oral and a written text. Transcribe the oral text if a transcription is not already available. Using the aforementioned guidelines, analyze the cultural context of your chosen oral and written practice texts. Save the texts for further analyses in subsequent sections of this book.

Suggested Reading

Coates, J. (1986). *Women, men and language.* London: Longman.
    A sociolinguistic introduction to the problems of language and sex. Particularly useful
    for providing insights into how sex-differentiated language arises.
Coupland, N., Giles, H., & Wiemann, J. (Eds.). (1991). *"Miscommunication" and
    problematic talk.* Newbury Park, CA: Sage.
    Contains useful articles on miscommunication resulting from a number of culture-related
    variables: sex, power, age, ethnicity, the professions, and others.
Fairclough, N. (1989). *Language and power.* London: Longman.
    A Marxist interpretation of the role of power in discourse.

Most people think there's only one way to help the developing world. We have 26.

You'd be surprised at what 26 letters can do for people in developing countries. They can mean food security, good health and job opportunities because they can provide knowledge and skills through education. CODE supports literacy in 16 countries in Africa and the Caribbean as a long-term investment in development. Call us at 1-800-661-CODE for more information. We could use your help.

CODE

Self-sufficiency through literacy in the developing world.

FIG. 1.3. The CODE advertisement. Reprinted with permission.

Fowler, R. (1985). Power. In van Dijk (1985), vol. 4, pp. 61–82.
   Clear and concise treatment of power in discourse as shown through lexical processes, transitivity, syntax, sequencing, complexity, modality, speech acts, implicature, turn-taking, reference, and phonology. Contains good examples.

Gumperz, J., & Roberts, C. (1980). *Developing awareness skills for interethnic communication.* Singapore: SEAMEO Regional Language Centre.
   Describes a program that was set up to improve the communication between Asian workers and their British managers.

Hall, E. (1959). *The silent language.* Garden City, NY: Doubleday.
   An excellent analysis of culture, what it is, and how to describe it. Also useful for those wishing to acquire cultural sensitivity to other cultures.

Halliday, M., & Hasan, R. (1989). *Language, context, and text: Aspects of language in a social-semiotic perspective* (2nd ed.). Oxford, England: Oxford University Press.
   Chapter 1 and the "coda" following chapter 3 both deal in part with Halliday's concept of the context of situation and are relevant in connection with discourse and culture, because Halliday often includes culture with situation. According to Halliday, the cultural context determines the way in which a text is interpreted within its situational context.

Kress, G. (1985). Ideological structures in discourse. In van Dijk (1985), vol. 4, pp. 27–42.
   A brief, clear overview of the major issues affecting the role of ideology in discourse.

Kress, G. (1989). *Linguistic processes in sociocultural practice.* Oxford, England: Oxford University Press.
   Excellent introduction to some of the major cultural concerns affecting discourse. Includes sections on power and ideology.

Poynton, C. (1989). *Language and gender: Making the difference.* Oxford, England: Oxford University Press.
   Good introduction to the problem of sex-differentiated discourse. Contains sections on the social construction of gender, lexis and sex, speaking about men and women, and speaking as woman/man, among others. Also contains a useful summary of research findings, according to different aspects of discourse.

Scollon, R., & Scollon, S. (1995). *Intercultural communication.* Oxford, England: Blackwell.
   Excellent all-encompassing discourse approach to the problems of communicating between cultures. Contains sections on "Interpersonal politeness and power," "Topic and face," "Ideologies of discourse," "What is culture?", "Corporate discourse," "Professional discourse," and "Gender discourse," among others. Examples are drawn largely from Western and Asian cultures.

Sykes, M. (1985). Discrimination in discourse. In van Dijk (1985), vol. 4, pp. 83–101.
   Contains syntactic and semantic analyses of examples of discrimination in discourse.

Tannen, D. (1985). Cross-cultural communication. In van Dijk (1985), vol. 4, pp. 203–215.
   Focuses on paralinguistic signals in communication between closely related cultural groups (Californians and New Yorkers).

Van Dijk, T. (1984). *Prejudice in discourse.* Amsterdam: John Benjamins.
   Provides an overview of the various theories of racial prejudice. Then examines how prejudice is realized in language. Contains sections on contexts; topics; stories about minorities; and semantic, pragmatic, and conversational strategies, among others.

West, C., & Zimmerman, D. (1985). Gender, language, and discourse. In van Dijk (1985), vol. 4, pp. 103–124.
A good brief overview of the major issues.
Wierzbicka, A. (1991). *Cross-cultural pragmatics: The semantics of human interaction.* Berlin: Mouton de Gruyter.
Thorough treatment of pragmatic issues in cross-cultural communication. Examines speech acts, cultural values, conversational routines, and many other kinds of speech patterns and shows how they are realized in different cultures.

DISCOURSE PARTICIPANTS

The discourse participants include the **producer(s)** and the **interpreter(s)**. The producer is typically the one who writes or speaks a text. This person may or may not be the actual **source** or author of the information. Instead, the producer may be an editor, illustrator, artist, photographer, or designer of any text or part of a text. In fact, a single text may have several producers, as in the case of news media texts. In the case of an advertisement, the producer is probably an individual or team hired for the purpose of creating the text. The source, on the other hand, is the management of the company whose product is represented in the text. Sometimes this kind of source is referred to as an **institutional producer.**

As illustrations, consider the following two texts:

(5) As soon as we came in, an older, thin peasant woman, probably the housekeeper, who at once recognized Mother, started to talk furtively in a thick dialect, and in her bewilderment flapped her arms like a wild duck. She was terribly excited and beside herself, and after a minute or so Nacia, who had heard the fuss, came running in.
She was a lovely, dark blond young woman: slim and graceful, like a ballerina. And though she was very simply dressed, to me she instantly became the Princess of all the fairy tales I had ever known.
(Baum, 1990, p. 115)

(6) Under Washington law, we are attorneys solely for [client] and owe duties solely to her.
(From a personal letter, signed by an attorney)

In Example 5, the producer is the narrator (writing as "I").[1] Little information can be obtained about her from the passage itself. However, further research would reveal that the story from which this

---

[1] For more information on the position of narrators in relation to their texts, see part II, chap. 7.

passage is taken, together with the other stories appearing with it, are true stories written from memory by a Jewish woman named Anna Baum. She lived in Poland during the Nazi period and was one of those who suffered at the hands of the Nazis, along with the others she portrays in her book. It is possible that in preparing these stories the author clarified her memories by discussing her stories with other Holocaust survivors. These other people are not coproducers of the stories, but they could have influenced the production process. Among the other people who contributed more directly to the production process of these stories and who may be said to be producers in their own right are an artist, who created drawings to illustrate some of the stories, and other persons, including editors and designers.

In Example 6, there is a source, or institutional producer ("we"), represented by the actual producer who signed the letter. If the text of the entire letter was presented, it would be possible to identify both the institutional producer (the law firm) and the actual producer (the signer).

In some kinds of texts, such as advertisements, it is often impossible to identify the actual producer. In others, such as instructions from cabin crews to airline passengers, it is not always possible to identify the source.

The producer directs the text to one or more interpreters. The interpreters are the intended receivers of the text, typically readers or listeners. The interpreter may or may not share the same cultural concepts as the producer, and may or may not have a shared knowledge of related texts. Take Example 5, for instance. The interpreter of that text is any mature reader. The text is probably intended for readers in their teens or older who have some knowledge of events in Europe during World War II. Readers from Africa or India might not share the same cultural concepts of place in the world and perception of the world with the producer of this text. Readers may or may not have read *The Diary of Anne Frank* or other works concerning the Holocaust. Some may have studied world history of the 20th century, and others may know only their local history. These readers will come away from the text with somewhat different interpretations.

Just as there are different kinds of producers, there are also different kinds of interpreters. The **addressee** is the interpreter to whom the text is directed, and the **target** is the interpreter whom the text is intended to affect. For instance, in Examples 5 and 6, the addressees and targets are probably the same people. However, consider a will

---

Practice 7:
Identify the producers and interpreters of the following text, which is the headline from an advertisement for an exercising machine:

Our machine takes care of your machine.
(*Newsweek* (international ed.), 25 May 1992, p. 6)

---

that makes a provision for an infant child. Although the will may be addressed to that child's legal guardian, the child is the target. In such cases where the target is not competent to interpret the discourse, the addressee will usually be someone empowered to act as interpreter on the target's behalf.

Finally, **overhearers** are those who may receive the text in some form but who are neither addressees nor targets. They may, however, function as subsidiary interpreters in their own right. One example would be persons not mentioned in a will, but who have been invited to attend the reading of the will nevertheless.

Guidelines for Analyzing Discourse Participants

Determine whether the producer is single, plural, institutional, or hidden.
Determine whether the interpreter is oneself or another; single, plural, or unenumerated.
Determine whether the interpreter(s) is also the target.
Determine whether there are any overhearers.

Sample Analysis: Discourse Participants

The CODE advertisement (Fig. 1.3) may be analyzed as follows:

Producer: Source is institutional, actual producer(s) is hidden.
Interpreter(s): Those readers of the magazine in which the advertisement appeared who might be persuaded to contribute money to CODE. These readers are also the target.
Overhearers: Any readers of the advertisement who are not potential donors to CODE.

Application

Using the aforementioned guidelines, analyze the discourse participants of your chosen oral and written practice texts.

Suggested Reading

Biber, D. (1994). An analytical framework for register studies. In D. Biber & E.
Finegan (Eds.), *Sociolinguistic perspectives on register* (pp. 31–56). Oxford,
England: Oxford University Press.
Biber's scheme is the only one to date for uniquely specifying the situation of a text,
including discourse participants. Some sections of the current book are strongly based
on Biber's situational scheme.

Brown, G., & Yule, G. (1983). *Discourse analysis.* Cambridge, England: Cambridge
University Press.
See the section on the elements of the situation for more information on how discourse
participants function in this context, esp. pp. 35–46.

Halliday, M., & Hasan, R. (1989). *Language, context, and text: Aspects of language
in a social-semiotic perspective.* Oxford, England: Oxford University Press.
Most relevant here is Halliday's description of tenor, another way of looking at the roles
of discourse participants, esp. p. 12 & pp. 24–26.

Hymes, D. (1972). Models of the interaction of language and social life. In J.
Gumperz & D. Hymes (Eds.), *Directions in sociolinguistics: The ethnography
of communication* (pp. 35–71). New York: Holt, Rinehart & Winston.
One of the first and most famous attempts to specify the situation of discourse, including
the discourse participants. Many subsequent approaches to situation are based heavily
on Hymes.

Renkema, J. (1993). *Discourse studies: An introductory textbook.* Amsterdam: John
Benjamins.
Like Brown and Yule, Renkema relied heavily on Hymes (1972) for a description of the
elements of the situational context, and specifically the participants. See pp. 43–45,
which include a discussion of "institution" and institutional participants.

PRODUCER–INTERPRETER RELATIONSHIPS

When looking at a printed text, such as a magazine article or a novel,
it is easy to think of it only as a finished product and not as the result
of a complex creative process. However, a great deal of discourse
analysis is concerned expressly with the process of discourse creation.
This process can be thought of as the interaction of two constituent
processes: the process of production and the process of interpretation.
Both processes work together to create a text. Because no two
interpreters have exactly the same experience of the world or their
culture, the same understanding of related texts, and the same pref-

erences for language use, there is an important sense in which what appears to be a unique text is in fact a different text to each person who interprets it. In this sense, a produced text is created anew by every attempt at interpretation. Of course, for the sake of communication, producers and interpreters generally trust that a large enough common core of meaning is shared among them so that a significant portion of the message is interpreted similarly by a majority of interpreters from the same cultural background.

It is easy to see that the processes of production and interpretation interact spiritedly in conversation, for example; but it is nonetheless true that the two processes interact in written forms of discourse as well, though in a less active way because of the situational distance between producer and interpreter. The dynamic interaction of these two processes continuously redefines the social, institutional, or intellectual relationship between the producer and the interpreter as the discourse proceeds. As Bakhtin (1981/1934–1935, p. 293) observed, "Language . . . lies on the borderline between oneself and the other. The word in language is half someone else's." This close dynamic relationship derives ultimately from the culture, and may be based on power, authority, position, and/or sex, among other things.

The producer's relationship to the text and to the interpreter(s) appears in the language of the text primarily as personal pronouns ("you," "they," and so on), modalities ("should," "perhaps," etc.), statements, questions, honorifics ("Dr.," "Your Honor," and so on), speech acts (requests, warnings, advice, and so on), registers (business language, legal language, and so on), hedgings (using modalities to "soften" a speech act), and polarity ("not"). The producer also manipulates the situation by using a variety of nonverbal means, such as manner of dress, choice and depiction of the setting, object of the text, and so on. The interpreter must consider all these when attempting to identify and to understand the producer.

Next comes an examination of some of the ways in which producers and interpreters can exercise culturally derived power over each other and actively intervene in the process of discourse creation to force a redefinition of the relationship between them.

The most common way in which an interpreter can pressure the producer toward a reevaluation of their dynamic relationship is through actively questioning one or more elements of the situational context that the producer is attempting to impose (or has imposed) on the discourse. Such questioning, called **monitoring**, is likely to be accompanied by appropriate body language, gestures, facial expressions, and so on (more on this later).

Monitoring is carried out to clarify the situation or to identify it as being in some sense unacceptable to the interpreter. It is, thus, most likely to occur when there is a perceived violation of the **assumed normality** of the world. Assumed normality exists as long as all variables of a situation conform to an individual's understanding, based on experience, of the world and how it behaves. Normality would be violated, for example, if a person heard or read a text about a situation in which trees fly, fish dance, mountains deliver lectures, and so on. People's experience of the world tells them that such events do not normally occur (but may be found in fables and children's stories). Two special cases of assumed normality are the **Principle of Analogy** and the **Principle of Local Interpretation**.

The Principle of Analogy states that things will behave according to people's expectations, based on their experience of the behavior of similar things. For example, if somebody hears that a person without a parachute fell out of an airplane at 4,000 meters and survived, the Principle of Analogy is violated. Any human being would be expected to die in such a situation.

The Principle of Local Interpretation, on the other hand, states that the smallest situational context required to form a reasonable interpretation is the correct one. So, for example, if some people are riding in an automobile and the driver suddenly shouts, "The brakes have failed!" meaning the brakes of some vehicle other than the one they are in, then the Principle of Local Interpretation is violated. The driver's statement would be expected to refer to the brakes of the vehicle in which the people are riding.

In general, violations of assumed normality occur whenever something improbable or contrary to the expected pattern occurs in a text. An interpreter will then usually respond by monitoring the text—often by referring to the offending element of the situation. Consider an example from classroom discourse. In this example, students monitor a teacher's comment merely by repeating some words relating to the place element:

(7) Teacher: Yes, write them down in your notebooks.
    Students: In our notebooks?
    (Author's notes)

The students were expecting to hear "exercise books," not "notebooks."

Practice 8:
Identify the monitoring in the following text.
(a) What principle is being violated?
(b) How does the monitoring reinforce the power relationships that exist in this text?
(c) What intonation, gestures, or body language might accompany such monitoring?

Teacher: Who did I give Ranya's piece of paper to yesterday with the tests I wanted her to do?
Students: (I did.
(You gave . . . You gave it to me but I had to go to Student Council so I gave it to Ellen.
Teacher: Is that right, Ellen?
Ellen: Yeah, but I forgot to give it to Ranya.
Teacher: Well, THAT is a LOT of use, isn't it? . . . When did you realise you forgot to give it to Ranya?
Ellen: Just now.
Teacher: Only just now? Ranya, why didn't you ask someone else in your FORM for it at afternoon registration?
Ranya: I forgot.
Teacher: And YOU forgot! It's MOST inconvenient because it now means that I cannot give those tests back. . . .
(Authors' notes, 1995)

In all texts, the producer has considerable control over the form and content of the text. Any choice in form and/or content that the producer makes to cause a text to be interpreted one way rather than another is called **staging**. Such devices as word choice, clause structuring, the ordering of words or information, intonation, choice of register and/or genre, and making information prominent can be used to achieve staging. Staging may draw on such techniques as the repetition of keywords, use of "loaded" synonyms (e.g., "queer" for "homosexual"), unsubstantiated interpretation (not based on any given facts, or based on deliberate or selective misinterpretation of facts), selective reporting of facts, and so on.

Texts that give facts or a point of view, such as news reports, may be staged to bring them in line with personal or institutional biases or ideologies or to show empathy with an individual, such as a victim. In texts that tell stories or anecdotes, the perspective of the storyteller or narrator is often used as a staging device. The narrator may appear to be omniscient, as in the novels of Dostoevsky, in which the deepest thoughts of the protagonist are revealed to the reader. Alternatively, the narrator may be one of the characters, as in the Baum text (Example 5). Such a narrator reports personal events and experiences only—seeing the world from one point of view. Another type of narrator acts as an unemotional recording machine, reporting words and actions but very little descriptive detail not related to the interactions of the protagonists. This type of narrator is typical, for example, in Hemingway's stories. (The narrative viewpoint is considered further in part II, chap. 7, this volume.)

Observe the following examples of two heavily staged texts on the subject of abortion:

(8) (a) "I have always believed that if television stations ever aired pictures of aborted babies it would begin to change many people's minds about the issue," [Republican congressional candidate Michael] Bailey explains. "People would focus on the evidence of abortion—which is the aborted baby—rather than this ill-conceived idea of women's choice. Choice is no choice to babies."

(b) "I have personally taken care of women with red rubber catheters hanging out of their uterus and a temperature of 107°F [42°C]," says Dr David Grimes, 45, of the University of Southern California School of Medicine. "Once a physician has watched that happening, he or she will never be willing to see the laws go back."

(Lacayo, R. [4 May 1992]. Explosion over abortion. *Time* [international ed.], p. 41)

In Example 8a, the speaker assumes that the sight of an aborted fetus is enough to convince anyone of the right to life of the baby. In Example 8b, on the other hand, the speaker assumes that the sight of a woman who has suffered from an illegal abortion is enough to convince anyone of the need to legalize abortions. In each case, staging is achieved by a selective reporting of information and by the choice of words intended to emphasize a personal bias or ideology. It is clear from these examples that staging may lead to two completely different interpretations, based on the same or very similar factual information.

Staging is particularly common in news reporting, where highly staged texts often masquerade as factual, unbiased accounts of events in the news. As van Dijk (1988, p. 71) observed: "Whereas negative implications are often associated with politically or socially defined them-groups, neutral or positive implications may be associated with the acts of those considered as we-groups. . . . [L]exical and semantic implications may involve evaluations based on the point of view and the ideology of the reporter."

Practice 9:
In the light of van Dijk's observation, examine the staging of the following news extracts from two British newspapers of 28 December 1986:

(a) What staging techniques are used?
(b) Who are the "them-groups" and "we-groups" in the two extracts?
(c) What word choices and meanings indicate point of view and ideology, as expressed by the two papers?
(d) Who, would you say, are the producers of these extracts? Who are the intended interpreters?

(i) INTENT ON REVENGE Colonel "Mad Dog" Gadaffi of Libya proclaimed in January that he would "train and equip Arab terrorists for suicide missions." He enflamed the United States' sensibilities, shut off the Gulf of Sirte and the war of words erupted to load the guns. In March, the final straw came with the bombing of American servicemen in a West Berlin discotheque. Reagan threatened and then ordered a strike in April—making controversial use of American air bases in Britain to launch his F-111s, and diluting the concentration of American tourists venturing to holiday in the United Kingdom. Tripoli was shattered as Gadaffi's adopted daughter was killed in an explosion and his private, luxury tent was completely devastated. Colonel Gadaffi went to ground.
(*Sunday Express*, quoted in Fowler, 1991)

(ii) Ronald Reagan got tough on terrorism when US planes bombed Libya in April. Alone of his NATO allies Britain gave direct support by allowing his F-111 bombers based at RAF Lakenheath to be used in an action which killed indiscriminately. As dead children were dug out of the rubble in Tripoli (photograph) British police massed at Lakenheath to repel protesters. Many people wondered who was the "mad dog" and who the "terrorists."
(*Observer*, quoted in Fowler, 1991)

One of the most effective and subtle ways of staging discourse is by placing certain elements of the text next to each other in order to show a contrast. For example, examine the following short texts:

(9) (a) Some scientists claim that the drug interferon shows striking results in the treatment of AIDS. Other scientists dispute this claim.
    (b) Two years ago, some scientists claimed that the drug interferon had shown striking results in the treatment of AIDS. More recently, other scientists have disputed this claim.
    (c) Kenyan scientists claim that the drug interferon shows striking results in the treatment of AIDS. U.S. scientists dispute this claim.
    (d) Two years ago, Kenyan scientists claimed the drug interferon had shown striking results in the treatment of AIDS. Last week, U.S. health

---

Practice 10:

Look for an example of the use of contrast as a staging device in the following extract from the speech of an American politician, Pat Buchanan. What is his probable intention in making such a contrast? (Consider the intended interpreters.) What is the unstated implication of his remark?

(At the 1992 Democratic Party Convention), 20,000 radicals and liberals came dressed up as moderates and centrists in the greatest single exhibition of cross-dressing in American political history.
(*The Seattle Times*, 19 August 1992, p. A2)

---

officials said that new tests had failed to confirm those findings and that interferon is not recommended for people with HIV infections. (*Time* [international ed.], 11 May 1992, p. 15)

Simply by contrasting the time "two years ago" with "more recently" in Example 9b, the producer stages the text heavily in favor of "other scientists" who dispute the claim. The unstated implication is that a more recent study is more reliable. Similarly, in Example 9c, contrasting the Kenyan scientists with the U.S. scientists might lead to the interpretation that the U.S. findings are more reliable simply because of the unstated but commonly shared belief that U.S. science is more advanced than Kenyan science. Both of these contrasts are contained in the actual article, which is given in Example 9d.

Using contrasts as a staging device is a particularly common technique in political discourse (including propaganda), the discourse of advertising, and the discourse of popular journalism.

Another device that a producer can use to exercise power over interpreters is **style**. Styles are personal choices that express who people are as individuals, who they think they are, or who they want others to think they are. The choice of one personal alternative rather than another, while maintaining essentially the same meaning, determines a style. Styles are chosen by individuals to achieve personal goals, such as assuming status, affirming group membership, and so on. Styles are often associated with greater or lesser prestige or formality. Gestures, body language, and so on, play an important role in spoken styles, and certain kinds of nonverbal behavior may come to be associated with certain speaking styles.

As an example of style, consider General Douglas MacArthur's famous utterance, as he was forced to flee with his troops from the

Philippines during World War II: "I shall return!" His choice of this style—rather than, for instance, "I'll be back," "I'm gonna come back," or some other more common phrasing—gave a greater indication of the determination, power, and prestige that he exercised as a military commander.

Van Dijk (1988) identified a number of styles; three types are considered here: **Personal style** is maintained by an individual through different situations. This may include a foreign accent, a preferred use of certain words or phrases, characteristic gestures, quality of voice, and so on. An example is Joseph Conrad's maintenance of a strong Polish accent in his speech while writing classics in English. **Ad hoc style** characterizes the discourse of a single person in a single situation. It may be revealed through indications of anger or other intense emotion, effective or ineffective attempts at achieving formality, and so forth. General MacArthur's utterance, already discussed, is an example of ad hoc style. **Group style** is a kind of personal style of an entire group, and is intended as an expression of group solidarity. An example is the speech style of the Quaker community in the United States. Quakers typically use a number of archaisms in their speech, including "thee." Any of these styles can be combined with any others.

Monitoring, staging, and style are all specific relational devices for expressing the power relationships between producer and interpreter. Within this relationship, the producer's purpose becomes quite prominent as a measure of power and is revealed to a large extent by the ways in which monitoring, staging, and style are used.

Along with the power relationships discussed earlier, an equally important part of the relationship between producer and interpreter(s) is the relevant prior knowledge of the world each possesses. Although such knowledge, too, can be used to maintain a power differential

---

Practice 11:
Examine a text by Henry James and one by Ernest Hemingway. Looking only at narrative passages (not dialogue), what can you say about the differences in the styles of the two authors? As an aid in this task, try writing a short passage from one author in the style of the other. Based on your findings, discuss how style communicates information and helps to create power relationships. For instance, what kind of power relationship does James' writing help to establish that Hemingway's does not? (*Hint:* Imagine persons of limited schooling attempting to read both.)

among discourse participants, its primary function is to provide a mental context for a text.

In the creation of a text, the producer must be aware of the intended audience of the text and must be able to make certain assumptions about the kinds of knowledge possessed by that audience (i.e., interpreters). For example, the reason why instruction manuals are often so difficult to understand is that the producer finds it difficult to think like the interpreter. The producer knows everything and the interpreter knows nothing. The producer simply cannot remember what it is like to know nothing about the object. As another example, a nuclear physicist, writing a paper for other nuclear physicists, may use a standard kind of technical language and a group style that are largely incomprehensible to the average reader but are easily understood by the intended audience. However, even in the least technical writing or conversation, a producer must make many important assumptions about the kinds of knowledge possessed by the interpreter(s); most of these assumptions are likely to be automatic, requiring no conscious thought on the part of the producer.

To see a simple but typical example of **participants' knowledge at work**, consider the following:

(10) Grandmother's response to my mother being dead for Christmas was to refuse to participate in the seasonal decoration of 80 Front Street; the wreaths were nailed too low on the doors, and the bottom half of the Christmas tree was overhung with tinsel and ornaments— ...
(Irving, J. [1989]. *A Prayer for Owen Meany.* New York: Ballantine, p. 147)

Note that the author writes "*the* seasonal decoration," "*the* wreaths," "*the* doors," "*the* Christmas tree," and so forth, instead of "seasonal decoration," "wreaths," "doors," and "a Christmas tree." Wreaths, doors, and Christmas tree have not been mentioned previously, so how is the author able to use the definite article "the" meaningfully in this text? Similarly, how is the reader able to understand what "80 Front Street" refers to without a more detailed description or a prior mention?

Clearly, the answer to these questions is that there *is* a prior mention of these things, but it is in the context rather than in the text itself. To be more precise, it is in the readers' minds and is part of their cultural knowledge of the world. People know, for example, that there are seasonal decorations at Christmas time and that doors, street numbers, and street names belong to houses and other buildings.

The ability to understand texts is derived from organized bodies of information related to common experiences that people store in their minds. These experiential organizations of information are called **frames**. Frames consist of slots and fillers. A house frame, for example, contains such slots as "door," "kitchen," "address," and so on. One possible filler for "address" is "80 Front Street." In this way, frames can be adapted to fit the situation by selecting relevant slots, eliminating others, and filling the selected slots with specific and pertinent details. Furthermore, frames can contain other frames. For example, a "Christmas tree" frame may fill a slot in a "Christmas decoration" frame.

Just as a frame highlights missing pieces of a thing and is expressed in terms of noun phrases, a **script** highlights missing pieces of a process and is expressed in terms of verb phrases. For example, a person who hears the utterance "she started the car" can fill in the missing processes: She inserted the key into the ignition switch; she turned the key while giving gas, and so on.

When frames and scripts are combined and placed within a situational context, they form **scenarios** or **schemata** (plural of "schema"). Scenarios are sequences of frames and scripts that describe situations. As structured sequences, they show people and things against a continuity of thought or action and help the interpreter to foresee or predict what will happen next by meaningfully connecting many frames and scripts. In the same way that individuals apparently conceptualize things, objects, people, and so on, as frames, and actions and processes as scripts, it would seem that they conceptualize the situational events of daily life as a combination of these (viz. scenarios). For example, they can conceive of a "grocery shopping" scenario, a "classroom learning" scenario, a "visiting the doctor" scenario, and countless others. And because discourse reflects thoughts and experiences, individuals perceive discourse in part as consisting of scenarios.

When thinking of a grocery shopping scenario, for example, people know that certain individuals are involved (e.g., shopper, stocker, cashier, bagger, etc.). Similarly, certain processes are involved and are associated with these individuals: stocker puts items on shelf, puts price tags on items, and so forth; shopper compares prices, selects items, puts items in cart, and so forth; cashier tallies the cost and makes change; bagger packs the groceries and may assist in taking them to the car. So in saying, "I went grocery shopping this morning," it is possible to imagine that this person experienced most of the individuals and processes related to this scenario, even though they were not mentioned explicitly.

Occasionally, a text is governed by a single dominant scenario. In such a case, all participants agree that the discourse itself, rather than merely the world it depicts, should follow a predetermined pattern. In other words, the scripts within the scenario are fairly rigidly preordained. Examples include marriage ceremonies, courtroom procedures, oaths of allegiance, State of the Union Addresses, and so on. Such examples differ primarily in the degree to which they stipulate the exact wording of texts. The wording of a marriage ceremony is usually rigidly predetermined by custom, whereas a State of the Union Address may resemble previous speeches only in the general topic and the approximate order in which the items are presented.

Like a scenario, a schema involves individuals and actions. However, it differs from a scenario in that it is related to general, rather than specific, situations. It is a description of people's knowledge of other people and the things they typically do in typical circumstances. Suppose Jim tells a joke about a shop owner and some shoes to Carol. A few days later Carol recounts the joke to a friend, but this time it is about a traveling salesperson and some hats. Carol remembers the point of the joke and gets the punch line right, but she changes the characters, the objects, and the processes to a certain extent. A psychologist might say that a schema has intruded on Carol's memory of the joke. It is a workable and situationally correct schema for the joke, but it has overridden the original scenario.

Tannen (1980) demonstrated that cultural differences affect schemata. She showed a film to American and Greek subjects. Then she asked them to recount it. The Americans tended to describe the actual events of the film in detail, whereas the Greeks invented additional events and explained the emotions and actions of the characters.

Frames, scripts, scenarios, and schemata encompass a person's general knowledge of the world. Without relevant knowledge of this kind, an interpreter would be unable to make sense of any text, no matter how simple. If an interpreter has the relevant knowledge for understanding a text, then the text seems (to that interpreter at least) to have **coherence**. In other words, it seems to make sense and to have meaning. People often speak of a text as being coherent, but in fact, coherence is as much a property of the interpreter's world knowledge

Practice 12:
To gain a better understanding of frames, scripts, scenarios, and schemata, repeat the classic experiment that was carried out in the early 1930s by the psychologist F. D. Bartlett. Bartlett presented the following story to a group of subjects. They were then distracted for a time and made to think about something else. Finally, they were asked to write down a retelling of the story.

Read the story to some classmates or friends. Then, for 15 minutes or so, do something else that will distract their attention. Finally, ask them to retell the story in writing. Each retelling will be an interesting composite of frames, scripts, scenarios, and schemata that will reveal some insights into the minds of your friends. In particular, schemata will tend to take over the retelling, substituting more common things and behaviors for the uncommon ones contained in the story. (*Hint:* Take special notice of which uncommon things and processes are replaced by more common ones. Also, what kinds of cultural knowledge, about Indians for example, might creep into the story.)

The War of the Ghosts

One night two young men from Egulac went down to the river to hunt seals, and while they were there it became foggy and calm. Then they heard war-cries, and they thought: "Maybe this is a war-party." They escaped to the shore and hid behind a log. Now canoes came up, and they heard the noise of paddles, and saw one canoe coming up to them. There were five men in the canoe, and they said:

"What do you think? We wish to take you along. We are going up the river to make war on the people."

One of the young men said: "I have no arrows."

"Arrows are in the canoe," they said.

"I will not go along. I might be killed. My relatives do not know where I have gone. But you," he said, turning to the other, "may go with them."

So one of the young men went, but the other returned home.

And the warriors went on up the river to a town on the other side of Kalama. The people came down to the water, and they began to fight, and many were killed. But presently the young man heard one of the warriors say: "Quick, let us go home: that Indian has been hit." Now he thought: "Oh, they are ghosts." He did not feel sick, but they said he had been shot.

So the canoes went back to Egulac, and the young man went ashore to his house, and made a fire. And he told everybody and said: "Behold I accompanied the ghosts, and we went to fight. Many of our fellows were killed, and many of those who attacked us were killed. They said I was hit, and I did not feel sick."

He told it all, and then he became quiet. When the sun rose he fell down. Something black came out of his mouth. His face became contorted. The people jumped up and cried.

He was dead.

(Bartlett, 1932; quoted in Renkema, 1993, pp. 161–162)

as it is a property of the text. Coherence is, therefore, a knowledge relationship between producer and interpreter. When the relevant knowledge of the producer matches the relevant knowledge of the interpreter, then coherence may exist. As an example, a person looks at a text on microbiology, nuclear physics, brain surgery, or any unfamiliar topic. Although many words and sentences may seem clear and well formed, longer sections of the text will not make sense to this individual. This person's world knowledge does not include the kinds of relevant knowledge that the producer is drawing on for an understanding of the text. For this individual, the text is incoherent. But for someone else who understands the topic, the text may be quite coherent indeed.

Many contextual and linguistic devices can work to facilitate coherence in texts, but undoubtedly the most important of these is the interpreter's world knowledge. However, saying that coherence is facilitated by the interpreter's knowledge of the world requires being careful about what is meant. Clearly, it does not mean the actual facts themselves. If that were the case, people would be able to make sense of only those things that they already know. They would never be able to learn anything new from texts. Rather, the kind of general world knowledge that facilitates coherence is the frame knowledge already discussed. Frame knowledge made it possible to make sense of the Christmas decoration text (Example 10), even though the reader has never met the people in that text and has never been in their house. Similarly, it allows a reader to make sense out of the following short (constructed) text:

(11) Aardvarks are fascinating. You should read Welda Leakey-Fawcett's latest book.

In their understanding that Leakey-Fawcett's book is about aardvarks, interpreters should have no difficulty finding this short text coherent. Following Stubbs (1983), be aware that texts of this kind cannot be based on any knowledge of the world that includes an author named Welda Leakey-Fawcett who writes about aardvarks. Such a person does not exist. Therefore, the only source of world knowledge that remains is the more generalized frame knowledge that people possess about books, authors, and topics. According to frame knowledge, it is just possible for an author to be named Welda Leakey-Fawcett and for a book to be about aardvarks. Therefore, people can find coherence in this text, even in the absence of specific knowledge about its topic.

People's understanding of a coherent text continues to grow and develop as they assimilate it. Everything individuals hear or read continues to awaken knowledge within them that contributes to the continuous reinterpretation of the text. These items of knowledge are called **activated features of discourse**. In the Christmas decoration text (Example 10), the mention of "Christmas" activates certain sets of ideas, or frames, in the readers' minds. Later, "decorations" reinforces this set and at the same time particularizes it. People constantly predict the kinds of information that follow, and once they have assimilated this information, their interpretation of the entire text so far is reshaped. As an interpreter moves through a text, it may be necessary to activate features of the discourse that were not required earlier. This process is known as **spreading activation**.[2]

Sometimes, of course, activation of knowledge leads to incorrect predictions. Look again at the Christmas text:

(10) Grandmother's response to my mother being dead for Christmas was to refuse to participate in the seasonal decoration of 80 Front Street; the wreaths were nailed too low on the doors, and the bottom half of the Christmas tree was overhung with tinsel and ornaments— ...

For example, imagine why the Christmas decorations are placed too low. Most people, when asked this question, assume that the decorating is being done by the children of the household, because Grandmother refuses to participate. That is a common enough assumption, based on scenario knowledge of many Western households and the kinds of tasks children do at Christmas. If you were one of these interpreters, however, the very next phrase of the text would cause you to reevaluate and reinterpret:

(12) ... —the result of Lydia applying her heavy-handed touch at wheelchair level.

The relationship between producer and interpreter is always, to some extent, a personal one. Understanding what kind of personal

---

[2]A study by Henry and Roseberry (1995) showed that an important difference between first- and second-language readers was their relative abilities to use word knowledge to activate appropriate background knowledge when reading. Readers in both groups were asked to rate the importance of sentences and clauses to the meaning of an entire text. Using the sentences and clauses rated highest by the readers, summaries of the text were created. The native-speaker summaries stressed pervasive and crucial ideas, whereas those by second-language speakers stressed specific, isolated, and often relatively trivial facts.

relationship exists can help shed light on the kinds of emotional response a text might evoke in an interpreter. And this, in turn, can help to define the kind of power relationship that might exist between producer and interpreter. According to Biber (1994, p. 40), the producer and interpreter(s) might be "kin, friends, enemies, colleagues, etc." The emotions they might feel for each other might include "like, respect, fear," and so on. Complex power relationships will arise out of any of the combinations of these relationships and feelings. People who are respected—such as a parent, a teacher, or a judge—exercise power over other individuals based on that respect. Similarly, if an individual likes someone, such as a friend, that friend is able to exercise a great deal of power over the individual in the form of persuasion.

A powerful tool for achieving power over an interpreter is politeness. Politeness clearly plays a major role in the degree of cooperation among participants in discourse. Politeness is, by its nature, cultural. What makes politeness necessary, according to Goffman (1956), is the fact that discourse often presents the interpreter with a **face threatening act**. Refusals are one example of such an act. If individuals request something and are bluntly told "no," then they may feel accosted or insulted. People of many cultures perceive such blunt behavior as a threat to one's **face**, meaning the personal image that the person projects in a discourse situation. If one person offends another by committing a face threatening act, the response, in current colloquial English, may be "Get outta my face!"

The degree of bluntness that a person may accept without feeling that a face threatening act has been committed appears to depend heavily on culture (as hinted at earlier in the discussion of Wierzbicka's analysis of self-assertion in Black American, Anglo-American, and Japanese cultures). Attempts that have been made to give a description of politeness that is general enough to be valid across cultural boundaries have been quite extensively criticized (Fraser, 1990). Nonetheless, the conversational-maxim, face-saving, and conversational-contract views of politeness, all taking as their point of departure Grice's Cooperative Principle, seem to be the most fully articulated. Lakoff's (1973) **Politeness Principle**, the conversational-maxim view, was elaborated by Brown and Levinson (1987) in their face-saving view, whereas Fraser and Nolen's (1981) conversational-contract view differs from Brown and Levinson's approach.

The Politeness Principle consisted of three maxims designed to explain the politeness strategies that people use in discourse. According to these three maxims, a producer who wishes to be perceived as being polite (a) will not impose on the interpreter, (b) will give the interpreter options to allow escape from undesired situations, and (c) will attempt to make the interpreter feel good. The following exchange exemplifies these maxims:

[13] A: Uh if you'd care to come and visit a little while this morning I'll give you a cup of coffee
B: Hehh Well that's awfully sweet of you, I don't think I can make it this morning. .hh uhm I'm running an ad in the paper and-and uh I have to stay near the phone.
(Quoted in Levinson, 1983, pp. 333–334)

Note that A does not impose on B, but rather offers something in return. Also, by stating the indirect request in the conditional ("if . . ."), A allows B an easier escape route than would a demand or a question. Finally, by making B feel that B's company is desirable, A attempts to make B feel good. B's reply is also polite. B shows appreciation intended to make A feel good and uses hedges and explanations to show that A's invitation is valued even if it cannot be accepted.

Brown and Levinson (1987) went on to develop Politeness Theory, claiming that power (P), distance (D), and ranked extremity (R), while remaining culturally specific, are the universal determinants of politeness levels. They identified 5 strategies, later reduced to 4, with

---

Practice 13:
In the following text, locate all the markers of politeness that you can find. Include choices of indirect speech acts, instances of hedging, and examples of the Politeness Principle. This text is part of a letter from a bank to its customers.

(a) What kind of power relation does the bank establish over the customer by using politeness markers in this way?
(b) What might be the effect of a more direct, less polite text?

There are increasing numbers of incidences where HongkongBank Global Access or ETC International Cards are lost or stolen along with written records of Personal Identification Numbers (PIN). This has resulted in unauthorised withdrawals of funds from accounts. We would like to remind you, as a valued cardholder, of the precautions that should be taken in order to ensure that such unfortunate circumstances do not happen to you.
(The Hongkong and Shanghai Banking Corporation Limited, Bandar Seri Begawan, Brunei, June 1994)

15 subvarieties of positive politeness and 10 of negative politeness. The 4 strategies are as follows:

1. Do the face threatening act (FTA) on record without redressive action, baldly.
2. Do the FTA on record with redressive action of the kind called positive politeness and/or of the kind called negative politeness.
3. Do the FTA off record.
4. Don't do the FTA.

Politeness Theory is exemplified in a number of examples already given. For example, Strategy 1 may explain the apparent rudeness of "Exact change, please" in Practice 1a, and Strategy 2 may explain Practices 1b and 13.

Fraser (1990) provided a critical overview of previous and subsequent refinements of politeness theories, dismissing the old social norm view, and concluding that the face threatening view is currently the most viable. A more interesting development, however, is the relation between positive and negative face and **affect**. Brown and Gilman (1989, p. 168), for example, found in their study of P, D, and R in Shakespeare's tragedies that "distance and affect had to be treated separately and, for the problems presented, affect was the more important variable by far." Furthermore, "politeness decreases with the withdrawal of affection and increases with an increase of affection" (p. 199). This relation between politeness and affect is of interest in any power relation.

To get a clearer understanding of power relations and the role that politeness plays in them, consider an example of a male doctor who is advising a young single woman about birth control choices. The patient probably respects her doctor, which is why she seeks his advice in the first place. This automatically provides the doctor with a great deal of power over his patient. Culture and situation—including age, gender, and many other factors—may determine the doctor's and the woman's ideas and viewpoints on the topic of birth control. However, exactly how the topic is expressed, what kinds of power indicators are used, what sort of relevant information is omitted, and so on, is no longer a general matter of discourse, but is rather a matter of a specific text that has developed between two people.

In order to have some control over a text at the interpersonal level, interpreters require not merely an awareness of the producer's actual

51

techniques and motives, but also a degree of assertiveness to establish their own viewpoint. First, interpreters must be able to see how the topic structure is developing and to what extent conscious staging is being used in the development of the exchange. If any such techniques are apparent, interpreters immediately need to explore possible reasons for the staging. For example, they may need to recall relevant information that has been purposely omitted from a text to further the producer's purpose. Second, having established that the producer is, indeed, attempting to stage the text, interpreters need to be able to monitor effectively in order to force some degree of compliance on the producer. Both of these strategies are difficult and are achievable much more easily in theory than in practice.

The first strategy is achievable through a mastery of the techniques of discourse analysis, which is the primary purpose of this book. As people grow, learn, and experience more of the world and of life, their understanding of other people and their intentions grows, and they become increasingly better able to perceive biases, staging, and other attempts at exercising power through texts. The second strategy is the more problematical one for many people, who simply feel unable to question authority figures. Authority figures are most likely to stage texts, and they do so in order to lead (or mislead) those over whom they have real or imagined power. For example, read the following two short extracts from an interview involving a male doctor and a female patient:

(14) Doctor: Would you like something called meprobramate? . . .
    Patient: I don't know what it is.
    Doctor: Fine, I'll call the pharmacy and [inaudible]. And you can mix that with aspirin. That's perfectly fine.

(15) Patient: And my mother, and my mother tends to be anemic.
    Doctor: Don't choose a diagnosis out of the blue. Buy a medical book and get a real nice diagnosis.
    (Borges, 1986, pp. 47–48)

In Example 14, staging is accomplished through the omission of relevant information, namely, the answer to the patient's question, "what is it?" The doctor is merely carrying on a monologue with himself, the result of which, most likely, will be to cause the patient to take a drug that she has never heard of and does not understand. In Example 15, staging goes a step further and violates cultural and situational norms of politeness. The patient can understand from the doctor's sarcasm that, as a relatively uneducated person without any medical training, she has no right to encroach on the doctor's domain and use technical terms like "anemia." It should be noted that, if the patient had been a man, it is very unlikely that the doctor would have responded in this way.

What can be learned from this patient's experience that can help someone else cope with similar situations that occur in daily life at school, at home, in the workplace, and elsewhere? Clearly, people do not want to say anything that will cause them to be "put down" or ridiculed, as in the doctor–patient interview. Probably, there are only two real options: *avoidance*, and *mastery*. Certainly, avoidance is not to be ruled out altogether. In this case, the patient would probably do very well to change doctors. Anyone who has such contempt for women and for patients generally, and whose view of medicine leads him to condescend to a person with limited medical knowledge, clearly has no business in a helping profession.

However, avoidance can never be a complete solution. There will always be difficult texts to negotiate, even between people who have no enmity toward each other. A more positive approach, and one that can benefit the victim in situations such as the doctor–patient interview, is assertiveness training. In this approach, a person learns to value and respect the self. A relatively uneducated person learns, for example, that questioning a doctor for the purpose of increasing personal knowledge is a positive, not a negative, act. A woman who has been brought up in a society where women defer to men learns that her own ideas and opinions count as powerfully as anyone's—especially when they concern choices that she must make about herself. She would then be able to say to the doctor in the previous situation, "Excuse me, doctor, but I am not going to take a drug without knowing precisely what it is and what it does. As for my mother, she *does* have anemia—at least if one can trust the diagnosis of her doctor. And as one final point, let me say that I do not like the nonprofessional tone of some of this interview today. I detected considerable and uncalled-for rudeness and contempt. If we are to continue to work together as doctor and patient, I would hope to see no further examples of this in our future meetings. Have a nice day."

As pointed out earlier, attaining the ability to manage discourse in this way is no easy task. However, once this ability is attained, it brings with it personal rewards that go even beyond the management of discourse. Individuals become more secure in the knowledge of who they are, they increase others' respect for them, and they learn how to intervene actively to improve their relationships with others.

Guidelines for Analyzing Producer–Interpreter Relationships

Determine the relative status and power of the producer and the interpreter(s), and try to identify any power relationships that are likely to exist between producer and interpreter(s).

Determine the extent of shared knowledge. How much specialist knowledge is shared? How much specific personal knowledge is shared?

Determine the extent of interactiveness between producer and interpreter(s).

Specify the personal relationship that exists between producer and interpreter(s), and indicate what kinds of emotional attachment characterize this relationship.

Identify any violation of assumed normality and any response to this in the form of monitoring.

Identify any instances of staging. Attempt to predict the intended interpreter(s)' reactions to this staging.

Identify the use of style. Attempt to predict the intended interpreter(s)' reaction to this style.

Identify typical frames, scripts, scenarios, and schemata that are likely to contribute to an interpretation of the text.

Attempt to assess whether the intended interpreter(s)' general world knowledge and knowledge based on frames, scripts, scenarios, and schemata are sufficient for the interpretation of this text. If not, attempt to assess the producer's purpose in requiring such knowledge.

Sample Analysis: Producer–Interpreter Relationships

The CODE advertisement (Fig. 1.3) may be analyzed as follows:

Interpreter exercises power over the producer, who is attempting to convince the interpreter to contribute money.

Knowledge of Third-World illiteracy must be shared by discourse participants.

There is no interactiveness between participants. This is typical of written texts.

The personal relationship is one of needy expert to generous layperson. The relationship may be characterized by admiration and/or pity and compassion.

No significant violation of assumed normality.

The letters of the alphabet are staged, both through the mystifying "We have 26" and then immediately in the photo, which explains this sentence by showing its meaning. The intention is to cause the interpreter to focus on the symbols of literacy, which is the focus of the text.

Style is typical for this type of text—literate yet informal.

Alphabet frame and scenarios tying education to job attainment are essential here. Also aid agency scenarios would be helpful in trying to form a picture of what CODE does and why.

World knowledge required for the comprehension of the text is well within the norms expected for readers of the news magazine from which the advertisement was taken.

Application

Using the aforementioned guidelines, analyze the producer–interpreter relationships of your chosen oral and written practice texts.

Suggested Reading

Biber, D. (1994). An analytical framework for register studies. In D. Biber & E. Finegan (Eds.), *Sociolinguistic perspectives on register* (pp. 31–56). Oxford, England: Oxford University Press.

Biber's scheme is the only one to date for uniquely specifying the situation of a text, including producer–interpreter relationships. Several sections of chapter 1 are strongly based on Biber's situational scheme.

Brown, G., & Yule, G. (1983). *Discourse analysis*. Cambridge, England: Cambridge University Press.

Contains a useful summary and explanation of work on frames, scripts, scenarios, and schemata (pp. 238–256).

Chafe, W. (1994). *Discourse, consciousness, and time*. Chicago: University of Chicago Press.

Most of the second half of Chafe's book deals with narrative point of view. Chafe provided a taxonomy of narrative viewpoints based on the role of consciousness in language and showed how different elements of the grammar come into play to realize these viewpoints. Studying the section on narrative viewpoints in chapter 7 of this book is recommended before attempting Chafe's work.

Fairclough, N. (1989). *Language and power.* London: Longman.
A Marxist approach to the kinds of power relations that can exist between discourse participants.

Scollon, R., & Scollon, S. (1995). *Intercultural communication: A discourse approach.* Oxford, England: Blackwell.
See especially chapter 3 ("Interpersonal Politeness and Power") and chapter 5 ("Topic and Face").

SETTING

Setting includes time and place. There are two main kinds of setting: **textual setting** and **metatextual setting**. The textual setting is the setting contained in the text itself, and metatextual setting is the setting *of* the text. As an example, consider a motion picture such as *Doctor Zhivago*. The opening scene of that film depicts the Steppes of Russia (textual setting), but the scene was actually filmed in the Canadian Prairies (metatextual setting). The novel and the film based on it portray the period of the Russian Revolution (textual setting); however, Pasternak wrote the novel many years after the revolution had ended (metatextual setting). Discussions of setting in this book are concerned primarily with textual setting, although occasional references to metatextual setting are necessary. A third type of setting is the time and place of the interpreter(s).

Time, as shown earlier, is greatly dependent on culture for its definition. Western cultures are among those that may indicate time in discourse through descriptions of clothing, furniture, weather, landscapes, music, and other objects or art forms commonly associated with a particular period, season, time of day, and so on. In the languages of these cultures, time is expressed primarily through tense and aspect, time adverbials, words such as "then" and "now," and time prepositions.

A typical example of the use of time in discourse is the following text, the first two paragraphs of which were given in Example 5 (Baum, 1990, pp. 115–116):

(16) As soon as we came in, an older, thin peasant woman, probably the housekeeper, who at once recognized Mother, started to talk furtively in a thick dialect, and in her bewilderment flapped her arms like a wild duck. She was terribly excited and beside herself, and after a minute or so Nacia, who had heard the fuss, came running in.

She was a lovely, dark blond young woman: slim and graceful, like a ballerina. And though she was very simply dressed, to me she instantly became the Princess of all the fairy tales I had ever known.

After some time her mother, old Mrs. Norski, trudged in, dressed all in black, leaning heavily on her cane. Crippled by arthritis, she walked slowly. I noticed her immaculate hair-do, and only now I assume that undoubtedly, it must have been a wig. And I could not help noticing the well polished, old-fashioned, tightly laced shoes reaching to her midcalf, a type that I had only seen in old photographs. We were taken at once to greet Mr. Norski himself, who presided in a heavy armchair at a massive rectangular oak table laden with well-worn Hebrew books. Dressed in black, broad-shouldered, he appeared to be very tall, even while sitting. Though he certainly must have been advanced in years, his thick beard was not all that gray.

This text employs the usual narrative past tense, which does not in itself tell much about the period being described. The contrast in Sentence 7 between "I noticed" and "only now I assume" suggests the passage of a significant amount of time in the life of a person, but remains imprecise. The fact that the old couple are both dressed in black might suggest in some cultures a period of mourning, but in others it simply may be the preferred color of dress for members of the older generation. The mention of "old-fashioned" shoes similar to those appearing in "old photographs" places it after the mid-19th century. The mention of arthritis may bring it closer to the present. If interpreters were to read the rest of the story and the other stories that appear with it in the collection from which it comes, they would see that the time is the period during World War II.

The other part of setting, **place**, is related to the cultural concept of territory. It is expressed primarily through adverbials, including words such as "here" and "there"; location verbs and nouns, such as "site," "locate," "place," "position," and so on; and prepositional phrases indicating location. In Example 16, the larger setting (if the whole story was read) turns out to be mid-20th-century Poland, and a small subset of that setting is the Polish-Jewish household depicted in that text.

The language of the text reveals a number of spatial clues. One of the most important is the pointing adverb "in" near the beginning of the text. Other examples of the same usage include "came running in" and "trudged in." All of these reinforce the concept of an enclosed space, such as a house. Other verbal clues that activate frame knowledge are "presided," "in a heavy armchair," and "at a massive rectangular oak table." This image is of a study—one of the rooms in a house. The fact that the people mentioned include typical household members such as a daughter, her mother, the mother's husband, and a housekeeper, again suggests a house into which the outsiders "we" have entered. Cultural items such as clothing and furniture and particularly the "well-worn Hebrew books" provide some further information, but again it would be necessary to read the entire book to see how this household fits into the larger setting.

The elements that comprise the situation are rarely static. Participants, time, place, and other variables of the situation to be discussed in later sections may change as the discourse progresses. If this happens, any words that refer to these elements will be subject to continually changing definitions. A typical example is the following:

```
(17) R:  Why don't we all have lunch
     C:  Okay so that would be in St. Jude's would it?
     R:  Yes
         (0.7 second pause)
     C:  Okay so:::
     R:  One o'clock in the bar
     C:  Okay
     R:  Okay?
     C:  Okay then thanks very much indeed George=
     R:  All right
     C:  // See you there
     R:      See you there
     C:  Okay
     R:  Okay // bye
     C:          bye
     (Quoted in Levinson, 1983, pp. 316–317)
```

Here, place is referred to alternately as "St. Jude's," "the bar," and "there." In this text, these words all mean "where we will have lunch." However, the context evolves with the varying specificity of the place words. "St. Jude's" is less specific than "bar." On the other hand, "there" has varying degrees of specificity because of being a pointing word. Depending on the situation, "there" could refer to "St. Jude's," the "bar," or even part of the street near the restaurant. Unlike the place element, the time element in this example does not evolve. The only reference to time is the specific designation, "one o'clock."

Conversations such as this text often contain the most complex examples of evolving contexts. Producer and interpreter exchange roles in every move, and usually the different elements of the situ-

---

Practice 14:
Analyze Example 4 (reprinted here) for an evolving context. Which elements of the situation are redefined as the text progresses? How are the words "now" and "the present" related?

Let us take as our starting point the calculation of the General Register Office that by 1985 there would be in this country 3½ million coloured immigrants and their offspring—in other words that the present number would have increased between two and three-fold in the next 17 years—on two assumptions, current rate of intake and current birthrate.

The first assumption is that the rate of net inflow continues at present. It has not indeed diminished since the estimate was made, but I am willing to suppose that, especially with the substantially greater limitations which a Conservative government has undertaken to apply, the rate would be markedly reduced during the period in question. For the purposes of argument I will suppose that it falls at a steady rate from 60,000 in 1968 to nil by 1985. In that case the total in the latter year would be reduced by about half-a-million, that is to 3 million.

I now turn to the second and more crucial assumption, the birthrate. . . . There are grounds for arguing that the immigrant birthrate is likely to rise during the next 2 or 3 decades: for instance the proportion of females must increase as dependents join male workers, so that a given total of immigrant population will yield more family units.

---

ation, and especially time and place, are redefined frequently during the interaction.

If one of the elements of the text situation (textual) does not match its counterpart in the immediate real situation (metatextual), this means **displaced context**. This is what is bothering Snoopy in Fig. 1.4. In the following (constructed) example, the place is displaced, because it does not match the current position of the husband and wife. As a result, the pointing word "here" in the discourse refers to a place other than where the husband and wife currently are:

(18) (Husband pointing to a place on a map that his wife is holding): Why don't we stop here for a few days on our trip south?

Aside from conversations that refer to the immediate situation, texts frequently grow out of situational contexts that are almost always displaced in some way from the real situation. The most common displacement occurs when the time mentioned in the text is not the same as the current time. Printed texts, movies (such as the one mentioned earlier), and television programs recorded for later broad-

FIG. 1.4. A displaced context may be described differently by different discourse participants. PEANUTS © United Feature Syndicate. Reprinted by permission.

casts are among the common examples of texts that exhibit this kind of contextual displacement. It is important to be aware of the distinction between current time and place of the producer, current time and place of the interpreter(s), and textual/metatextual time and place in and of the text. Any differences among these can cause problems of interpretation.

Guidelines for Analyzing Setting

Determine if the place of discourse is private or public.

Identify the domain of the discourse: business, education, government, etc.

Determine what type of mass media carries the discourse: television, printed book, newspaper, etc. Determine what kind of a contextual displacement, if any, results from this.

Identify the extent to which the participants share the place of the discourse: immediate, familiar, removed.

Identify the extent to which the participants share the time of the discourse: immediate, familiar, removed.

Identify the specific time and place of the discourse (metatextual), and in the discourse (textual). Determine what linguistic features of time and place are most prominent. Examine why these features are prominent.

Identify any evolving contexts. Determine what elements of the situation are affected. Determine why the context evolves as it does. Determine if this is typical for the type of discourse under scrutiny.

Identify any displaced contexts. Determine if the use of displaced contexts is within the range of expected normality.

Sample Analysis: Setting

The CODE advertisement (Fig. 1.3) may be analyzed as follows:

It is a public text, involving political and educational matters and carried in the visual mass media (magazine). The time lapse between production and interpretation can therefore probably be measured in weeks.
The time of the discourse is immediate; the place may be familiar to some interpreters; for others, it is removed.
The specific time and place of the discourse (metatextual) is *Time* magazine, 27 July 1992.
Time: governed by aspect rather than by tense. The interpreter assumes that the given information has continuing validity and is not restricted to a specific time frame. This aspect is shown grammatically through the present simple tense.
Place: the "developing world" indicated specifically by the phrase "in 16 countries in Africa and the Caribbean." The phone number for CODE itself may also be taken as a spatial reference here, especially as it is prefixed by the spatial preposition "at."
Evolving context is indicated by "developing world," "developing countries," and "16 countries in Africa and the Caribbean." This serves to guide and focus the interpreter's attention.

Application

Using the aforementioned guidelines, analyze the settings of your chosen oral and written practice texts.

Suggested Reading

Biber, D. (1994). An analytical framework for register studies. In D. Biber & E. Finegan (Eds.), *Sociolinguistic perspectives on register* (pp. 31–56). Oxford, England: Oxford University Press.
Biber's scheme is the only one to date for uniquely specifying the situation of a text, including setting. Several sections in chapter 1 are strongly based on Biber's situational scheme.

Brown, G., & Yule, G. (1983). *Discourse analysis.* Cambridge, England: Cambridge University Press.
  Pages 35–58, in particular, clearly describe setting and evolving context.
Chafe, W. (1994). *Discourse, consciousness, and time.* Chicago: University of Chicago Press.
  A penetrating philosophical study of the relation of consciousness to discourse and music. This is definitely an advanced text.
Halliday, M., & Hasan, R. (1989). *Language, context, and text: Aspects of language in a social-semiotic perspective.* Oxford, England: Oxford University Press.
  The section by Halliday (chaps. 1–3) discusses situational context in light of his concept of "field."

CHANNEL

Channel is the physical means by which a text is conveyed to an interpreter. The two most common channels are writing and speaking. But texts may also be conveyed through **sign language**, body language, code, and so forth. Often, a mixture of channels is used to convey a text, as in a movie. A channel may be permanent, as in writing or recording, or transient, as in unrecorded speech. Various **media** may be used for transmissions through a given channel. Paper is the common medium of the written channel. But radio, television, e-mail and many others are also common media of the modern age.

Many elements of the context affect writing, speaking, and other channels in various ways. One of the most important of these elements is the culture (discussed earlier). For example, a culture that has access to writing is able to develop advanced economic, political, and technological systems. Written discourse in such societies provides the foundation for further advancement. On the other hand, oral cultures depend on the memory of the custodians of their history, which means the foundation shifts from generation to generation, given the transient nature of unrecorded speech.

By contrast, oral discourse in all societies, whether literate or not, gradually socializes individuals into their cultures, from infancy onward. Even when, in literate societies, children start formal schooling and learn to read and write as they mature, talk continues to be a major force in self-development. And the pervasiveness of nonprint media such as radio and television has a major impact on individuals' self-development.

On the other hand, in literate societes, individuals and groups may appear to be able to choose between oral and written channels for their self-preservation and development. However, in technologically advanced societies, the illiterate have few opportunities, because so much value is placed on the ability to produce and interpret sophisticated written discourse in many spheres of life. Nonliterate societies, as already noted, cannot develop complex institutions.

Within any culture, situational contexts have an important relation to channel. For one thing, spoken texts, and especially conversations, offer a wider scope for monitoring than written ones. Monitoring is more effective if it can be carried out as the text progresses. It loses much of its power if there is a delay between production and monitoring, as there would be in an exchange of personal letters, for example. Spontaneity is a powerful tool here, and to monitor by saying something like, " 'X'? What do you mean 'X'?" places a great deal of pressure on the producer to justify "X" immediately. In an exchange of personal letters, on the other hand, the producer has time to think and to justify "X," and most of the power that monitoring gives to the interpreter is lost.

Of course, in many forms of written discourse, monitoring is impossible. If the author is dead or otherwise inaccessible to the interpreter, the only monitoring that is likely to take place is between two interpreters who may be citing part of a written text as support for an argument. Of course, there are oral texts that do not permit monitoring. Among these are lawyer's summations in court, many kinds of formal speeches (e.g., the State of the Union Address), ceremonial language (e.g., a marriage ceremony), and so on.

From the producer's point of view, staging is more central than monitoring; the choice of written or spoken channel is significant only to the extent that it helps to determine how the staging should be accomplished. Staging, and especially thematization, can be aided by intonation and stress in spoken language, whereas in written language certain orthographic conventions such as underlining and italicizing may be used as a feeble substitute for paralinguistics. It is also likely in face-to-face conversation, for example, that conversationalists will use body language to further highlight certain elements of the text. In both spoken and written texts, information can be further thematized by placing it in prominent positions in clause groups.

Participants' knowledge also influences written and spoken texts differently. Halliday (1989) observed that writing is built largely around noun phrases. Talking, on the other hand, is structured in clause complexes and represents phenomena as processes. Each is conducive to its own kind of knowledge structures. Noun phrases and products are realized more easily as fillers in frame slots, and frame knowledge is predominant in written texts. On the other hand, clause complexes and processes are more easily realized as parts of scripts. These form the basis of most oral texts as well as of texts that imitate the spoken channel—namely, narrative.

Halliday (1989) pointed to the relation between situation and channel. He noted that spoken language is much more closely bound to current, evolving situational contexts than written language. The contexts of writing are almost always situationally displaced, especially with regard to time. The textual and contextual times of written texts are typically far apart. Finally, how topics are structured varies greatly from oral to written texts.

Halliday's descriptions of written and oral texts are based on contrasts between academic writing and spontaneous conversation. However, as Biber (1988) demonstrated, between these extremes lie many types of written and spoken discourse with widely varying characteristics. Some types of spoken discourse, such as formal speeches, are much more similar to academic writing than they are to spontaneous conversation. On the other hand, personal letters resemble conversation more than they do most other kinds of writing. Biber's study of variation across speech and writing is discussed further later.

One of the most powerful channels of communication is sign language as used by the deaf. Sign language is more than a mere channel. Contrary to popular misconceptions, most sign languages for the deaf are not merely elaborated systems of gestures. Instead, sign languages, such as American Sign Language (ASL), are fully developed languages.

Sign languages consist of signs in much the same way as verbal languages consist of words. Just as a word is formed out of sounds, each of which is produced by varying the place and manner of articulation, so signs are constructed of **articulatory parameters**. In

---

Practice 15:
Consider as many different ways of advertising a product as you can think of. Divide these ways according to channel and medium. What are the advantages and disadvantages of each channel and medium combination?

ASL, there are four: shape of the hand, orientation of the hand, location relative to the body, and movement. Thus, two signs formed with the same shape, orientation, and movement may have two different meanings depending on the position of each relative to the head, for example. In a similar way, many spoken languages assign different meanings to words of identical sound sequences, depending on whether they are spoken with a high or low tone, among others. An example of this from Mandarin is the word "ma," which means "mother" when spoken with a high tone, and "hemp" when spoken with a low rising tone. Similarly, in ASL, the signs for "summer," "ugly," and "dry" are identical except for their height relative to the eyes, as shown in Fig. 1.5.

A common misconception is that ASL is merely some kind of visual rendition of English. In fact, it is not related to English or to any other spoken language at all. The closest analogy between a sign language such as ASL and a written language would be with a language like Chinese, which represents each word as a complete symbol or character. A sign can be thought of as a gestured character. ASL also has a way of "spelling" new or technical words that are not in common use. In this, it may be compared with the written system of a language like Japanese, which uses Chinese characters to represent common words, but also has a set of symbols for spelling out the syllables of technical and foreign words.

Like all languages, ASL has its own grammatical patterns and syntax. These are accompanied by facial expressions that influence the meaning of sentences. Thus, the signs for "me," "borrow," and "book," when arranged in that order and accompanied by a facial expression that stands for "question," produce the meaning, "Can I borrow the book?"

Sign languages are as complex and sophisticated as any of the world's spoken languages. Subtleties of art, literature, philosophy, politics, and any other subject can be discussed as readily in ASL as in English, French, or Japanese. Consider simultaneous sign translators, who may be seen in the corner of a television screen, translating complex political speeches at remarkable speed without missing anything said by the speaker.

All the defining properties of human language are present in sign languages. Such languages have complete phonologies, morphologies, and syntactic systems. They have dialects; they change with time (as old photographs have shown); and they are learned through

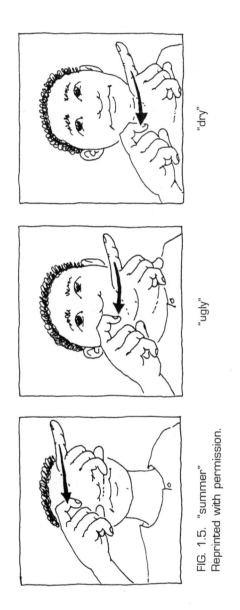

FIG. 1.5. "summer" "ugly" "dry"
Reprinted with permission.

65

Practice 16:

(a) Sign languages such as ASL have fully developed systems of phonology, morphology, and syntax. In the case of spoken languages, phonology refers to the sound system, morphology refers to the way words and roots of words are related, and syntax refers to the way sentences are constructed. What do these concepts mean when applied to a sign language?

(b) Invite to class a person fluent in ASL. Ask the person to teach the class a few basic words and sentence patterns. Ask about some of the most important linguistic and discourse-related problems faced by deaf people. Alternatively, visit a school or class where deaf children are learning through ASL. Ask about the importance of bilingualism (ASL and written English) for such children. What issues of power in discourse are especially applicable to people who use sign languages?

---

the same stages that children go through in learning spoken languages. (However, children learning a sign language as their first language move through some of these stages faster than speaking children.)

A serious study of sign languages and signed discourse has begun only in the last several years. As yet, most of the issues discussed in this book with respect to spoken languages have not been investigated in connection with sign languages. When such studies are carried out, they will most likely show that sign languages are as much a part of their cultural and situational contexts as spoken languages, and meanings in these languages work in much the same way and play the same roles as they do in spoken languages. Even the study of tones of voice and gestures will have something to say about sign languages. After all, it is possible to shout in ASL: All you have to do is make a very large sign!

Guidelines for Analyzing Channel

Determine the primary channel of the text.
Note whether the text is recorded or transient.
Indicate the medium of transmission.
Indicate whether the text is part of a larger text having a different purpose.

Sample Analysis: Channel

The CODE advertisement (Fig. 1.3) may be analyzed as follows:

The channel is writing and the text is therefore recorded.
The medium is a news magazine and therefore has a different overall purpose than the CODE advertisement itself.

Application

Using the aforementioned guidelines, analyze the channel of your chosen oral and written practice texts.

Suggested Reading

Biber, D. (1994). An analytical framework for register studies. In D. Biber & E. Finegan (Eds.), *Sociolinguistic perspectives on register* (pp. 31–56). Oxford, England: Oxford University Press.
    Biber's scheme is the only one to date for uniquely specifying the situation of a text, including channel. Several sections of chapter 1 are strongly based on Biber's situational scheme.
Brown, G., & Yule, G. (1983). *Discourse analysis*. Cambridge, England: Cambridge University Press.
    See, especially, pp. 6–9 on written and spoken texts.
Chafe, W. (1994). *Discourse, consciousness, and time*. Chicago: University of Chicago Press.
    Chapter 4 is concerned with the differences in the activities of speaking and writing and in the attitudes discourse participants have toward speaking and writing. Chafe's observations and ideas provide an enlightening backdrop to analyses of spoken and written texts themselves, such as the study carried out by Biber.
Halliday, M. (1989). *Spoken and written language*. Oxford, England: Oxford University Press.
    Halliday contrasts spontaneous conversation with formal writing to show that formal writing is lexically denser, whereas conversation is grammatically more complex.

PARTICIPANT–TEXT RELATIONS

An earlier section showed how the knowledge and power relations between producer and interpreter(s) help to shape discourse. Another important influence on discourse involving the participants is the relation between the participants and the text.

Participant–text relations are analyzable in two ways: by viewing the text as one of a set of similar texts involving similar producers and interpreters, and by viewing the text as a process of communication that arises in the mind of the producer and is imperfectly transmitted in some way to the mind of an interpreter. The first of these ways is known as the study of **intertext**, and the second is the study of production and interpretation.

As an example of intertext, consider the sermon, which is familiar especially to Christian audiences. The intertext of a sermon contains all similar sermons, and particularly those on the same topic or by the same preacher, especially if the one at hand was intended as part of a series. But the concept of the intertext can be further extended to include all other texts related in any way to the sermon at hand. This intertext would, of course, include the Bible, other Christian books and teachings, other religious texts generally, and even secular works such as speeches, histories, news articles, and so on that relate in some way to the form or content of the given sermon. A series of news articles on teen drug abuse, for example, might be a crucial part of the intertext of a contemporary sermon on the same subject.

In general, then, the intertext is the knowledge derived from examining similar texts, growing out of similar situations. This knowledge influences the production and/or interpretation of the given text. For example, if individuals read a poem, their knowledge of the intertext tells them to have different expectations than those they would have for a news article or a telephone conversation. And the more they know about poetry in general, the more informed their interpretation of a specific poem. At the same time, the more shared knowledge of intertext they have with the poet, the closer their interpretation is likely to be to that aimed at by the poet.

A striking example of the function of shared knowledge of intertext by both the producer and interpreters of a text is a three-word message sent by a British officer, in 1940, when troops were trapped on the beaches of Dunkirk: "But if not . . ." As it turned out, it was not necessary for the message to be any more explicit. Those familiar with the biblical book of Daniel (3:16–18) recognized that the complete message was: "O Nebuchadnezzar, we are not careful to answer thee in this matter. If it be so, our God whom we serve is able to deliver us from the burning, fiery furnace, ... BUT IF NOT, be it known unto thee, O king, that we will not serve thy gods, nor worship the golden image which thou has set up."

Söderbergh (1992) demonstrated the importance of the intertext to reading acquisition and noted how one text can "trigger" another in the mind of a beginning reader even after a period of several months. As the reader matures, according to Söderbergh, a network of interconnected texts gradually develops, until for the mature reader "every text carries a potential associability to an infinite number of other texts, and every one of these texts is in its turn associated with still more texts" (p. 12).

The intertext usually calls on the interpreter's partial remembrance of many texts similar to the one under scrutiny, and that is probably what the man in Fig. 1.6 is doing, while generating a little original intertext of his own. It is often possible to spot texts that depend so heavily on one or two other texts that a large amount of intertextual information may be gleaned from a small body of intertext. One striking example occurs whenever a specific text is part of a series. When this is the case, individuals may understand the text better if they are familiar with the other texts in the series. These other texts may precede the text in question and thus give it a historical background, or they may be contemporaneous with it and provide additional information or different viewpoints.

FIG. 1.6. "Don't mind Dad. He's just reciting a little intertext related to the operation manual." (Intertext may arise out of knowledge of a series of similar or related texts.) Reprinted with permission.

Practice 17:
Read the following opening paragraphs (Paragraphs 1, 2, 3, and 8) from a full-page article appearing in *The Seattle Times*, August 19, 1992, p. A3:

Houston—Four years after George Bush promised a kinder, gentler America, he'll be nominated for a second term as president tonight by a Republican convention that revels in drawing a hard line between wrong and right.
    These Republicans have seen the enemy, and it's not them.
    "The other side," as defined in speeches and platform planks this week: feminists, gays and lesbians, environmentalists, cross-dressers, women who choose abortion, the black residents of inner cities, people who make or enjoy the wrong kind of art, and anybody whose culture comes from other than Judeo-Christian roots.

· · · · ·

    But "defining your opponent," in the euphemism of the craft, remains a far cry from mounting a holy-war attack on fellow Americans who happen to be a little bit "different."

The writer devotes most of the rest of the article to an evaluation of the keynote address by Pat Buchanan, one of the speakers who opened the convention. The following are a few relevant excerpts from Buchanan's keynote speech, given on the day before the news article appeared. (A part of this text appeared in Practice 10):

"There is a religious war going on in our country. It is a cultural war, as
    critical to the kind of nation we will one day be as was the Cold War
    itself."
"[At the Democratic Convention], 20,000 radicals and liberals came dressed
    up as moderates and centrists in the greatest single exhibition of cross-
    dressing in American political history."
"The agenda Clinton and Clinton [referring to the Democratic party presi-
    dential candidate and his wife] would impose on America—abortion on
    demand, a litmus test for the Supreme Court, homosexual rights, dis-
    crimination against religious schools, women in combat units—that's
    change all right. But it is not the kind of change America needs . . . it is
    not the kind of change we can abide in a nation we still call God's
    country."

(a) How does a knowledge of Buchanan's speech contribute to an under-
    standing of the news article?
(b) What kinds of bias indicators can you perceive in the news article to
    suggest the writer's opinion of what the Republican party, and Buchanan
    in particular, stand for? (Note especially the use of the term *cross-dressing*
    in both texts.)
(c) What other kinds of intertextual information do you need to draw on to
    understand the news article?

An example of preceding texts in a series was a set of black-and-white television commercials that appeared in North America a few years ago. Each lasted only a few seconds and featured youthful, sexy, "with-it" individuals in partylike surroundings. The word "black" was stressed and associated with these individuals and their lifestyles, but a product name was not mentioned. Each commercial was shown for a day or two and then replaced by a slightly different one. At the end of a few weeks the advertised product was finally shown. It was a beverage with the word "black" in its name. Other common examples of the kind of intertext provided by a series of preceding texts include installments of articles in popular magazines and newspapers, novels that form part of a set or series (such as Galsworthy's *The Forsyte Saga*), and sequels and "prequels" of motion pictures (such as the *Star Wars* series). Of course, a lifetime of conversations between close friends or family members may also be regarded as such a series.

In addition to intertext, the other crucial way of looking at the relations between the participants and the text is to consider what a text is and how it results from the processes of production and interpretation.

Texts evolve out of the discourse process and are products of the interaction between a producer who structures the content as words, images, and so on, and one or more intepreters who take in the words and images and make sense out of them. A text is not restricted to words and images but may include nonverbals, sounds, gestures, silences, or any combination of these. As becomes clear in the next section, there must also be a purpose or intention behind the text. Clearly, a producer intends that the text communicate some information, even if that information consists of emotional states or attitudes, rather than statements of fact. And the interpreter's purpose must be to understand the message content the producer intended to convey, even though the producer's exact intentions might never be knowable. Finally, as noted in the previous section, to specify a text it is also necessary to stipulate the channel chosen by the producer. A text might be spoken, written, signed, mimed, and so on, or some combination.

It is easy to see that the **physical text** itself (the sounds, gestures, written words, and so on) act merely as a bridge between producer and interpreter. As Stoddard (1991) pointed out, they may be said to have their own text. The **producer's text** is the complex pattern of meanings and intentions that exist in the producer's mind and that the producer has attempted to reproduce in the form of a physical text. Similarly, the **interpreter's text** is the complex (but not identical) patterns reconstructed in the interpreter's mind on the basis of the physical text. As an analogy, think of the world maps in atlases, where the three-dimensional planet is projected with distortions onto a two-dimensional surface: Topographical features such as mountains, valleys, and rivers are symbolically indicated by flat patterns of lines and colors. Similarly, the producer's text is a multidimensional construct generated in the human brain and reflecting the brain's ability to process information in many directions and patterns simultaneously. It draws on the producer's existing frames and scripts, such as those examined earlier; but, ultimately, it must be reduced to a linear arrangement of language, in whatever channel. This is the physical text, which is then taken in by the interpreter, who generates a multidimensional pattern of meaning out of it based on another personal set of frames, scripts, and so on. To the extent that the mental patterns of both producer and interpreter are alike, the interpreter's text will resemble the producer's text. But both will be far more complex than the visible or audible physical text, which is the only direct link between them.

An important consideration in the production and interpretation of texts is the circumstances in which they are produced or interpreted. A producer's text may be planned or scripted, such as a thoroughly prepared public lecture or an article prepared for publication in an academic journal. Alternatively, it may be online, such as a conversation or interactive e-mail. The time constraints on production are always self-imposed by the producer. On the other hand, the interpreters' text obviously cannot be planned or scripted, but interpreters can control the time they spend on interpreting by, for example, deciding to put down the book, rereading a passage, or reading more slowly. However, in the case of a conversation, interpretation is, like production, online, in the sense that the interpreters cannot slow down the producer, even though they can ask for repetition, clarification, and so forth.

In order for the physical text ("the text") to seem to be a text, it must have **texture**. Texture is the complex interrelation of the elements that an interpreter judges as important to the "smoothness" and "meaningfulness" of the text. When interpreters hear or read a text, they recognize it to be something more than mere words, gestures, or images arranged haphazardly. Everyone would probably agree that Lincoln's Gettysburg Address is a text. But what about the list of the synonyms of "stone" in *Roget's Thesaurus*, or every fifth sentence in the eighth volume of the *Encyclopedia Britannica*? Something is missing from these two examples that is very much present in Lincoln's speech, and that something is referred to as "texture." Although texture remains extremely difficult to define in any scientific way, a few important statements can be made about it. First, texture is a defining property of texts: People are able to recognize it when they see or hear it, and anything that has texture in this sense is a text. Second, different interpreters may perceive the texture of the same physical text differently: An interpreter who has greater experience in reading, greater experience in life and the world, and a greater storehouse of relevant knowledge may perceive a far more complex and intricate pattern of texture than, for example, an immature or beginning reader. Finally, it is clear that whatever texture is found in interpreters' texts, it must grow out of the connections between and among the words, gestures, silences, and so on of the physical text, because typically that is all that is shared between the producer and the interpreter.

In a study of interpreters' perceptions of texture, Roseberry (1995) isolated six elements (called "indexicals") of texture. These indexicals are **conjunction, conjunctive reach, connectivity, specificity, topic**, and **topic shift**. In brief, these six indexicals provide measures of the way parts of a text are connected and of the way information is organized in a text. Roseberry then devised an index that could be calculated numerically on the basis of an analysis of these six indexicals. Having calculated this texture index for several essays written by students, he gave the essays to native-speaking teachers of English language skills and asked them to rate the texture of the essays. The teachers' ratings correlated closely with the calculated index. Roseberry concluded from this experiment that the six indexicals play a crucial role in enabling interpreters to perceive texture in informational writing, such as students' essays.

It seems then that texture is largely dependent on **cohesion**, or the ways parts of a text are linked with each other, and coherence, which refers to the interpreter's ability to make sense out of the information contained in the text. Cohesion is a surface feature of texts. This means it depends on mechanical devices, such as the way word meanings are related to each other and arranged throughout a text.

Later sections look at some of the most important linguistic devices for helping to achieve cohesion. Coherence, on the other hand, goes beyond matters of language and organization. It depends on the knowledge shared by the producer and interpreter(s).

As a complex interrelation of cohesion and coherence, texture ultimately depends on participants' knowledge and is something that is reconstructed in the interpreter's mind, as part of the interpreter's text. It is this process of reconstuction, according to Stoddard (1991), that brings about synergism in a perceived text. *Synergism* here means that all of the linguistic and contextual elements of a text interact in complex relations to create a dynamic, evolving text that can be recreated in somewhat different ways by different interpreters.

Both as part of its intertext and as a texture-bearing product of the production and interpretation processes, a text is evaluated by those who interpret it. If it is perceived as an accurate reflection of the culture, if it is perceived as responding meaningfully to the situation and intertext that gave rise to it, and if it seems to have sufficient texture, then an interpreter will judge it to be appropriate. Deciding whether or not a text is appropriate is something that only interpreters can do. Producers may attempt to structure their texts to be appropriate, but the final judgment rests with the interpreter alone. In judging appropriateness, an interpreter makes a personal evaluation of a text. As Biber (1994) pointed out, the interpreter may find the text to be "important, valuable, required, beautiful, popular, and so on." In this, the interpreter may or may not agree with the producer.

Practice 18:

Stoddard (1991) devised a system for indicating different kinds of texture. She claimed that her system showed that different kinds of texturing devices were prominent in different kinds of writing.

(a) Collect several examples of two very different kinds of written texts, such as personal letters and product advertisements. Using your own personal judgment, rate the amount of texture in each on a scale of 1 to 10.
(b) Try to state what devices are responsible for creating texture.
(c) Try to indicate how these devices might be used differently in the two kinds of texts under examination.
(d) Read Stoddard's book to see whether your results and methods agree with hers. If not, what do you see as the advantages and disadvantages of each method?

Finally, the interpreter's judgment may be colored by a perception of the producer's own attitude and commitment to the text.

Guidelines for Analyzing Participant–Text Relations

Identify other important texts in the intertext, including texts in the same series. (*Note:* The text may be part of more than one series.)

Identify the kinds of general background knowledge of other texts that would be needed to understand the given text.

Identify direct references to other texts.

Identify topics, the use of conventional (sourceless) ideas, and literary allusions that tie the text to other known texts.

Identify structural ties with other known texts. These may include stylistic devices, use of certain words, imitation of a standard form such as a sonnet, and so on.

Identify the use of proverbs, clichés, and "portemanteau" words (words that have different meanings for different people and that are in common use in certain recognizable registers and types of discourse, e.g., Thatcherism, Reaganomics, and so on).

Determine the circumstances of production.

Determine the circumstances of interpretation.

Compare and contrast the producer's and interpreter's evaluations of the text.

Determine the producer's attitude toward the text.

Determine the producer's commitment to the text.

Sample Analysis: Participant–Text Relations

The CODE advertisement (Fig. 1.3) may be analyzed as follows:

The intertext would typically include other advertisements soliciting funds for CODE or for other similar causes and agencies. It would also include factual information about literacy, poverty, and so on in the countries named as well as in others. There is no information available on whether or not this advertisement is part of a series. However, in a general sense, all other texts about CODE could be considered part of a general series relating to this text.

Necessary background knowledge would include the concepts of illiteracy, poverty, and how they are related, and so on; general information about the Third World and the specific countries named; knowledge that nongovernmental helping agencies exist; and so on.

The topics of poverty and illiteracy tie the text to many other known texts, such as similar advertisements, lectures, government documents, and so on.

Language and structuring devices are similar to those employed in other advertisements. Much intertextual information can thus be derived from advertisements generally.

Circumstances of production: planned (as opposed to edited), scripted (following a set form), or online.

Circumstances of interpretation: self-imposed time constraints (as opposed to online). In other words, the interpreter can decide how much time to devote to interpretation.

Producer's and interpreter's personal evaluation of the text: probably "important" for both. (But not necessarily important for overhearers.)

Producer's attitude toward the text: emotionally somewhat involved (not detached); not reverent, little excitement.

Application

Using the aforementioned guidelines, analyze the participant–text relations of your chosen oral and written practice texts.

Suggested Reading

Biber, D. (1994). An analytical framework for register studies. In D. Biber & E. Finegan (Eds.), *Sociolinguistic perspectives on register* (pp. 31–56). Oxford, England: Oxford University Press.

Biber's scheme is the only one to date for uniquely specifying the situation of a text, including participant–text relations. Several sections of chapter 1 are strongly based on Biber's situational scheme.

de Beaugrande, R., & Dressler, W. (1981). *Introduction to text linguistics.* London: Longman.

Chapter 9 (pp. 182–208) in particular covers many of the issues relevant to the intertext.

Stoddard, S. (1991). *Text and texture: Patterns of cohesion.* Norwood, NJ: Ablex.

Contains a thorough discussion of texture and a description of the complexities of interaction that can occur in a texture-forming process.

PURPOSE AND INTENT

To be effective, a text must be perceived by the interpreter(s) to achieve the **purpose** that its producer intended. Although **intent** can never be known absolutely without consulting personally with the producer, it will usually be clear enough from the recognizable form and content of the text. Only in rather unusual instances will purpose and intent turn out to be different. "Intent" means the purpose the producer intended, and "purpose" means the purpose the interpreter perceives. Note that intents and purposes are properties of the producer and interpreter(s). Texts themselves do not have purposes, but they may reveal them.

To take an example, one of the authors once had the occasion to write a letter of recommendation for a night watchman who had been fired for repeatedly falling asleep on the job and being very difficult to awaken. The letter stated that the gentleman in question was very honest, always prompt, admirably respectful, and so on, but pointedly neglected to say anything about his abilities as a watchman. The writer's intent was to warn prospective employers that this person might not make the best watchman. However, "it is not typically appropriate to express overt reservations about a candidate. Within this context, a 'faceless' letter indicates a certain degree of reservation" (Biber & Finegan, 1989, p. 113), and the perceived purpose of a letter of recommendation for employment is clearly to help a person to get a job. So the intent and purpose of the discourse were at odds. The interpreter of the letter (a prospective employer) failed to notice the discrepancy between the producer's intent and the perceived purpose of the letter, and hired the gentleman as a night watchman. Happily, the man, having learned his lesson, turned out to be an admirable night watchman after all.

Purpose and intent are related to the functions of language. There are several well-known theories of language functions (see Halliday & Hasan, 1989, p. 17, for a concise description). Biber's (1988) list of language functions helps to classify a text by specifying its degree of factuality and the purposes it reveals.

In relation to factuality, a text may be based on fact (such as a course textbook), on speculation (such as a horoscope), on imagination (such as a short story), or on some combination of these three. Most texts involve more than one of these attitudes to factuality. News articles and political speeches, for example, may combine fact with speculation;

novels may combine fact (descriptions of a city, names of famous people, and so on) with imagination; science fiction stories may combine imagination with speculation and fact; and so on.

Together with attitude toward factuality, four distinct purposes may be noted in texts. A text may persuade or sell (such as a product advertisement); transfer information (such as an academic lecture); entertain or edify (such as a drama); or reveal the producer's self (such as a personal letter). Again, various combinations of these purposes occur frequently in texts, with the different purposes being represented in different degrees of importance or dominance. For example, some advertisements may have the perceived purpose of entertaining as well as selling, but clearly the more dominant purpose is selling. An autobiography usually has the primary purpose of revealing the self. However, to a lesser degree it may have the purpose of entertaining; and an even lesser purpose may be to transfer information or to persuade. A good example of such an autobiography is *The Diary of Anne Frank,* in which all of these perceived purposes are clearly present. Different interpreters, however, may see them represented in the text to different degrees. And, Anne Frank's own intent in writing the diary was clearly quite different from any of those mentioned.

In order to specify intent and purpose, a discourse analyst must discover and identify all of the relevant elements of the context that gave rise to the text in question. These elements include everything described so far in this book—namely, the culture, the discourse participants and the relations between them, the setting, the channel, and the relations between the participants and the text. When these are known, and when the intent and purpose are accurately specified, the discourse analyst is in the position to recognize and describe the genre of the text.

The genre of a text refers to its type. Personal letters, poems, political speeches, sermons, e-mail messages, prescriptions, telephone conversations, prayers, laws, court summations, recipes, and countless others are examples of genres. They are all recognizable by their purposes, and each has a specific form. Furthermore, each contains certain topics and arranges its topics in fairly predictable ways. The remainder of this section examines the forms of genres to see how they work; the following section investigates the concept of topic, which provides the crucial link between the genre of the text and the kind of language used to realize the text.

Basing his work on the fact that a genre is defined largely on the basis of its specific purpose, Swales (1981) showed how the purpose of any definable genre is realized through a progression of **moves**. Each move accomplishes some part of the purpose. For example, referring to the text given in Practice 19, Swales showed that it contains four recognizable moves. These moves establish the field of research, summarize previous research, open the way for present research, and introduce the present research.

The text in Practice 19 is an introduction to a scientific research article. Swales found by studying many such introductions that they all more or less follow the same pattern and contain the same moves. However, his research carried him a step further because he noted that the introductions to all kinds of research articles also follow more or less the same pattern and contain the same moves. On this basis, Swales defined the genre of research article introduction as one in which the four moves, and no others, are used in approximately the order given to achieve the specific purpose of introducing research.

Practice 19:
In the following text, locate the four moves that were identified by Swales:

The thermal properties of glassy materials at low temperatures are still not completely understood. The thermal conductivity has a plateau which is usually in the range of 5 to 10K and below this temperature it has a temperature dependence which varies approximately at T2. The specific heat below 4K is much larger than that which would be expected from the Dabye theory and it has an additional term which is proportional to T. Some progress has been made towards understanding the thermal behaviour by assuming that there is a cut-off in the phonon spectrum at high frequencies (Zaitlin and Anderson 1975 a, b) and that there is an additional system of low-lying two level states (Anderson et al, 1972, Phillips, 1972). Nevertheless more experimental data are required and in particular it would seem desirable to make experiments on glassy samples whose properties can be varied slightly from one to the other. The present investigation reports attempts to do this by using various samples of the same epoxy resin which have been subjected to different curing cycles. Measurements of the specific heat (or the diffusivity) and the thermal conductivity have been taken in the temperature range 0.1 to 80K for a set of specimens which covered up to nine different curing cycles.

(Kelham and Rosenberg, 1981: 1737)

(Quoted in Bhatia, 1993, p. 30)

TABLE 1.1
Moves and Strategies of Research Article Introductions

Move	Strategy
1. Establishing the research field	by asserting centrality of the topic, by stating current knowledge, or by ascribing key characteristics
2. Summarizing previous research	by making the author's name prominent, by not making the author's name prominent, and/or by using a subject orientation
3. Preparing for present research	by indicating a gap in previous research, by question-raising (about previous research), or by extending a finding
4. Introducing the present research	by stating the purpose of present research or by outlining the present research

One factor seemingly linked to the ability to produce highly textured writing (see the previous section) is knowledge of the move structure of a genre. Henry and Roseberry (in press-a) found that knowledge of the move structure of a particular genre enabled second-language learners to improve their ability to texture their writing. In other words, they were able to link information in their texts more effectively.

Identifying the moves contained in a genre is only part of what genre analysis can do. Swales showed that it can also identify the limited sets of the actual ways in which each move is accomplished. These ways, called *strategies*,[3] are shown in Table 1.1 for the four moves of the genre.

Bhatia (1993) extended Swales' work by showing that it applied generally. In particular, Bhatia dealt primarily with genres of business and law, and demonstrated among other things that the discourse types of "letter of application" and "promotional letter" are members of the same genre. In showing this, Bhatia provided an important way of delimiting a genre. Previously, genre designations had been arrived at almost haphazardly. For example, "letter," "business letter," and "letter of application" have all been referred to as genres. Clearly, however, each of these is contained in the one mentioned before it.

---

[3]Swales' term is *realizations*.

Practice 20:
Use Table 1.1 to specify the strategy or strategies of each of the moves of the text in Practice 19.

In other words, a letter of application is a type of business letter which, in turn, is a type of letter. The question arises: Which of these is actually the genre, and which are subgenres or supergenres? Bhatia's work suggests that such a question is irrelevant. If two types of discourse have the same general purpose but exhibit exactly the same moves, and in the same order, then the two are examples of the same genre. Of course, it is still possible to argue that promotional letters have somewhat different purposes from letters of application, and on that basis it would be justifiable to classify them as two subgenres of the same genre.

Hasan (Halliday & Hasan, 1989) noted that in some genres certain moves may be obligatory and others may be optional. She further noted that in the service encounter genre, such as a conversation involving buying and selling, moves or move complexes may be repeated. She referred to this as the *iteration of elements.* Taking into consideration obligatory, optional, and iterative move structures, Hasan was able to show the allowable limitations on move structure variation in conversations about buying and selling. Her work suggests strongly that all genres may be described in the same way, showing not only what kinds of moves must exist or may exist, but also what allowable variations may be found in the ordering and repetition of moves.

In another study, Henry and Roseberry (in press-b) collected and analyzed large collections (corpora) of a number of common written genres in daily use. They noted two further move characteristics: move splitting and move joining. *Move splitting* occurs when one move is embedded within another. This usually occurs only when a move contains several strategies. Another move sometimes may be inserted between two of the strategies. However, Henry and Roseberry did not find any examples where strategies themselves were split.

The opposite phenomenon, *move joining,* occurs when two moves appear to combine into one. In such a case, a single phrase or clause acts to combine the functions of two separate moves.

Genre provides information, through the intertext, about other texts of the same genre. For example, if a company receives a letter of

Practice 21:

In a study of the move structure of the genre "brief tourist information," Henry and Roseberry (1996-b) found that the following moves may be represented: motivation (emotional enticement to visit a place), identification (name of place), location (where it is), explanation (what it is), short history (brief historical background), description (what it contains that makes it an example of its kind), facilities/activities (conveniences, together with special fixtures, not part of "description," that give the visitor something special or interesting to do), and directions (information on how to get there). Analyze the following texts to determine which moves are obligatory and which are optional, and the preferred order of the moves.

(i)
Sights on Stilts

Kampong Ayer, generally recognised as the world's largest water village, extends from both banks of the Brunei River and is home to around 30,000 people. Centuries old, the settlement was described by early European visitors as the "Venice of the East." Pigafetta, who sailed in with the explorer Ferdinand Magellan in 1521 was impressed then by its size. Today, most of the houses on stilts are well furnished and equipped with modern amenities inside but the atmosphere remains traditionally lively and colourful. Hire a water taxi to take you around or stroll on the raised wooden walkways which link the houses. Over the water, visitors find modern schools, a clinic, police station and a mosque.
(*Brunei Darussalam*, n.d., Royal Brunei Airlines)

(ii)
Muara Beach

As the coast of Brunei Darussalam is caressed by the glistening waters of South China Sea, it is only natural that a trip to the beach will be an essential part of any visit to Brunei.

Less than 27 km. from Bandar Seri Begawan, Muara Beach is perhaps the most popular with adults and children alike. The beach is a stretch of light golden sand and is perfect for sunbathing. The South China Sea stretches as far as the eye can see and the water is calm and clear for pleasant swimming or boating.

The area's facilities include a well-developed picnic ground, changing rooms, toilets, children's playground and food and drink stalls which are open at weekends. This is an ideal place for a family outing.
(*Explore Brunei*. (1992). Economic Development Board, Ministry of Finance, Brunei, p. 19)

(iii) Another impressive national park is the Kinabalu Park in Sabah. Here lies Mount Kinabalu (4101 metres), one of the highest mountains in South-East Asia. Dominating the Sabah skyline from every angle, the mountain, together with its surrounding area make up the Kinabalu Park, a reserve covering an area of 754 sq. km. and home to an incredibly diverse range of flora and fauna, including the Rafflesia (the largest flower in the world) and more than a thousand species of exotic orchids.

(Continued)

Practice 21 (*cont.*):
The main attraction here is the conquest of Mount Kinabalu. The climb to the summit is a 2-day affair. Climbers usually start early in the (morning) as the cabin at Panan Laban (3350 metres above sea-level) needs to be reached before nightfall. Early the next morning, it is time to start again. After a 2-hour climb, the climber reaches the shelter at Sayat-Sayat. Another hour of climbing and the summit, Low's Peak, is reached. Although the view from the summit is breathtaking and many climbers would like to linger much longer, it is important that the descent be commenced before noon if the power station is to be reached before dark.

The less adventurous visitor can explore sections of the Park using graded trains near the Park Headquarters. Kinabalu Park is a haven for doing nature study. It is home to a variety of plants, animals, and birds such as the Mountain Blackeye, Warbler Blackbird and the Argus Pheasant.

Another attraction of the park is the Poring Hot Spring, situated about 43 km from the Park Headquarters. Here are found open-air sulfur baths amidst a beautiful landscaped garden.

(*Fascinating Malaysia*. (1992). Tourist Development Corporation of Malaysia, pp. 53–54)

---

application, its personnel workers' knowledge of the purpose of such a letter and how that purpose is typically expressed in moves helps them to understand the current letter. The letter might, for instance, neglect to mention experience or qualifications (as in the example given at the beginning of this section). In that case, they ought to become rather suspicious concerning the applicant's suitability for the job. Because of their knowledge of genre in the intertext, they learn to be as attentive to what the letter does not say as to what it does say. Similarly, when reading a murder mystery, readers can expect at least one murder, the identification of suspects and motives, a considerable number of misleading clues, eventual untangling of the evidence, and the identification of the killer. Although there may be some variation in the structure of such stories, the producer must present a commonly recognizable pattern of the necessary moves in order for interpreters to recognize the story as a murder mystery.

Not all texts are pure examples of a given genre. There are many texts that combine the purposes and moves of more than one genre, and even a few that adopt the disguise of a genre they do not represent at all. If it were not for people's knowledge of genre and its relation to the intertext, they might be "taken for a ride" by such texts, which are often designed to exploit the interpreter in various ways.

Practice 22:

Henry and Roseberry (in press-b) identified the following moves and strategies for the genre "Encylopedia Article About a City":

MOVES	STRATEGIES

(I)   Identification   State the name of the city or town.

(L)   Location   State where the city or town is located.

(E)   Explanation   Briefly state one or more characteristics that differentiate the city or town from all others.

(H)   History
- (ev) Give a brief history of events, battles, and so on, from the founding of the city to the present, usually in chronological order.
- (pe) Give a brief history of, or historical facts about, the ethnic groups that live in the city.
- (la) Briefly give the history of the city's layout.

(R)   Raison d'être   Explain why the city exists, especially with regard to its location.

(D)   Description
- (ar) Describe the city's architecture.
- (la) Describe the city's layout.
- (pe) Describe the city's people or ethnic groups.
- (pr) Describe the city's economy, production, and/or livelihood of the people.
- (In) Describe the major landmarks and/or institutions in the city.
- (cl) Describe the city's climate.
- (to) Describe the city's topology, elevation, and so on.
- (ff) Describe the city's flora and fauna.

(PP)   Population   Give population statistics.

All moves are required and, in most cases, they appear in the order given. Any given strategy of History or Description is optional.

Examine the following encylopedia article and identify the moves and strategies. Which move or moves are split? Which move or moves are joined?

> **Vancouver** 49 13N 123 06W A city and port in W Canada, in British Columbia on Burrard Inlet and the Fraser River delta. Established in 1862 on a beautiful site at the S end of the Coast Mountains, it has developed a rich tourist industry. Vancouver is Canada's largest Pacific port and railhead. With a large airport, it is a centre for international trade and warehousing. It is the commercial and industrial centre of British Columbia, important especially for its timber, paper, and associated industries. Other industries include food processing, ship repairing, and fishing. Vancouver has two universities and a thriving cultural life. Population (1986): 431 147.
> (*Macmillan Encyclopedia* (rev. & updated). (1991). London: Macmillan, p. 1257)

Practice 23:
What is the actual purpose of the following text? Is it a personal letter, or is it
more closely related to some other genre? How do you know?

Dear Jinny,
   I'm so glad you introduced me to Glo-Quick's Super-Facial. It's just
unbelievable what a difference it has made to me in less than a week.
I must say it's a new and a very pleasant sensation to be noticed with
envious admiration . . .
(Halliday & Hasan, 1989, p. 98)

As pointed out earlier, all the elements of the context combine
with the purpose to specify the genre. Closely related to the purpose
of a text is its topic, which is discussed in the next section.

Guidelines for Analyzing Purpose and Intent

Determine whether the text is based on fact, speculation, imagination, or some combination of these.
Rate the degree to which the purpose of the text appears to be to
persuade or sell, to transfer information, to entertain or edify, or
to reveal the producer's self.
Name the specific purpose of the text.
Identify the genre or mix of genres.
Identify the moves and attempt to determine to what degree the move
structure deviates from what might be considered a normal move
structure for the genre.

Sample Analysis: Purpose and Intent

The CODE advertisement (Fig. 1.3) may be analyzed as follows:

The text is based on fact but is also speculative in its predictions that
literacy will improve lifestyle.
To a high degree, the text attempts to persuade. To a lesser degree,
it transfers information.
The specific purpose of the text is to persuade interpreters to contribute money to CODE.

The specific genre is "printed advertisement for soliciting contributions." It may be possible, by Bhatia's reasoning, to group this advertisement with other kinds of printed advertisements, however. The moves are a "grabber" that attracts the interpreter's attention, which consists of the large, bold headline and the visual; solution to a problem; description of an agent (CODE); a call to action; logo; and a motto that acts as a "clincher" by reaffirming the message. No move seems out of order or unexpected for this kind of text.

Application

Using the aforementioned guidelines, analyze the purpose and intent of your chosen oral and written practice texts.

Suggested Reading

Bhatia, V. (1993). *Analysing genre: Language use in professional settings.* London: Longman.
An excellent introduction to the concept of genre as reflected in professional discourse (including business and law).

Biber, D. (1994). An analytical framework for register studies. In D. Biber & E. Finegan (Eds.), *Sociolinguistic perspectives on register* (pp. 31–56). Oxford, England: Oxford University Press.
Biber's scheme is the only one to date for uniquely specifying the situation of a text, including purpose and intent. Several sections of chapter 1 are strongly based on Biber's situational scheme.

Halliday, M., & Hasan, R. (1989). *Language, context, and text: Aspects of language in a social-semiotic perspective.* Oxford, England: Oxford University Press.
Halliday's section (pp. 16–23) examines the various approaches to the functions of language. Hasan's section (chaps. 4–6) deals clearly with genre, cohesion, and the identity of a text.

Swales, J. (1990). *Genre analysis—English in academic and research settings.* Cambridge, England: Cambridge University Press.
A detailed examination of the genres of academic discourse.

TOPIC

It is impossible to conceive of a genre without knowing something about the topic it contains. Any given genre contains only a limited range of topics. Personal letters contain personal topics; academic lectures contain academic topics; legal genres contain legal topics;

and so on. Up to this point, the text has dealt with topic in a very general way without trying to define it. Indeed, for most practical purposes, topic can be thought of as the answer to the question, "What is the text about?" However, this section tries to be more rigorous in describing the topic. It tries to show more precisely what topic is and how it works.

A good starting point in the discussion of topics is Biber's (1994) specification of "level of discussion" of a topic as "specialized," "general," or "popular." Together with this is the specification of the specific topic area itself, such as finance, science, religion, and so on. Consider the following two texts as examples:

(19) K: ... Did you grow up in Philadelphia?
      B: In the Philadelphia area. Not really *in* Philadelphia. (*pause*) Uhm, (*pause*) this is embarrassing to admit, I was a Main Line kid. (*pause*) in the uh—n'there's a stream—of—of cities or towns—that go around Philadelphia.
      K: Um hmm/
      B: That are called the Main Line and (*pause*) they range from suburban to rural.
      K: Um::!
      B: As rural as you get—in Philadelphia an' the—Pennsylvania farms don't look anything like Wisconsin farms. You don't see a lot of—of fields with—wheat and corn. You see a few—but—there are a lot of horse farms. ...
      (Craig & Tracy, 1983, p. 314)

(20) Burns are usually classified as first-degree, second-degree, or third-degree. First-degree burns show redness, increased heat, tenderness, and pain. There may be swelling but no blistering. Second-degree burns show all of the first-degree burn signs, plus blistering. In third-degree burns, the area is charred, coagulated, or light and lifeless (as in scalding). Burns may show combinations of damage at different areas.
      (Dvorine, W. [1983]. *A dermatologist's guide to home skin treatment.* New York: Scribner's, p. 31)

In Example 19, the topic level is "general" on Biber's scale. In other words, it is not intended for an audience of specialists, such as lawyers or scientists; and it is not "popular" in the sense that it is not intended for the public. Popular topics would tend to appear in television programs, tabloids, and other media that cater to widespread interests. Example 20, on the other hand, contains a specialized topic. Although it is probably not intended for scientists or doctors, this text is likely to be of interest only to a limited group of people.

Practice 24:
Examine Examples 19 and 20 for patterns of new versus old information, and theme versus rheme. Which of the two texts thematizes information more prominently? Why?

The specific topic of Example 19 is something like "growing up" or "the place where I grew up." The specific topic of Example 20, on the other hand, is clearly "burns," which is a subtopic of "medicine."

Two important concepts in tracing the development of a topic through a text are **new** versus **old information**, and **theme** versus **rheme**. To illustrate, look closely at the first two sentences of Example 20:

(21) Burns are usually classified as first-degree, second-degree, or third-degree. *First-degree burns* show redness, increased heat, tenderness, and pain.

Here, we have italicized "first-degree burns" in the second sentence to indicate that it contains old information. That is to say that it repeats a concept introduced in the previous sentence. The new information in the second sentence is the rest of that sentence, which mentions "redness, increased heat, tenderness, and pain."

Theme and rheme, on the other hand, are primarily structural concepts. The *theme* is the first element in a sentence. This may be a single word, a phrase, or an entire clause. But it must be the focal point of the sentence. In other words, the rest of the sentence, called the *rheme*, must be about the theme. In Example 21, the theme of the first sentence is "burns," and the theme of the second sentence is "first-degree burns." When old information and theme coincide, as they do in the second sentence of that text, the topic is being thematized. This means that whatever the text appears to be about is being put at the front of the sentence.

Thematizing is a common method of staging. Brown and Yule (1983) pointed out that this method is often used by producers of encyclopedia entries, obituaries, and children's books, among others. For a typical example, refer back to the encyclopedia article in Practice 22 in the previous section. Another typical example is the following:

(22) *E.A. "Ted" Ellis*, the Norfolk-based naturalist, author and broadcaster, who wrote the Guardian Country Diary regularly for two decades, died yester-

day aged 77. *He* was a world authority on microfungi, and for some years presented the radio programme, Nature Postbag.
(*Guardian*, 23 July 1986; quoted in Fowler, 1991, p. 123)

In this example, the staged information, which has been italicized for clarity, refers to the person who is the topic of the text. Topic, however, is more than merely what a text is about. It is also, as shown earlier, an indicator of how information is structured in a text. Similarly, it is an indicator of how this structuring of information is understood by an interpreter. Strictly speaking, texts themselves do not have topics; only producers and interpreters have topics.

In most kinds of texts, topic information is structured according to what van Dijk (1977) called **normal ordering**. According to van Dijk, there is a normal or natural ordering of elements within a text that is judged as well textured. In a normal ordering, certain elements are considered more likely to be mentioned before certain other elements. The following list by van Dijk indicates the order in which these elements are likely to occur:

general—particular
whole—part/component
set—subset—element
including—included
large—small
outside—inside
possessing—possessed

Practice 25:
R. Anderson, Reynolds, Schallert, and Goetz (1977) showed that titles are one of the most powerful thematizing devices. Read the following text.

A Prisoner Plans His Escape

Rocky slowly got up from the mat, planning his escape. He hesitated a moment and thought. Things were not going well. What bothered him most was being held, especially since the charge against him had been weak. He considered his present situation. The lock that held him was strong, but he thought he could break it.
(R. Anderson et al., 1977, p. 372; quoted in Brown & Yule, 1983, p. 139)

Now give the text to a friend or colleague to read, but first change the title to "A Wrestler in a Tight Corner." Compare notes about the topic. What effect does title thematization have on the topic in this case?

Consider how the elements in the following text conform to van Dijk's criteria for normal ordering:

> (23) Not only the floors, but the walls ... as well, were full of colourful coverings, which, to Mother's eye, seemed to be original Persian rugs. They were fascinating, not thick, but of a dense weave. The rich soft colours and intricate designs were a feast to the eyes. The one on the dining room wall felt like rich velvet to the touch, and must have been a representation of the eternal Garden of Eden, with exotic trees, some never-seen flowers, and splendidly featured mythical birds, drinking and flapping their magnificent wings around small aquamarine pools. (Baum, 1990, p. 71)

Table 1.2 indicates some of the items in this text that contribute to the pattern of normal ordering. To establish that normal ordering is crucial to texture, try reversing the order of some of the elements in this text. A great deal of explanation and clarification will be necessary to maintain an acceptable degree of texture, as in the following (partial) attempt: "Flapping their magnificent wings around small aquamarine pools, splendidly featured mythical birds *appeared among* exotic trees and some never-seen flowers. *All this, from what* must have been a representation of the eternal Garden of Eden, *was portrayed in a hanging,* velvet to the touch, on the dining room wall." Note that the added phrases, given in italics, contain prepositions, which are needed to establish the relations between items that are no longer in normal, or expected order. Even so, it is obvious that texture has suffered somewhat in this experiment. Normal ordering of topic information is clearly a part of what is perceived as texture.

Topic structuring varies across several different kinds of discourse. Examine once again the text given as Example 19:

TABLE 1.2
Normal Ordering in Example 23

Mentioned first	Mentioned next
floors, walls (general)	coverings (particular)
Persian rugs (whole)	thickness, weave (components)
Persian rugs (set)	one on dining room wall (elements)
Garden of Eden (including)	trees, flowers, birds (included)
mythical birds (possessing)	wings (possessed)

Practice 26:
In a study by Tyler (1992), the discourses of Korean and American English speakers of English were analyzed for texture, including normal ordering. The following two texts were spoken by graduate teaching assistants in botany who were pointing to and explaining a photograph of a particular species of plant to their classes. Text (i) is by a native speaker of Korean, and Text (ii) is by a native speaker of American English. Judge the relative acceptability of both texts. Then, examine them for violations of normal ordering. In particular, pay attention to the presentation of general and specific information. Do you find a relation between normal ordering and the acceptability of the texts? If not, can you suggest why the rules of normal ordering may not apply in the same way to such texts?

(i) Korean: And ok . as you know aa . . like . . . aa gingkophyta and . a cycadophyta . they are both division characteristically . dioecious . so they have separate female and male plants. This is aa . the male plant which has a male cone here.

(ii) American: This is a close up of the same plant . um showing you in more detail . the male cones aa . . In both divisions. cycadophyta and gingkophyta. the plants are dioecious. You have male and female plants . so that you have male cones produced on one plant . female cones produced on separate plants.

(Tyler, 1992, pp. 4–5)

---

[19] K: ... Did you grow up in Philadelphia?
 B: In the Philadelphia area. Not really *in* Philadelphia. (*pause*) Uhm, (*pause*) this is embarrassing to admit, I was a Main Line kid. (*pause*) in the uh—n'there's a stream—of—of cities or towns—that go around Philadelphia.
 K: Um hmm/
 B: That are called the Main Line and (*pause*) they range from suburban to rural.
 K: Um::!
 B: As rural as you get—in Philadelphia an' the—Pennsylvania farms don't look anything like Wisconsin farms. You don't see a lot of—of fields with—wheat and corn. You see a few—but—there are a lot of horse farms. ...

The topic is clearly centered on the Main Line suburbs and rural areas around Philadelphia. This understanding is achieved by applying one of van Dijk's (1977, 1988) methods. Van Dijk regarded topic as a macrostructure drawn from all the information contained in a text. To arrive at the topic, the interpreter assembles all the factual statements of the text and summarizes them in a statement called a **macroproposition**. This is then the topic statement or topic macroproposition. Three kinds of rules are used to reach the macroproposition: deletion, generalization, and construction rules. Deletion removes information the interpreter considers to be relatively unimportant or too detailed to be part of the topic statement. Generalization allows items in a set to be replaced by the name of the set; and construction, which is similar in some respects to generalization, replaces the individual acts in a scenario with the scenario name. These three rules can be applied repeatedly and in any order until a sufficiently concise topic statement has been derived. Knowing how far to go in reducing the topic in this way depends on interpreter's knowledge—in other words, how much the interpreter is able to supply from frames and scenarios. Applying van Dijk's method to the previous conversational extract, the following statements of fact can be derived:

(24) you grew up somewhere
[I grew up] in the Philadelphia area
I was a Main Line kid
stream of towns goes around Philadelphia
towns are called the Main Line
Main Line ranges from suburban to rural
Pennsylvania farms are unlike Wisconsin farms
few wheat and corn fields exist
a lot of horse farms exist

Next, apply any of the three rules. Construction can be ruled out, because there is no sequence of acts that can be described by a scenario name. If the text had contained propositions such as, "I was born in the Main Line," "I spent my childhood in the Main Line," "I went to school in the Main Line," and so on, the construction rule could be used to reconstruct this as "I grew up in the Main Line." However, both participants in this conversation have already made this reconstruction, as is clear from the first two lines of the text. Therefore, begin by applying the generalization rule. This rule can be used to change "wheat and corn" to "crop," "cereal," or "food." However, there is not much more room here for generalization, because a great deal of the text has already been generalized by B herself. The final rule, deletion, is the most powerful in creating macrostructures. It is also the most variable, because it depends on the interpreter's view of what is general and specific in the text. By applying that rule on top of the generalization, the following set of macropropositions can be identified:

(25) I grew up in the Philadelphia Main Line
Main Line is a suburban to rural stream of towns around Philadephia
Pennsylvania horse farms versus Wisconsin cereal farms

It is important to note that a different interpreter, with a different view of what is general or specific in this text, might well arrive at a somewhat different set of macropropositions and, hence, a different concept of the topic. As indicated earlier, it is more realistic to speak of a producer's topic and an interpreter's topic than it is to speak of a text topic. Note also that the fact that Philadephia (city) is in Pennsylvania (state) is presupposed both in the original conversation and in the last of the three macropropositions in the reduction. Different producers and interpreters with different sets of frame knowledge are likely to presuppose different kinds of information in constructing a topic.

Van Dijk's three macrostructure rules may be repeatedly applied until only a single all-encompassing macroproposition is left. One possible final macroproposition, based on the three given, is the following:

(26) I grew up in the Main Line horse-farming area around Philadephia.

Note in passing that the final macroproposition resembles written text much more than it resembles the original conversation from which it was derived. This should hardly be a surprise, because topic reduction based on macropropositions closely resembles the kinds of thought processes used when trying to put spontaneous thoughts in written form. In this sense, as Halliday (1989) stressed, spontaneous conversation is very much like a first draft of written text.

Another problem with Example 26 is that it does not capture the emotional state of the speaker. Clearly, she was embarrassed to admit that she had grown up in the Main Line. Back-channel signals, pauses, false starts, and her use of the word "embarrassing" all combine to make this clear.

In deriving the previous macropropositions, interpreters relate the propositions in texts to the frames, scenarios, and schemata of their own previous knowledge. Psychological experiments on recall have shown that interpreters rely on these mental constructs to structure information in memory in such a way that several statements of fact are subsumed into a larger, more encompassing statement of fact, as has been indicated. It is this larger macroproposition that is recalled. The small individual statements on which the macroproposition is built are much more difficult to recall. When called on to state the topic of a text, it is likely that this macroproposition would be named, or perhaps only a part of it, such as "growing up in the Main Line," "growing up near Philadelphia," "a horse-farming area near Philadelphia," and so on. Each of these partial representations of the topic is called a **topical focus**.

Different kinds of discourse tend to structure topics in different ways. Argumentative and informational discourse often identify the topic early on and then provide support in the form of reasons, solutions, and so on. The topic frequently reappears throughout the text. This type of structuring pattern was prominent in Example 20, as seen earlier. However, much argumentative and informational writing contains considerably more complex patterns of given versus new information, and theme versus rheme, than was found in Example 20. Nevertheless, in order for argument or exposition to work, the topic must be thematized predominantly at pivotal points throughout the text. A typical example of how this is accomplished in informational writing is shown by the following paragraph from a student's essay.

> (27) Despite its promise, [Project] Head Start still meets with a great deal of criticism. Many local school boards and teachers complain that they sometimes do not get the money the government promised for supplies and salaries. The general public complains that disorganization in the program wastes public funds. Then, although the idea of the program generates much enthusiasm, in some places parents at first refuse to help. This is a great handicap, and members of the program struggle valiantly to overcome it. Parents simply have to help if Head Start is going to work. If a child leaves his pre-school center only to return home to a suspicious and uninterested family, much of the progress he has made is lost. One of the things parents object to most is the age of many Head Start teachers. Some parents and community leaders feel that youthful teachers mean inexperienced teachers. Parents also complain that the grouping in classrooms is too homogeneous, an inevitable effect since the program was of course developed specifically for poor people. And finally, cynical observers note that once Head Start children enter primary school, the gains they register during the pre-school period tend to disappear.
> (Orlando, L. [1980]. Project Head Start. In Bruffee, 1980, p. 144)

To show the topic thematization of this paragraph more clearly, each sentence can be started on a separate line and all the sentences that do not contribute greatly to thematization can be indented. The topic-bearing sentences are then aligned in a vertical column on the left:

(28) (1) Despite its promise, [Project] Head Start still meets with a great deal of criticism.

(2) Many local school boards and teachers complain that they sometimes do not get the money the government promised [Project Head Start] for supplies and salaries.

(3) The general public complains that disorganization in the [Head Start] program wastes public funds.

(4) Then, although the idea of the [Head Start] program generates much enthusiasm, in some places parents at first refuse to help.

(5) This is a great handicap, and members of the program struggle valiantly to overcome it.

(6) Parents simply have to help if Head Start is going to work.

(7) If a child leaves his pre-school center only to return home to a suspicious and uninterested family, much of the progress he has made is lost.

(8) One of the things parents object to most is the age of many [Project] Head Start teachers.

(9) Some parents and community leaders feel that youthful teachers mean inexperienced teachers.

(10) Parents also complain that the grouping in classrooms is too homogeneous, an inevitable effect because the [Project Head Start] program was of course developed specifically for poor people.

(11) And finally, cynical observers note that once [Project] Head Start children enter primary school, the gains they register during the pre-school period tend to disappear.

This arrangement stresses the topic structure of the text and clearly identifies the topic, in Sentence 1, as "criticism" of Project Head Start. It should be clear that Sentences 2, 3, 4, 8, 10, and 11 contribute to this topic by thematizing it. Most of these sentences begin with something like "X complains, objects, and so on." This restates the concept of criticism and is, therefore, the old information, because criticism was already mentioned in the first sentence. The rest of each sentence is the new information, indicating what it is they complain about or object to. Because "X complains, objects, and so on" is also the theme of most of these sentences, it is clear that the topic is thematized. The function of the indented sentences is to provide additional support in the form of reasons, details, and so forth. In spite of its added complexity, the basic topic structure of this paragraph closely resembles that of the simpler "burns" paragraph examined earlier.

In texts that give instructions, topic structuring is usually handled quite differently. As a rule, the topic is given as a heading or title, and the text itself consists of sequential steps in a process. It is also possible for the topic to occur in the first sentence, as in informational texts. However, because all the steps together are required for the process to be complete, no single step is usually associated directly with the whole topic and, therefore, the topic cannot easily reoccur meaningfully in subsequent sentences, as it does in argument and exposition. A common instructional genre is the recipe, of which the following is a typical example:

> (29) FISH CAKES
>
> Ingredients:
>
> 2 slices of bread grilled and made into bread crumbs (about ⅓ c.)
> ⅓ c. mashed potatoes
> 2 small fish fillets boiled for 3 minutes in water
> 2 T. chopped green onions
> 1 T. chopped fresh parsley
>
> Instructions:
>
> Mix fish with potatoes. Add onions and parsley. Mix thoroughly. Mold into patties. Roll in bread crumbs. Fry in hot oil, turning over, until golden brown on both sides. Makes 4 to 6 cakes.
> (Authors' notes)

Although "[fish] cakes" is mentioned in the final sentence, in recipes a general noun such as "servings" is often used instead. The only place in this text where the topic is indicated clearly is in the title "Fish Cakes." It would, of course, be possible to include it in the opening sentence: "To make fish cakes, mix fish. . . ." To include it in subsequent sentences, however, would require relating the particular step to the topic, as in "The next step in making fish cakes is to add onions and parsley." Such redundancy is unnecessary and disturbing. Therefore, it is usually avoided in this kind of writing. In instructional texts, the topic is rarely thematized. Instead, the topic structure of the text almost entirely depends on connections between adjacent sentences. Each sentence answers the question, "What do I do next?"

If a text is purely descriptive, then its topic structure will usually be similar in many ways to the structure of instructional texts. However, instead of steps in a process, there are items making up a whole.

Therefore it is expected that the topic would be named early in the text, as in informational texts; but it is expected that the rest of the text would maintain the topic structure almost exclusively through normal ordering with little or no further reference to the topic. An example (in which the topic is italicized) serves to illustrate.

[30] In *the silent gardens of the old houses in Kakunodate* the tops of the stone lanterns are lumpy and green, the stone wells drip with dark water drops that congeal in the summer heat. The moss is black-green and thick as a poultice. Not a single flower blooms, though the cherry trees are in full leaf, and beyond the mounds of twig and rock stands a small, empty veranda from which to view their blossoms.
[Booth, A. [1985]. *The roads to Sata: A 2000-mile walk through Japan.* Harmondsworth: Viking, p. 89; quoted in Virtanen, 1992, p. 299]

This text begins with all the gardens taken together. Within these gardens are objects and plants. Finally, there is a single veranda. This structuring clearly follows van Dijk's normal ordering.

The type of discourse that exhibits the most complex topic structuring is narration. In Western cultures at least, narrative is concerned primarily with time sequences and consecutive events. However convoluted the time presentation, as a result of flashbacks, flashforwards, simultaneous narratives, and so on, there must be enough time clues (adverbs, adverbial phrases and clauses, tense, etc.) in the text to enable the interpreter to unravel the tangle of events and arrange them in chronological sequence. However, even then it will usually be necessary to extract the topic structure from a complex weave of time adverbials and other nontopical text, as in the following familiar example:

[16] *As soon as we came in,* an older, thin peasant woman, probably the housekeeper, who *at once* recognized Mother, started to talk furtively in a thick dialect, and in her bewilderment flapped her arms like a wild duck. She was terribly excited and beside herself, and *after a minute or so* Nacia, who had heard the fuss, came running in.
She was a lovely, dark blond young woman: slim and graceful, like a ballerina. And though she was very simply dressed, to me she *instantly* became the Princess of all the fairy tales I had ever known.
After some time her mother, old Mrs. Norski, trudged in, dressed all in black, leaning heavily on her cane. Crippled by arthritis, she walked slowly. I noticed her immaculate hair-do, and *only now* I assume that undoubtedly, it must have been a wig. And I could not help noticing the well polished, old-fashioned, tightly laced shoes reaching to her midcalf, a type that I

had only seen in old photographs. We were taken *at once* to greet Mr. Norski himself, who presided in a heavy armchair at a massive rectangular oak table laden with well-worn Hebrew books. Dressed in black, broad-shouldered, he appeared to be very tall, even while sitting. Though he certainly must have been advanced in years, his thick beard was not all that gray.

The time adverbial constructions have been italicized to make it easier to separate them from the rest of the text. The same can be done with tense markers and other indicators of time. Still, deriving the topic of this text is not an easy matter. Van Dijk's macrostructuring rules might produce a topic statement such as, "Mother and I visited the Norskis, who live among the trappings of Jewish tradition." (Note that the word "Jewish" is not in the text and must be supplied by frame knowledge based on "Hebrew books" and possibly also Mr. Norski's patriarchal image.)

Frequently, time is thematized in narratives (as in the previous example). In sharp contrast with informational texts, narratives rarely, if ever, thematize their topics.

Topic, however it is derived, has its basis in the producer's and interpreter's knowledge and may well vary in some ways from producer to interpreter and from one interpreter to another. In addition, there are difficulties involved in identifying topics. Is it any easier to identify shifts in topic? In writing in English and in a number of other languages, topic shifts are often indicated by the indentation that begins a new paragraph. But, such indentations are used to indicate shifts of speaker, rather than topic, in quoted discourse as well. And, many writers appear to follow different conventions of paragraphing and divide the same text into paragraphs differently.

Nevertheless, it would appear that detecting a topic shift, at least in narrative prose, is much easier than identifying the topic itself. Topic shifts in narrative prose are frequently indicated by a dependent adverbial expression of time, the beginning of a description, or occasionally, a shift of speaker. All three are usually indicated by an indentation in the text. To see an example, look back at Example 16. Note that the first paragraph of the extract begins with the time clause "As soon as we came in." The second paragraph begins with a description of Nacia, and the third begins with the time phrase "After some time."

Detecting topic shifts in expository or argumentative writing can be much more difficult. For this reason, producers of these kinds of

---

Practice 27:

Examine your chosen oral text for paratones. Indicate the intonation and stress at the place where a paratone begins and again at the place where it ends. (*Note*: More than one concept may be stressed at the beginning of a paratone, especially if the speaker intends to include them in the topic macroproposition.)

---

texts are encouraged to indicate shifts of topic with topic moves, which show clearly where and how a topic has shifted. As in narrative, topic shifts are often indicated through indentation.

In spoken discourse, according to Brown (1977), topic shifts are usually accompanied by recognizable shifts in intonation. The totality of spoken discourse between two topic shifts is called a **paratone**. A paratone typically begins with high pitch on the first main concept, which is usually the topical focus. In addition, pauses between phrases within the spoken text are brief. The paratone ends with a significant drop in pitch and a longer pause. A certain kind of gesturing may also accompany topic moves and topic shifts.

Related to topic and topic shift, a third concept that is a partial determiner of texture is specificity. Obviously, an informational text that clearly thematizes its topic but never gives any specific information would probably not be valued highly by an interpreter. Specificity, however, presents a rather difficult problem of definition. Just as it is difficult to apply van Dijk's deletion rule because of not being able to define the absolute degree of specificity of a statement, it is difficult for the same reason to determine how specific any part of a text might be. Furthermore, in certain kinds of texts some parts of the text may be expected to be more or less specific than others. A good working rule for determining specificity is to look for examples, reasons, anecdotal information, names, and other similar details. This kind of information is the most specific. At the other end of the scale, statements that include more than the topic are the least specific. Anything between these two extremes is probably closely related to the topic macroproposition and is at an intermediate level of specificity. As an example, consider the following sentences from a student's essay:

(31) [15]and evaluation becomes impossibly biased. [16]To one teacher a grade of 79 is a low B, ...
(Sackrowitz, B. [1980]. To number or not to number. In Bruffee, 1980, pp. 136–137)

Sentence 15 is clearly less specific than Sentence 16, which is a specific example. Assume the topic macroproposition of this student's essay is "A numerical grading system is fairer than an alphabetical one." Then the first sentence in the same essay:

(32) Modern advances in technology and science have led to an increase in the amount a student must learn.
(Sackrowitz, B. [1980]. To number or not to number. In Bruffee, 1980, pp. 136–137)

is even less specific than Sentence 15. Most genres require at least the middle level of specificity at critical focal points within the text. If this level of specificity is missing, there is little to tie the text to its situational context. Interpretation thus becomes difficult or impossible (for more on specificity, see Roseberry, 1995).

Guidelines for Analyzing Topic

Determine if the topic level is specialized, general, or popular.
Determine the specific topic of the text.
Determine to what extent the topic is thematized.
Determine the extent to which normal ordering is used.
Determine the topic macroproposition and assess the likelihood of finding the existing topic structure in this type of text.
Identify any topic shifts.
Determine if existing patterns of specificity are acceptable for this type of text.

Sample Analysis: Topic

The CODE advertisement (Fig. 1.3) may be analyzed as follows:

The text contains a specialized topic: literacy in the Third World.
There is some thematization of the topic ("they," "CODE"), which is indicative of informational texts.
A more normal ordering would be to introduce the concept of literacy before discussing the letters of the alphabet. This reversal of normal ordering seems to be intended to captivate the interpreter(s)' attention. The confusion that could occur is immediately removed

by the photo and by explanations, so no interpretive problems are likely to occur. The topic macroproposition could be "CODE is an agency that promotes literacy in developing countries," or "CODE needs your help in promoting literacy in developing countries," and so on. It is sharply focused with no subtopics. This type of topic structure is typical of solicitation advertisements such as this and brief arguments generally.
No topic shifts.
Normal specificity.

Application

Using the aforementioned guidelines, analyze the topic of your chosen oral and written practice texts.

Suggested Reading

Biber, D. (1994). An analytical framework for register studies. In D. Biber & E. Finegan (Eds.), *Sociolinguistic perspectives on register* (pp. 31–56). Oxford, England: Oxford University Press.
Biber's scheme is the only one to date for uniquely specifying the situation of a text, including topic. Several sections of chapter 1 are strongly based on Biber's situational scheme.

Brown, G., & Yule, G. (1983). *Discourse analysis.* Cambridge, England: Cambridge University Press.
Pages 68–124 contain an in-depth presentation of the relation between topic and discourse content.

Chafe, W. (1994). *Discourse, consciousness, and time.* Chicago: University of Chicago Press.
Chapters 5–11 give a penetrating look at information structure and topics in spoken discourse. However, study the section on nonverbal meaning in chapter 2 in the current text to gain a necessary foundation in prosody before attempting Chafe's work.

Coulthard, M. (1985). *An introduction to discourse analysis* (2nd ed.). London: Longman.
Pages 79–88 contain a helpful section on "topic," including discussions of some of the most important work in this area.

Renkema, J. (1993). *Discourse studies: An introductory textbook.* Amsterdam: John Benjamins.
Pages 62–66 contain an easily understandable discussion of "new versus old information," "theme versus rheme," "topic," and "topic shift."

2

THE LANGUAGE OF DISCOURSE

Genre is a description of the structure of a text and results from the culture and situation of the discourse participants. Topics are closely associated with genres, and only certain topics are likely to appear in certain genres. Topic and genre together select the language of a text. Certain kinds of words and grammatical forms are likely to appear with certain genres. For example, discourse markers such as "well" and "umhmm," and tag questions (". . . isn't it?," "doesn't she," and so on) are much more likely to occur in conversational genres than in written academic genres.

The specification of the language that belongs with a genre is called the *register* of that genre. Registers indicate the language items that have a high probability of occurring in a given genre. Among the kinds of language items specified in describing a genre are words and other lexical units such as idioms, grammatical items, devices that provide connections between different parts of the text, ways of using language nonliterally, ways of implying unstated information, and even nonverbal ways of communicating.

Once the genre and topic are identified and the accompanying register is specified, a full description of the text has been achieved. And, because this description is based on a thorough understanding of the discourse process that created it, it opens the way to a fuller and more penetrating interpretation of the text, including a better understanding of the power structures and purposes associated with it.

Evaluation of the text as a whole becomes possible. Just as interpreters can judge the genre to be more or less appropriate, they can judge the language to be more or less grammatical. Together, these judgments add up to the total evaluation of the text as more or less acceptable for what it is.

REFERENCE AND COREFERENCE

Texts are semiotic. That is to say that they are among the many things, natural and artificial, that communicate information by means of **signs**. The various codes that have been devised to transmit information can be included among semiotic communicators: signal flags and semaphores, such as international road signs; measures of physiological activity, such as heart rate and body temperature; mating and warning calls of animals; symbolic "dances," such as the mating dances of some birds and the dance of the queen bee; and many more.

All of these semiotic communicators use signs. A sign may be defined as a communication unit consisting of a **token** and a **referent**. The token is the part of the sign intended to stimulate a sense organ of the interpreter. For example, certain insects indicate readiness to mate by secreting a specific odor. The mate, perceiving this odor, pursues the emitter and follows natural mating instincts. In the case of a text, a token may be an arrangement of symbols on a piece of paper, for example. These may stimulate people's visual sense and be transmitted to their brains to be interpreted accordingly. A token may be either an **icon** or a **symbol**. Iconic tokens resemble the things they are supposed to represent. Thus, a road sign showing a drawing of schoolchildren walking hand in hand is an iconic token representing schoolchildren. A symbolic token, on the other hand, bears no obvious resemblance to the thing it represents. The word "schoolchildren" itself does not resemble actual schoolchildren, but may be used symbolically to represent them, as in the current text, for example. The referent is the idea to which the token refers. In this case, actual schoolchildren would be the referent of both the iconic road sign and the symbolic word.

A text may be of any length whatever. A single token, such as a shriek, may constitute a text. At the opposite extreme a lengthy novel, such as Tolstoy's *War and Peace*, may be said to constitute a single text. When focusing on one part of a text, the surrounding parts are called the **cotext**. In other words, the cotext consists of the nearby parts of the text just before and after the part being examined. Cotexts of various lengths are possible in a long text such as *War and Peace*.

If a text is very short, say two or three words long, traditional grammar could be used as a tool of analysis. First, traditional grammar can help in understanding the meaning. Thus, if somebody shouts, "Behind you!" this text might be interpreted to mean there is some reason to look behind. Perhaps something dangerous is approaching. The words "behind" and "you" are linked in meaning; the phrase cannot mean "in front of you" or "behind somebody other than you." Next, the syntax is also determined by traditional grammar. This text is a prepositional phrase, and as such its form is strictly determined by English syntax rules. Finally, the forms of the words are determined by the grammar. Forms such as "behinds you," "behind the you," or "behind yous" are not likely to occur in standard English.

If a text extends over more than one sentence, however, then traditional grammar no longer applies. If the text consists of "Behind you! Use your gun!", for instance, there is no way that grammar rules can tie the two sentences together. As a text, it would be equally acceptable to say, "Behind you! Use my gun!" or "Behind you! Run!" Grammar restricts each individual sentence, but it does not restrict the way sentences are attached to each other. For example, a bear is chasing you and your friend sees it and shouts, "Behind you! Use your gun!" Clearly, this is somehow a more sensible thing to say in this situation than, for instance, "Behind you! And by the way, do you take cream and sugar?" There is nothing grammatically wrong with either of these texts. However, something other than grammar is clearly wrong with the second one, and it is the business of this section to try to discover what that something is. To do this, it looks at a different kind of grammar, or a *grammar of the text*, rather than a grammar of the sentence. This grammar of the text is concerned largely with signs and with ways of tying meanings together across sentence boundaries.

In texts, there are two kinds of meaning relations involving signs: those tying tokens within the text to referents in the world, and those tying together tokens and referents that both exist within a text and do not reach directly into the world at all.

When a sign refers from a text to the world, the referent is an object, concept, and so forth that exists in the world or in common knowledge. In such a case the token is called a **referring expression**. For example, if someone says, "A cat has climbed the apple tree," there is a meaning relation between the text and the world: the word "cat" refers to an actual (or imagined) cat, and the word "tree" refers to an actual (or imagined) tree. Thus, the symbolic tokens "cat" and "tree" are referring expressions.

In addition to referring to real things, referring expressions can refer to concepts that are not things at all. For example, each of the following is a referring expression: "midafternoon," "when Lincoln died," "thirty-seven," and "to Hell and back."

Furthermore, it is possible for referring expressions to refer to things that are nonexistent in the real world, in which case they refer to things that exist in imaginary worlds. However, for imaginary worlds to be comprehensible, they must be similar to the real world, differing from it only in small defined ways. For example, in the sentence, "Martians landed in the neighboring town last night," the word "Martians" refers to beings that do not exist in the world with which we are familiar. At the same time, however, such concepts as "landing" and "town" are very much a part of the real world. Without such a similarity of worlds, fantasy and science fiction would be incomprehensible.

Referring expressions refer outward from a text into the world, but different people may understand the world differently, may select different parts of it to refer to, or may create different worlds within their minds. The world that producers assume that they are talking about at the time is known as the **universe of discourse**. It may be a real or imaginary world, or a world partly real and partly imaginary. For the sake of simplicity, a partly fictitious world, such as the world of the Martian landing (described earlier), is referred to as being fictitious. Misunderstandings commonly arise when participants in a conversation make different assumptions about what universe of discourse is being discussed. Here is an example in which such a misunderstanding is eventually resolved:

(33) A: Is it very rough down there though?
   B: Well there are no cobbles as far as I can remember. Have you tried riding on the cobbles?
   A: Yes, yes.
   B: You must have done.
   A: I went down to Muirhouse.
   B: Which is almost all cobbles, isn't it?
   A: It was rather rough.
   B: Hmm.

A: No, but I was—I was thinking rather more in terms of the, em, people.
B: Oh, I see. You—well, I don't think so. I don't know. I—I—eh—parts of it
are quite poor—particularly the Pilton area.
(Brown & Yule, 1983, p. 93)

In this text, the referent causing difficulty is the concept associated with the token "rough." Each participant has a different idea of what is meant by "rough." Thus, although "bicycle riding at Muirhouse" may be said to be the universe of discourse for this text, the different concepts of "rough" create a slightly different universe of discourse for the two speakers. Note that A temporarily accepts B's concept of "rough" when she says, "It was rather rough." This is a politeness strategy designed to further cooperation and maintain the conversation. She then explains her different meaning, bringing the two universes of discourse together; and B then tries to be equally cooperative by returning to the original question and interpreting it as intended. B's hesitations indicate the confusion caused by redefining the universe of discourse.

Regardless of what universe of discourse is being assumed, when **reference** is to referents outside the text, as with the words "there," "I," and "you" in the previous conversation, it is known as outward reference, or **exophora**. Exophoric references often include pointing gestures, especially when used with "this" and "that," in which case the gesture is part of the referring act. It is reasonable to assume that in face-to-face communication (the most common form of verbal communication), the use of "pointing" words is much more natural than verbal repetition. It is clear that a great deal of situational knowledge must be shared by producer and interpreter before exophoric references in a text can make sense, as Fig. 2.1 clearly demonstrates.

The reflection of this situational knowledge in the words and grammar of a language is called **deixis**, and exophora may be accomplished through the use of deictic expressions, such as the words already mentioned. Languages vary in the types of deixis they use in order to achieve exophora. Culture often plays a significant role in specifying the types of deixis available within a language. Honorifics, tense and aspect choices, and ways of talking about time are examples of cultural deictics. In English, deixis makes considerable use of pro-forms, such as pronouns, but it can also make deictic use of certain syntactic categories, such as tense. The traditional categories of deixis in all languages are person deixis, place deixis, and time deixis. These clearly relate to the discourse participants and to the

FIG. 2.1. "And it was this big and next to that one but facing toward those over there ..." (Deictic terms cannot be understood by conversationalists who do not share knowledge of the situation.) Reprinted with permission.

setting. Three other deictic categories may also be noted: social deixis, attitudinal deixis, and discourse deixis. Most of these types of deixis are contained in the following telephone conversation:

(34) Marcia: Hello.
     Tony: Hi Marcia.
     Marcia: Yeah?
     Tony: This is Tony.
     Marcia: HI Tony
     Tony: How are you?
     Marcia: OHhhh hh I've got a paper b- (0.2) the year paper due
                tomorrow.
     Tony: How about that.
     Marcia: Heheheh hh I can tell you a lot ab(h)out th(h)at ...
     (Wong, 1984; quoted in Hatch, 1992, p. 9)

The pronoun "you" in Tony's question, "How are you?" is an example of person deixis. To see this more clearly, imagine talking with Marcia face to face. It is possible (though impolite) to point to Marcia while asking, "How are you?" If a word can be accompanied by a pointing gesture, then it is certainly a deictic expression. Similarly, Tony could point to himself while saying, "This is Tony." Therefore, "this" is another deictic word, although in this case the word refers to position rather than person and means "here at this place." Tony could equally well have said, "Tony here." Consequently, "this" is an example of place deixis. Both speakers refer to themselves as "I," which of course is another example of person deixis.

When Marcia says she has a paper due "tomorrow," she is in effect pointing to time. There is no way of knowing what day "tomorrow" is without being shown, for example, by means of a calendar. Therefore, "tomorrow" is an example of time deixis. There is also an example of attitudinal deixis in Tony's comment, "How about that." The word "that," rather than "this," shows that Tony is distancing himself slightly from the event. If he had said, "How about this" (with no stress on "this"), he would have been indicating a greater degree of personal involvement with Marcia's paper. Choosing "this" rather than "that" to show emotional nearness is a common device in children's stories, for instance, where the narrator might say something like, "And then the wolf blew down the little pig's house. *This* was a very naughty thing to do."

Social deixis involves the use of terms indicating the social status of one or more participants in the discourse. Such status may be shown in English by the use of address terms (e.g., "Your Honor," "Madam Chairperson," "Mr. President," and so on), names and nicknames (e.g., "Bob," "Robert," "Dr. Smith," "Smithy," "Sweetheart," "Doc," and so on), and even certain lexical and syntactic choices of style (e.g., "I shall return" vs. "I'm comin' back," and "am not" vs. "ain't"). In many other languages, honorifics are used to show social deixis. Unequal status can be shown in a variety of contexts, such as a doctor–patient interview, a lawyer–client interview, and a teacher–class lesson. For example, the following is an exchange typical of what takes place at the beginning of classes:

(35) Teacher: Good afternoon, Year Eight.
     Pupils: Good afternoon, Mrs. W.
     (Authors' notes)

In the telephone conversation in Example 34, both participants refer to each other by their first names, indicating a social informality

In addition, short forms (e.g., "hi"), informal greetings, personal style, exaggerated intonations, mild sarcasm, and a pun all count as informal social deictics here.

Of the various kinds of deixis listed earlier, only one kind, discourse deixis, is not present in the telephone conversation between Marcia and Tony. Discourse deixis typically uses "this" and "that" to refer to a text or a part of a text in discourse. If, for example, Marcia had brought an end to the conversation by saying, "I have to end this conversation now and get back to work," that would have been an example of discourse deixis. The underlined words are a deictic expression that in effect point to the text produced by Marcia and Tony. Note that the names of genres are typically used in discourse deixis: conversation, joke, story, anecdote, novel, and so on.

In English and a number of other languages using **tense** and **aspect**, subtle instances of time deixis can occur. Time deixis may be shown by the tense alone, as in the present-tense verbs in the telephone conversation (Example 34). This use of the present tense means that everything being discussed is happening "now." Alternatively, aspect may be combined with tense to indicate whether a process is completed, continuing, repeating, and so on. Consider the deictic use of tense and aspect in the following extract from a conversation:

> (36) B: ... This is the first time I'll have been to Florida.
> K: Hmmm::! I meant to ask you the other day, are you flying down?
> B: Um hmm, and I hate planes.
> (Craig & Tracy, 1983, p. 306)

Combining the future tense with the perfect aspect, as in "I'll have been to Florida," indicates a completed action seen from some point farther in the future. In other words, if someone goes into the future and looks back, that person will see that B's Florida trip is completed. At that time, she will be able to say truthfully, "I have been to Florida." However, at the time when B is speaking, the trip has not yet taken place. Time (tense) and completion (aspect) are seen here from the point of view of the deictic "now." It is not possible to know what time is being referred to or when the trip will be completed unless the time at which the conversation is taking place is known. When K replies "Are you flying down?", she uses the present tense combined with a continuous aspect. Typically, this combination is used in English to describe processes continuing at the present moment ("now"), such as "Right now I am sawing wood." In this case, however, it is used to describe a future process. What Levinson (1983) called the **linguistic tense** (LT) diverges from the real, or **metalinguistic tense** (MT), which is the time frame existing in the real situation outside the language. A further complication arises when the conversation is given at some point in time after it actually took place. It may be received as a tape recording or as a printed text in a book, for example. This is referred to as **coding time** (CT), which is the time at which it was spoken, written, recorded, and so on. All deictic references to "now" are actually pointing to the coding time. Therefore, in this conversation, B and K are actually talking "now" (CT) about a trip that will occur in the future (MT), but are using the present tense (LT) and the continuous aspect to refer to this trip. The moment at which someone reads the transcript of this conversation is called the **receiving time** (RT).

A special case of time deixis in English occurs when there is no MT at all. Consider the following:

(37) K: Oh!—Ferriers are horse doctors.
(Craig & Tracy, 1983, p. 317)

This utterance is metalinguistically tenseless (M-tenseless), because the meaning is that ferriers are, always were, and always will be horse doctors. In English, the simple present tense (LT) is usually used to convey this meaning, though sometimes the future is used (e.g., "Boys will be boys").

In order to be perceived as a text, the various elements comprising the text must have cohesion. That is, they must appear to be related meaningfully to each other. One of the most important tools a producer can use to make a text cohesive is **coreference**. Coreference concerns meaning relations within parts of a text. It contrasts with

---

Practice 28:
Identify the deictic expressions in the following short conversation (already seen as Example 13).

A: Uh if you'd care to come and visit a little while this morning I'll give you a cup of coffee
B: Hehh Well that's awfully sweet of you, I don't think I can make it this morning. .hh uhm I'm running an ad in the paper and-and uh I have to stay near the phone.

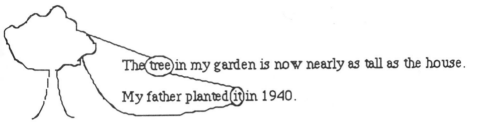

The (tree) in my garden is now nearly as tall as the house.

My father planted (it) in 1940.

FIG. 2.2. Reference and coreference.

reference, because the latter is concerned with the meaning relationships between parts of a text and the world. Hence, whereas a word
like "tree" is referential and refers to a real or prototypical tree, the
pronoun "it" can be both coreferential by referring to the word "tree"
and referential by referring to the actual or prototypical tree itself, as
Fig. 2.2 shows.

The phenomenon of exophora, where the referring expressions can
only be interpreted in the context of situation, has already been
considered. However, when the referring expressions can refer both
within the text and to the real world, then this is **endophora**—that is,
reference within the text. Endophoric coreference is further split into
two categories: **anaphoric** and **cataphoric**. Anaphoric coreference
happens when the **node** (usually a noun) comes before the **cohesive
element** (a pronominal form), as in Fig. 2.2, where the word "tree" is
the node and "it" is a cohesive element referring anaphorically to "tree."
The link between them is called the **cohesive tie**. Unlike in anaphoric
coreference, in cataphoric coreference the node comes after the
cohesive element. This ordering is much less common.

Halliday and Hasan (1976) included three subcategories of reference and coreference in their analysis of cohesion: **personal, demonstrative**, and **comparative**. Each is represented in the following text,
which was presented by a British police department as part of a
transcribed confession of a suspect:

(38) I could not see Chris when I shouted to him—he was behind a wall. I
heard some more policemen behind the door and the policeman with
me said: "I don't think he has many more bullets left." Chris shouted "Oh
yes I have" and he fired again. I think I heard him fire three times altogether. The policeman then pushed me down the stairs and I did not see
any more. I knew we were going to break into the place. I did not know
what we were going to get—just anything that was going. I did not have

a gun and I did not know Chris had one until he shot. I now know that the policeman in uniform is dead.
(Coulthard, 1992b)

A number of examples of personal coreference in this text involve the connection between "Chris" and "he" or "him." For example, the pronoun "he" in the second sentence ("I don't think he has many more bullets left") refers to "Chris" in the first sentence and provides a potential for tying the two sentences together.

Demonstrative coreference is often shown by the use of "this," "that," or "the," modifying a noun. In this text, one example is "The policeman" in the middle of the text that refers back to "the policeman with me" and helps tie these two parts of the text together meaningfully.

The third type of coreference, involving comparatives, is shown here by the expression, "I did not see any more." This provides a general tie to all the previous text, which is a description of what the narrator saw.

Coreference, as shown by the example, provides ties between words based on their meanings and helps the interpreter to recognize the parts of a text as being related and meaningfully connected to each other, rather than as a random collection of words or sentences. However, for coreference to work, it must be perceived as cohesive by the interpreter. According to Stoddard (1991), a producer cannot guarantee cohesion. The producer can only give a text a potential for cohesion. In order for cohesion to exist, an interpreter must see the text as cohesive. In general, the more cohesive ties there are to

---

Practice 29:

(a) Identify the deictic and coreferential expressions in the following excerpt from an advertisement. Explain how these are related to the purpose of the advertisement.

(b) How might a knowledge of these expressions help to protect a potential consumer?

(c) Compare your results with those of a classmate or friend. Do both of you perceive the same cohesive ties? Which of you is likely to be more "immune" to the message contained in the advertisement?

Imagine a washing machine that's easy to use. More economical, more efficient. More reliable. And more durable. One that really cares for your wash. That washing machine is waiting for you.
(Quoted in Fairclough, 1989, p. 204)

a single node, the more likely an interpreter is to perceive cohesion with respect to that node. Likewise, the more specific a producer's choice of cohesive element, the more likely the interpreter is to establish cohesion. Thus, while speaking of the potential for cohesion in the producer's text, reference is made to the likelihood of cohesion being perceived by the interpreter in the interpreter's text. Ultimately, textual cohesion must lie with the interpreter, because if interpreters cannot identify cohesion in their own mental construct of the text, then cohesion cannot be said to exist for that particular interpreter (although it may exist for a different interpreter).

Guidelines for Analyzing Reference and Coreference

Identify any instances of exophoric reference or deictic terms or expressions and their referents.

Consider whether all referring expressions have clear referents in a commonly recognized universe of discourse. If not, consider the possible dangers of interpretation. Determine what misunderstandings could arise.

Determine whether the universe of discourse is the real world or a world that is at least partly imaginary. Determine what elements of the real part of the universe of discourse are particularly susceptible to misinterpretation.

Identify all instances of personal, demonstrative, and comparative coreference and their coreferents.

Sample Analysis: Reference and Coreference

The CODE advertisement (Fig. 1.3) may be analyzed as follows:

Coreference: personal coreference: "They" corefers to "letters." Demonstrative coreference: "the . . ." uses the neutral demonstrative to limit the meaning of "world" to "developing" (i.e., reference rather than coreference). Comparative coreference: "Most people" is compared endophorically with "We"; "one way" is compared with "26"; "more information" is compared with the information already given.

Universe of discourse: clearly the real world, but with possible variations within this universe of discourse. For example, participants in conversation may make different assumptions about the universe of discourse of "education." Therefore, interpreters from different societies attempting to make specific claims about the benefits promised by the advertisement might arrive at mutual misunderstandings of specific points.

Exophora: "You" and "your" can only be exophoric, referring to readers in whatever situation they find themselves in. "We" and "us" would be exophoric in other circumstances, but are endophoric in this case given the reference to CODE.

Deixis: *Person deixis*: "You," "your," "We," and "us" refer to the interpreter(s) and producer(s) of the advertisement respectively. "Most people" refers to those others who don't read this particular magazine. *Social deixis*: Seen in the more relaxed, familiar, contracted forms of the verbs "there's" and "You'd." *Time deixis*: Coding time is the time when the advertisement was first produced; receiving time is the time when it is first read by any particular reader; probably the distance between CT and RT should be measured in days, weeks, or months, rather than years, decades, and so on, for a typical advertisement of this kind; linguistic tense is simple present for the most part, with a hint of the future in "you'd be surprised" and "We could use . . ."; metalinguistic tense is probably future, expecting the future support of the reader. *Place deixis*: seen in the C of CODE, which in this context refers to Canada and Canadian.

Referring expressions include: "developing," "letters," "literacy," "opportunities," "knowledge," "skills," "education," "CODE."

Application

Using the aforementioned guidelines, analyze reference and coreference in your chosen oral and written practice texts.

Suggested Reading

Fox, B. (1987). *Discourse structure and anaphora: Written and conversational English*. Cambridge, England: Cambridge University Press.
  Examines, from a sociolinguistic perspective, the anaphoric uses of pronouns and noun phrases in conversation, magazine articles, and psychoanalytic biography.

Halliday, M., & Hasan, R. (1976). *Cohesion in English*. London: Longman.
This text is seminal. Much of its analysis of cohesion is, however, being refined by other researchers. (The authors use the term "reference" to refer both to reference and to coreference.)
McCarthy, M. (1994). It, this and that. In M. Coulthard (Ed.), *Advances in written text analysis* (pp. 266–275). London: Routledge & Kegan Paul.
Claiming that no distinction should be made between endophoric and exophoric reference, McCarthy attacks, and apparently solves, the previously unsolved problem of specifying rules for the selection of "it," "this," and "that" in discourse.
Stoddard, S. (1991). *Text and texture: Patterns of cohesion*. Norwood, NJ: Ablex.
Stoddard has refined some of Halliday and Hasan's concepts, especially concerning the nature of text and the potential for cohesion. Her understanding of cohesion focuses largely on coreference by pronouns and definite articles.

WORDS AND LEXICAL UNITS

Misunderstandings may arise when participants in conversation make different assumptions about what universe of discourse is being discussed. An even greater potential for misunderstanding occurs when words are chosen that have different meanings for different people, as in Fig. 2.3. The word "democracy," for example, may seem fairly well defined to the Americans, British, Canadians, Australians, or New Zealanders; they should be able to speak about it easily with one another without serious misunderstanding. But suppose one of the participants in the conversation is a government representative from a small one-party state in the developing world. The government of that state may well describe itself as democratic, but would someone from one of the countries mentioned agree? Words such as

CALVIN AND HOBBES / BILL WATTERSON

FIG. 2.3. Words may have different meanings for different people.
CALVIN AND HOBBES © Watterson. Dist. by UNIVERSAL PRESS SYNDICATE. Reprinted with permission. All rights reserved.

"democracy" are strongly entrenched in different universes of discourse, as the following utterance clearly indicates:

> (39) We believe we are already within a democratic system. Some factors are still missing, like the expression of the people's will.
> (President Roberto Eduardo Viola of Argentina, from a *Time* magazine interview, September 1982)

Following Leech (1981), **word meanings** may be divided into **conceptual** and **associative** meanings, where associative meanings may be further subdivided into **connotative, social, affective, reflected,** and **collocative** meanings.

Conceptual meaning is the logical, cognitive, or denotative meaning of a word. In other words, it is the meaning most predominantly given in a standard dictionary. For example, the *Franklin/Merriam-Webster Language Master* (electronic dictionary) gives for its first meaning of "democracy" the definition, "government in which the supreme power is held by the people."

Some or all of the associative meanings of a word may be added to conceptual meaning. The connotative meaning includes meanings imposed by ideology, cultural use, belief systems, and so on. Thus, the Anglo-American connotation of "democracy" would probably include the concept of a bicameral legislature in which more than one party is represented. The word may not carry these connotations in other societies or ideologies.

The social meaning of a word is reflected in stylistic choices as well as in such matters as dialect differences and differences in usage due to historical periods. For example, democracy surely had a very different meaning in Elizabethan England, when the monarch and Parliament were competing for power. Also, as a result of social meanings of words, producers may choose to use euphemisms, or words lacking some of the conceptual and associative meanings that might be deemed offensive to an individual or group. Consider, for example, the many words that replace "toilet" in polite conversation: cloakroom, restroom, bathroom, comfort station, and so on. Ironically, the word "toilet" itself was originally a euphemism.

Closely related to social meaning is affective meaning, which reflects the producer's attitude toward the communication. The producer may indicate—possibly through gestures, intonation, and surrounding text—that the concept of "democracy" is a "good" one or one not yet adequately realized, or is merely a term used to pull the wool over the eyes of the electorate. A producer who believes that democracy has become a dead issue, institutionalized by the "establishment," may clamor instead for "people power" or use some other emotive term associated with a personal set of beliefs.[1]

The meaning of a word may be reflected in other meanings carried by the same word. "Democracy," for instance, can refer either to a form of government or to a political unit having that form of government. Thus, the phrase "the European democracies" may cause people to think of the countries themselves, their governments, and the government institutions that serve the people. All of these meanings are present to some degree, even when one is singled out by the producer as the intended meaning in the utterance.

Finally, collocative meaning derives from the meanings of other words normally associated with the word in question, as is discussed later. Thus, "democracy" may be found in the same immediate cotext with "Parliament," "legislature," "election," "representative," "elected member," and so on. And deriving from the connotative, social, and affective meanings of some individuals or groups, additional collocations such as "justice," "liberty," "capitalism," and so on, on the one hand or, on the other, "socialism," "workers' rights," or "equitable division of wealth" may arise.[2] Indeed, as S. Chimombo and M. Chimombo (1996, chap. 3) pointed out, in Malawi, during the totalitarian regime of Hastings Banda, the governing party collocated "democracy" with "anarchy."

All the different kinds of meaning discussed combine in some way to form semantic meaning. Thus, for example, before the word "gay" can be related as a synonym for the word "homosexual," all the meanings of both terms must be combined to discover how they overlap. According to Fairclough (1989), the way in which words group together with other words, and the relations between words in such groups, is a crucial determining factor of word meanings.

---

[1]Related to connotative, social, and affective meanings is van Dijk's (1988) concept of "lexical stylistics" in news reporting—the deliberate choice of one of a set of words of similar meanings to emphasize a particular bias. Thus, a newspaper may use "terrorist" to describe one type of individual, usually in the enemy camp, whereas similar individuals approved of by the paper or by the society at large may be termed "freedom fighters."

[2]It is unusual for dictionaries to indicate the different ideologically and socially charged meanings of words, but one notable exception is R. Williams' *Keywords* (1976), which is somewhat in need of updating.

Practice 30:
Examine the meanings of the keywords in the following sentence from the American political speech already given in Practice 10. Remember that the speaker, Buchanan, is widely considered to be ultra right-wing. What kinds of meanings are most significant? How does a knowledge of Buchanan's political bias help you to interpret the meanings of the words? (*Hint:* Look particularly at "radicals," "liberals," "moderates," and "centrists." What kinds of associative meanings would you expect these words to have to a right-wing thinker?)

(At the Democratic Convention), 20,000 radicals and liberals came dressed up as moderates and centrists in the greatest single exhibition of cross-dressing in American political history.
(Pat Buchanan, quoted in *The Seattle Times*, 19 August 1992)

Just as personal, demonstrative, and comparative coreference can contribute to textual cohesion, so too, according to Halliday and Hasan (1976), can the meanings of words in a text. This is called **lexical cohesion**, and it results from **meaning relations** between pairs of words or phrases. Lexical cohesion can be achieved by repeating words, by using **synonyms** (words having similar meanings), or by using constellations of words related to each other in some sense. Consider the following three examples of lexical cohesion:

(40) A thunder being nation I am, I have said.
A thunder being nation I am, I have said
You shall live.
You shall live.
You shall live.
(Sioux battle cry to aid in rescuing comrades under fire. From *Black Elk speaks*. [1961]. Lincoln, NE: University of Nebraska Press, p. 258)

(41) Every pet deserves the benefit of life long dietary management. When you provide high-quality pet food like _____, you are giving your dog the nutrition it needs for a long and healthy life.
(From a dog food flyer)

(42) A good fire must have good firewood if it is to burn well. So must a person be stoked with good food if he is to be healthy and strong and happy.
(Cole-King, S. M., from the Foreword to A. Shaxson, P. Dickson, & J. Walker, [1985]. *The Malawi cookbook*, p. X. Zomba: Government Printer)

Example 40 is clearly a rather extreme case of lexical repetition. Such repetition not only welds the text into an obvious unity, but serves the purpose here of psychological, or perhaps even magical, enhancement. It seems if something is repeated often enough and loudly enough, then people really do begin to believe it. Believing that comrades can be rescued is obviously a necessary first step in actually rescuing them.

In Example 41, repetition is used as well (pet—pet; life—life). However, here there is also a use of synonyms (food—nutrition) and **hyponyms**, where a specific word is included in a more general one (dog—pet). There is also an example of **collocation**, where two words or phrases are neither synonyms nor hyponyms, but are perceived as belonging together in some sense (dietary management—pet food) and hence as having a greater than average chance of occurring in the same cotext. Collocations are usually restricted to very small cotexts consisting of only five or six words. They are directional, meaning that the probability of the first word occurring with the second is usually quite different from the probability of the second word occurring with the first. For example, the lexical frame "rancid _____" predicts that the word "butter" has a very great probability of occurring in the blank space. Very few other words could fit here. The probability of finding "rancid" in the lexical frame "____ butter" is, however, much smaller. Many other words (e.g., "fresh," "sweet," "salted") are also very likely to occur.

Example 42 depends almost entirely on collocations focusing on "fire" (fire—firewood—burn—stoke). Note that "stoke" is in the second sentence and is the major lexical cohesive tie relating that sentence to the first one.

Halliday and Hasan (1989) showed that one of the most powerful devices for creating a high potential for cohesion in a text is a special set of meaning relations known as **lexical chain interaction**. Halliday and Hasan used the following two texts as an illustration:

(43) Once upon a time there was a little girl, and she went out for a walk, and she saw a lovely little teddybear, and so she took it home, and when she got home she washed it, and when she took it to bed with her she cuddled it. . . .

(44) The sailor goes on the ship, and he's coming home with a dog, and the dog wants the boy and the girl, and they don't know the bear's in the chair, and the bear's coming to go to sleep in it, and they find the bear in the chair. . . .

They showed that there is roughly the same amount of cohesion in Examples 43 and 44, yet clearly the texts vary greatly in texture.

Simplifying their procedure somewhat, the keywords in the texts can be mapped as follows:

(45) girl ↔ went
girl ↔ got home
girl ↔ saw   ↔ teddybear
girl ↔ took home   ↔ teddybear
girl ↔ washed   ↔ teddybear
girl ↔ took to bed ↔ teddybear
girl ↔ cuddled   ↔ teddybear

(46) *Sailor* ↔ goes
Sailor ↔ comes with ↔ dog
dog ↔ wants ↔ *boy & girl*
boy & girl ↔ know ↔ *bear* ↔ *chair*
boy & girl ↔ find ↔ bear ↔ chair
bear ↔ come
bear ↔ sleep

Here the subjects, verbs, and objects of the two texts have been arranged in columns and have been connected with arrows to show the lexical meaning relations. The pattern in Example 45 is one of **unity of meaning**. This occurs when the text is relevant to one topic or a small set of closely related topics. In terms of lexical chains, unity of meaning exists when there is a close relation (shown by multiple arrows in the diagrams) connecting sets of words. In Example 43, "girl" (called the **agent**) is connected many times with "teddybear" (called the **patient**) through a number of verbs (called **processes**). And because there are no other sets of words that are not connected, unity of meaning exists.

Example 44, on the other hand, clearly does not demonstrate much unity of meaning. Another problem with Example 44 is indicated by the words in italics in Example 46. These are words accompanied in the text by the definite article "the." However, there has been no

---

Practice 31:
Outline the lexical chains in the "Vancouver" text of Practice 22.

(a) According to this outline, would you be justified in saying that this text has unity of meaning?
(b) Does it seem reasonable to you that texts of this genre should normally have unity of meaning? Why or why not?

prior mention of these words, nor is there any prior frame from which these words can be derived, as in the Christmas text (Example 10), examined earlier. Thus, these words can only be interpreted by looking outside the text.

In any language there are certain kinds of phrases that behave as though they were individual words. These are referred to as **lexical phrases**. Becker (1975) was one of the first to suggest that much of the language people use in everyday talk is processed in the form of prefabricated chunks rather than as individual words arranged in grammatical patterns. Each of these chunks, just as individual words, appears to be assigned a meaning by convention. However, the meaning of a lexical phrase is not necessarily derivable from the meaning of the individual words contained in it. Examples include "the oldest profession" (prostitution), "a (long) song and dance about (X)" (a not totally truthful account of [X]), and ". . . , that's all." (don't get flustered). Becker and his followers classified lexical phrases into a number of categories from very rigid phrases whose wording cannot change (idioms), to very flexible ones containing slots that can be filled by a number of words or other phrases. It is these flexible phrases that are most significant in language learning, because they provide patterns that can be easily modified to fit different cotexts. The theory of lexical phrases thus offers a view of language acquisition that is simpler than the one offered by traditional linguistics.

As elements of discourse, lexical phrases are significant in a number of ways. Nattinger and DeCarrico (1992) pointed to the importance of lexical phrases as signaling devices in complex texts. As idioms, they function as lexical units and enter into the same kinds of meaning relations as individual words do. As phrase and sentence builders, they are capable of generating meaning relations among the words that comprise them. To take one example, Example 42 (reproduced here), uses a parallel structure to repeat a lexical phrase that generates collocations:

(42) A good fire must have good firewood if it is to burn well. So must a person be stoked with good food if he is to be healthy and strong and happy.

The lexical phrase here has the pattern "X must have Y in order to Z." In this pattern, "X," "Y," and "Z" are expected to co-occur. When the same pattern is repeated in the second sentence, a different set of collocates is expected. But, in fact, one of the items ("stoked"), as already noted, belongs to the first set and thus provides an additional cohesive potential between the two sentences. Thus, lexical phrases can be summarized by noting that they act as individual words and enter into the same meaning relations that words enter into, but at the same time they act as patterns of words and generate meaning relations among the words they contain. Lexical phrases are discussed further later.

Entire statements, as well as individual words and lexical chains, can combine to provide meaning relations. More properly, such statements are called **propositions**. A proposition may be defined as the smallest unit of meaning that contains both a theme and a rheme. It is usually a statement that can be evaluated as being either true or false. For example, the following is a proposition:

(47) Dogs need nutrition.

Usually, more than one proposition is included in an utterance or sentence. The following are examples of sentences containing multiple propositions:

(48) Dogs need calories and fiber. (*dogs need calories + dogs need fiber*)
A good fire must have good firewood if it is to burn well ([condition] *a good fire must have good firewood: a good fire burns well*)
When you provide high-quality pet food like _____, you are giving your dog the nutrition it needs for a long and healthy life. ([condition] *you provide high quality pet food: you give your dog nutrition + dog needs nutrition + nutrition [causes] long life + nutrition [causes] healthy life*)

Together with multiple propositions, complex propositions can exist in virtually all languages. Complex propositions often look at first glance as though they must be multiple propositions. In fact, they are single propositions with multiple parts. As an example, the following sentence from a news report may appear to be a multiple proposition, but actually it is a single (and incomplete) proposition:

(49) Relatives have been called upon to provide the committee with all available information about the abduction victims.
(*International Herald Tribune*, July 12, 1984; quoted in Fairclough, 1989, p. 45)

The process indicated by the verb "call upon" ("ask," "request") requires several parts for completeness. The full form of this proposition is: W calls upon X to provide Y with Z. The passive voice form of the verb in Example 49 has removed, and thus mystified, the agent (W). Note that the following forms of this proposition would also be incomplete:

(50) (a) Relatives have been called upon to provide all available information about the abduction victims.
(b) The government has called upon the relatives to provide all available information about the abduction victims.
(c) Relatives received a government request to provide all available information about the abduction victims.

The "Y" part of the proposition, in this case "the committee," is missing from each of these versions. The problem of incomplete complex propositions is discussed in a later section.

Analyzing propositions enables people to describe meaning relations between units of text longer than single words. For example, in Example 41, some propositions of the second sentence repeat the meaning of the propositions of the first sentence. Both say essentially that you should give your dog a good diet because it needs this for good health. Expressing the same meaning in different words is called **paraphrase**. Thus, the second part of Example 41 is primarily a paraphrase of the first part, and vice versa.

Another kind of meaning relation between propositions is **parallelism**, in which two adjoining propositions with different meanings are given similar structures. A good example of this can be found in Example 42, where the structure of the first sentence (fires must have firewood) parallels the structure of the second (person must have food).

One last kind of phrasal or clausal meaning relation described here is **entailment**. Entailment exists when the truth of one proposition requires another proposition to be true. For example,

(51) (i) Dogs need nutrition.
(ii) Dogs need calories and fiber.

In this example, (ii) entails (i), because if (ii) is true, then (i) must be true. Note that in order to make this connection, the inference that nutrition is made up of calories and fiber (among others) must be understood. This type of inclusion relation is called *hyponymy*. Hyponymy often provides the basis for entailment relations in texts.

The following text is merely a more complex (and real) version of Example 51. In this text, the second sentence also entails the first, for the reasons already given. Whether you prefer to think of this as

Practice 32:
Identify the meaning relations that help tie the following text together.

(a) Analyze the sets of meaning relations that refer to "people," "leader," and "enemy."
(b) How does the producer characterize each of these three concepts?
(c) How does a knowledge of these concepts, as characterized by the producer, help interpreters to protect themselves?

> As a whole, and at all times, the efficiency of the truly national leader consists primarily in preventing the division of attention of a people, and always concentrating it on a single enemy. The more uniformly the fighting will of a people is put into action, the greater will be the magnetic force of the movement and the more powerful the impetus of the blow. It is part of the genius of a great leader to make adversaries of different fields appear as always belonging to one category only, because to weak and unstable characters the knowledge that there are various enemies will lead only too easily to incipient doubts as to their own cause.
>
> As soon as the wavering masses find themselves confronted with too many enemies, objectivity at once steps in, and the question is raised whether actually all the others are wrong and their own nation or their own movement alone is right.
>
> Also with this comes the first paralysis of their own strength. Therefore, a number of essentially different enemies must always be regarded as one in such a way that in the opinion of the mass of one's own adherents the war is being waged against one enemy alone. This strengthens the belief in one's own cause and increases one's bitterness against the attacker.
>
> (Adolf Hitler, *Mein Kampf*; quoted in Fairclough, 1989, pp. 86–87)

an example of entailment or hyponymy, the result is the same: the establishment of a cohesive potential linking the two sentences:

> (52) Dogs that are less active or have a tendency to gain weight have different nutritional needs for their specific situation. They need fewer calories, and increased fiber to provide bulk and a "full" feeling after eating. (From a dog food flyer)

Guidelines for Analyzing Words and Lexical Units

Locate all keywords and phrases in the text—especially those that reoccur or clearly play a dominant role. Be on the lookout for unusually frequent repetition as a clue to words and concepts the producer considers crucial.

Consider whether all referring expressions among these keywords and phrases have clear referents in a commonly recognized universe of discourse. If not, consider the possible dangers of interpretation. Determine what misunderstandings could arise.

Derive the meaning set (conceptual and associative meanings) for each of the keywords and phrases identified. What scope for misinterpretation is provided by the associative meanings?

Examine the lexical cohesion linking sets of keywords. Determine how this lexical cohesion is achieved.

Look for critical sentences in which keywords are used. Examine meaning relations relating to these sentences. Are sentences repeatedly paraphrased? Is any possibly significant information entailed but not expressly stated? Does any contradiction or ambiguity exist in the text? If you can answer "yes" to any of these questions, determine what effect such meaning relations may have on the text. One way to do this is to rewrite part of the text, removing the meaning relation that is under scrutiny, and then to compare and contrast the two versions.

Determine if there are any instances of sentences joined by a meaning relation that is made explicit only by use of structural parallelism.

Sample Analysis: Words and Lexical Units

The CODE advertisement (Fig. 1.3) may be analyzed as follows:

Word meanings: Keywords include "developing," "letters," "literacy," "opportunities," "knowledge," "skills," "education," and "CODE." Many of these words could have associative meanings that differ from one interpreter to another, yet their conceptual meanings are fairly stable. Even where different interpretations exist, most interpreters would agree that the concepts offered by the advertisement are desirable ones.

Lexical cohesion. *Reiteration*: "developing," "countries," "26" are repeated; "developing" is also reiterated as "development"; "world" is repeated and also reiterated as "countries"; "developing countries" is a general term for countries readers know to be in "Africa and the Caribbean"; "literacy" is repeated, but is also a superordinate of "letters" and is included within the meaning of

"education." Note that "people" is repeated but is not lexically cohesive because it is referring to two different groups—those likely to read the advertisement and those in the developing world. *Collocation*: "One" way collocates with "26" as the ordered series of the letters of the alphabet, for which there is the further collocation of the symbolic blackboard with the letters written on it in chalk; "developing" collocates with "food security, good health and job opportunities," "knowledge and skills through education," "literacy," and so on; these further collocate with "Self-sufficiency." Paraphrase: No noticeable paraphrasing, because adverts typically depend on succinctness.
Entailment: The statement that CODE supports literacy. This entails that CODE solicits funds, aid, and so on, and distributes these to targeted groups. (Note that "funds" is never mentioned and must be derived through this entailment.)

Application

Using the aforementioned guidelines, analyze words and lexical units in your chosen oral and written practice texts.

Suggested Reading

Fairclough, N. (1989). *Language and power.* London: Longman.
    The sections on the relation of word choice and word meaning to power are recommended, especially pp. 93–97 and 112–119, and also the various sections on vocabulary, including racist vocabulary (pp. 69, 116).
Halliday, M., & Hasan, R. (1989). *Language, context, and text: Aspects of language in a social-semiotic perspective.* Oxford, England: Oxford University Press.
    Hasan's section of this book, and especially chapter 5, gives a clear and concise description of the major devices of cohesion with special focus on lexical chains.
Hoey, M. (1991). *Patterns of lexis in text.* Oxford, England: Oxford University Press.
    Hoey provides a detailed hypothesis of how lexical patterning might occur in texts.
Hurford, J., & Heasley, B. (1983). *Semantics: A coursebook.* Cambridge, England: Cambridge University Press.
    A clear introduction to the major concepts of semantics, with many definitions and examples.
Leech, G. (1981). *Semantics.* Harmondsworth, England: Penguin.
    A more advanced book than that by Hurford and Heasley, but still very readable. The section on the "Seven Types of Meaning" is especially recommended.
Stubbs, M. (1983). *Discourse analysis: The sociolinguistic analysis of natural language.* Oxford, England: Blackwell.
    Contains a particularly clear treatment of propositions and entailments (pp. 203–204).

Van Dijk, T. (1988). *News as discourse.* Hillsdale, NJ: Lawrence Erlbaum Associates.
van Dijk's sections on how words are chosen and used in news reporting are recommended, especially pp. 81–82. Also consult sections on propositions and proposition sequences (pp. 59–60), and macropropositions (pp. 31–32).
Williams, R. (1976). *Keywords: A vocabulary of culture and society.* London: Fontana/Croom Helm.
A "dictionary" of the associative meanings of keywords in modern English-speaking societies.

SUBSTITUTION AND ELLIPSIS

Halliday and Hasan (1976) showed that, together with coreference and lexical cohesion, **substitution** and **ellipsis** provide two additional, closely related ways of enhancing the cohesive potential of a text. Substitution means replacing a word, phrase, and so on, by a different word or phrase. Ellipsis is similar to substitution, except that no word or phrase is substituted. In this sense, it may be regarded as substitution by nothing.

Both substitution and ellipsis may operate on the noun phrase, on the verb phrase, or on the clause. This means they result in either word replacements (substitution) or word omissions (ellipsis) in part of a noun phrase, verb phrase, or clause. The usual substitution for a noun phrase is "one," for a verb phrase is some form of "do," and for a clause is "so" or "not." The following text contains an example of verbal substitution by "did" (underlined in the last line):

```
(53) B: It was a horse I'd never seen before.
     K: .hhh I remember when you said that! He attacked you. ((laugh))=
                                                               [ ]
     B:                                                       (Hm::)!
        = He did! He just came running up out of ((laughing)) nowhere
(Quoted in Craig & Tracy, 1983, p. 318)
```

Here "did" substitutes for the actual verb "attacked." The substitution provides a potentially cohesive link between B's and K's comments (although a possibly stronger link is provided by the repetition of "he"). In the following text, ellipsis dominates:

```
(54) A: I think he's been the least quiet in the group, don't you think?
     B: Uh hum.
     C: Ge::zz,really?
     A: Who do you think has been (0.5) ya you have (2.0) who do you think
        has been the most talkative in our group?
```

C: I won't say anything but wait (1.0)*le:::ssst* quiet?
A: Ya, you're the//
B: No, most//quiet
A: You're the most quiet
C: I didn't think so
(Quoted in Beach, 1983, pp. 210–211)

To see the ellipsis more clearly, look at the following version of the same text. Here the various ellipses have been filled out with words in brackets and the one clausal substitution "so" has been underlined in the last line:

Practice 33:
Look at the following poem by D. H. Lawrence and identify all the potential cohesive ties that help to bind the poem into a unity. Include coreference, lexical cohesion, substitution, and ellipsis. What is the relation between the types of cohesive ties used by the poet and the conversational structure of the poem?

                    What Is He?
What is he?
—A man, of course.
Yes, but what does he do?
—He lives and is a man.
Oh quite! but he must work. He must have a job of some sort.
—Why?
Because obviously he's not one of the leisured classes.
—I don't know. He has lots of leisure. And he makes quite beautiful chairs.
There you are then! He's a cabinet maker.
—No no!
Anyhow a carpenter and joiner.
—Not at all.
But you said so.
—What did I say?
That he made chairs, and was a joiner and carpenter.
—I said he made chairs, but I did not say he was a carpenter.
All right then, he's just an amateur.
—Perhaps! Would you say a thrush was a professional flautist, or just an amateur?
I'd just say it was a bird.
—And I say he is just a man.
All right! You always did quibble.
(Pinto, V. de S., & Roberts, W. (Eds.). (1964). *The Complete Poems of D. H. Lawrence, Volume One.* London: Heinemann, pp. 452–453.)

(55) A: I think he's been the *least* quiet in the group, don't you think [that he has been the least quiet in the group]?

B: Uh hum, [I think that he has been the least quiet in the group].

C: Ge::zz, [do you] *really* [think that I have been the least quiet in the group]?

A: Who do you think has been [the most talkative in our group] (0.5) ya you have [been the most talkative in our group] (2.0) who do you think has been the most talkative in our group?

C: I won't say anything but wait (1.0) [do you really mean] le:::*ssst* quiet?

A: Ya, you're the// [least quiet in our group]

B: No, [you mean] most//quiet

A: You're the most quiet [in our group]

C: I didn't think so [that I am the most quiet in our group]

In this text, ellipsis in particular provides a number of potential cohesive ties helping to cement the text together.

In contrast, written narrative seldom exhibits a great deal of substitution or ellipsis. These cohesive devices arise more naturally in conversation, where the various participants make use of ways to avoid repetition. When one person is narrating, the danger of undesired and unnecessary repetition is not so great, because the narrator has complete control over the structure of the narrative and the presentation of information. In other kinds of written text, nominal, rather than verbal, substitution and ellipsis may be characteristic.

Guidelines for Analyzing Substitution and Ellipsis

Identify all instances of nominal, verbal, and clausal substitution. Consider for each instance what information has been retained from the node in the cohesive element and what has been changed.

Identify all instances of nominal, verbal, and clausal ellipsis. Consider for each instance what information has been retained from the node in the cohesive element and what has been changed.

Consider whether the producer had a choice between substitution or ellipsis or was required by the grammar of the language to select one in preference to the other.

Sample Analysis: Substitution and Ellipsis

The CODE advertisement (Fig. 1.3) may be analyzed as follows:

Substitution: no instances in the CODE advert. (Note that "do" is a lexical verb in "You'd be surprised at what 26 letters can <u>do</u>. . . .") Ellipsis: nominal ellipsis: "one way" is tied to "26 _____" by nominal ellipsis. No other instances of ellipsis.

Application

Using the aforementioned guidelines, analyze how a potential for cohesion through substitution and/or ellipsis is achieved in your chosen oral and written practice texts.

Suggested Reading

Halliday, M., & Hasan, R. (1976). *Cohesion in English.* London: Longman.
Contains a very detailed description of subsitution and ellipsis.
Hatch, E. (1992). *Discourse and language education.* Cambridge, England: Cambridge University Press.
Hatch gives an extremely clear synopsis of substitution and ellipsis on pp. 224–225.

CONJUNCTION AND CLAUSE RELATIONS

Another powerful way in which cohesion can contribute to texture is through the way in which clauses or sentences are linked. Combined clauses, along with their meaning relations, comprise what Halliday (1985) referred to as "clause complexes." By constructing clause complexes in ways that strengthen cohesion between clauses, a producer can contribute to the texture of a text.

Halliday and Hasan (1976) identified four types of meaning relations, called conjunction, between clauses or sentences: *additive* (e.g., "and"), *adversative* (e.g., "but"), *causal* (e.g., "because"), and *temporal* (e.g., "before"). By adding one of these four meanings to the clause complex, conjunction differs greatly from the other kinds of cohesive devices examined so far. Other cohesive devices link meanings together but do not add meanings of their own.

Another important way in which conjunction differs from other types of cohesive devices is that it creates ties not between nodes and cohesive elements but rather between entire segments of text of various lengths. To get a better idea of the importance of conjunction and how it works, consider the linking strategies of the following children's narratives (Examples 43 and 44):

(43) Once upon a time there was a little girl, and she went out for a walk, and she saw a lovely little teddybear, and so she took it home, and when she got home she washed it, and when she took it to bed with her she cuddled it. . . .

(44) The sailor goes on the ship, and he's coming home with a dog, and the dog wants the boy and the girl, and they don't know the bear's in the chair, and the bear's coming to go to sleep in it, and they find the bear in the chair. . . .

Example 43 uses additive ("and"), causal ("and so"), and temporal ("when") meanings to bind the clauses. Example 44, on the other hand, relies exclusively on additive conjunction, producing what might seem to be a mere list of unrelated things and events. It is likely, therefore, that conjunction, as well as lexical chain interaction, plays an important role in creating the different degrees of texture that are perceived in these texts. As a further example, consider the following extract from a student's essay:

(56) [24]Because of its greater accuracy, the numerical grading system also gives a more reliable account of a student's potential. [25]If alphabetical grades do not give a clear picture of what a student has achieved in the past, how can they possibly give an idea of what the student is likely to achieve in the future? [26]The main reason for this is that grades are computerized.
(Sackrowitz, B. [1980]. To number or not to number. In Bruffee, 1980, 136–137)

It is clear that all the clauses in this extract are meaningfully related. Arranging the student's text as follows may help to show the kinds of clausal relations that an interpreter may perceive:

(57) (i) Because of its greater accuracy, the numerical grading system also gives a more reliable account of a student's potential.
(ii) If alphabetical grades do not give a clear picture of what a student has achieved in the past, how can they possibly give an idea of what the student is likely to achieve in the future?
(iii) The main reason for this is that grades are computerized.

Here, indentation is used to indicate adversative, causal, or temporal links, whereas additive links are shown by placing the related clauses directly above and below each other. In the example, (ii) is related to (i) as a continuation of a list (additive). It is an additional and independent piece of information. Sentence (iii), on the other hand, is related causally to (ii). The writer could have begun (iii) with "this is true because" or something similar. This was not necessary, however, because the meanings contained in (iii) show the causal relation clearly enough.

Notice that in the arrangement of the three sentences of Example 57, there are only two ways in which adjacent sentences can relate to each other with regard to dependency. They can either be in some sense parallel to each other, like sentences (i) and (ii); or one can depend on another, like sentence (iii), which depends on sentence (ii) for its meaning. Only sentences related additively can have equal status. Causal (e.g., "because"), adversative (e.g., "however"), and most temporal links (e.g., "before") automatically create a dependency on the previous sentence. In Example 57, the third sentence has a causal dependency on the sentence before it.

Halliday (1985) used the term **paratactic** for the relation between two elements that are equal in status, like sentences (i) and (ii). If there is a dependency between two elements, as between (iii) and (ii), their relation is said to be **hypotactic**. Note that, in general, any item in a paratactic set can be removed without disturbing the mutual dependencies of the items. Thus, either (i) or (ii) can be removed from the example text without disturbing the meaning of the other. In general, any paratactic clause or sentence together with its dependencies (such as [iii]), can be removed from a text without greatly disturbing the meaning of the rest of the text. This is not true of hypotactic items, however. For example, because (iii) is dependent on (ii), removing (ii) causes (iii) to shift meaning such that it refers to (i) instead. But this is not the meaning intended by the writer. Its original meaning depends on a sentence that no longer exists. For one thing, the coreferent for "this" has been changed by the removal of (ii). More important, however, is the faulty causality that now results. This is easier to see if the sentence is rewritten in such a way that it no longer needs a coreferent:

(58) The main reason is that grades are computerized.

Clearly the shift of meaning is the result of the cause stated in this sentence that has now been shifted to (i). By asking "Reason for what?", it is found that "alphabetical grades do not give a clear picture of what a student has achieved in the past," and so on. Instead, the conjunctive reference now shifts to "the numerical grading system also gives a more reliable account of a student's potential." This is a completely different meaning from the one that was intended.

In addition to the dependency relations of parataxis and hypotaxis, another formal relation among clauses is **embedding**. Embedding occurs when one clause is inserted within another. The following sentence (clause complex) from the text of Practice 4 provides a clear example of embedding:

> (59) This book, *which is written especially for use in Malawi using ingredients which are locally available,* is designed to give the housewife some ideas and suggestions to improve her "firewood."

The embedded clause complex has been italicized for clarity. An embedded clause complex such as this can easily be removed and made into a separate independent clause complex, as follows:

> (60) *This book was written especially for use in Malawi using ingredients which are locally available.* It is designed to give the housewife some ideas and suggestions to improve her "firewood."

Different genres typically use different degrees of parataxis, hypotaxis, and embedding. In general, genres that involve ongoing production, such as telephone conversations, have few embeddings. As Halliday showed, such genres typically contain complex relations of parataxis and hypotaxis between clauses instead. Carefully constructed literate genres, such as academic writing, on the other hand, are more likely to contain embeddings.

Dependency relations between sentences or clauses are not the only clausal relations that contribute to texture, however. There are also meaning relations between the clauses or the sentences. Any two adjacent elements are linked by meaning, just as they are linked by the presence or absence of dependency. The meaning of the clauses depends ultimately on coreference and reference to the situation.

As an example, look again at Examples 43 and 44. Both refer to their situation to a greater or lesser degree because both were produced by children who were asked to use a set of dolls (sailor, dog, children, and so on) to tell a story to a teddybear. Presumably, to an individual present at the telling of these stories, Example 44's exophoric use of "the" would not have seemed as disturbing to the texture as it does when the story is removed from the situation that produced it. This does not solve the problem of the story's lack of unity, however; and a closer inspection would suggest that the rapid shift of topic (sailor, ship, dog, boy, girl, bear, chair) detracts from situational reference, and hence from texture. Reference, therefore, depends on the stability of situational elements. If one or more of the situational elements of a text are altered, a clear indication is needed of how the altered elements relate to those they replace. In this connection, Example 44 fails to clarify the connection between "sailor," "dog," "boy," and so on. In general, there is a lack of connectivity between the elements of this text.

Connectivity, as Bruffee (1980) explained, can be provided in a text by answering questions that can be generated by previous information. For example, the segment, "he's coming home with a dog," can generate such questions as "what kind of dog?", "where did he get the dog?", "where is 'home'?", "how long had he been away?", and so forth. If the next segment answered one or more of these questions by stating something like, "It was a dog that he had found on a magic island," and if the next segment answered a question generated by this segment, and so on, the text would gain in connectivity, and hence, texture. Note that Example 43 has a high degree of connectivity in this sense.

The meaning of a clause or a clause complex, and the way clauses are related to each other, is conditioned by the degree of **functional transitivity** exhibited by the clause or clause complex. In its simplest sense, transitivity refers to whether or not the verb, known as the

---

Practice 34:
Examine the following text for conjunction and connectivity. Which of these features seems to be more closely related to problems of texture in this text? This text is by a schizophrenic speaker. What other kinds of producers might be expected to produce texts with similar patterns of conjunction and connectivity?

Interviewer: A stitch in time saves nine. What does that mean?
Schizophrenic: Oh! That's because all women have a little bit of magic to them—I found that out—and it's called—it's sort of good magic—and nine is sort of a magic number. Like I've got nine colours here you will notice—I've got yellow, green, blue, grey, orange, blue, and navy—and I've got black—and I've got a sort of clear white—the nine colours to me they are the whole universe—and they symbolise every man, woman, and child in the world.

(Rochester, S., & Martin, J. (1979). *Crazy talk: A study of the discourse of schizophrenic speakers.* New York: Plenum, p. 95. In Brown & Yule, 1983, p. 74)

process, carries its meaning to a direct object, as in "We demolished the house," where "house" is the direct object of the process "demolish." This view of transitivity stipulates whether or not a process is transitive. However, Tsunoda (1994), following Halliday (1985), explained that there are degrees of transitivity, which depend on the following factors: the number of participants in the process; how heavily the meaning of the process impinges on one of the participants; whether or not a change takes place in one of the participants; whether or not there is a transitive pattern of subject–verb–direct object; and whether the clause can be expressed as a passive, a reflexive (e.g., using "-self"), and/or a reciprocal (e.g., using "each other"). Tsunoda's examples include "Brutus killed Caesar," which exhibits all of these characteristics and is thus highly transitive; and "It is cool today," which exhibits none of the characteristics listed and is thus highly intransitive. An intermediate example is "Di looked at Kay," which, on the positive side, has two participants. In addition, it has forms that can be passive ("was looked at"), reflexive ("looked at herself"), and reciprocal ("looked at each other"). But, on the negative side, it has no direct impingement of the process on Kay, no change of condition, and no transitive pattern. Therefore, such a process as "look at" must be considered to be only partially transitive in this sense.

In general, Tsunoda noted that the more highly transitive a process is, the more easily the clause containing it can be transformed into a passive construction. This is of interest in discourse analysis, because passives provide one way of removing the agent, or subject, from the clause. Passives are often used for this purpose in newspaper articles, especially if there is some reason for wanting to mystify the agent. This is apparently the case in the following excerpt from an article in the official government organ of a previously dictatorial African state in which a free press was not, at the time, permitted. (In this extract, comprising Paragraphs 15–20 of the article, the passive constructions are underlined):

(61) ... Thereafter, [the three Ministers and one M.P.] were believed to be travelling to Soche; however, they were not seen there.

When by that evening the gentlemen had not reported at the Police Station in Blantyre, the Police Force was alerted.

As a result, it became necessary to make a special radio announcement at 10 p.m. on that evening, and again at 6 a.m. the following morning.

The purpose of the announcement was to appeal to the members of the public to assist the Police in locating the whereabouts of the gentlemen.

It was in the course of this intensive search that the car in which the gentlemen were travelling <u>was found</u> to have overturned several times, badly wrecked and the people in it dead.

The Police came to the scene of the accident and after some time managed to retrieve the bodies from the wrecked car which <u>was mangled</u> a hundred feet or so down a steep gradient. . . .

(Malawi *Daily Times*, 25 May 1983; quoted in S. Chimombo & M. Chimombo, 1996, Appendix A, p. 196)

Of the five passive constructions contained in this segment, only one, "was found," is clearly linked to an agent ("Police") mentioned in the previous sentence. The other four cannot be connected to any agent in the text. Not all interpreters will instantly spot the fact that possibly important information—namely, who did the believing, seeing, alerting, and mangling—is missing here. This is all the more disturbing considering that this information may have been omitted deliberately for political or other reasons; as S. Chimombo and M. Chimombo (1996) explained, the men may have been the victims of a political assassination, and the car appeared to have been "mangled" only after the "accident."[3]

A related device, as Chimombo and Chimombo pointed out, is **extraposition,**[4] because this, like the passive, contributes to mystification by distancing the producer from the content. There are two examples of this in the previous extract:

(62) . . . <u>it became necessary</u> to make a special radio announcement at 10 p.m. on that evening . . .

(63) <u>It was in the course of this intensive search</u> that the car in which the gentlemen were travelling was found to have overturned several times, badly wrecked and the people in it dead.
(Malawi *Daily Times*, 25 May 1983; quoted in S. Chimombo & M. Chimombo, 1996, Appendix A, p. 196)

A more direct (and highly transitive) way of stating the second of these, for example, is the following:

(64) The police conducted an intensive seach. In the course of this search the car . . .

---

[3]Subsequent to S. Chimombo and M. Chimombo's (1996) work, Hastings Banda, former "Life President" of Malawi, and his Minister of State, John Tembo, were arrested in connection with this incident and were tried on the charges of murder and of conspiring to defeat justice by tampering with evidence.

[4]Extrapositions, also called cleft constructions, are a fruitful source of presuppositions. See Levinson (1983, pp. 182, 217–222).

By observing the differences between the real and the constructed examples, note that the extraposition ("It was . . .") in the actual example fulfills several functions. First, it enables the agent "police" (or whoever the actual agent was) to be omitted. Second, it allows producers of the passage to place a greater distance between themselves and the truth of the propositions contained in the passage, namely, that there was a search and the car was found presumably as a result of the search. And third, it aids the writer in passing off onto the interpreter the idea that the search (if there was one) was "intensive."

An additional point to be noted about Example 63, in which the producer uses both extraposition and a passive construction, is the obvious difficulty the producer is having with the language of the text. The sentence collapses into a jumble of ungrammaticality as its parallel structure breaks down (". . . overturned several times, badly wrecked and the people in it dead"). Problems in ideology and belief may easily result in a breakdown of grammar, as Kress (1989, p. 81) noted.

One final phenomenon related to transitivity is **nominalization**, which, as Fowler (1991) and Thom (1989) pointed out, is potentially capable of mystifying the agent, the patient (direct object of the process), and even an entire clause. To see an example of this, examine . Paragraph 4 of the same news article from which the extract was taken:

> (65) In view of the importance to the Government to dispel any false rumours and unsubstantiated speculation, the Department of Information is under instruction to release the facts as they are known to the authorities up to this point in time.

Here, such nouns as "speculation" and "instruction" serve effectively to mystify agents and other information. As pointed out earlier, a verb such as "speculate" yields a complete proposition something like

X <u>speculates</u> about Y

When the nominal form is used, both X and Y can quietly disappear. Similarly, the verb "instruct" can form a complete proposition such as

Under the authority of A, X <u>instructs</u> Y to do Z for reason R

Who are A and X in the news article mentioned? By using the nominal form, the producer can omit this information, probably without arousing the suspicions of most interpreters.

Halliday (1989) showed that the clause connections in spontaneous conversation are more complex than those of many written genres.

Practice 35:

In a study of newspaper coverage in Malawi before and after 1993, when a free press was permitted to begin operating in that country, S. Chimombo and M. Chimombo (1996) observed that much greater use of passives and extrapositions characterized the nondemocratic press, whereas the later democratic press was more direct and used fewer such obscuring or mystifying devices in its reporting. Read the following extract from a free press article in Malawi reporting on the same "accident" that was reported in the previous examples. Examine the degree of transitivity, as shown by passive constructions, extrapositions, and nominalizations. What evidence can you find to support S. Chimombo and M. Chimombo's conclusion regarding the free press in Malawi? (In the following text, "Mr. X" refers to an eyewitness who does not wish to be named.)

> Both the government statement and Mr. X's story do, however, agree that the Peugeot was in the Mwanza area on or about 18 May 1983. According to Mr. X's description, the car was facing the Thambani direction as it leant against the tree. This suggests that it may have been going uphill. The spot is so steep that the car could not have been travelling at high speed, even supposing that the men were on the run. An accident leading to overturning at this spot, if the car was indeed going uphill, could lead to the death of all four occupants only in the most bizarre circumstances.
> (*The Nation* (Malawi), 23 August 1993; quoted in S. Chimombo & M. Chimombo, 1996, Appendix B, p. 199)

For this reason, among others, it is important to look in some detail at **conversation structure** in genres such as face-to-face conversation and telephone conversation.

It is obvious that participants in a conversation take turns speaking. This is known as turn-taking. There has been a great deal of investigation into exactly how turn-taking is accomplished. Sachs, Schegloff, and Jefferson (1974) established three rules, based on empirical investigation, to describe how speakers relinquish turns in conversation at points known as *Transition Relevance Places* (TRPs):

1. If the current speaker S selects the next speaker (N) in the current turn, S is expected to stop speaking, and N is expected to speak next.

2. If S's utterance or behavior does not select the next speaker, then any other participant may self-select. Whoever speaks first gets the floor.

3. If no speaker self-selects, S may continue.

These rules apply recursively at each TRP in the order in which they are given. Note that, according to Rule 2, a speaker may select the next speaker by an utterance or by a variety of nonverbal behaviors (considered later). A speaker who does not wish to give up the floor may use such terms as "but," "however," and so on, to indicate that the utterance is not yet complete. Similarly, beginning an utterance with a subordinator such as "although" or "if" signals that at least two clauses must follow before completion. Signals such as "first" or "to begin with" also indicate that extended information is likely to follow. As a last recourse, a speaker may resort to paralinguistic features such as increased loudness or higher pitch to retain the attention of the listener(s).

Exactly how turn-taking is done is largely a cultural matter. The rules for turn-taking given previously apply to most English-speaking cultures, but they vary greatly from the norms of turn-taking found in many parts of the world. Within any cultural norms, however, violations of standard turn-taking behavior may be examined as an indicator of power relations between discourse participants. One well-known pattern of violation of turn-taking norms in England and North America involves male dominance in conversations between men and women.

A turn that consists of two related utterances, each spoken by a different person, is known as an **adjacency pair** if the first utterance belongs to a set of utterances known as *first pair parts*, and the second utterance belongs to a corresponding set of utterances known as *second pair parts*. The first pair part might be an announcement, a challenge, a complaint, a greeting, an invitation, an offer, a question, or a request. The second pair part·may in some cases be reciprocal, as when a greeting results in a return greeting. Some first pair parts may give the respondent a choice of second pair parts. For example, an invitation may lead to either an acceptance or a refusal. And others leave the respondent with no choice. For example, a question must be followed by an answer.[5]

In those cases in which a first pair part allows for a choice of second pair parts, it has been shown that some second pair choices are preferred over others. Preference in this case is based on human psychology and culture with the preferred choices being structurally

---

[5]In actual conversations, this idealized view of adjacency pairs is not always followed by speakers. This has led to questions concerning the status and form of adjacency pairs and has resulted in a great deal of current research into this question.

simpler than dispreferred ones. For example, the preferred choice following an invitation is an acceptance. A refusal, the dispreferred choice, is typically more complex, as seen in Example 13:

> (13) A: Uh if you'd care to come and visit a little while this morning I'll give you a cup of coffee
> B: Hehh Well that's awfully sweet of you, I don't think I can make it this morning. .hh uhm I'm running an ad in the paper and-and uh I have to stay near the phone.

If B had accepted A's invitation, B's response would probably have been much simpler and more direct. A typical acceptance in such a case might be "I'd love to."

Levinson (1983) listed preferred and dispreferred parts corresponding to several first pair parts (see Table 2.1). Quite often, additional sequences of speech exchanges will occur between the first pair part and the second pair part of an adjacency pair. Many of these are simple in form and resemble the adjacency pair itself, as in the following example in which a question–answer **insertion sequence** (Qi-Ai) is inserted in the middle of a question–answer adjacency pair (Q-A):

> (66) A: I don't know where the—wh—this address //is   Q
> B: Well where do—which part of town do **you** live?   Qi
> A: I live four ten East Lowden   Ai
> B: Well you don't live very far from me   A
> (Quoted in Coulthard, 1985, p. 73)

Many insertion sequences are much longer and more complex than the one given here and may exhibit a number of levels of embedding (insertion sequences within insertion sequences). In addition, as Levin-

TABLE 2.1
Parts of Common Adjacency Pairs

First Parts	Second Parts	
	Preferred	*Dispreferred*
request	acceptance	refusal
offer/invite	acceptance	refusal
assessment	agreement	disagreement
question	expected answer	unexpected answer or non-answer
blame	denial	admission

son pointed out, questions in insertion sequences do not always result in answers. Respondents may claim not to know the answer or may refuse to answer; the speaker may be advised to ask a different person or may be challenged about the sincerity of the question.

Some types of conversation, especially those in which talk is the main purpose of the social event of conversing, exhibit a fairly rigid or predictable overall organization. Telephone conversations, chats over the fence, and conversations that result from chance meetings on the street are among those that contain an opening section, a series of topic slots, and a closing section. Each of these has its own characteristic features or parts. An opening typically begins with a summons, a response to the summons, and an exchange of greetings. In a telephone conversation, the summons (the ringing of the phone) will typically be followed by an identification exchange in which the summoned person is given an opportunity to recognize the caller. One variant of this structure is shown in the following example:

```
(67)  C:  ((rings))            ((SUMMONS))
      R:  Hello                ((ANSWER)) + ((DISPLAY FOR RECOGNITION))
      C:  Hello Rob            ((CLAIM THAT C HAS RECOGNISED R))
          This is Laurie       ((IDENTIFICATION))
          How's everything     ((GREETING 1ST PART))
      R:  ((sniff)) Pretty good ((CLAIM THAT R HAS RECOGNISED C))
          How 'bout you        ((GREETING 2ND PART))
      C:  Jus' fine. The reason ((INTRODUCING 1ST TOPIC))
          I called was ta ask ...
      (Schegloff, 1979, p. 47; quoted in Levinson, 1983, p. 312)
```

Topics should be clearly related to each other if the conversation participants are to have the impression that the conversation is going smoothly. Occasionally, a participant will perform a topic jump by using an expression such as "hey" and then abruptly switching to a nonrelated topic. If this happens frequently during the conversation, participants will probably begin to feel uncomfortable as they realize that the conversation is forced and not really spontaneous.

After all topics are exhausted and closed or shifted, one by one, the conversation will arrive at a closing section, whose purpose is to allow all participants to synchronize their exits from the conversation. Levinson presented a four-part scheme for closings, including (a) a closing down of a topic—indicating that the end of the conversation is near (e.g., making arrangements, inquiring after the health of family members, etc.); (b) one or more pairs of preclosing turns involving such terms as "Okay," "so," and so on; (c) if appropriate, a summarizing expression referring to the type of conversation (e.g., thanking for a favor, inquiring after health—"Well, I just wanted to know how you were . . . ," and so on); and (d) a final exchange of closing terms, such as "bye." The following example (examined in Example 17) contains all of these. (The symbol = indicates that no pause occurred between the end of one utterance and the beginning of the next, and the symbol ::: indicates a greatly lengthened vowel):

(68)	R: Why don't we all have lunch	(topic closing)
	C: Okay so that would be in	
	St Jude's would it?	(topic closing)
	R: Yes	(topic closing)
	(0.7 second pause)	
	C: Okay so:::	(preclosing turn)
	R: One o'clock in the bar	(summarizing expression)
	C: Okay	(summarizing expression)
	R: Okay?	(preclosing turn)
	C: Okay then thanks very much	
	indeed George=	(summarizing expression)
	R: All right	(summarizing expression)
	C: // See you there	(preclosing turn)
	R: See you there	(preclosing turn)
	C: Okay	(preclosing turn)
	R: Okay // bye	(preclosing turn; final exchange)
	C: bye	(final exchange)

Consider **presequences**, a final conversational structuring device. These are a special kind of psychologically motivated conversation structure used by conversation participants to minimize the chance of embarrassment that might result from dispreferred responses to certain types of first-pair parts. For example, if you invite someone to dinner and that person declines your invitation, you may feel somewhat hurt or rejected, as seen in connection with politeness strategies. To prevent this, you might preface your invitation with a preinvitation, such as "Are you doing anything on Saturday evening?" If the respondent then makes a reply such as "We're planning to spend the weekend at the lake," you may be able to soften your invitation or get out of making it altogether, and thus escape from the situation without any embarrassment. In addition to preinvitations, Levinson listed prerequests, prearrangements (for future contacts), and preannouncements (such as "guess what") among possible types of presequences. All of these are a fruitful source of inferences in conversational discourse. For example, a preinvitation allows the interpreter to infer that an invitation will follow. The answer to the pre-invitation may allow the individual inviter to infer whether the inter-preter intends to accept or to reject the invitation. In general, prese-quences can increase politeness by maximizing the Politeness Principle, while at the same time mutually reducing the power of the conversation participants to threaten each other's face.

Halliday's (1989) work on patterns of hypotaxis and parataxis in spontaneous conversation shows clearly how this genre's clause connections differ markedly from those of more formal written gen-res. The following, provided by Halliday (p. 85), is a typical example of an extended, spontaneous, spoken text :

(69) So we rang up the breeder, and she sort of tried to describe the dog to us, which was very hard to do over the phone, so we went over to have a look to see what they were like, and we bought Sheba, because at that stage Bob was away a lot on semi-trailers with the army and it used to get quite bad with the exercises—you'd have prowlers and perverts through the married quarters, so if we—you know—got a dog, which we could do because it didn't matter what sort of dog anyone had, it'd bark and they wouldn't bother us.

If the hypotactic connections are indented in this text, as in Ex-amples 28 and 57, the following pattern emerges:

(70) So we rang up the breeder,
     and she sort of tried to describe the dog to us,
         which was very hard to do over the phone,
     so we went over
         to have a look
             to see
                 what they were like,
     and we bought Sheba,
         because at that stage Bob was away a lot on semi-trailers with the army
         and it used to get quite bad with the exercises—
         you'd have prowlers and perverts through the married quarters,
     so if we—you know—got a dog,
         which we could do
             because it didn't matter what sort of dog anyone had,
     it'd bark

and they wouldn't bother us.
(Halliday, 1989, p. 85)

Clearly, the sentence grammar of this text is far more complex than that of the written texts analyzed earlier. In texts of this sort, the pattern of clause connections is likely to be much more intricate than that of written texts. The intricacy largely depends on how conjunction is realized as parataxis or hypotaxis. In written texts, on the other hand, the relatively simpler sentence grammar yields a simpler pattern of conjunction, yet one capable of linking larger chunks of text, including embedded clauses.

Guidelines for Analyzing Conjunction and Clause Relations

Identify the patterns of conjunction in the text. Determine the text segments (phrase, clause, sentence, paragraph) in which conjunction is used. Examine the meaning relations between the clauses, sentences, or longer stretches of text joined by conjunction. Locate any uses of conjunction that may be intended to weaken the interpreter's position by forcing a point (e.g., adversative concession).
If the text is a conversation, attempt to identify major parts of the structure. Does the conversation follow normal patternings of structure? If not, attempt to explain the effect this has on the communication.

Sample Analysis: Conjunction and Clause Relations

The CODE advertisement (Fig. 1.3) may be analyzed as follows:

Conjunction: "only," in the first sentence of the headline, creates adversative conjunction with the second sentence. "Because" creates causal conjunction between the two clauses in the second sentence below the visual. Other meaning relations between sentences are made explicit by word meanings, meaning relations, and other cohesive means.

Application

Using the aforementioned guidelines, analyze conjunction and clause relations in your chosen oral and written practice texts.

Suggested Reading

Fowler, R. (1991). *Language in the news*. London: Routledge & Kegan Paul.
   Contains one of the clearest introductions to the concept of transitivity (pp. 70–80).
Halliday, M. (1985). *An introduction to functional grammar*. Baltimore: Edward Arnold.
   For an in-depth description of transitivity and its types, see chapter 5.
Halliday, M., & Hasan, R. (1976). *Cohesion in English*. London: Longman.
   See chapter 5 for a description of the four types of conjunction.
Hatch, E. (1992). *Discourse and language education*. Cambridge, England: Cambridge University Press.
   Hatch gives an extremely clear synopsis of conjunction on pp. 225–226 of her text.
Sanders, T., Spooren, W., & Noordman, L. (1992). Toward a taxonomy of coherence relations. *Discourse Processes, 15*(1), 1–35.
   An interesting attempt to provide a meaningful basis for the classification of the different kinds of conjunction.
Winter, E. (1994). Clause relations as information structure: Two basic text structures in English. In M. Coulthard (Ed.), *Advances in written text analysis* (pp. 46–68). London: Routledge & Kegan Paul.
   Winter identifies two primary clause relations in English: the matching relation, in which significant parts of two adjacent clauses are the same; and the logical sequence relation, similar to the hypotactic connections of Halliday. There is a third type, the multiple clause, which combines these two. Winter then goes on to develop patterns of basic text structure: situation and evaluation, hypothetical and real, and a structure that combines these two. Winter's work is recommended as a logical extension of the information presented in this section.

LINGUISTIC FEATURES

The discussion of language in texts, up to this point, has been concerned only with cohesive elements. These, as has been shown, link clauses and clause complexes, sometimes over large stretches of text. These features (including coreference, lexical cohesion, substitution, ellipsis, and conjunction) are sometimes referred to as the elements of discourse grammar, because they affect the discourse as a whole, rather than merely a clause or a sentence. But knowledge of the patterns of language in texts is incomplete unless the grammar of the clause and sentence is also investigated. Obviously, physical texts are comprised of words and grammar, and anyone who wants to understand or produce texts must pay considerable attention to this fact.

A major breakthrough in the understanding of how patterns of words and sentence grammar are used in various genres was provided by Biber (1988). Biber made use of extensive computerized corpora (collections) of texts, consisting of nearly a million words. The corpora consist of authentic texts of many kinds, collected from various sources. These enabled Biber to study actual uses of language and not ideas of teachers and linguists about how language ought to be used.

As a first step in the study, each word in each corpus was "tagged," meaning that it was labeled according to its part of speech, grammatical function, and so on. Next, Biber identified 17 written genres and 6 spoken genres[6] contained in the corpora. He also identified 67 **linguistic features** spread across these genres. He measured the relative frequencies of all the linguistic features in the corpora and recorded each frequency as the number of instances of that feature per 1,000 words of text. To take the past tense, for example, Biber found that in some genres it was not used at all, whereas in others it was used as often as 119 times in 1,000 words. The mean (average) turned out to be 40.1 uses per 1,000 words. In the same way, he calculated the frequencies of all 67 linguistic features in his study.

Using these frequency counts, Biber then performed a complex statistical operation called *factor analysis*. Factor analysis is a way of determining what groups of things tend to cluster together. What Biber learned was that there are some linguistic features that are commonly found together, like members of a gang, and there are others that also group together but that are rarely found when the first group is present, like members of a rival gang. For example, past-tense verbs, third-person pronouns, perfect aspect verbs (e.g., "has seen"), public verbs (e.g., "say"), synthetic negation (e.g., "no" + noun), and present participial clauses (e.g., "*Tripping over the stone*, he cursed") tend to occur together. If one of these features is

---

[6]Biber's use of the term *genre* is very close to the use defined earlier and that is used throughout this book. The only differences are that Biber tends to pay more attention to general, rather than specific, purpose, and he does not take the move structure of the genre into consideration. This means that Biber's genres tend to be more general and more inclusive. For example, he identified a genre called "professional letters." In contrast, this volume considers that several different genres (e.g., "letters of application," "letters of complaint," etc.) are contained within this group. Biber considered these to be subgenres.

present in a text, then there is a strong probability the others will be too. But there is also a strong possibility that the following will not be present in the same text, although they tend to group together in other texts: present-tense verbs, attributive adjectives (e.g., "large" + noun), past participial deletions of "which is" (e.g., "The problems ~~which are~~ caused by . . ."), and long words. Biber observed that the distinction here seems to be between narrative and nonnarrative texts. Narrative texts contain considerable numbers of past-tense forms and third-person pronouns, for example, but few present-tense forms or adjectives placed before nouns. These features are more common in other genres.

In all, including Dimension 2, the narrative dimension just discussed, Biber identified six dimensions of linguistic features. He labeled them as follows:

Dimension 1: involved vs. informational production
Dimension 2: narrative vs. nonnarrative concerns
Dimension 3: explicit vs. situation-dependent reference
Dimension 4: overt expression of persuasion
Dimension 5: abstract vs. nonabstract information
Dimension 6: online informational elaboration

Any given genre can be uniquely identified in relation to these six dimensions. It will have a different combination of values for each of the six dimensions, and no other genre will share that combination of values. As an example, consider Biber's genre "official documents." This genre has a high negative score on Dimension 1, indicating a high degree of informational content as evidenced by the kinds of linguistic features used to convey information. It has a negative value on Dimension 2, indicating that it is nonnarrative in nature. On Dimension 3 it shows a high positive value, meaning that its patterns of reference and coreference are strongly explicit, with little or no dependency on the immediate situation. With regard to Dimension 4 it is neutral, suggesting that some official documents may be persuasive and others are not. A significant positive value on Dimension 5 suggests that abstract information is more usual in such documents than nonabstract information. And, finally, a fairly neutral value on Dimension 6, tending toward the negative, suggests a certain looseness of style and lack of revision and editing, such as one commonly finds in memos, for example.

Biber observed that no genre or collection of genres can be differentiated by means of a single dimension alone. It is only their cross-dimensional patterns that differentiate genres from each other and show the unique way in which they use various linguistic features to accomplish their specific purposes. It follows, therefore, that there are no distinguishing characteristics that separate written from spoken language in English. Only by taking specific genres of speaking and writing, such as spontaneous conversations and academic writing, is it possible to show how these differ from each other over Biber's six dimensions. In fact, as Biber noted, there are some genres of writing, such as personal letters, which are very similar to spontaneous conversation; conversely, some genres of speaking, such as rehearsed lectures, bear a great resemblance to academic writing.

Biber showed not only how each genre can be characterized in terms of the six dimensions, but also how much variation occurs within a single genre. To do this, he defined "subgenres" within each of his genre categories. For example, within the genre "press reportage" six subgenres were represented in the data: political, sports, society, spot news, financial, and cultural press reportage. Each of these differs from the others in complex ways along each of the six dimensions. Cultural press reportage, for instance, scores higher on involved production than spot news reportage, which exhibits higher informational values than cultural press reportage. Similar differences may be found along each of the other five dimensions.

It is possible for members of one subgenre to exhibit similar values on all dimensions to members of another subgenre. One example of this, according to Biber, is an academic article in a field such as history. Such an article may exhibit many of the qualities of fiction and receive similar scores to fiction in each of the six dimensions. This phenomenon led Biber to distinguish between genres and what he called "**text types**." A text type is a category that contains all texts that exhibit similar linguistic characteristics and similar values across the six dimensions of variation. Thus, a text type may include examples from a number of genres or subgenres, which in turn are identified on the basis of their purposes and move structures, rather than on their linguistic patterning.

In a study of the lexical and grammatical marking of evidentiality and affect in the same data, Biber and Finegan (1989, p. 117) found "two major grammatical styles of marking stance: adjectivally in planned informational texts, and verbally/adverbially in interactive, informal texts." The stance styles identified were: emphatic expression of affect, faceless stance, interactional evidentiality, expository expression of doubt, predictive persuasion, and oral controversial persuasion.

Thus, of the six styles, only the first reflects the marking of affect, suggesting that affect is not generally marked by lexical and grammatical means, except in personal letters (p. 105), which they concluded "are less face-threatening than conversations, simply because of the physical separation of the interlocutors" (p. 107). The third style, interactional evidentiality, includes most notably face-to-face and telephone conversations, and "is affective in the sense that the participants are clearly emotionally involved in the interaction [but] the affect is not lexically encoded" (pp. 108–109). On the other hand, the second style, faceless stance, is by far the most common, "including large majorities of most written expository and fiction genres," such as press reviews and editorials, suggesting that "the prevailing norm is to leave stance lexically and grammatically unmarked, thus putting the burden on addressees to infer a speaker's stance" (p. 108). The fourth style, expository expression of doubt, like the second, includes primarily "informational written exposition" (p. 111), but unlike the second, expresses doubt when it exists. The overt marking of stance in this style "reflects the opportunity for planned production and editing in the communication situations of written expository texts" (p. 112), as it does in the fifth style, predictive persuasion. The fifth style was discussed earlier in connection with letters of recommendation, "where an overt emphasis on certainty is required in order to be convincing" (p. 113). The last style, oral controversial persuasion, is aimed at creating "a sense of solidarity with listeners when discussing issues that are in fact divisive" (p. 115). All the styles clearly interact with the dimensions already discussed.

Although the studies by Biber and Biber and Finegan include only the kinds of linguistic items commonly associated with clause and sentence grammar, it should be possible to extend them to include the discourse texturing devices described in the previous four sections. This would give a complete picture of the register of texts, which means the way language is used to realize a genre. Armed with such information, together with the structural descriptions of genre moves, it would then be possible to give a complete description of any genre, including affect and stance. Such information applied to English-language genres, for instance, would be invaluable to teachers of English for specific purposes; students of English as an additional language; students of law, business, and other professions; and many others.

Registers may be either relatively restricted or relatively open. A relatively restricted register is severely limited in topic, vocabulary, syntax, and discourse functions. Examples of such registers include the register of air traffic controllers and the register of bridge playing—to name two. Relatively open registers, on the other hand, have much more freedom. They are still limited in various ways, however, and it is these limitations that give institutional registers their distinctive characteristics. A genre's defining purpose determines the extent to which a register will be restricted or open. The purpose of air traffic instructions, for example, is to guide planes safely into and out of landing fields. To do this, a restricted vocabulary and grammar are sufficient, and unneeded words or complex sentence constructions could in fact impede the communication rather than facilitate it. Air traffic safety, therefore, dictates that the register must be severely restricted.

Power may be associated with registers. Consider, for example, the registers of various legal genres. Only a trained lawyer or legislator can understand, produce, and use such registers effectively. Registers such as these are at once easy for members of the cultural in-group to recognize, and difficult for members of cultural out-groups to learn. For this reason, writers or speakers who are fluent in a particular register are able to wield considerable power over readers or listeners who are not. If people require legal services, for instance, they are dependent on lawyers and judges.

Describing registers is a complex undertaking involving painstaking analyses and the help of computers. Fortunately, Biber's work provides descriptions of the patterns of linguistic features in the several most common genres in English. If, however, texts that do not belong to any of Biber's genres, or texts written by unskilled writers, must be analyzed, then individuals must rely on their own abilities to identify the salient features of a register. As a first step toward understanding how to perform a simple register analysis, examine the partial descriptions of the registers "press reportage" and "legislation" in Table 2.2.

An examination of the elements listed here shows that these two registers differ most clearly in topic, type of communication, vocabulary, and syntax. Additional information can be obtained about "press

TABLE 2.2
Comparison of Two Common Registers

Press Reportage	Legislation
Discourse	
impersonal:	impersonal
no "I"	no "I"
has an institutional voice	has an institutional voice
impartial	impartial
reader not addressed:	reader not addressed
no "you"	no "you"
no reader-addressed speech acts	no reader-addressed speech acts
large amount of general and political	large amount of legal knowledge
knowledge presupposed	presupposed
restricted topics:	restricted topic: law
politics, war, society, violence, disaster,	
sports, arts, human interest	
standard formal communication:	nonstandard communication:
no colloquialisms	no colloquialisms
no spoken language style	no spoken language style
	no standard written style
	repetitions
	extreme clarifications
	long initial case descriptions
	many qualifications
Words & Syntax	
long complex sentences	excessively long sentences
embeddings	syntactic discontinuities
relative clauses	complex prepositional phrases
nominalizations	extreme nominalizations
news vocabulary:	legal vocabulary:
technical words	binomial expressions (e.g., "will
jargons	and testament")
language of politics	
new coinages	
routine syntax and word choices (to	extreme choices in syntax and
avoid errors under the pressure of	wording to avoid ambiguity
deadlines)	

151

Practice 36:
(a) Select a newpaper article that reports on an event (press reportage). Analyze the register according to Table 2.2 together with Biber's information about the language of this genre. To what extent does your article conform to the partial description of register given? (Ignore the reference to speech acts, discussed later.)
(b) Now add to your register description any relevant linguistic information you can think of that is not included either in Table 2.2 or in Biber's description. These may include cohesive devices, such as pronoun coreference, ellipsis, and substitution; the use of words with loaded meanings (e.g., "terrorist" rather than "freedom fighter"); topic structuring (e.g., "top-down processing" rather than enumeration of items); distinctive patterns of parataxis, hypotaxis, and/or embeddings; a preference for one type of conjunction over another; and so on.

---

reportage" from Biber, because that is one of the genres he analyzed. Most notably, press reportage receives a very low value on Dimension 1. This means that it contains language typically used to convey information. Such language includes nouns, long words, prepositions, attributive adjectives, place adverbials, agentless passives (as noted in the previous section), and past and present participial deletions of

---

Practice 37:
You have already seen the following text in Practice 23. There you were asked to judge the purpose of the text. Now have a closer look at the text and try to analyze its register. From the point of view of discourse, the language of this text suffers from ungrammaticality. Although there are no errors in the sentence grammar, and words are used correctly, the discourse grammar, or register, is clearly wrong. What errors in the register can you find that would lead you to judge this text ungrammatical as discourse? (*Hint*: Make a partial description of the register of personal letters and compare the register of this text with your description. To begin with, consider what kinds of topics are typically found at the beginnings of personal letters.)

Dear Jinny,
     I'm so glad you introduced me to Glo-Quick's Super-Facial. It's just unbelievable what a difference it has made to me in less than a week. I must say it's a new and a very pleasant sensation to be noticed with envious admiration . . .

FIG. 2.4. "Ms. Hood, realizing that the prominent frontal skeletal structure and, in particular, the elongated proboscis and incisors corresponded in no way to those of an octogenarian female *homo sapiens*, immediately recognized that the creature occupying her grandmother's bed was in fact a mature male of the species *Canis Lupus* and not her grandmother at all." (Matching the wrong register with a genre can result in confusion or unintentional humor.) Reprinted with permission.

"which is." All of this is important linguistic information that is missing from the previous description.

Judgments made by interpreters about the acceptability of the language or register of a genre are referred to as grammaticality judgments. These judgments include all standard notions of what constitutes a well-formed sentence or a correct use of a word or phrase for a particular interpreter. However, grammaticality also includes all the other elements of register already discussed. In judging grammaticality, interpreters are reacting to the way the language of a text fulfills its purpose and realizes the genre. A register that would be grammatical in one genre might be considered ungrammatical and even ludicrous in another, as illustrated by Fig. 2.4. For example, the register of a personal letter would simply appear wrong in a formal letter written to a judge. Conversely, the carefully constructed language of a sermon would appear wrong in a friendly telephone chat between neighbors.

Guidelines for Analyzing Linguistic Features

Examine a number of examples of the genre in order to draw up a partial description of the register being analyzed.
Use Biber's information about linguistic features of the register, if applicable and available.
Add any cohesive features that appear to be significant for the genre.

Sample Analysis: Linguistic Features

The CODE advertisement (Fig. 1.3) may be analyzed as follows:

Although Biber provided no analysis of advertisements, the following linguistic items appear in a large number of advertisements: present tense, use of "you," use of "we," modal verbs, omission of "that" in noun clauses, contractions, incomplete sentences, clauses of cause and result, attributive adjectives, and avoidance of passives. Most of these features are present in the CODE advertisement.

In addition, there is a predominantly paratactic pattern of information, salient use of ellipsis, and pronoun coreference. There is an avoidance of substitution. Lexical choices and collocations reflect the topic: literacy education. There is a top-down information structure, with a headline providing a topic macroproposition for the text.

This genre would be expected to receive low scores on Biber's Dimensions 1 and 5, and high scores on Dimension 4, with relatively neutral scores on the other dimensions. This text generally follows this pattern, but would seem to have a neutral to low score on Dimension 4 (persuasion). The typical suasive features, infinitives, prediction modals, suasive verbs, conditional subordination, necessity modals, split auxiliaries, and possibility modals are in part missing. Of these, only infinitives, possibility modals, and one suasive verb ("call") appear in this text.

Application

Using the aforementioned guidelines, analyze the linguistic features of your chosen oral and written practice texts.

Suggested Reading

Biber, D. (1988). *Variation across speech and writing*. Cambridge, England: Cambridge University Press.
This is the text that contains the complete description of Biber's work on registers.
Virtanen, T. (1992). Issues of text typology: Narrative—a "basic" type of text? *Text*, *12*(2), 293–310.
Another way of looking at variation within texts, and the difference between Biber's "genre" and "text type," is to consider, as Virtanen did, how the different modes of discourse (argumentation, exposition, instruction, description, and narrative) can intermingle in a text. Virtanen explained how some modes are more restricted than others in the ways in which they can mix. Whereas narrative can occur in almost any kind of text, argumentation rarely occurs in nonargumentative texts. Virtanen distinguished between "discourse modes" and "text modes." The discourse mode is the dominant mode of a text, as exposition, for example, is the dominant mode of this book. Text modes can mix with discourse modes according to certain patterns. For example, a short narrative anecdote could be included in this book without disturbing its expository nature.

LITERAL AND NONLITERAL MEANING

Human language is full of expressions that appear to mean something different from what the words themselves would suggest. This leads to the question of how an interpreter knows what **nonliteral meaning** is actually intended by such **figures of speech**. The following list includes a few of the most common types of figures of speech, with examples and their intended meanings:

Metaphor (Words that normally do not collocate are brought together to imply a comparison)

I couldn't hear the laugh but the hole in her face when she unzippered her teeth [= opened her mouth] was all I needed.
(Chandler, R. [1953]. *The long good-bye*. Harmondsworth, England: Penguin, p. 75)

Simile (A comparison is made between two dissimilar things, using "like" or "as")

He had a jaw like a park bench. (= He had a very large jaw.)
(Chandler, R. [1949]. *The little sister*. Harmondsworth, England: Penguin, p. 165)

Metonymy (Use of one word in a collocation to stand for another)
Ben: Go and light it.
Gus: Light what?

Ben: The <u>kettle</u>. (= the gas)
Gus: You mean the gas.
Ben: Who does?
(Pinter, H. *The dumb waiter*, quoted in Coulthard, 1985, p. 183)

Overstatement (Deliberate exaggeration)
To say she had a face that would have stopped a clock would have been to insult her. It would have stopped a runaway horse. (= she had an unattractive face.)
(Chandler, R. [1949]. *The little sister*. Harmondsworth, England: Penguin, p. 166)

Sarcasm   (Critical remark based on extremes in meaning)
"I don't think I'd care to employ a detective that uses liquor in any form. I don't even approve of tobacco."
      "<u>Would it be all right if I peeled an orange?</u>" (= Is there anything you do approve of?)
(Chandler, R. [1949]. *The little sister*. Harmondsworth, England: Penguin, p. 7)

In addition to being literal or nonliteral, texts may also be direct or indirect. An utterance such as "You know where the door is" may be used as an indirect request to leave. In this example, the indirect request is also literal. But it is possible for a communication to be both indirect and nonliteral, as in "I'm sure the baby loves it when you scream at her like that," which means that the baby "hates" it and also doubles as an indirect request to stop screaming.

Interpreters must follow some kind of strategy in deriving inferences about the meanings of utterances such as the examples given. They must somehow determine how much of the utterance may be taken as direct and how much may be taken as indirect. Similarly, the amount of literalness and nonliteralness the interpreter is willing to ascribe to the utterance must be determined. Psychological, cultural, and other contextual processes examined earlier in this book are at work in this kind of interpretation.

Another important source of nonliteral meanings is **idioms**. Idioms are a type of lexical phrase that seem to behave like individual words and are invariable. For this reason, Nattinger and DeCarrico (1992) referred to them as *polywords*. Some of these, such as "hold your horses," obey the grammar rules of English, and others, such as "by and large," do not. Of the following three lexical phrases, the first is an idiom:

(71) kick the bucket

Practice 38:
Analyze the following extract from a novel to determine how much of the meaning is literal, nonliteral, direct, and indirect.

> "You'd better sit over here beside me."
> "I've been thinking that a long time," I said. "Ever since you crossed your legs, to be exact."
> She pulled her dress down. "These damn things are always up around your neck."
> I sat beside her on the yellow leather chesterfield. "Aren't you a pretty fast worker?" she asked quietly.
> I didn't answer her.
> "Do you do much of this sort of thing?" she asked with a sidelong look.
> "Practically none. I'm a Tibetan monk, in my spare time."
> "Only you don't have any spare time."
> "Let's focus," I said. "Let's get what's left of our minds—or mine—on the problem. How much are you going to pay me?"
> "Oh, that's the problem. I thought you were going to get my necklace back. Or try to."
> "I have to work in my own way. This way." I took a long drink and it nearly stood me on my head. I swallowed a little air.
> "And investigate a murder," I said.
> (Chandler, R. (1940). *Farewell, my lovely*. Harmondsworth, England: Penguin, p. 115)

---

(72) break down barriers between X and Y

(73) I would like some ice cream.

Example 71 is totally nonliteral. Its meaning is not related in any way to the meanings of the words it contains. Furthermore, if any word within it is changed, the idiom no longer exists. Expressions such as "kick the pail" or "boot the bucket" do not have any idiomatic meaning. Idioms therefore have meanings unrelated to their parts. This idiom is a polyword having the same meaning as the verb "die."

Example 72, on the other hand, allows for some flexibility. "Walls" or "obstacles" could be substituted for "barriers," though "barriers" is much more common. These substitutions would not change the meaning. The text would still mean something like "remove hindrances or impediments between X and Y." This text is recognized to be a metaphor based on an unlikely collocation of "barriers" with the individuals "X" and "Y." The metaphor leads to an implied comparison

---

Practice 39:
Read the following text and identify any lexical phrases that you can find. Indicate whether they are more like Examples 71, 72, or 73. In other words, assess the extent to which they exhibit nonliteral meaning.

CAPRICORN
Friends may come through for you in a big way and because of their assistance, your affairs should benefit. In respect of something you are aiming towards it could be important not to burn bridges behind you. (*Borneo Bulletin,* 28/29 October, 1995)

---

between "barriers" and whatever it is that prevents "X" and "Y" from getting together or agreeing on something.

Example 73 is freer still. Without changing the basic meaning, "want," "desire," or "wish for," could be substituted for "would like." In addition, the flexibility of this lexical phrase allows the substitution of other agents, such as "she," or "Elizabeth" for "I," and other objects such as "pizza" or "beer" for "ice cream." In this lexical phrase, there is no nonliteral meaning. Lexical phrases of this type are called "sentence builders."

The text in Practice 39 may suggest to you that different degrees of nonliteral meaning may occur in different genres. In fact, many more idioms have been found in conversation, personal letters, narrative fiction, horoscopes, and business-related documents than in instructions, recipes, and research articles. For this reason, include types of nonliteral and indirect meaning in any description of register.

Guidelines for Analyzing Literal and Nonliteral Meaning

Determine to what extent the text is direct, indirect, literal, and/or nonliteral.
Identify idioms, figures of speech, and other lexical phrases that are important in the text.

Sample Analysis: Literal and Nonliteral Meaning

The CODE advertisement (Fig. 1.3) may be analyzed as follows:

The text is direct and literal, but the reference to the 26 letters of the alphabet is used nonliterally to stand for literacy education in general.
There are no remarkable lexical phrases or idioms.

Application

Using the aforementioned guidelines, analyze the literal and nonliteral meaning of your chosen oral and written practice texts.

Suggested Reading

Moon, R. (1994). The analysis of fixed expressions in text. In M. Coulthard (Ed.), *Advances in written text analysis* (pp. 117–135). London: Routledge & Kegan Paul.

> In this analysis, which focuses largely on press reportage, Moon concluded that a great deal of information about a text may be derived from an analysis of idioms.

Nattinger, J., & DeCarrico, J. (1992). *Lexical phrases and language teaching.* Oxford, England: Oxford University Press.

> This is a study of the acquisition of language in the form of lexical phrases (including idioms) rather than as the phrase structures of conventional transformational grammar. The second part of this book is devoted to an application of this theory to language teaching.

IMPLICATURE, PRESUPPOSITION, AND INFERENCE

In almost all texts it is possible to infer information that is not stated in the text. In fact, such inferences, called **implicatures**, are crucial to interpretation. To take a simple example, if somebody mentions "the president of XYZ Corporation," it must be possible to infer that XYZ Corporation exists, and that it has a president. If individuals cannot make these inferences, the text will remain largely meaningless to them.

One kind of implicature is known as **conventional implicature**. Nonliteral expressions are part of this group. Conventional implicature refers to any inferences that are easily and typically made by an interpreter, without having to refer to the situation in which the utterance is couched. Thus, a figure of speech such as "All hands on deck!" always has essentially the same meaning for all interpreters, regardless of whether they are on a ship at sea or in some other situation.

Another important type of conventional implicature is **presupposition**. Presuppositions are certain kinds of truths that may be inferred on the basis of what is stated in a text. They are unstated propositions that must be true in order for the stated proposition to be either true or false. The "XYZ Corporation" utterance is one example. As another, to say "My sister's yoga class took a day trip to the India Culture Center" may give rise to the following presuppositions: I have a sister, my sister is studying yoga, my sister belongs to a yoga class, there is an India Culture Center, the India Culture Center is not far from where my sister and her class study yoga, the class obtained the necessary transportation to get to the Center, the class returned the same day, and so on. All these unstated propositions must be true in order for the utterance itself to be either true or false.

Unscrupulous producers may attempt to embed presuppositions in a text in such a way as to bias the interpretation in favor of a particular point of view or perspective they wish to communicate. For instance, a news report containing the sentence, "When the dictator of Slobovia was asked when he planned to introduce democracy, he refused to comment," contains, among others, the presupposition that the leader of Slobovia is a dictator and the method of government is undemocratic. Neither of these presuppositions may, strictly speaking, be based on fact, but may instead reflect the personal or institutional bias of the producer. Presupposition is a common part of communication, and for the most part the presuppositions of statements are interpreted without individuals even being aware they are doing so. Therein, of course, lies the danger for the unwary interpreter.

The Chandler text in Practice 38 contains a number of presuppositions. Looking at one small part of the text,

(74) "How much are you going to pay me?"
"Oh, that's the problem. I thought you were going to get my necklace back. Or try to."

the following presuppositions can be derived: He expects her to pay him. The payment will be in money or something else quantifiable. There is a problem. She owns a necklace. The necklace is missing. She expects him to retrieve the necklace.

Presuppositions contain information not actually stated in a text. They differ in this way from entailments, which are rooted in the meanings that are stated. For example, the sentence

(75) "I thought you were going to get my necklace back"

contains, as already noted, the presupposition "I own a necklace." This is not actually stated. This presupposition, in turn, entails "I own jewelry." The entailment is derived by hyponymy from the meaning of the word "necklace," which appears in the text; a necklace is a piece of jewelry. On the other hand, the presupposition "I own a necklace" is derived purely by inference.

Another difference between presuppositions and entailments is that presuppositions can be canceled, whereas entailments cannot. For instance, it is possible to say meaningfully "I thought you were going to get my necklace back—well, it isn't actually mine. It belongs to my mother." This cancels the presupposition, "I own a necklace." On the other hand, it is not possible to say meaningfully, "I own a necklace, but I don't own any jewelry." The entailment cannot be canceled.

Hornby (1974) showed that it is easier for interpreters to be misled by incorrect presuppositions than by incorrect propositions actually stated in a text. This fact is frequently employed by unscrupulous advertisers who seek to mislead buyers. Consider, for example, the following excerpt from a newspaper advertisement (familiar from Practice 2):

(76) ELIMINATE BALDNESS
Enjoy a full head of hair in only 3 hours!

One of the presuppositions contained in this text is that the hair is real hair, growing on the buyer's scalp. This presupposition can be defeated by biological knowledge, which pronounces that such a thing is medically impossible in most cases of baldness, and regardless of other factors, it cannot be accomplished in 3 hours. Nevertheless, if potential customers are desperate enough, they might find themselves ignoring the presuppositions and sending money to the advertiser to purchase a product or to receive further information.

Another type of pragmatic inference arises from what have been called **speech acts**. The concept of speech acts is based on the

---

Practice 40:
Find all the presuppositions contained in the text in Practice 38. Together with the literal, nonliteral, direct, and indirect meanings that you have already uncovered in this text, what do these presuppositions tell you about what is happening in this text? Can you explain what is going on?

understanding that sentences have three definable functions: declarative sentences make statements, interrogative sentences pose questions, and imperative sentences issue commands. A statement is based on a proposition and can usually be evaluated as being either true or false. If a person who utters a statement is committed to the truth of it, then that person has made an assertion. There are three kinds of assertions: *constatives*, which describe some aspect of the world (e.g., "Grass is green"), and are either true or false; *ethical propositions*, which impose an ethical force, usually through the use of a modal verb like "should" (e.g., "An immature person should not attempt to raise a family"); and *speech acts* ("performatives"), which perform an act merely through the use of words (e.g., "I warn you that that car is dangerous").

When a speech act is performed, an interpreter automatically makes a set of inferences known as **felicity conditions**. These are the conditions in the surrounding world that must be met in order for the speech act to have force. For example, if someone requests that Jesse close the door, it can be inferred that the door is open, the speaker is in a position to make such a request, Jesse is capable of shutting the door, Jesse is likely to be willing to accede to the speaker's request, and so on. These are felicity conditions for that particular request. It would be quite odd to attempt to make speech acts for which the necessary felicity conditions cannot be met, as for example, "I order you to keep breathing until you die!" One of the felicity conditions for both orders and requests is that there must be a choice of action. The previous speech act fails precisely because no option exists.

Both Austin (1962), who invented the concept of speech acts, and Searle (1969), who modified Austin's work after the latter's death, noted that certain types of verbs are closely associated with speech acts and seem to contain the core of the meaning or force of a speech act. These verbs are called *performatives*, and include such verbs as "warn," "promise," "request," and so on. In fact, any verb that can be used meaningfully together with the words "I hereby," as in "I hereby order you to . . . ," is likely to be a performative.

Austin noted that performatives perform three kinds of act: the **locutionary act**, the **illocutionary act**, and the **perlocutionary act**. The locutionary act is the physical (phonological) act of uttering the speech act; the illocutionary act is the act performed by the speech act (e.g., promise, threat, request, etc.); and the perlocutionary act is the (nonlinguistic) effect that the illocutionary act has on another person. The force of the illocutionary act is called the **illocutionary force** of the speech act. For example, if someone says "How about letting me have a slice of your pizza?", then that person performs a locutionary act by pronouncing the words, intonations, and so on of the utterance. The illocutionary act has the illocutionary force of a request, and the perlocutionary act could be any of a number of possibilities: The individual might give the person a piece of the pizza, might say "Get your own pizza!", and so forth. It may be possible to determine what perlocutionary act was intended by the speaker, but it is rarely possible to predict what perlocutionary act will actually occur.

Searle (1976) classified speech acts into five groups: **Directives** are requests to do something or to stop doing something; **commissives**, such as promises and refusals, commit the speaker to future action; **representatives** are statements of propositions and have varying degrees of truth value; **declaratives** are the same as Austin's performatives; and **expressives**, such as thanking and apologizing, are statements expressing emotion. The following are some actual examples from a school lesson:

(77) Directive: Can you turn to page one hundred and fifty-one, please?
     Commissive: . . . I'll tell you in a minute.
     Representative: Now there are ways, aren't there, of measuring really accurately.
     Declarative: [I hereby warn you that] You all need to work very, very hard . . .
     Expressive: Thank you. Good afternoon, Year 8.
     (Authors' data)

Expressions known as **hedges** are often used with representatives in order to put distance between the producer and the truth of the statement. In the previous example, "now" and "aren't there" are hedges that serve to protect the producer against the full force of the interpretation of her utterance. They do this by calling on the interpreters to agree with what the producer is saying. Hedges are commonly constructed with modal verbs (may, might, could, etc.), modal lexical verbs (think, imagine, feel, suppose, etc.), modal adjectives and adverbs (possible, likely, maybe, perhaps, etc.), tag questions (. . . isn't it? . . . aren't there? etc.), and phrases and clauses that serve a modal function (in my estimation, it seems to me, etc.) As noted earlier, there may be a tendency, in Western cultures at least, for women to use more hedges.

One problem with declarative speech acts is the fact that many declarative utterances that lack performatives altogether still have illocutionary force. To illustrate this point, here are just three ways of wording the declarative given in Example 77:

> (78) I hereby warn you that you all need to work very, very hard.
> Work very, very hard, because it's the only way to avoid the failure that you're headed for.
> Do you think you'll ever amount to anything if you don't work very, very hard?

Note that only the first of these examples contains the performative verb "warn." The second example is in the form of a command, and the third is a question. Yet, it seems clear that all three contain the illocutionary force of a warning.

Speech act theorists explain this phenomenon by differentiating between **direct illocutions** and **indirect illocutions**. The direct illocution is identified from the literal meaning of the grammatical form and vocabulary of the utterance, whereas the indirect illocution derives from its nonliteral meaning. Thus, in the utterance "Can you tell me where to find a hotel?", the direct illocution is an inquiry concerning someone's ability to do something, and anyone who responds "Yes" is merely attending to the direct, literal meaning. But the indirect illocution is clearly a request for information, and the person making the request expects the interpreter to attend to the nonliteral meaning.

This distinction between direct and indirect illocutions is an attempt to align speech acts with the structural forms of sentences. But as is clear from the three examples of a warning, the problem is a messy one; and no entirely satisfactory solution has yet been proposed. Furthermore, taking indirect illocutions to their extremes, it can be postulated that any utterance must be an illocution (declarative) of some kind. Thus, a constative utterance such as "Grass is green" has the illocutionary force of an affirmation if it is assumed that the complete utterance is "I affirm that grass is green," because "affirm" is a performative verb.

Levinson made the interesting point that prerequests are nothing other than what has been examined as indirect speech acts of request.

Practice 41:
Analyze the first sentence of the text in Practice 38 in the previous section. The sentence is repeated here:

"You'd better sit over here beside me."

(a) What category of speech act should it be classified as?
(b) What illocutionary force, if any, does it have? What are its direct and/or indirect illocutions?
(c) What perlocutionary act results from it? (If you have forgotten, look back at the original text to answer.)
(d) What felicity conditions must be met in order for the utterance to function as an illocutionary act?
(e) Note the way it is worded. How does this contribute differently to the meaning of the text, than, for instance, a direct command, a question, a polite request, etc.?

From the point of view of conversational analysis, they are simply initial turns in requests such as the following:

(79) A: Hi. Do you have uh size C flashlight batteries? (*Prerequest*)
     B: Yes sir.   (*Go-ahead*)
     A: I'll have four please.   (*Request*)
     B: (*Turns to get*)   (*Response*)
     (Merritt, 1976; quoted in Levinson, 1983, p. 357)

Often the "go-ahead" and "request" stages are omitted, and a response is given to the prerequest itself, as in the following example:

(80) S: Have you got Embassy Gold please? (*Prerequest*)
     H: Yes dear. (*Provides*)   (*Response*)
     (Sinclair, 1976; quoted in Levinson, 1983, p. 361)

As Levinson pointed out, contrary to speech act theory, the meanings of initial prerequests may be clearly understood without resorting to questions about whether they have indirect meanings.

In conversation, strings of speech acts are joined in such a way that several different illocutionary forces combine into one or two predominant illocutionary forces that characterize the purpose and content of the conversational exchange. A speech act derived in this way out of a combination of speech acts in discourse is called a **macrospeech act**. Van Dijk (1977) defined a macrospeech act as "the global speech act performed by the utterance of a whole discourse, and executed by a sequence of possibly different speech acts." In the following dialogue (familiar from chap. 1), a number of speech acts are used, yet the entire dialogue is primarily an invitation or suggestion, followed by an acceptance:

```
(17)  R:  Why don't we all have lunch
      C:  Okay so that would be in St Jude's would it?
      R:  Yes
          (.7 second pause)
      C:  Okay so:::
      R:  One o'clock in the bar
      C:  Okay
      R:  Okay?
      C:  Okay then thanks very much indeed George=
      R:  All right
      C:  // See you there
      R:     See you there
      C:  Okay
      R:  Okay // bye
      C:          bye
```

This dialogue opens with an indirect illocution having the force of a suggestion or invitation. This then dominates the rest of the exchange. Other speech acts in the sequence include a request for clarification, affirmation, specification, agreement, thanking, promising, acknowledging, and leave-taking.

Practice 42:
(a) What appears to be the predominant macrospeech act in the text of Practice 38?
(b) Describe the apparent purpose of the following text by listing the speech acts it contains and the predominant macrospeech act they comprise:

If you knew how much good you could do just by joining us, you wouldn't hesitate. So if you've read this far and you're not already a member of Amnesty, we ask you again, please cut the coupon.
Don't do it tomorrow, do it today. Don't have a cup of coffee first. Do it now. If you can't find a pen, pick up the phone.
But do it now.
(Advertisement for Amnesty International, in *Times Higher Education Supplement*, 25 March 1994)

Van Dijk observed that macrospeech acts are an important component of coherence in a text. He also suggested that the reason macrospeech acts emerge clearly from segments of text, as in the previous example, is that text producers cannot plan or predict the totality of speech acts that such a text will contain. Much of the patterning of the text depends on the responses of the corespondent. However, the originator of the text can plan the primary purpose of the text—in this case requesting something—and that, therefore, becomes the main illocutionary force of the text.

Lexical phrases, examined earlier, are another source of pragmatic information that helps to explain indirect illocutions. As indicated, the problem with indirect illocutions is that some language forms are used in preference to others to achieve a specific illocutionary force. For example, Searle (1975) noted that when making a request, people typically say things like

[81] Can you hand me that book?
Could you hand me that book?
Can you reach that book?

and so on, rather than, for example,

[82] I request that you hand me that book.
Are you in a position to be able to hand me that book?
Fulfill my request by handing me that book, please.

The first sentence in Example 82, "I request that you hand me that book," contains the performative verb "request," and is therefore the form expected to be most common in making requests. In fact, however, it is hardly ever used. Nattinger and DeCarrico (1992) explained this apparent anomaly by suggesting that as people gain competence in a language, they learn one or more **lexical phrase frames** that are associated by convention with a particular illocutionary function. In this case, the lexical frame

Modal Verb + *you* + Verb Phrase?

covers the first three examples of indirect request, and appears to be one of the forms commonly employed to serve the function of making requests. When this form is modified to take into account the several other common question forms for indirect requests, the more complete lexical frame is the following:

Auxiliary Verb (*not*) + *you* (*mind/kindly/be willing to*) + Verb Phrase

This phrase is flexible enough to allow for such other indirect requests as

(83) Do you want to hand me that book?
Would you mind handing me that book?

and a number of others. To this frame, Nattinger and DeCarrico added the frame

I {want/would like/would rather} you (to) (not) Verb Phrase (for me)

as an additional common form of indirect request as in

(84) I would like you to get that book for me.

And there are several others. In the same way, lexical phrase frames exist for a whole range of indirect illocutions. They provide patterns that allow appropriate words to be slotted in. This flexibility of the phrase frame may explain why utterances that fit the frames are more common than other utterances when used as indirect illocutions.

Yet another type of inference deriving from text pragmatics is **conversational implicature**. Conversational implicature, unlike conventional implicature, depends on the particular context in which an

---

Practice 43:

Nattinger and DeCarrico (1992) pointed out that indirect illocutions, like all pragmatic meanings, are either conventional or nonconventional. If they are conventional, their meanings are derived by common agreement within a speech community. Thus, all the examples of indirect requests given are conventional. They are recognized as indirect requests regardless of who is saying them or under what circumstances. Look again at the first sentence of the text of Practice 38:

(a) Is it a conventional or nonconventional request?
(b) What circumstances are required to make it a request?
(c) Can you think of other circumstances in which it would not be a request?

utterance occurs. Because of this context dependency, conversational implicature, like all sources of pragmatic inference, depends on the cultural context. In the discussion that follows, examples are restricted to Anglo-American culture.

In an attempt to take a broader view of pragmatic inference than is possible through speech act analysis alone, the philosopher Grice (1975, 1978) took an important step toward the generation of a general theory of inference. He began by observing that conversationalists normally make an effort to cooperate with each other in order for the conversation to facilitate their goals. According to this **Cooperative Principle**, conversationalists typically make their contributions appropriate to the stage in a conversation in which they occur. Grice suggested that, to do this, conversationalists cooperate in four ways, which he described as the maxims of relation, quality, quantity, and manner.

The **maxim of relation** states that conversationalists are normally expected to cooperate with each other by making their contributions relevant to the part of the conversation in which these contributions occur. In other words, each participant in a conversation typically assumes that the other participants are saying things relevant to the current topic. This relevance is assumed by the interpreter. If this is not the case—if one of the participants deliberately says something not relevant to the current topic—then that participant is flouting the maxim of relation. Interpreters, however, try to find relevance in utterances, even if the utterances could easily be construed as not relevant, as in the following example:

(85) W: Heard you're falling in love
     D: (*laughing*) I wish I had recordings of those meetings!
     [Beach, 1983, p. 198]

Interpreters are likely to infer from this that at one of the meetings D speaks of, somebody said something about D falling in love.

In the Chandler text in Practice 38, several inferences can be made based on the conversation of the two characters. Consider the following exchange from that conversation:

(86) "Do you do much of this sort of thing?" she asked with a sidelong look.
     "Practically none. I'm a Tibetan monk, in my spare time."

Inferences based on the previous text indicate that "this sort of thing" could mean either detective work or flirting with women. The second sentence of the detective's reply gives the clue that the detective at least understands the question to refer to flirting. For interpreters to arrive at this conclusion, however, they require first a belief that the reply is relevant, and second, an understanding that a Tibetan monk leads a celibate existence. It is thus possible to understand the reply to be a humorous figure of speech suggesting that the detective, too, leads a mostly celibate existence. Grice called this type of inference a conversational implicature. Conversational implicatures depend on the assumption that conversational participants are cooperating with each other and that their utterances, therefore, are meaningful.

A second source of conversational implicatures is the **maxim of quality**. According to this part of the cooperative principle, conversationalists normally speak the truth to each other and do not state as facts anything for which they do not have adequate evidence. Consequently, an utterance will normally be interpreted to be as accurate an expression of the truth as is possible in the wording given. By telling small fibs now and again, everybody is probably guilty of violations of this maxim.

Among those people who frequently flout this part of the Cooperative Principle, however, are habitual liars (such as the man in Fig. 2.5), schizophrenics, and writers of metaphor. Literary metaphors such as "I hid my heart in a nest of roses" (Swinburne) are not intended to confound or confuse, however, and are usually interpreted meaningfully without difficulty. The interpreter assumes that the producer is making a meaningful remark and thus rejects the literal interpretation as being bizarre or absurd. The detective's statement, in the example, that he is "a Tibetan monk" obviously flaunts the maxim of quality. But because his statement is clearly a metaphor and the woman perceives it as such, it does not impede communication.

The **maxim of quantity** is another part of the Cooperative Principle and one that recognizes the fact that interpreters usually expect producers to make their contributions just as informative as is required, providing neither too little nor too much information. In the Chandler text, the following example of minimal informativeness occurs:

(87) "Aren't you a pretty fast worker?" she asked quietly.
     I didn't answer her.

The woman is referring to the way the detective is flirting with her. By the maxim of quantity, the lack of an answer to her question

FIG. 2.5. "Just collecting for charity, Ma'am." (According to Grice's Cooperative Principle, we typically accept as fact what other people say, unless we have some reason to think otherwise.) Reprinted with permission.

becomes an answer in itself. In this situation, she might draw from his silence the conversational implicature that the detective agrees with her statement but feels that a verbal answer is unwarranted. Not all floutings of the maxim of quantity are so innocent. For example, what about individuals who, when asked if they know where the nearest post office is, merely reply, "Yes," and walk away? And many have met the dreaded bore who replies to the harmless question, "How are you?" with a litany of complaints, laments, and detailed descriptions of medical operations. Neither of these flouters of the quantity maxim is likely to have many friends.

The last of Grice's maxims, the **maxim of manner**, states that conversation participants expect each other to be brief and orderly without being obscure or ambiguous. As a consequence, an utterance will normally be interpreted as being as clear an expression of its content as its wording will allow in the situational context. Thus, in the following example, the patient clearly accepts the doctor's utterance as being as short and accurate a description of what occurred as is possible under the circumstances:

> (88) Doctor: ... hear from Dr. _____, uh, I know you had the class three
>   Pap and he had / cauterized it and /
>   Patient: / and then, he had / cauterized it, and then ...
>   (Borges, 1986, p. 36)

Clearly, the patient understands what the doctor is telling her. In spite of his use of technical jargon, the doctor's utterance does not seem to the patient to be obscure or unorderly. Indeed, she uses the same technical language to continue the account of the medical process.

Some individuals, and indeed professions, appear to be dedicated to flouting the maxim of manner. The speeches of politicians are usually full of examples, as is much legal discourse, and a good deal of the discourse of education, among others. The following text, from an autobiographical essay by Jacques Derrida, the founder of deconstructionist literary criticism, would probably be judged by most interpreters to be in violation of the maxim of manner:

> (89) The raw utterance, to dispute with it over what crudeness is, as if never
> to raise it again, and the word "raise," the poker term, belongs only to
> my mother, as if I hung onto it to pick a fight over what crude talk means,
> as if, deep in my blood, I strove to remind her, for He knows it, *cur
> confitemur Deo scienti*, what the crude (credited) requires of us. . . .
> (Quoted in *Newsweek* (international ed.), 25 May 1992, p. 45)

This last example shows that, although Grice specifically addresses conversation, even in written discourse the interpreter approaches the text with the expectation that the four maxims will apply. Take, for example, the extracts from a Malawian government newspaper quoted in Example 61. An educated reader familiar with Malawian politics would find it very difficult to accept that the maxim of quality had not been violated in that report, simply by the reporter not giving the "whole truth." The maxim of quantity is also violated because the reader would have expected far more detail of the accident, along the lines of the information provided in the opposition newspaper quoted in Practice 35. Teachers are likewise familiar with the problems students have in selecting relevant facts and opinions, and presenting them clearly, unambiguously, and in sufficient detail, when learning to write essays.

Practice 44:

(a) Write short texts that appear to flout each of Grice's four maxims. Give your texts to another student and ask him or her to try to derive meaningful conversational implicatures for them.

(b) Analyze the following conversation for inferences based on conventional implicatures, speech acts, the Cooperative Principle, and conversational structure. In particular, what can you infer from the doctor's (D) apparent violation of the maxim of quantity in his last turn? If you were the patient (P) and could afford to have a dermatologist or plastic surgeon perform the operation, would you do so? Why or why not? (*Note*: The doctor is in training in a teaching hospital where treatments are subsidized and thus less expensive for the patients than a private practice would be.)

D: What other problems or questions do you have?

P: Okay. Um I was wondering if you could take some moles off for me?

D: Okay. Where abouts?

P: (*unintelligible*) There's one on my forehead. Right there. ___ (*unintelligible*).

D: Any others?

P: Um, how many can you do at once?

D: Half dozen. Well, the problem is that, ah, on ah, young attractive females I don't usually take them off the face. But I can do it and probably everything will go well, but those are best done by either a dermatologist or a plastic surgeon. But I'll be glad to do it. We can do one in another location and see how it goes, and if you feel comfortable with it and I feel comfortable with it we'll do the one on your forehead.

P: I would not be afraid to have you do it at all. First of all I can't afford anybody else.

It should be clear from the discussion and examples that it is helpful for purposes of analysis to break the Cooperative Principle down into the four maxims. However, it should be equally clear that these maxims are not separate entities, but overlap in complex ways. Indeed, Brown and Yule (1983) pointed out that the maxim of relation seems to cover all the other maxims, because something that is not relevant may well not be true, and can hardly be appropriately informative or clear.

Speech act theory, the Cooperative Principle, and conversational analysis all deal with typical or expected patterns of verbal behavior, but they fail to describe a large number of real conversational exchanges—such as the following extract from Haldeman's testimony in the Watergate hearing:

(90) Q: You saw all of the papers that were being reviewed, did you not?
A: Not all the working papers of the committee. I saw the recommen-
dations that went to the President.
Q: Did you read the recommendations that went to the President?
A: I am not sure I did or not. If I did it was not in any detail.
(*The New York Times*, 1973; quoted in Levinson, 1992, p. 76)

According to the Cooperative Principle, if someone admits to having
seen some papers in such a context, the conversational implicature
can be drawn that this person also read those papers. The last part
of the exchange, however, contradicts the implicature. The implicature must therefore be abandoned and the Cooperative Principle does
not apply. As another example, consider the kind of questioning
exchange typical of classroom situations:

(91) T: Now there are ways, aren't there, of measuring really accurately.
There's an instrument ... the ruler is one instrument. There's also
em something called a ... Any of you can think of anything else?
S: Ah the the em sort of wheel thing that you roll along the ground.
T: There's the wheel thing that you roll along the ground if you're marking
out the length of a hockey pitch or something like that. Yes?
S: Eh er a metre ruler.
T: There's a metre ruler.
S: Tape measure.
T: There's a tape measure.
(Authors' data)

This type of exchange violates certain felicity conditions stipulated
by speech act theory. Requests for information are supposed to be
made by someone who does not know the answer to the questions
being asked. The purpose of asking the questions is to obtain wanted
information. It is clear, however, that such a purpose does not pertain
to classroom questioning. There, the purpose of asking questions is
more likely to be a check on students' knowledge.

Levinson (1992) proposed a framework for overcoming these perceived problems in analyzing texts for implicatures. He suggested that
discourse should be evaluated in the context of its **activity type**. An
activity is a part of the situational context and thus has its basis in the
culture. Different activities require different amounts and types of
discourse. For example, a foot race may require little or no discourse,
a card game may be accompanied by a small set of standard expressions, and a trial in court may require a great deal of language. Other

activities, such as guiding an airplane to a loading dock or identifying ships at sea, may be accompanied by nonlinguistic semiotics, using signaling devices such as semaphores, flags, pennants, and lights. Different activity types are associated with different degrees of cooperativeness and with different patterns of speech act behavior. A knowledge of the activity type enables the interpreter to decide the degree of application of Gricean maxims and felicity conditions, as well as the substitution of some rules and conditions in place of others. Thus, in a court of law, the interpreter expects instances when cooperation breaks down almost completely, as when defendants resist answering a question that could harm their case in the eyes of the jury. Similarly, in classroom situations, an interpreter expects some questions to be asked by people who know the answers to them. Thus, the very same question (e.g., "How old are you?") may be asked and answered under completely different felicity conditions and with greater or lesser degrees of cooperativeness—in a classroom, in a doctor's office, or in a court of law.

Practice 45:
The activity type in the following dialogue is a courtroom trial. The expert witness is an x-ray technician who had photographed the body of a murdered child. The lawyer, the witness, and all other persons present in the court already know the answers to all the questions being asked. Analyze the text with regard to speech acts and Gricean maxims, but without taking the activity type into consideration. Next, analyze the text again, but this time adjust the application of felicity conditions and Gricean maxims to fit the activity type. What additional information can you derive from your analysis when you take the activity type into consideration? Finally, note any patterns of reference, ellipsis, and conjunction, and explain how such patterns might be explained in connection with the activity type.

Lawyer:	Can you identify these?
Witness:	They are the pictures I took.
Lawyer:	And what are they of?
Witness:	A 3-year-old child.
Lawyer:	And what was the child's name?
Witness:	R___ M___.
Lawyer:	And when were they taken?
Witness:	The evening of September nineteenth, uh . . .
Lawyer:	1981?
Witness:	Yes.

(Nofsinger, 1983, p. 254)

The concept of activity types helps the interpreter to predict the kinds of actions and discourses that might co-occur. At the same time, it aids in drawing appropriate inferences from texts. It does this by bringing together culture and situation in determining the meanings of texts.

It is clear from the examples given in this section that implicature is an important part of the meaning of texts. It is therefore a crucial part of any register description and should be added to the other linguistic phenomena examined when describing a register.

Guidelines for Analyzing Implicature, Presupposition, and Inference

Identify important inferences that are crucial to the meaning of the text. These may be conventional implicatures, felicity conditions, and/or conversational implicatures.

Determine to what extent inferences may reflect a personal bias on the part of the producer.

Determine whether or not it is likely that the Cooperative Principle is being observed, and if not, consider what effect this has on the communication.

Determine the effect the activity type has on the meaning of the discourse.

Sample Analysis: Implicature, Presupposition, and Inference

The CODE advertisement (Fig. 1.3) may be analyzed as follows:

The most important inference is that the 26 letters mean literacy education or literacy generally. Although inferences in the advertisement are likely to be institutionally biased, it is clear that the advertisement is not intended to mislead.

It is clear that the Cooperative Principle is being observed.

Understanding that the activity type of advertising is taking place enables the interpreter to be watchful of biases, persuasion, possible attempts to mislead, and so on.

Application

Using the aforementioned guidelines, analyze the implicatures, presuppositions, and inferences of your chosen oral and written practice texts.

Suggested Reading

Coulthard, M. (1985). *An introduction to discourse analysis.* London: Longman.
  The chapter on "Speech Acts and Conversational Maxims" is a clear, straightforward account of the topic.
Green, G. (1989). *Pragmatics and natural language understanding.* Hillsdale, NJ: Lawrence Erlbaum Associates.
  An intermediate-level text containing sections on the topics covered in this section.
Levinson, S. (1983). *Pragmatics.* Cambridge, England: Cambridge University Press.
  An advanced text covering all the topics discussed here.
Levinson, S. (1992). Activity types and language. In P. Drew & J. Heritage (Eds.), *Talk at work* (pp. 66–100). Cambridge, England: Cambridge University Press.
  A revealing and illuminating discussion of the relation between discourse and the activities in which it occurs.

NONVERBAL MEANING

It has been suggested that language is only one kind of semiotic system, or way of communicating information through signs. Furthermore, linguistic meaning can be either related to the situation surrounding the text or bound to the words and phrases themselves. Almost all linguistic communication is a combination of these. This section takes a brief look at nonverbal ways of communicating information in texts.

Nonverbal language, like its verbal counterpart, consists of a mixture of meanings drawn from convention as well as from situational and cultural norms. Often, linguistic and nonlinguistic strands of discourse can be thought of as two parallel texts, reinforcing each other as they proceed. Sometimes, however, nonlinguistic meaning contradicts linguistic meaning. When this happens, nonlinguistic meaning is the more significant. An earlier section showed how important these parallel texts can be in cross-cultural communication.

Here each of the forms of nonverbal communication is examined: **Prosody** examines voice features of pitch, pitch movement, loudness, and length. These are collectively referred to as **intonation**.[7] **Paralanguage** concerns voice quality and such signals as silences and emphasis. And **nonverbal language** involves examining specifically facial expressions, visual behavior, and gestures. Brief consideration is given as to how both prosody and paralanguage may co-occur with verbal texts, and how paralanguage may, on occasion, substitute for verbal texts in communicative situations.

The modern study of discourse intonation is primarily the work of Brazil (1973, 1975, 1978, 1985a, 1985b), who examined the relation of intonation patterns to the structuring of information in spoken English. Brazil identified four sets of options related to a **tone unit**: **prominence**, **tone**, **key**, and **termination**.

A tone unit, according to Brazil, consists of an optional "proclitic segment," followed by the "tonic segment," followed by an optional "enclitic segment," as in the following examples:

(Proclitic Segment)	Tonic Segment	(Enclitic Segment)
	HELP	
	HELP	me
please	HELP	me
well	for PETE'S sake HELP	me

The last example contains all four of the syllable classes recognized by Brazil:

> unaccented: "for," "sake"
> accented: "well," "me"
> prominent: "PETE'S"
> tonic: "HELP"

(Note that prominence is indicated with uppercase letters and tonicity with uppercase letters plus underlining.)

Prominence is the deliberate act of raising the pitch of a word. Both prominent and tonic syllables carry prominence. And prominence certainly has something to do with informativeness in exchanges such as the following:

---

[7]Prosody also includes tone, a feature of tone languages. The discussion here, however, is restricted to English, which is a nontonal language. For more information on tone languages, consult any standard text on introductory linguistics.

Practice 46:
Before going any further, see how much of intonation you understand merely through intuition. Encourage friends, family members, or classmates with a dramatic flair to give dramatic recitations of the following lines from Shakespeare. Each line should be spoken only once and tape recorded. Listening to the recordings, try to identify the proclitic, tonic, and enclitic segments in each utterance. Is there more than one tonic segment in any utterance?

To be or not to be
Our doubts are traitors
Tomorrow and tomorrow and tomorrow
Out, out, damned spot!
Shall I compare thee to a Summers day?

---

(92) A: What kind of mouth?
     B: The mouth of a RIVER.

In this exchange, "river," which is pitch prominent, is the word that supplies the required information.

In addition to prominence, speakers of English use tones to differentiate between common, shared knowledge, and new information. Tone choice thus provides an alternate way of differentiating between new and old information. The new information is usually signaled with a rising tone. For example, the utterance "After my birthday I went to the lake" may answer either of the two questions "When did you go to the lake?" or "What did you do after your birthday?" If it answers the first question, then the word "birthday" will normally have a rising intonation. If it answers the second question, then the rising intonation would attach to "lake."

The third option, key, refers to relative pitch as selected from a three-tier system: high, mid, or low. A speaker's key is measured

---

Practice 47:
Record or videotape a few minutes of a television program in which one person is questioning another (e.g., a talk show or a news analysis program with expert guests). Play back a question–answer exchange. Listen for the pitch prominent word or phrase in the answer. Why is that word or phrase pitch prominent? (*Note*: Any answer that contains more than one word will have at least one pitch prominent word.)

Practice 48:
Working with a friend or classmate, silently choose one of the two following questions. Pretend that someone has just asked you that question. Keep your choice of question a secret from your partner, but answer it out loud with the answer given. Ask your partner to specify which of the two questions you were answering. How could your partner tell which one it was? Exchange roles and repeat the exercise two or three times. Can the interpreter always tell which of the two questions is being answered?

Question (a): Who is standing in the driveway?
Question (b): Where is the gardener standing?

Answer: The gardener is standing in the driveway.

---

relative to the pitch of the cotext that preceded it. A high key is an indicator of contrastive information, a mid key indicates additive information, and a low key indicates equative information. The following exemplify each of these:

(93) (a) (high)   //p He threw a BONE at the dog, and it ^{BIT} him//
                   (Contrastive: You would not expect such a thing.)
      (b) (mid)   //p He threw a BONE at the dog, and it BIT him//
                   (Additive: No causal connection between the two events.)
      (c) (low)   //p He threw a BONE at the dog and it $_{BIT}$ him//
                   (Equative: It is what you would expect.)

Finally, the high, mid, or low pitch with which a speaker begins a falling tone or ends a rising tone is called termination. Because there is typically a high degree of concord between the termination of the final tone unit of an utterance and the beginning key choice of the following utterance, termination is a way for a speaker to request a particular key choice from a respondent. Key choice carries meaning, so a speaker can mediate toward a particular meaning in

---

Practice 49:
Again in pairs, recite the following utterance to your partner, who should try to determine whether you intended to give it a contrastive, additive, or equative meaning. Take turns reciting it to each other, alternating among the three key meanings. Can the interpreter always understand the intended meaning? Why or why not?

She invited me, and I went.

---

this way. Consider the following exchange from a doctor–patient interview:

(94) D: //p VERy ^{IRritating you say}// P: //p ^{VERy irritating}//
(Coulthard, 1985, p. 116)

By choosing high termination, the doctor forces the patient to respond with a high key contrastive utterance whose meaning is "very definitely yes, rather than no." Clearly, this use of termination is potentially cohesive. More importantly, it gives power to the speaker, who is then able to control to some extent the outcome of the exchange.

A variety of paralinguistic signals may also co-occur with prosodic features to coordinate the progress of conversation. Silence can indicate the end of a turn, but there is a marked difference in preferences for long or short silences between turns across cultures. It is important to remember, however, that although "silence counts," it can in no sense be considered to constitute a speech act.

There are also other paralinguistic markers used for turn-taking. For example, apart from the producer's control of terminal pitch to determine the respondent's answer, the last syllable or the stressed syllable in a clause may be drawn out in a paralinguistic drawl, or there may be a drop in loudness accompanying the use of a statement like "you know." There are, furthermore, paralinguistic cues that co-occur with vocalizations such as "mm" and "uh-huh," which the interpreters may give to the producer to signal that they understand what is being said.

Apart from these paralinguistic signals, voice quality can change significantly to the point of turning an ordinary statement into a threat, warning, joke, and so forth. In other words, voice quality can actually change the meaning of statements in conversations. Think about the role voice quality can play in changing the meaning of an innocuous statement into sarcasm.

Practice 50:
Attempt to control responses to a question by using high and low terminations. Ask several of your friends a question such as "Great (lousy) movie (meal, trip, game, etc.), would you say?" Use high termination when asking some of your friends and low termination when asking others. Do you notice any difference in the responses? What conclusions can you draw from this practice concerning the power relations between participants in a discourse?

Finally, a paralinguistic cue may occasionally substitute for verbal behavior, as the following example shows:

(95) (J wants to pay S for the stamps that she has given her.)
S: I think you better just keep it because I don't have change anyway.
J: Well, next time I'm in the money as far as stamps are concerned.
S: ((laughs))
(Tsui, 1989, p. 554)

The laugh constitutes an acknowledgment of J's acceptance of S's suggestion. Very little research has yet been done on this aspect of the relation between paralanguage and verbal behavior, probably because such nonverbal behaviors as laughs or facial expressions "are often not recorded on transcriptions, giving the illusion that the follow-up move is absent" (Tsui, 1989, p. 554).

Like prosody and paralanguage, nonverbal language contributes to the meaning of much discourse. Nonverbal language includes the nonlinguistic elements of discourse, related to the five senses, that contribute to the meaning of a text. These nonlinguistic elements used to be viewed as completely independent of the discourse, but now it is realized that they have a considerable bearing on an understanding of how producers and interpreters process information and manipulate impressions.

Occasionally, nonverbal language contradicts the verbal message. In such cases, the nonverbal language seems to speak more loudly. Consider the following example drawn from an experience of one of the authors. While giving directions, her informant assured her that the building she was seeking was "on the left." But the (second language) speaker was gesturing very emphatically with her right arm, at the same time giving such features as "a high white wall with a gate in the side." Noting the gestures as well as the words, the author found the building on the right, not on the left!

Practice 51:
Record a 5-minute conversation with at least three people. Transcribe it, noting very carefully the length of pauses between the turns, the length of any silences, the use of terminal pitch, the presence of a paralinguistic drawl, and any drop in loudness, whether or not accompanying a statement such as "you know," at turn changes. Interpret the meanings of any of these paralinguistic features that you find.

Although nonverbal behaviors may be manipulable by the producer who is conscious of them, they are probably much less manipulable by the interpreter. Many people are unaware of the power of nonlinguistic elements to moderate the meaning of text. However, if interpreters are aware of their power, they are less likely to be disturbed by them. This discussion concentrates on two types of nonverbal behavior: facial expressions and visual behavior, and gestures.

Unfortunately for the study of the relation between nonverbal behaviors and discourse, the co-occurrence of facial expressions and verbal behavior has not yet been examined. The research on facial expressions has focused instead on the depiction of emotions. Several attempts have been made to determine which is more important, the facial expression or the context, in providing information; results suggest, although inconclusively, that facial cues are more important.

Researchers look at facial cues as expressive of particular emotions. Ekman and Friesen (1975) provided a list of clues to surprise and disgust:

Surprise:
The brows are raised, so that they are curved and high.
The skin below the brow is stretched.
Horizontal wrinkles go across the forehead.
The eyelids are opened; the upper lid is raised and the lower lid drawn down; the white of the eye shows above the iris, and often below as well.
The jaw drops open so that the lips and teeth are parted, but there is no tension or stretching of the mouth.

Disgust:
The upper lip is raised.
The lower lip is also raised and pushed up to the upper lip, or is lowered and slightly protruding.
The nose is wrinkled.
The cheeks are raised.
Lines show below the lower lid, and the lid is pushed up but not tense.
The brow is lowered, lowering the upper lid.
(Ekman & Friesen, 1975, pp. 45, 76; quoted in Druckman, Rozelle, & Baxter, 1982, pp. 55–56)

What needs to be done now is to correlate these facial cues with verbal behavior.

Fortunately, unlike facial expressions, **visual behavior** has been found to serve a number of functions in discourse. These include regulating conversational turn-taking and seeking information. For ex-

---

Practice 52:

Attempt to identify the meanings of the facial expressions and gaze behaviors of discourse participants in a 5-minute segment of a video. (It may, for example, be a recording of a television conversation.) You may need to play through the same segment several times to do this. Determine whether these meanings are identifiable independent of the words or only in conjunction with them. If the recorded program is a talk show or something similar, observe how the moderator controls turn-taking, in part through the use of gaze behavior.

---

ample, directing a gaze at a discourse participant signals the speaker's willingness to relinquish the floor, and looking away signals the desire to maintain the floor. Then discourse participants who need information but do not want to reveal anything about themselves will throw short, frequent gazes at the speaker, whereas those who need information and are willing to reveal something will throw frequent sustained looks. It is worth noting in passing that cultural differences in gaze behaviors can cause significant problems in cross-cultural communication.

Just as gaze behaviors are often synchronized with speech behavior, so too is **body language**, which can be a powerful tool of communication (Fig. 2.6). In fact, body cues serve similar functions of regulating the flow of conversation and helping the speaker formulate thoughts into words. One category of body movements, gestures made with the hands, is considered to be particularly relevant in the study of nonverbal behaviors associated with discourse. Quintilian, as early as the first century A.D., wrote, "For other portions of the body merely help the speaker, whereas the hands may almost be said to speak. Do we not use them to demand, promise, summon, dismiss, threaten, supplicate, express aversion or fear, question or deny?" (Quoted in Feyereisen & de Lannoy, 1991, p. 1).

Despite this early view, gestures were, for a long time, considered as mere accompaniments to conversation. Recently, however, Feyereisen and de Lannoy (1991), Levy and McNeill (1992), and Bavelas, Chovil, Lawrie, and Wade (1992), among others, have begun to examine the relation of gestures to the structuring of information in spoken English. Feyereisen and de Lannoy saw, in particular, that gestures may be used to maintain coherence by providing gestural anaphora, deixis, and even conjunction. McNeill (1985), likewise, viewed gestures as indispensable to referential acts, thus contributing to the cohesive potential of discourse. Levy and McNeill found that

FIG. 2.6. "Which is the man, and which is the monkey?" (Body language can be a powerful tool of communication.) Reprinted with permission.

during the early stages of any conversation, prior to agreement on the topic, participants gesture a great deal as they search for common ground. Subsequently, they find less need for gestures.

It is necessary to distinguish between two kinds of gestures: **emblems**, which are stereotypical hand signals that substitute for words, such as those of a traffic police officer; and **illustrators**, which accompany and contribute to the flow of conversation. Illustrators are the main concern, and they can be further subdivided into **topic gestures** and **interactive gestures**. Topic gestures are clearly related to the topic of the conversation, and may happen even during long monologic stretches, such as during a lecture. They may help speakers to formulate what they want to say. Here is an example:

(96) . . . then you <u>look up</u> the author or the title . . .
(The speaker makes a gesture of skimming through a drawer of cards.)
(Bavelas et al., 1992, p. 473)

In this example, the gesture reinforces the concept of "looking something up" in a card catalogue.

Interactive gestures, on the other hand, tend only to happen in dialogic, face-to-face communication, such as a question–answer session toward the end of a lecture or, more informally, a conversation between friends. They are the gestures primarily responsible for regulating the flow of conversation. An example of an interactive gesture is:

> (97) ... and of COURSE there were chances that they would, uh, write something WRONG, you know? (speaker flicks hand outward toward the listener; index finger points at the listener; palm faces up; other fingers are curled)
> (Bavelas et al., 1992, p. 471)

Here, the gesture is deictic and reinforces the concept of interaction by indicating the other participant in the discourse.

Norms of prosody and paralanguage can vary considerably from culture to culture. Similar variations affect nonverbal language, including body language. A striking example was shown in a study by Garratt, Baxter, and Rozelle (1981). In this study, white police officers were trained in the characteristics of Black nonverbal behavior and asked to conduct interviews with Blacks. Some of the interviews were conducted using white nonverbal behavior, and some were conducted using Black nonverbal behavior. The officers received the following instructions for the two kinds of behavior in interviews:

Anglo-American Interviews

1. Open the door moderately wide, step through, continue facing and looking at the subject (S), and close the door behind you.
2. Approach the S quickly while continuing to look at him.
3. Stand four and one-half feet away from the S while asking for his identification.

Practice 53:
In lectures and conversations over the next few days, try to identify some common topic and interactive gestures. Then watch part of a television talk show with the volume turned off. Try to see the difference between topic and interactive gestures. In your estimation, how much of the information in spoken discourse is carried by gestures?

4. Approach the S quickly and directly to receive the identification card, and stand directly facing him while close to him, perusing the card.
5. Position yourself four and one-half feet away from the S again after returning the card.
6. Upon leaving, turn and walk quickly away to the door, open the door moderately wide, step through, and close the door behind you.

Black American Interviews

1. Open the door widely when entering the room, swing completely around and close the door slowly with your back to the ·S.
2. Approach the S slowly and deliberately while averting your gaze.
3. Stand six feet away from the S while asking for identification.
4. Approach the S slowly to receive the identification card and stand at right angles to the S while close to him, perusing the card.
5. Position yourself six feet away from the S again after returning the card.
6. Upon leaving, turn and walk slowly away, open the door widely, step back, turn and then walk out, closing the door.

(Quoted in Druckman et al., 1982, pp. 104–105)

Blacks who experienced both of these interviewing techniques showed a significant preference for the "Black American Interview" style and rated the interviewers using this style as having greater personal, social, and professional competence.

As a result of studies such as the one by Garratt et al., it has become clear that body language is a text in its own right, even in the absence of much spoken or written text. It can be used to communicate important and powerful information. And, like all texts, its meanings can be strongly influenced by cultural bias.

This section has examined the relation of nonverbal language to spoken discourse. But what about its relation to writing? Literary authors who are able to convey the paralanguage and gestures of their characters realistically in their writing are often praised for the verisimilitude of their books.

Remembering that language is primarily oral, one of the most important uses of written discourse is to make a permanent record of oral discourse. The most difficult aspects of oral language to record in this way, however, are prosody and paralanguage. The use of punctuation marks, different type sizes and type faces (e.g., advertisements and comic strips), physical layout (e.g., a metered poem), and even color may suggest intonation patterns and other paralinguistic signals. Sometimes, authors simply have to resort to description, for example, of voice quality. Still, with all these aids, it may take a skilled reader or actor to produce the desired effect.

It is just as difficult to record facial expressions, visual behavior, and gestures in written texts as it is to record prosody and paralanguage. Virtually the only way for nonverbal language to be effectively recorded in written form is for readers to accept written descriptions of the facial expressions, visual behavior, and gestures accompanying the written texts.

In the case of sign language, chapter 1 indicated how sign size, speed of signing, and so on can substitute in some ways for the paralinguistic features of spoken discourse. Another special case is that of the blind, who are deprived of the use of visual verbal and nonverbal texts. For them, other senses such as hearing and touch can often be used instead as channels of communication.

Nonverbal elements of meaning form a parallel text in all spoken discourse and in much written discourse as well. A description of a genre's register cannot be considered complete without an analysis of the nonverbal meanings contained in the text.

Guidelines for Analyzing Nonverbal Meaning

Divide the text into probable tone units, indicating any proclitic, tonic, and enclitic segments.

Identify all instances of prominence and mark them. What information is given by the prominence?

Identify all tones. What information is given by the patterning of these tones?

Identify the key of each segment under scrutiny. What meaning is given by the key?

Identify the termination of the utterance. How does it affect the following key choice? What meaning is suggested in contrast to other meanings that would be suggested had a different key been used?

Identify all instances of silences, hesitations, and pauses, determining the length of each. What is the significance of the different lengths of silences?

Identify any paralinguistic markers used to indicate turn-taking, and any used with or without vocalizations to indicate that the discourse participants understand the speaker.

If the text is written, look for punctuation marks, different type sizes and type faces, physical layout, and color as indicators of probable intonation choices and other paralinguistic signals.

Describe facial expressions and visual behavior in as much detail as possible, stating their functions where possible.

Examine carefully the relation between the words and the facial expressions and visual behavior. Does a specific facial expression or visual behavior occur at exactly the same time as a particular word? Or does it come immediately before or after the word(s)?

Identify and describe all instances of gestures. Separate these instances into the two categories, topic and interactive gestures, on the basis of your description. Do you notice any differences in contexts for topic and interactive gestures? If so, are these differences simply a question of the difference between monologic and dialogic discourse, or are they related to other factors? Specify any factors.

Examine carefully the relation between the words and the gestures. Does a specific gesture occur exactly at the same time as a particular word? Or does the gesture come before or after the word(s)?

If the text is written, look for any words that serve as indicators of the facial expressions, visual behavior, and gestures of discourse participants.

Sample Analysis: Nonverbal Meaning

The CODE advertisement (Fig. 1.3) may be analyzed as follows:

Prominence is suggested through the use of bold lettering of larger size than the lettering of the main body of the text. The word "26" achieves additional prominence by juxtaposition with "one way" in the segment of text that precedes it.

With regard to silence, the spacing before the line "We have 26" suggests a significant pause.

The CODE logo could be conceived as an example in writing of a gesture, but it is an emblem rather than an illustrator.

Application

Using the aforementioned guidelines, analyze the paralinguistic features of your chosen oral text. To save time, focus particularly on one short and meaningful segment of the transcript. If you have had the good fortune to be able to videotape your oral text, review the video to note down details of any gestures.

Suggested Reading

Bavelas, J. B., Chovil, N., Lawrie, D. A., & Wade, A. (1992). Interactive gestures. *Discourse Processes, 15*(4), 469–489.
    Brings Druckman et al.'s survey of body language up to date. A particularly useful summary diagram of typical interactive gestures is given on pp. 474–475.
Coulthard, M. (1985). *An introduction to discourse analysis* (2nd ed.). London: Longman.
    A clear, concise treatment, bringing together most of the main points of Brazil's contribution to an analysis of discourse intonation. See especially pp. 100–119.
Druckman, D., Rozelle, R. M., & Baxter, J. C. (1982). *Nonverbal communication: Survey, theory, and research*. Beverly Hills, CA: Sage.
    A useful survey of the state of the art of research into nonverbal communication up to 1982. See especially part I.
Edmondson, W. (1981). *Spoken discourse: A model of analysis*. London: Longman.
    An interesting study of the relation between linguistic and nonlinguistic behavior in discourse.
Feyereisen, P., & de Lannoy, J-D. (1991). *Gestures and speech: Psychological investigations*. Cambridge, England: Cambridge University Press.
    Chapters 1–3 give a comprehensive survey of the state of the art of research into the relation between gestures and speech.
Halliday, M. (1989). *Spoken and written language*. Oxford, England: Oxford Univesity Press.
    Halliday provides an alternative view of discourse intonation to Brazil's. See especially chapter 4 of Halliday's text.
Yule, G. (1985). *The study of language*. Cambridge, England: Cambridge University Press.
    Chapter 17 (pp. 158–166) provides a clear, concise introduction to sign languages and how they work.

Conclusion to Part I: The Acceptability of Discourse: Genre and Register

Part I opened with a discussion of textual acceptability as a function of the grammaticality and appropriateness of texts. Their relationship was sketched like this:

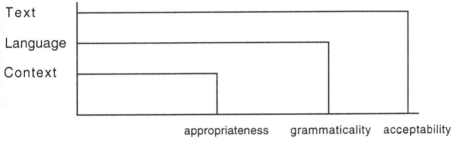

Appropriateness is a judgment about how a text relates to its context. In other words, it is a judgment about the genre of a text. If interpreters judge a text to be appropriate, they are expressing the belief that the genre is the correct one for fulfilling the intentions of the producer. This means that it is well founded in the culture, it has the expected producer(s) and interpreter(s), the relations between these are within the allowable range for such a genre, the setting and channel are the ones stipulated by the genre, the text is a recognizable part of its intertext, the purpose is the one assigned to the given genre, and the topic is within the range of topics belonging to that genre. In short, the text conforms to the limitations discussed in chapter 1.

Grammaticality is the other component of acceptability. It is a judgment about the register, or allowable language, of a genre. If the

191

interpreter judges the register to be grammatical, this means that the cohesion patterns of the text are what one would expect for that register, the linguistic features conform to Biber's factor analysis, and the patterns of literal and nonliteral meanings, inferences and implicatures, and nonverbal meanings are within the allowable range for that register. In other words, the limitations described in chapter 2 apply to the register of the text.

Of course, few interpreters are aware that the judgments they make are based on the elements discussed so far in this book. However, interpreters who are familiar with specific genres routinely make such judgments on the basis of this familiarity. For example, an employer is likely to recognize an acceptable letter of application, even without the help of discourse analysis. But an employer who is also a discourse analyst will more quickly spot unacceptable features of the text. Such an employer might have spotted the information missing from the letter of application described earlier.

If the text is judged to be both appropriate and grammatical, this means the interpreter finds the text to be acceptable. It is both well structured and well styled. It is poised to fulfill the intentions of the producer.

Part I of this book has enumerated the elements of genre and register that comprise a text. In addition, it has shown how these elements are combined with each other in the discourse process. The final product of this process is the text. Readers are now in the position to make expert judgments about the appropriateness, grammaticality, and acceptability of texts. More than that, readers are now capable of producing many such texts more effectively than they have ever done before.

II

DISCOURSE IN USE

Introduction to Part II: From Process to Product

Part I discussed how the producer and interpreter, in the process of discourse, draw on context and language in order to create text. Part II moves on from the process to the product. It is even more concerned with the acceptability of text, because if a text is not acceptable within the culture, then it will have no role to play in the ongoing development of that culture. In each of the institutional discourses to be examined (education, medicine, law, news media, and literature), it becomes evident how the process of arriving at appropriateness in the context and grammaticality in the language results in acceptability of the product.

The relation between the concepts of acceptability and text is diagrammed in Fig. II.1, which is an expansion of Fig. I.1. It presents in graphic form how the process of achieving appropriateness and grammaticality results in an acceptable product in each one of the institutional discourses examined.

It is, however, extremely important to realize that the product is unchangeable in one sense only: Each text that is produced (most recognizably when in written form) is an unchangeable product. Thus, each individual teacher who teaches a particular topic produces a very different class lesson (the product) than any other teacher. Again, whereas one physician may prescribe a particular treatment (the product) following a diagnosis, another may prescribe a different treatment. Yet again, the precedent established by a particular court decision (the product) can be interpreted differently by different lawyers in subsequent cases. Then the reports people read in their favorite newspapers every morning at breakfast (the products) may cover the same topics, but they will differ from each other because

195

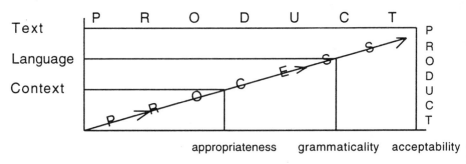

FIG. II.1. The relation of product to process.

each journalist will focus on different aspects of the topic. Finally, although the essential themes of literature may remain the same over the centuries, different novels (the products) remain quite distinctive.

In another sense, the product, in general, changes over time, such that a text that is unacceptable in one age may become acceptable in a later age. This is true of literature as well as all institutional discourses. In the case of education, witness the shift of focus from passing on facts to learning how to learn; in medicine, notice the move from the clinical approach of the physician to the relational approach of the psychiatrist and counselor; in law, witness the debate on how best to conduct interviews; in the news media, notice the current debate on ethical issues. Another way of saying this is that the rules on what is acceptable change. In each generation, people begin to ask questions such as: "Why do such rules exist? Whose interests do such rules serve? Have these rules been contested? Do these rules limit possibilities for our [culture]? Are there other sets of rules that can expand possibilities?" (Pierce, 1989, p. 406).

The following five chapters put to use the skills of discourse analysis acquired in part I to analyze the acceptability of institutional discourses of a variety of kinds, in addition to advertising. Although just five institutional discourses are considered, it is possible to apply the same techniques to any institutional discourse in order to understand it better.

3

THE DISCOURSE
OF EDUCATION

It has been possible, throughout history, to see education as "a communication process between society and the individual" (Hills, 1979, p. 10). Society has used teachers to communicate its standards, and the current store of human knowledge, by using the community's language. Thus, educational discourse provides discourse analysts with a source of a variety of texts very much tied to a context, the school. In the Western and Western-educated world of the late 20th century, this context is virtually inescapable for children age 5 to 18. An analysis of educational discourse begins to show how text interacts with context and language in textbooks and classrooms, schools and education offices. Although not denying the importance of the analysis of educational decision-making discourse—such as in the case of educational referrals (Mehan, 1986), placement (Hertweck, 1986), and policy-making (McHoul, 1986)—the focus here is on the text–context–language interface in textbooks and classrooms.

Notice the power relation that exists between teacher and students, which is different from that between doctor and patient, or lawyer and client. People are already aware of this relation from their student days, from earliest memories of elementary school. As children, most individuals probably played "teacher," with all the right words and tone of voice! As Simon and Boyer (1970, p. 2) noted: "Any school-child playing teacher will produce most of the behaviour used by most teachers. Typical behaviours are: standing in front of a group of relatively passive onlookers . . . doing most of the talking . . .

197

asking questions to which they already know the answers . . . and evaluating by passing judgements." The power relation between the administrative and academic staff in a school, between the school psychologist and the teacher, and between the textbook writer and the teacher who uses the writer's materials may not be so obvious to nonteachers. In addition, the language of the classroom varies according to the subject being taught, the age and sex of the students, the educational level, and so on.

There are, thus, a number of different ways in which discourse analysts can make themselves useful. For, according to Barnes (Barnes, Britton, Rosen, & the L.A.T.E., 1971, p. 11), "as the complicated commerce within the [teacher–class] group is largely carried on through language, so it is largely through language that society explicitly or covertly defines and limits the activities of the group. Thus, to study the language of the classroom is to study both the learning processes and some of the internal and external constraints upon it." First, those who write textbooks in the full range of subjects taught at the different educational levels can make use of discourse analysis to determine the appropriateness and acceptability of the content and form for each level. Second, teachers of any language, whether a first, second, or foreign language, can profitably study discourse analysis so as to better teach the interaction between grammar, meaning, and context in both listening and reading comprehension and writing skills. Third, teachers of all subjects can analyze their own use of language in the classroom in an attempt to balance their use of the different functions of language; their use of the full range of verbal and nonverbal means available to them; and their understanding of the cultural, situational, and relational contexts in which they are teaching. Of course, in one sense these three different ways are not, strictly speaking, separable. Every teacher needs textbooks in the classroom, and likewise teachers are, whether or not they like it, teachers of language. For one thing, language is the means by which teachers convey the content of the subject, and the means by which students relay back their understanding, or otherwise, of the teacher's material. In Postman and Weingartner's (1971, p. 103) words, "Biology, maths and history teachers, quite literally, have little else to teach but a way of talking and therefore seeing the world." Finally, going beyond the more narrow confines of textbook and classroom, anyone involved in education can make use of discourse analysis to answer questions about the relation

---

Practice 54:

Record on audio- or, if possible, videocassette, one lesson in a subject that interests you. If the teacher uses group work at all, make sure to move the microphone close to ONE group, so that that group's discussion is recorded clearly. Transcribe a 10-minute segment of the lesson, giving as much detail as possible of use of visual aids, the textbook, and the chalkboard, and noting prosody and body language. Also get hold of copies of the textbook materials and any other visual aids the teacher may have used. Use these materials to compare with the lesson discussed later.

---

between the narrow confines of the classroom and the wider school and societal context, such as the impact of the physical setting on communication between staff and students.

This chapter refers to the transcript of one mathematics lesson, taught at the beginning of the 1993–1994 academic year to a Year 8 class of 21 girls, age 12 to 13, in a private boarding convent school in southern England, and to the textbook used by the teacher in that class (Vickers, Tipler & van Hiele, 1993, chap. 11). Although some may feel that the nature of the school limits the transferability of results to other state school settings, the "culture of the school" is such that, in the Western world, classroom procedures and language are very much the same. Furthermore, in England, with the National Curriculum being in force now, the content does not vary from one school to another as much as in the past. In fact, Silberman (1973, p. 122) stated that "Schools differ, of course, according to the nature of the community they serve, the education of the children's parents, the school's own history and tradition, the outlook of its teachers and administrators, and so on. But the differences tend to be differences in degree, not in kind; in any case, they are relatively trivial compared to the uniformities and similarities."

THE CONTEXT OF EDUCATION

The focus here is on Western-type school education, so its context is considered, but remember that elsewhere there is still a very different tradition of nonformal education. The latter coexists with the former in the West, but may be the only educational tradition in non-Westernized cultures. Until fairly recently, however, as Silberman (1973, p. 119) pointed out, nonformal education was the norm. There are still cultures where "instruction depends more on watching, imitation, and silent practice than on an endless stream of words" (Edwards & Furlong, 1978, p. 10). This nonformal education differs, however, both in the context and in the role of language from the formal education that is the focus of attention in this chapter.

Culture

As McDermott and Tylbor (1986, p. 123) put it, the school is one of the "culturally most well-formulated" contexts for language use. Western-style education has had the potential to act as a cultural leveler, in that, at least since the United Nations' Universal Declaration of Human Rights (1948, see United Nations, 1983, p. 81), education has been seen as a right for all children, schooling has been compulsory, and free schooling has been available from the age of 5–7 to the age of 16–18 in the West, so that, regardless of family background, children have attended school. Thus, Silberman (1973, p. 5), for example, purported that "the public schools . . . as the one publicly controlled educating institution with which virtually every child comes into close and prolonged contact, . . . occupy a strategic, perhaps critical, position in . . . society." In the Third World, many countries have attempted to introduce free compulsory education at least at the primary level, for about 7–8 years, for this very reason.

Narrowing the discussion down to education in the West, Barnes (Barnes et al., 1971, p. 11) clearly showed the cultural context of the teacher: "Not only is the teacher–class group a social microcosm, but one which also interacts with the social macrocosm of which it is a part." Because education is one of the main channels for the maintenance and/or change of cultural values, it clearly has a major role to play, outside the immediate family, in influencing people's perception of the world. Ideologies, whether consistent with or counter to the mainstream of culture, arise out of people's experience of education. Prejudices toward those who are different in any way, regardless of the fact that many of these prejudices originated in the family, may be reinforced in school by exposure to teachers and/or textbooks. Attitudes to territory and time are shaped by daily childhood journeys to and from school, and within school from one classroom to another, from the classroom to the playground, and from the playground to the dining hall, each activity closely regulated by the clock. As Heckman (1987, pp. 66, 77) put it, "Teachers, principals, and even students have views of their world that help them understand and guide what they do, what they do not do, and why. Certain teaching practices correspond to these views, which develop as a consequence of experience. . . . These views are derived in large part from the current culture of each school, conspiring to maintain the status quo."

Perception of the world is influenced by education in the mathematics lesson, and in the textbook chapter. Ideologies, prejudices, and attitudes to territory and time are all apparent, to greater or lesser extents, in the lesson itself, as the following extract (most of which was already presented in chap. 1, Practice 8) shows:

(98) T: Who did I give Ranya's piece of paper to yesterday with the tests I wanted her to do?
S 1:   You gave it to me but I had to go to Student Council so I gave it to er Ellen.
T: Is that right, Ellen?
S 2:   Yeah, but I forgot to give it to Ranya.
T: Well, THAT is a LOT of use, isn't it? ... When did you realize you forgot to give it to Ranya?
S 2:   Just now.
T: Only just now? Ranya, why didn't you ask someone else in your FORM for it at afternoon registration?
S 3:   I forgot.
T: And YOU forgot! It's MOST inconvenient because it now means that I cannot give those tests back to Year 8. (*Knock on door*)
T: Hello?
S 4:   Sorry, I'm late.
T: Okay, Michelle. So it means, I'm sorry, girls, that because Ellen and Ranya both forgot something, that you can't have your results until tomorrow, which is very inconvenient because I wanted to go over that toDAY ... because no one, besides you being Set One, no one, not one, got 10 out of 10.
(Authors' data)

Ideologies may not be immediately obvious, but even readers from other Western cultures may note some ideological differences. Consider, first, the reference to the student council, which means the school believes in giving the students a say, however minimal, in the day-to-day running of the school. Then there is the more subtle revelation of a belief in streaming students into Sets, which entails the expectation that Set One will perform well. Attitudes to territory

are revealed in the assumption that students are expected to help
each other by giving to those who miss a class details of readings
and assignments. Frequent references to time, such as "just now" and
"tomorrow," with the use of verb tenses to reinforce the adverbials,
suggest the importance in the Western world of sticking close to a
schedule, made initially by the administration of the school, in the
timetabling, and later by the teacher, in Schemes of Work. Such
control by the clock reflects the perception that "school is a place
where things often happen not because students want them to, but
because it is time for them to occur" (Jackson, 1968, p. 13). Prejudices
are more clearly seen in the textbook. To take just one example, of
the five pictures of people shown measuring or being measured, two
are of the same Asian-looking girl, and the others are of white,
presumably British, teenagers. Why is it that no pictures show a Black
British teenager? Some people might be led to read into that omission
a belief among the textbook author and/or publisher that Blacks are
not as good at mathematics as whites or Asians.

In much the same way, a person's place in the world is to a large
extent determined by experience of the culture of the school. In fact,
ironically, people's perception of their place in the world is probably
much more shaped by the procedural aspects of classroom activity,
shown in the previous extract, than by the instructional content that
is the main purpose of education. However, consider, for example,
sexual discrimination. Discrimination on sexual grounds is often
found in unsuspected places. For example, the mathematics textbook,
in the same five pictures already mentioned, shows four girls—possibly to counter the widely held belief that girls are not good at
mathematics, and to reinforce the ideology that all should be offered
equal educational opportunity. Interestingly, in this respect, a study
comparing the performance in mathematics of single-sex groups in
a coeducational secondary school with the performance of mixed
groups (in a developing country) revealed that the girls performed
much better when taught separately (Hyde, 1993). In the lesson
discussed in this chapter, the teacher's high expectations of the
students, all girls, is evident in the following:

> (99) The work was very careless indeed, and I don't expect that sort of thing
> from the lovely reports I've had of you from Mrs B. I gave you ALL the
> time in the world. Some of you didn't write your methods. Some of you
> didn't write your working. I DO not expect that sort of standard. Doesn't
> apply to everyone. Quite a few of you got 9 out of 10. The lowest was

3 out of 10, which I think's apPALling.
(Authors' data)

It would be interesting to have comparable lessons with a group of boys and a mixed group to find out whether the teachers have equally high expectations in all cases, and whether or not the sex of the teacher has any effect, which research suggests it might well have (Rosenthal, 1976). Teachers' expectations not only indicate their perception of their place in the world, they are also very important for students to develop their own sense of place (Rosenthal & Jacobson, 1968).

Students' perception of their place in the world is a factor in their self-development. Ethnicity plays an important role in language use in daily life, which may or may not carry over into the classroom. Much research has shown how middle-class children enter school knowing the functions of language needed to enable them to benefit from education, thus making their language and learning congruent with the expectations of the teacher, whereas lower middle-class children do not have the same advantage. Some researchers jumped to the conclusion that lower middle-class children suffered from a "language deficit" that was hindering their development (e.g., Bereiter & Engelmann, 1966). Others, however, contended that lower middle-class children do not suffer from a deficiency, but rather that they use language differently than middle-class children in what appears to researchers to be the "same" context (Bernstein, 1972, p. 142). Kochman (1972, p. 229) specifically stated that "an oral language program that attempts to replace nonstandard forms with socially preferred forms does **not** develop the child's ability to use language beyond what he is already capable of doing. This is also true of attempts to teach standard dialect as a second dialect, which attempts to augment, rather than replace, his nonstandard forms with standard forms, attempting to create a new set of language habits" (emphasis added).

Labov (1972) was particularly, and justifiably, critical of the linguistic and cultural deficit views, as hindering the self-development of Black children: "There is no reason to believe that any nonstandard vernacular is in itself an obstacle to learning. The chief problem is ignorance of language on the part of all concerned. . . . That children should be the victims of this ignorance is intolerable" (pp. 239–240).

In the lesson transcript, there are plenty of examples of congruence between teacher and pupils in their use of the language of the classroom. In Extract 98, a student, Michelle, excused herself for being late, rather than just barging into the classroom and sitting down without saying anything. In Extract 100, it is clear that all the students understand the teacher will call on individuals who raise their hands to answer, rather than all trying to answer at the same time, although occasionally a student forgets to raise her hand:

(100) T: . . . Did any of you get different answers to each other yesterday? Rebecca.
S 1: Em I em mine was 1 millimeter longer than the other.
T: So one was 1 millimeter longer than the other. What about you, Louise?
S 2: Well I got 14.1 and Lydia got 14 centimeters.
T: So some of you were a little bit out. . . . Why do you think you got different answers, Catherine?
S 3: Because some of us aren't exactly accurate.
T: Some of you aren't exactly accurate. Why do you think you're not accurate? (5 seconds) What what bits of your instruments aren't accurate, em . . . Eleanor?
S 4: Em we have blunt pencils.
T: You might have a blunt pencil. What sort of pencil did I say to use?
S 5: H.
T: Judith.
S 6: 2H.
T: 2H pencil, and a nice sharp 2H pencil as well.
(Authors' data)

In spite, or perhaps because of, the congruence between teacher's and students' language use, the typical power relation between them is maintained, such that the teacher preserves her position, and the students are expected to preserve theirs. Thus, for example, in Extract 100, the teacher uses the second-person pronoun to emphasize that it is the students who are inaccurate and use blunt pencils, not herself, in "Some of you aren't exactly accurate" and "You might have a blunt pencil." However, the teacher does allow for the fact that she may be at fault sometimes, as in the following extract:

(101) Maybe I was trying to make you go too fast. Maybe we need to go a little slower. We'll have to see how we go.
(Authors' data)

On the other hand, she very quickly reestablishes her position of authority when a student is out of line, as in this extract:

(102) You've left your notebook in your jotter. RG, you may go and get your notebook from your locker, and I will put you in my notebook as an offender.
(Authors' data)

The student in this case unsuccessfully tries to defend herself. When another student admits to an offense, the teacher is more positive, while still maintaining her authority:

(103) Well at least Rebecca you have the courage to own up because do you know if you make a mistake with me and you own up, it's actually a lot better than if you don't own up.
(Authors' data)

Thus we can see how the language of self-preservation is used in the classroom.

Discourse Participants

Educational discourse presents discourse analysts with an interesting perspective on discourse participants. First, analysts might hope for a single producer and a single source, something that may superficially be the case in the classroom, but is actually rare. Then they might hope for a high degree of homogeneity in the interpreters, which probably happens infrequently, except in schools that still believe in ability streaming. Even then, the ability streaming can only achieve homogeneity at the academic level, bearing little or no relation to, for example, family background and socioeconomic status.

　　Teachers select the information to be taught from a wide variety of sources. We are all aware, from our own school experience, how teachers make use of textbooks in their classes, an example being Extract 104:

(104) Anyway, today we're going to be working on chapter 11, Measurement. Can you turn to page 151, please?
(Authors' data)

However, teachers must in many cases refer to other sources as well while preparing. In this case, dealing with a topic that is relatively simple for a teacher who has a degree in mathematics, the teacher did not need to refer to other sources. But for more complex topics, such as those on the SAT mathematics subject test or the entrance examinations for specific universities, a teacher might have to consult not only other texts but also other teachers who have taught these topics. Then also, there is the question of the sources of the methods a teacher uses in the classroom. Some of these may have been learned in graduate school, others picked up at conferences, yet others from the head of department at the school, and so on. Thus it is that teachers who stand up in the classroom and "teach" the lesson they have prepared are the producers of the lesson, but there are other sources (e.g., heads of department, other members of the department, school principals, inspectors, textbook writers) and other important people (e.g., audiovisual technicians who might help in the use of audiovisual aids) behind the scenes who play greater or smaller roles in this preparation. These contributors may or may not be directly referred to in the classroom, but nonetheless, teaching is not something teachers do alone with students, which traditionally is how many teachers have perceived their work (Heckman, 1987, p. 66).

Students are the interpreters of educational discourse. Heckman (1987, p. 65) pointed out that many teachers still perceive students to be passive recipients of the knowledge teachers impart. Fortunately, he went on to report on longitudinal research in a school system where there was a major shift in perception of students' role, from that of mere spectator to that of participant: "Today . . . [the teacher] often uses cooperative learning strategies that reflect her changed perspective. Some students teach other students; others ask for help from peers. The teacher clarifies and supports group activities. The student has become a worker, not merely a passive listener" (Heckman, 1987, pp. 66–67). This is the situation depicted in Fig. 3.1. There are, however, many classrooms in the world where the students continue to be mere spectators. For cultural and other reasons, many countries still prefer rote-learning methods of teaching, which require the students merely to memorize and regurgitate, and thus preserve the power relation between teacher and learner in an authoritarian rather than an authoritative way (cf. Stevick, 1974).

Producer–Interpreter Relationships

It is useful to consider the metaphors that have been used to describe people's perceptions of the teaching–learning process and the role of teacher and student, because they elucidate their view of the power

FIG. 3.1. Stevick (1980) said that the learning process should be cooperative, like a teacher and student working together to fell a tree. Reprinted with permission.

relationship between the participants in the process. The most well-known metaphor of the child entering the school is the behaviorist tabula rasa, or blank slate. In this metaphor, clearly the teacher is all powerful, controlling the knowledge that is to be "written on" the slate. A similar metaphor describes the teacher as "shaping, forming, or molding" the child, who is seen as clay in the hands of the teacher as potter (Scheffler, 1960, pp. 50–51). A simile for a different view of the process is Stevick's (1980) one of two people sawing down a tree as shown in Fig. 3.1. In this case, the teacher and student are seen as cooperating in the teaching–learning endeavor.

In the transcript, there is clear evidence that the teacher perceives the students as active participants in the construction of knowledge (cf. Griffin & Mehan, 1981, p. 213). First, she is sensitive to the fact that at times she may be at fault, even though she is careful to establish her authority with the class, as is evident in Extracts 101 and 102. Second, she makes extensive use of group work, in which students teach and/or help other students, and that she supports by being available to individual groups for clarification of certain points. This strategy parallels the cooperative learning strategies recommended by Heckman (1987). Third, she has not assumed that knowledge lies outside her students (Postman & Weingartner, 1971, p. 98), as is revealed by her elicitation of students' examples to illustrate the importance of accuracy in measurement:

> (105) T: So em can you think of a situation where someone you know, or maybe yourself you've measured inaccurately and this has mattered? . . . Can you think of something, Caroline?
> C: Well, em, . . . at my old school we were trying to make these like em chocolate like sort of frying things [and
> T: [Yes
> C: we did it, we measured it all out and we did it and it didn't look much so we did it again but we forgot to put em some extra sugar in
> T: [(*laughs*)
> C: [and then we were trying to get it to look right but it all looked pretty odd and we had to throw it all away.
> T: Well that's a good example. We'll just, we'll just have three more, then, 'cause I can see three hands. . . .
> (Authors' data)

The fact that a number of students described instances illustrating the importance of accuracy suggests that the teacher is aware of the need for the students to absorb the meaning of the topic for themselves, individually, because they come to class with different degrees of background knowledge. Fourth, in order to achieve as much congruence as possible between her "producer's text" and the students' "interpreters' texts," she is careful to monitor her communication of the content and her students' understanding of it. This is shown, for example, in the following, in which she paraphrases a question the students do not immediately understand:

> (106) Why do you think you're not accurate? (5 seconds) What, what bits of your instruments aren't accurate?
> (Authors' data)

Clearly, the teacher is not just a "teacher" but a "facilitator" of the students' learning. She is helping the students find out their own meanings.

Setting

Classrooms are probably universally recognizable from their layout, although there are two fundamentally different layouts possible, paralleling the teacher–student power relationship already discussed. The layout may reinforce the teacher as totally in charge, as in the traditional concept of a classroom with teachers at the front, possibly with their desk on a dais, the blackboard on the front wall, and the students in neat rows, with enough space for teachers to walk between the desks. This is the classroom layout shown in Fig. 3.2. Alternatively, the layout may reveal the teacher as a facilitator, with a more flexible "open classroom" feel, where students sit round tables, and the teacher may walk from table to table, only calling students' attention to the blackboard at the "front" of the classroom when need arises. Interestingly, a study by C. Mitchell (1995) of beginning teachers' perceptions of a typical classroom as revealed in their drawings of teachers found that most of the drawings depicted the first layout.

In this case, the teacher had to work within the confines of desks and chairs arranged in the traditional manner, which were not that easy to

FIG. 3.2. The traditional classroom arrangement, such as this one in southern Africa, is familiar to most of us.

rearrange for group work, but she nonetheless organized group work, because of her philosophy of teaching as facilitating learning.

Just as space may be organized in two very different ways, so too may time. Traditionally, particularly at the secondary level, the school day is divided up into "subject" slots, with each subject being allocated so many periods per week of a specified length of time, such as six 40-minute periods of mathematics per week. The other way is to organize time around themes, although this method of time allocation is more often implemented at elementary level, if at all. It allows teachers the flexibility of looking at a theme from all the different subject perspectives (e.g., the history, geography, music, art, science, religion, and mathematics of the Romans), without the constraint of the bell telling the students they must arbitrarily move from one subject to another.

The traditional timetable followed by the school at which the transcript was recorded constrained the teacher to teach for one 40-minute period of mathematics on a Monday afternoon. Even though she was covering a topic, measurement, which in a thematic approach would have allowed consideration of a historical perspective and possibly an examination of old measuring instruments, the constraints of the timetable made this flexibility even less possible than the spatial flexibility she achieved for group work.

Channel

The channel used in classrooms varies somewhat from teacher to teacher, from subject to subject, and from level to level. The variation from teacher to teacher depends on any particular teacher's use of a combination of oral + nonverbal + written materials in any particular class. The variation from subject to subject may be much greater. Take, for example, the differences between a science lesson and a lesson in a second language. The science lesson may allow the students the opportunity to learn by doing an experiment, where instructions may be spoken or written but otherwise language may well not be a major factor. By contrast, the channels of the second language lesson may well be almost exclusively linguistic, whether spoken or written, with far fewer uses of pictures and realia. Then there is a third source of variation: the level of the students (i.e., whether they are at a beginning, intermediate, or advanced level in a particular topic). For most subjects there is much less use of the written word at lower levels. The higher the level, the more likely the student is to be able to work independently with the written word rather than depending on the teacher.

Obviously, in schools for the deaf, sign language is the main channel of teaching and learning, along with use of the written word. However, lip-reading is still taught, and some schools for the deaf also attempt to teach their students how to speak through feeling the voice box. Some students are able subsequently to function in the hearing world. Blind students will have no problems with oral communication in the classroom, but have to use Braille (i.e., touch) for reading and writing, rather than sight.

In the transcript, the teacher uses predominantly oral communication and accompanying prosody and nonverbal language. The prosody and nonverbal language is discussed in greater detail in the next section, but notice the uppercase letters in Extract 98, signaling stress on certain words for emphasis. As happens in the majority of classes around the world, the teacher speaks around 70% of the time, giving the students about 30% of the time for responding and for group work discussion (cf. Bellack, Bliebard, Hyman, & Smith, 1966, p. 41).

However, the teacher also makes use of the textbook. She does so in Extract 104 and it can be seen even more clearly here, where she is actually reading sentences from the textbook:

(107) T: ... Em so em there's a little statement here: "No measurement is exact." Do you agree with that?

Ss: [Yes.

Ss: [No.

T: Well, it's something to think about. Now, just underneath those pictures, "A student estimated the length of a corridor to be 20 meters." Now he ESTIMATED it. Now how do you think he might have done that? Abigail.

S 1:   Because of lockers and they're the same size, you just measure one of them and count how many are there.

T: He could have done that, couldn't he? He could have measured one of the lockers. Nazila, how might he have measured one of the lockers?

S 2:   The em use a er em er ...

T: Well, what have you got in your hand there?

S 2:   Ruler.

T: Could have used a ruler, couldn't he? Okay, em Lydia.

S 3:   He could estimate like em his stride's about a meter and walk.

T: That's a good idea. He could estimate that his stride is about a meter and then pace, pace it out, couldn't he? (5 seconds) Any other ways? (10 seconds) Anyway those are two good ways. Now "When the student MEASURED [teacher emphasis] the length of

this corridor he got an answer which was quite different from his
estimate." Now "What might have gone wrong?" Em, Loretta.
S 4:   It's not a great idea, but the lockers might have been of a slightly
       different size.
T: That would be a good idea, yes ...
(Authors' data)

She also refers to the graphics and assigns a group work task in the
textbook.

Participant–Text Relations

The previous discussion of the sources of information teachers may
refer to in their preparation of lessons hinted at the complex intertext
surrounding any one lesson. There are several references in the lesson
being analyzed that place it in a series. Extract 98 refers to tests given
the previous day, which the teacher has now marked. The teacher
explains that she had planned to go over the test, but because one
student had not yet written it, she had to postpone that activity to
the next day. There is the further point that she is, in the transcript,
teaching Set One, the group of more advanced students. This suggests
she also teaches other Sets, or someone else does. These other Sets
will presumably have to cover the same content either in the same
week or at some date in the near future.

In Extract 100, the teacher asks students about their answers to a
task undertaken during class time the previous day. Part of the
intertext is the students' findings on the task. Another aspect of
intertext is indicated by the teacher calling on the students to explain
why their findings are different and/or inaccurate. To answer this
question, the students have to refer back to something the teacher
may have told them with reference to a completely different topic:
"What sort of pencil did I say to use?" In this case, however, the
reference is still to a previous school experience. Extract 105, on the
other hand, shows how teachers can call on students to analyze past
experiences outside school in a way that has a bearing on a current
topic in school. This is particularly interesting because the teacher
could not know beforehand what experiences her students had that
might be relevant. In other words, in this case, the students' and
teacher's intertexts are completely different.

Extract 99 makes a reference to the students' previous teacher, Mrs. B. In addition, the current teacher's expectations are based not only on Mrs. B's assessment but also on her own experiences with previous Year 8 classes, whether at this school or elsewhere. Her expectations may even be partly based on vague memories of her own experiences as a mathematics student in secondary school.

Extracts 104 and 107 show how teachers make use of published materials in the classroom. In this case, the teacher actually refers to the students' textbook, and every student has a copy. But during preparation for lessons, teachers often refer to other textbooks dealing with the same topic, texts that may or may not be available to the students. If these other sources are either simpler or more difficult, teachers might have to adapt them for use in a particular lesson at a particular level.

All these examples serve to show that, in what Schegloff (1972, p. 76) called "conditional relevance": "The meaning of an utterance arises partly from something else which has been (or will be) said, perhaps some distance away in the interaction, in relation to which it is understood" (Edwards & Furlong, 1978, p. 41).

Purpose and Intent

In traditional educational jargon, the intent of any lesson is the objectives the teacher sets out to achieve through careful selection of tasks. The purpose is the students' perception of these objectives. The intent of the mathematics lesson under examination is to instruct the pupils in how to measure accurately and to help them to understand the importance of accuracy in measurement.

Most lessons will be based more on fact, although creative writing lessons may be based more on imagination. Creative teachers will attempt to strike a balance between fact and imagination. In language lessons, particularly lessons in listening or reading comprehension, such teachers may call on the students to predict the content of the passage on the basis of the title prior to actually working on the passage. In science lessons, they might encourage their students to speculate, even though they base their tasks on fact. In the transcript, the basis in the facts of measurement can be observed, including specific measuring tasks and the instruments for measuring. On the other hand, the teacher also encourages the students to relate the facts to their imagination, which may or may not be based on previous experience. In Extract 105, imagination is based on previous experience, and in the following example, which follows the same question that begins Extract 105, the student is speculating:

> (108) Well if a buil ... (2 seconds) er em er an architect was building a bridge and he g ... (1 second) em got the measurement wrong, then it wouldn't work.
> (Authors' data)

Classroom lessons clearly constitute one genre of educational discourse. Bellack et al. (1966) identified four specific moves—structure, solicit, respond, react—which teachers basically follow recursively throughout their lessons. Extract 109, which extends Extract 104, gives a typical example of the sequence of moves:

> (109) T: Anyway, today we're going to be working on chapter 11, Measurement. Can you turn to page 151, please?
> Ss: (Noise as students open books. Whispering)
> T: Okay ... Now ...
> (Authors' data)

The teacher starts with a structuring move: She states what is going to happen during the lesson. She then immediately follows it up with a soliciting move: She sets a task, which is again typical. The students respond by noisily opening their books, and some of them whisper to each other, possibly repeating the page number. Responses may be both verbal and nonverbal, in this case the appropriate response being nonverbal. Finally, the teacher reacts with a curt "Okay," to bring the students back to the task at hand.

Structuring moves typically mark topic shifts, so normally there is only one structuring move at the beginning of a sequence in which other moves may recur. The moves that tend to occur recursively are the soliciting, responding, and reacting moves. Extract 100 shows this recursive pattern of "teacher solicits, student responds, teacher reacts," which is so typical of classroom discourse. Part of that extract is repeated in table format, adding the initial structuring move:

> (110) T: So, em, looking at page 150, we were first of all   structure
> doing that exercise about em drawing that square
> and measuring the diagonals.
> T: Did any of you get different answers to each   solicit1
> other yesterday? Rebecca.

S 1:	Em I em mine was one millimeter longer than the other.	respond1
T:	So one was one millimeter longer than the other.	react1
T:	What about you, Louise?	solicit2
S 2:	Well I got 14.1 and Lydia got 14 centimeters.	respond2
T:	So some of you were a little bit out.	react2

In this case, the structuring move states what happened yesterday, rather than what is going to happen today. The soliciting move, rather than telling the students to do something, asks a question. The responding move is verbal this time. The reacting move, as frequently happens in classrooms, repeats the student's response in the first cycle, and paraphrases in the second cycle.

In passing, it is worth noting that Fanselow (1987) demonstrated how the same moves are observable in other situations not normally considered to be teaching situations but having an element of instruction in them. For example, on flights it is common for the pilot to report to the passengers that the plane will be landing in a few minutes, and the flight attendants follow this structuring move with a solicit to fasten seatbelts and put seats in the upright position. The passengers respond by doing as asked, and the flight attendants react by moving quickly through the cabin to check on everything.

Topic

The topic of any lesson is almost always specified by the teacher close to the beginning of the lesson. Although a lesson topic may not be specialized in the academic sense at elementary or secondary level, at the same time, it cannot be considered to be general or popular. It is specialized in the sense that it is intended for a specific audience at a specific point in their education.

In educational discourse, there is an interesting problem in considering the question of new versus old information. A common piece of advice given to new teachers is to move from the known to the unknown (i.e., from old to new information), but in classrooms all over the world, teachers commonly do not move from the known to the unknown. They themselves are expected to know all the information about the topic, at least for the level at which they are teaching. It is only the students who have to move from the known to the unknown.

In order to help their students move from the known to the unknown, teachers will often plan their lessons to follow one of the principles of normal ordering, general → particular, whole → part/component, set → subset → element. However, some topics may require the reverse order, to allow teachers to build up the information for their students in manageable units, so that the general, the whole, or the set comes in a revision lesson after a series of lessons covering the particular, part/component, or subset/elements. A certain amount of controversy has been generated in language teaching, for example, about whether it is better to teach students chunks of language that they analyze into their parts, as is supposed to happen in communicative language teaching, or to teach the students small components one at a time and expect them to synthesize these components together into the whole after a series of lessons, as in the Audio-Lingual Method (see, e.g., Wilkins, 1976).

In the transcript, it is clear that the lesson is one of a series on the topic of measurement. The lesson starts with a quick review of the previous day's task, for which the students had drawn squares and then measured their diagonals. This review allows the teacher to move on to the focus of this lesson, accuracy in measurement, by asking about differences in the students' measurements. A lengthy exchange on the reasons for inaccuracy in measuring follows, culminating in the teacher reading from the textbook:

> (111) T: Em so em there's a little statement here: "No measurement is exact." Do you agree with that?
> Ss: [Yes.
> Ss: [No.
> T: Well, it's something to think about.
> (Authors' data)

This exchange comes at the end of one subtopic, with the last statement by the teacher being marked by a drop in pitch and a pause. It is followed by a topic shift—marked by a structuring move—to a discussion of estimating rather than using accurate instruments for measuring. After discussing how to estimate distances, the teacher and students exchange experiences with inaccurate estimates leading to various degrees of disaster. The teacher ends this subtopic with a summary statement—another structuring move—prior to setting a follow-up task that the students work on in groups:

Practice 55:
If possible, obtain two transcripts of the same topic being taught by two different teachers in two different classes, and analyze carefully all the different features of context that make the two lessons similar and/or different. You might want to consider finding one male and one female teacher teaching in the same school, or two teachers of the same sex, one teaching in a boys' school and the other in a girls' school.

---

(112) So anyway, the accuracy in our measurements must be important if we're cooking or if we're building em and in other situations as well. And there'll be other examples later on in the book. Now can you see at the top of page 51 [sic], Okay, there's another little pink bit to write in your notebooks. So can you put the title in your notebooks "Measurement Activity"?
(Authors' data)

The next step is to discuss the different tools for measuring really accurately, after which the teacher sets another discussion task on "the effect of measurement errors." She finally sets a revision assignment for homework.

Experienced teachers typically prepare lessons similarly focused on a topic, with shifts in subtopics being highlighted by structuring moves. As pointed out in the next section, the coherence of such lessons is reinforced by the linguistic features of educational discourse. Of particular interest in the analysis of the language of education is the variety of meanings teacher and students together make of their lessons.

THE LANGUAGE OF EDUCATION

Much research has focused on the language of the classroom—from Bellack et al. (1966), Cazden, John, and Hymes (1972), and Fanselow (1987) in the United States to Barnes et al. (1971), Sinclair and Coulthard (1975), Stubbs (1976), and Edwards and Furlong (1978) in Great Britain. A great deal of progress has been made in describing the language. For example, it is now recognized that in the traditional classroom, as already mentioned, teachers generally talk about 70% of the time. Also, the structure of classroom discourse has been described, showing the nature of turn-taking in that context to be very different from that of ordinary conversation (Edwards & Furlong, 1978, p. 13).

Classroom discourse research has often, in establishing categories for describing communication, paid little attention to the fact that "making sense of what is said depends on locating language in the contexts in which it is used" (Edwards & Furlong, 1978, p. 62). Fanselow (1987), however, showed how his descriptive observation tool, Foci for Observing Communications Used in Settings (FOCUS), may be applied not only to the classroom but also in other settings as a way of enabling the teacher to generate alternatives, and if necessary "break rules" in the classroom by comparison with these other settings. Particularly useful in his categories is the elaboration of the mediums teachers use, and discussion of different combinations of medium with function and content. Few other researchers have specified categories for the coding and analysis of nonverbal language in classroom communication (e.g., Hills, 1979; Neill, 1991). Hopefully, this section will help to rectify the problem by considering the combined semantic, pragmatic, and nonverbal meanings the teacher and students make in collusion (cf. McDermott & Tylbor, 1986).

Reference and Coreference

A major way for teachers to use language to maintain authority is in the use of deixis, in particular, social deixis. Torode (1977) explored the differences between strong and weak teachers in their use of deictics, and showed that the former make extensive use of them to define their relationships with their students, whereas the latter fail to do so. The previous section already noted the use of the personal deictics to indicate the power relationship between teacher and students in the data. There is asymmetry not only in the use of the personal deictics but also the social deictics, such that whereas the teacher is always referred to by her title, "Mrs. W" (and likewise refers to the students' previous teacher with her title, "Mrs. B"; Extract 99), she consistently calls on the students using their first names, without a title (Extracts 98, 100, 103, and 104); she also, as is typical of teachers, uses the full name of a student as a reproof, in Extract 102 (cf. Edwards & Furlong, 1978, p. 25).

Apart from maintaining control, there is obviously a need for teachers to make clear to the students the semantic meanings of the referring expressions they are using, so that there can be no misunderstanding. There is the danger that "teachers tend to assume that *their* meanings are shared—that when they initiate interaction (as they usually do), pupils are seeing things in their terms, or are willing to learn how to do so" (Edwards & Furlong, 1978, p. 56). Weak teachers will be more likely to fail to take into account differences between their own and their students' universes of discourse.

Words and Lexical Units

As already mentioned, a clearer picture of the relationship between the teacher and the student, and their quest to match meanings, emerges from a study of the language of the classroom. Establishing a common universe of discourse is achieved by congruence between the students' meanings and the teacher's. Barnes (Barnes et al., 1971, p. 74) specifically asked, "Can specialist terminology hinder learning? . . . How do children learn new concepts, and what part can terminology play in this?" Extract 106 is an example of how the teacher paraphrased to clarify; and, in fact, one of the most important skills teachers need to develop is the ability to make available to their students the meanings they find difficult to grasp, most frequently by paraphrase.

In the sciences, terminology, at least at the elementary and secondary levels, will need to be defined in terms of conceptual rather than associative meaning; but, in the social studies and literature, associative meanings will be an important part of the promotion of learning. Here is an example of how teacher and students can together work toward common associative meanings:

(113) TEACHER: We have spent a few sessions exploring the shifting meanings of the word "right" in the sentences, 1. It is right for a man to give a woman his seat. 2. It is right for children to be vaccinated. 3. It is right for citizens to vote. Now I have written a fourth sentence on the board, which I would like you to look at: "It is right to say 'he doesn't' instead of 'he don't.'" And what we'll be exploring today is what the "right" means in that sentence. Now who will start us off? You might, if you like, compare its meaning there to its meaning in any of the other sentences.

MARCIA: I think that in that sentence saying "he doesn't" instead of "he don't" that "right" means "accepted." This is what educated people do, or people who have been brought up well.

I think that number 1 about the man giving up his seat is pretty much the same thing.

TEACHER: Are you saying that in Sentence 4 we are dealing with a question of etiquette just as we are in Sentence 1?

MARCIA: No, it's not exactly etiquette; it's more a reflection of your training and the way you've been brought up. If you've been brought up by hillbillies, you'd probably say "he don't," but if you've been brought up by parents who went to Oxford, you'd say "he doesn't."

TEACHER: Okay Dan?

DAN: I'd like to ask one question. She said, "If you've been well educated." Who decides who is well educated?

MARCIA: Who decides whether you are well educated? Okay. Well, let me give you a couple of examples! Would you say that someone who had a sixth-grade education was well educated?

DAN: I wouldn't know.

MARCIA: You wouldn't know?

DAN: It depends on the individual. A person who didn't even go to school but went around the world and just discovered things and read and everything might know more than a person who went to college all his life!

TEACHER: We may have here then right at the beginning a problem with another word. We started out exploring the word "right" and in just three or four minutes of conversation we've come across the word "educated." . . .

(Postman & Weingartner, 1971, pp. 75–76)

This extract contains examples of social meaning ("he doesn't" vs. "he don't"), affective meaning (the association of "he doesn't" with "educated"), collocative meaning (the collocation of "sixth-grade" with "well educated"), quite apart from the basic connotative meaning. Notice that the teacher also makes use of paraphrase, but in this case, unlike Extract 106, it is to clarify the meaning of the student's words rather than their own meaning. Incidentally, in this way the teacher maintains a different kind of control than that exhibited in the previous extracts.

Substitution and Ellipsis

A notable feature of educational discourse is the enormous amount of redundancy resulting from teachers repeating their own questions, the students answering these questions in full sentences without the normal substitution and ellipsis of everyday conversation, and teachers then repeating the students' answers, either exactly, or by para-phrasing, or correcting the students' mistakes.

This redundancy in the endless repetition of students' answers in a great many lessons led Gattegno to develop his Silent Way of teaching (1972). Language teachers in particular have been guilty of requiring their students to respond with full sentences, ignoring the normal communicative use of substitution and ellipsis to reply to questions. The following is a typical (constructed) example of such solicits and responses in the language class:

> (114) T: Repeat after me, "I am sitting by the window."
> S1: I am sitting by the window.
> T: S2, where are you sitting?
> S2: Where are you sitting?
> T: I am sitting by the window. Now ask S1.
> S2: Where are you sitting?
> S1: I am sitting by the window.

But even teachers of other subjects are guilty of violating the normal use of substitution and/or ellipsis in students' responses to questions, as can be seen in this example from the mathematics lesson:

> (115) S4: Em we have blunt pencils.
> T: You might have a blunt pencil. What sort of pencil did I say to use?
> S5: H.
> T: Judith.
> S6: 2H.
> T: 2H pencil, and a nice sharp 2H pencil as well.
> (Authors' data)

Notice how the teacher ignores the common practice of ellipsis by saying "You might have a blunt pencil," instead of "Yes, you might." And when Judith uses the normal elliptical form of response the teacher actually fills it out, although she does not make it into a full grammatical sentence in this case.

It is particularly interesting to compare segments of the lesson similar to Extract 115, where the teacher is strictly following the planned content for the lesson, with those segments of the lesson where the teacher is calling on students to narrate their experiences. In these segments, the teacher does not repeat the students' experiences but rather comments on them as they are being narrated, with

"Oh yeah," "Oh no!", and "Oh dear! Oh dear!" An example is Extract 105. Such exchanges are closer to normal conversation, with the occasional use of substitution and/or ellipsis.

Lesson textbooks, on the other hand, tend to use patterns of substitution and ellipsis that are more typical of informative texts generally and less like teacher–student discourse. In the textbook for the mathematics lesson, for example, there are several instances of ellipsis, such as the following. Example 116a gives the actual text version, whereas 116b shows the elliptical expressions filled out in square brackets:

> (116) (a) To build a house, what measurements are needed? How accurate
> do these have to be? Do some have to be more accurate than
> others?
>
> (b) To build a house, what measurements are needed? How accurate
> do these [measurements] have to be? Do some [measurements]
> have to be more accurate than other [measurements have to be]?
> (Vickers et al., 1993, p. 154)

Conjunction and Clause Relations

Marked conjunction is found infrequently in classroom discourse. When it is found, it is quite typical of conversational discourse, with the teacher asking the question and the student merely giving the answer immediately, without repeating the question in statement form. However, here again language teachers often deliberately distort the normal conversational pattern by requiring students to repeat the question in statement form before answering, in the misconception that such an abnormal pattern of discourse will help the students to master the grammar of the language. In the transcript, there are a few uses of marked conjunction across teacher–student moves, such as the following (emphasis added):

> (117) (a) T: Is that right, Ellen?
> S: Yeah, *but* I forgot to give it to Ranya.
> (b) T: Why do you think you got different answers, Catherine?
> S: *Because* some of us aren't exactly accurate.
> (Authors' data)

The most common conjunction is causal, usually represented as "because," possibly because in mathematics and science the focus is on scientific cause–effect relations.

In the course textbook for the mathematics lesson, marked conjunction is found only in the sections giving explanations, not in the exercises, which are numerous. Here are just two examples (emphasis added):

> (118) (a) All measurements are approximate. *For instance*, a length could be measured to the nearest mm or nearest cm or nearest m or nearest km. *Whether* we choose to give the length to the nearest mm or cm or m or km depends on how accurate we need the measure to be.
> (Vickers et al., 1993, p. 154)
>
> (b) The first of the modern day timing devices was the pendulum clock. This was invented in the 17th century. *Before this*, many other devices were used to measure time.
> (Vickers et al., 1993, p. 157)

Again, these patterns are typical of informative text.

It is not a problem for experienced teachers to maintain the cohesion of a lesson with a group of students from a similar ethnic and socioeconomic background, because they control the allocation of turns, allowing or disallowing students' contributions, usually by naming who is to speak. In Extract 100, for example, the teacher calls on six different students to respond to particular questions. Dispreferred sequences in the classroom include students calling out answers without raising their hands, and students answering "I don't know" to questions they should be able to answer. Also, generally dispreferred in the West is the student who chooses not to participate verbally in classroom exchanges. Most such students are assumed to be dull, but they may just be shy.

Linguistic Features

One of the genres that Biber (1988) described in his analysis of the linguistic features of genres is academic prose, a specific subgenre of educational discourse. As would be expected, Biber's analysis finds academic prose informational (Dimension 1), nonnarrative (Dimension 2), explicit (Dimension 3), and highly abstract (Dimension 5). Although some of the features associated with these dimensions may be observed in the lessons being analyzed, a distinction must be made between academic prose by intellectuals and the academic discourse of young students. For example, comments have been made on the way the teacher of the lesson involved the students in narrating their own experiences relevant to the topic of measurement, as in Extract 105. Even more significantly, whereas "narrative writing is not [normally] found in science textbooks," Martin (1993, pp. 197–198) noted that the New South Wales (Australia) *Writing K-12 Syllabus* recommends the use of narrative in writing science, both in the textbooks and in writing assignments given to students. Martin went on to give an example of textbook narrative, "Journey to the Brain," and two of writing assignments, one of which is "I am Joe's heart." Thus, secondary school classroom discourse is probably distinguishable from academic prose to a greater or lesser degree on at least three dimensions: the first, the second, and the fifth.

Then again, classroom discourse will reveal different features from textbook discourse. The register of the classroom is obviously that of teaching and learning, as it is in textbook discourse. Any child of schoolgoing age quickly learns the register of the classroom, and most are able to mimic teachers and students without any difficulty. The teacher for the most part uses standard formal communication with no colloquialisms, as does the textbook. On the other hand, parts of the lesson are less formal, such as when the teacher recounts an occasion in her life when inaccuracy in measuring led to a problem and the students then are likewise encouraged to recount their stories. Here is just one example of the teacher's:

> (119) I can remember a case I think where I was making chocolate cakes and I was doubling the ingredients to make sort of two chocolate cakes and I think I forgot to double the self-raising flour. Didn't work out very well.
> (Authors' data)

Notice the teacher's use of "sort of," and her omission of the subject in "Didn't work out very well," which are both typical of unscripted conversation. These colloquialisms contrast significantly with the scripted segments of the lesson, such as in Extract 107, where the teacher is reading from the textbook and commenting or asking planned questions. However, in neither case are the sentences excessively long or complex. This again distinguishes classroom and textbook discourse from higher level academic prose.

Inferencing, Implicature, and Presupposition

At least by the beginning of secondary education, if not before, teachers are able to use figures of speech and other forms of indirect and/or nonliteral communication with the knowledge that the students will understand. Students are less likely to use such forms as over-statement or sarcasm than teachers, for fear of the consequences. In Extract 98, the teacher's "Well, THAT is a LOT of use, isn't it?" is a typical example of sarcasm. The following extract shows the teacher's use of both overstatement and sarcasm:

> (120) So if you know if you've missed a lesson for any reason whatsoever, it is YOUR responsibility to catch up before the next lesson, unless you are DYING in the infirmary, or dying at home, in which case I suppose that I'll have to allow you to carry on dying, won't I? Okay. But if you're ill, then, of course you can't catch up before the next lesson. But if it's another reason, orthodontist, drama lessons, music lessons, you catch up. Right.
> (Authors' data)

In this case, the teacher softens the overstatement and sarcasm by her subsequent literal communication, which can be taken as a form of hedging. Thus, she makes the students aware of how much of her utterance may be taken as direct and how much may be taken as indirect. This constitutes one of the ways in which the teacher observes the Politeness Principle, giving the students an escape route. But the students also use a hedging strategy to save face for them-selves, as is shown by S4's contribution in Extract 107.

There are many other examples of politeness in the lesson being used to avoid presenting the interpreter, whether teacher or student, with a face threatening act. These include frequent use of "please" to soften a command, "sorry" (from both teacher and students) to apologize, and modal verbs and adverbs (particularly "might" and "maybe") as hedges. Examples can be seen in the various extracts.

Obviously, textbooks do not exhibit the same degree of repetition and redundancy as normal classroom discourse, but there is a form of redundancy in the classroom that could be said to flout the maxim of quantity. This redundancy occurs when the teacher reads out loud what is written in the text, yet the students, at least by the upper elementary level, should be quite capable of reading it silently. In the data, the teacher does this in only a short segment of the lesson, with each extract she reads out from the text, shown in italics, being interspersed with discussion. Extract 107 was used in the subsection on channel, but it is repeated here for reexamination:

(107) T: ... Em so em there's a little statement here: "*No measurement is exact.*" Do you agree with that?

Ss: [Yes.

Ss: [No.

T: Well, it's something to think about. Now, just underneath those pictures, "*A student estimated the length of a corridor to be 20 meters.*" Now he ESTIMATED it. Now how do you think he might have done that? Abigail.

S 1: Because of lockers and they're the same size, you just measure one of them and count how many are there.

T: He could have done that, couldn't he? He could have measured one of the lockers. Nazila, how might he have measured one of the lockers?

S 2: The em use a er em er ...

T: Well, what have you got in your hand there?

S 2: Ruler.

T: Could have used a ruler, couldn't he? Okay, em Lydia.

S 3: He could estimate like em his stride's about a meter and walk.

T: That's a good idea. He could estimate that his stride is about 'a meter and then pace, pace it out, couldn't he? (5 seconds) Any other ways? (10 seconds) Anyway those are two good ways. Now "*When the student MEASURED* [teacher emphasis] *the length of this corridor he got an answer which was quite different from his estimate.*" Now "*What might have gone wrong?*" Em, Loretta.

S 4: It's not a great idea, but the lockers might have been of a slightly different size.

T: That would be a good idea, yes ...

(Authors' data)

But it is not unknown for teachers to spend a great deal of time reading out loud from texts that the students have immediate access to, and could read much more quickly on their own. Such levels of redundancy are probably acceptable, however, in the context of the classroom.

Another way in which teachers consistently flout the Cooperative Principle is to ask questions to which they already know the answers, as seen in several of the previous extracts.

Students generally learn quickly what the teacher considers "relevant" as an answer. But research by Philips (1972) and, more recently, Michaels and Collins (1984) has shown the differences between white and nonwhite children's approaches to communication in the classroom. The latter researchers refer specifically to the difficulties that the Black children in their study had in adopting a non-face-to-face approach in their contributions to "sharing time." The teacher clearly had an underlying schema, shown by her questions and comments, which required a decontextualized account focusing on a single topic. Although the white children used a topic-centered style in their "sharing time" contributions, which the teacher therefore perceived as cohesive, coherent, and relevant, the Black children used a topic-associating style, which gave the teacher enormous problems perceiving the overall cohesion, coherence, and relevance of their contributions.

Nonverbal Meaning

Turning finally to the role of nonverbal language in the classroom, there are some fascinating insights that have been gained by researchers who look beyond the surface communications. P. Byers and H. Byers (1972, pp. 21–25) commented on nonverbal behaviors they observed in a film of a teacher and four children in her nursery school class, with particularly interesting observations on gaze behavior and physical contact. The discussion of gaze behavior is revealing: "Both the black girl and the [white] teacher look toward each other often (more often, in fact, than the white girl and the teacher) but rarely achieve eye contact and the exchange of expressions that would follow. Although this behavior may be summed up by a casual observer as 'the black child gets less attention,' it is more useful to see that there is a mismatching or difference in communication systems."

Michaels and Collins (1984), whose study of "sharing time" was mentioned in connection with coherence and relevance, likewise found a mismatch of communication systems. The white children's use of sustained rising tones to establish the scene, changing tones to elaborate on the topic, and low falling tones to close matched the teacher's own discourse styles. On the other hand, Black children's use of rhythm and high holding pitches to organize their information thematically gave the uninitiated the impression of having no beginning, middle, or end. In other words, Michaels and Collins found that Blacks tend to use prosodic signals where whites would use structure or lexis to maintain discourse cohesion.

McDermott and Tylbor (1986) found a contradiction between the verbal and nonverbal behaviors of one child, Rosa, in their study of a first-grade reading lesson. They described the situation as follows:

> Rosa constantly calls for a turn to read by shouting "I could" or "I could do it." . . . [But] upon careful examination, it seems that Rosa is doing much work to arrange *not getting a turn*: everyone is on page 5, Rosa on page 7 (as everyone can tell with a first grade illustrated reader); as the teacher begins to call on another child, Rosa calls for a turn, just a fraction of a second behind; as the other children move up from their books to face the teacher and to call for a new turn, Rosa lowers her head into the book with her face turning away from the teacher. The ploys are numerous in kind and fast in occurrence. (McDermott & Tylbor, 1986, pp. 128–129)

In this case, it appears that the teacher and the other students are aware of Rosa's avoidance strategies, although in a larger class it might not be possible for the teacher to become aware of such ploys.

Love and Roderick (1971, quoted in Hills, 1979, pp. 39–40) developed a tool for recording the nonverbal behaviors of teachers in 10 categories, including the following:

1. Accepts student behavior
   Smiles, affirmatively shakes head, pats on the back, winks, places hand on shoulder or head.
2. Praises student behavior
   Places index finger and thumb together, claps, raises eyebrows and smiles, nods head affirmatively and smiles. . . .
4. Shows interest in student behavior
   Establishes and maintains eye contact. . . .
7. Shows authority toward students
   Frowns, stares, raises eyebrows, taps foot, rolls book on the desk, negatively shakes head, walks or looks away from the deviant, snaps fingers. . . .

In the data, the teacher used quite a lot of contrastive stress, indicated by capitals in the extracts, but also had interesting intonation patterns. In Extract 99, for example, Sentences 2, 3, 4, 6, and 7 were ended by an exaggerated rising tone, whereas Sentences 5 and 8 were ended by an exaggerated falling tone. The use of the rising tone clearly indicates that the teacher has not finished detailing the problems, marking an

> **Practice 56:**
> Select a segment of your lesson and analyze all the linguistic, paralinguistic, and nonlinguistic features of the teacher's communications as compared with those of the students. Consider, in particular, the use the teacher makes of parallel oral and written language, for example, by reading aloud from the textbook, or by paraphrasing orally other written sources.

additive conjunctive strategy, and the falling tone marks the end of a particular additive set. During the discussion of different personal experiences of inaccuracy in measuring, both the teacher and the students laugh at certain points, and the teacher also expresses sympathy to some students over the consequences of the mistakes they made. It seems that the teacher and students share an understanding of the meanings of their nonverbal behaviors.

Nonverbal features are also expected in educational texts. In the data, the textbook makes extensive use of diagrams, pictures, and photographs to accompany the words of the text, in some cases to illustrate, in others to provide tasks. In fact, on only one page out of the eight there is no illustration at all, and on every other page there are several.

This examination of nonverbal meaning in the classroom ends a brief survey of the most significant features of the genre and register of educational discourse. But consider briefly some pertinent questions about the future of formal education.

CONCLUSION: SOME REMAINING QUESTIONS

This brief examination of educational discourse has done little more than hint at questions about the future of formal education. Of particular interest is whether teachers generally will come to accept the role of colluding with their students in the making of meanings. Given that schools have a strong inclination to preserve the status quo in the societies in which they operate, there could be widespread opposition to the general adoption of such a perspective.

If students are more frequently perceived to be makers of their own meanings, then to what extent will this empower them to change the content of the curricula, syllabi, and texts? Such a question has enormous implications for a major upheaval in any society that makes a move in this direction. What happens to all the "expert" curriculum, syllabus, and textbook writers in such a situation? And what happens to all the educational publishers, who would have to either seek to employ students to write the educational texts or go out of business? What major changes in perspective will be demanded of teachers, and, working backward, of schools of education and the professors who lecture therein?

Of more immediate relevance, in a text on discourse analysis, is the question of how such a shift in perspective will change classroom discourse. The transcript enumerated instances revealing the teacher's perception of students as participants in the teaching–learning endeavor, but there were still instances when she asserted her authority. This authoritative (but not authoritarian) role may have to be maintained simply so that the teacher can guide the discussion, acting somewhat as the chairperson of a meeting, calling on individual students so that they each get an opportunity to contribute, but otherwise doing little more than setting the initial task. The discourse in such a situation will be, if it is not already, much more collaborative, showing many more of the features of ordinary conversation than the familiar classroom discourse.

A third question concerns the extent to which educational media will impact the discourse of the classroom in the future. At the moment, distance learning and formal school-based education rarely meet. What could each learn from the other about the meaning-making capacities of their respective students? And what role could such technological innovations as e-mail and interactive computers play in both distance learning and formal school-based education, possibly narrowing the gap between them? Finally, what impact would each technological innovation have on features of the discourse produced in each educational setting?

Already in the late 1960s and early 1970s, researchers were aware of major problems in the Western classroom. Most significant are those researchers who saw, in classroom discourse, "the inseparability of what is said, and how it is said, from the social relationships in which the speech is embedded" (Edwards & Furlong, 1978, p. 24). Hopefully, the teachers of the future will pay increasing attention to their students as makers of their own meanings. The greatest irony is that in some sense teaching is going "back to the future." After all, it is not dissimilar to the way in which Socrates taught in Ancient Greece: "His aim was to guide students through various processes of thought to an awareness of truth discovered by themselves" (Hills, 1979, p. 10).

4

THE DISCOURSE OF MEDICINE

There are many lessons that the discourse analyst can abstract from the study of a wide variety of types of medical encounter, from diagnosis and prescription to counseling, which would be of benefit to those training to become medical professionals. According to Mishler (1984, p. 11), "Since the discovered illness is . . . partly a function of the talk between a patient and a physician, the study of this talk is central to our understanding." Of particular importance, with the advent of the AIDS epidemic, is a balance between the clinical, problem-oriented approach adopted by most doctors, and needed in the treatment of specific, identifiable medical problems, and the relationship-centered approach preferred by counselors, and needed in helping patients come to terms psychologically with their condition (cf. Robinson, 1982, p. 24). There is likely to be a greater shift toward the latter, an approach that was hitherto largely limited to psychiatry and clinical psychology, and generally unusual in other types of medical discourse. Issues of learning to live positively with an incurable and probably fatal illness, as well as facing up to an early and harrowing death, confronted many fewer people in the past. Furthermore, though some could trace their problem to a specific behavior, such as smoking in the case of lung cancer, many could be seen as innocent victims of circumstances beyond their control. Now, faced with AIDS, many more medical professionals have to deal with their own feelings about and attitudes to certain sexual behaviors, rather than simply avoid them: "AIDS, more than any other illness, challenges our most basic beliefs about health, infection,

Practice 57:
Record, on audio- or, if possible, videocassette, one medical interview on a case that interests you, using a consent form similar to the one here. If you cannot find anyone willing to serve as a subject, then the next time you go to see the doctor for a not-too-serious reason ask to record the interview.

Transcribe a 10-minute segment of the interview, giving as much detail as possible of use of gestures and facial expressions, and noting prosody and body language. Also ask the patient and the doctor for permission to read the medical file. Use these materials to compare with the medical interview data to be discussed.

The University of _____

Consent to Act as Human Subject

Subject's name: _____

Date: _____

This study examines, for research and educational purposes, how doctors or counselors and patients communicate.

I. I hereby authorize (*YOUR NAME*) to gather information in the following ways:
    (a) to audiotape, videotape, and observe interactions between me and my doctor or counselor;
    (b) to review my medical records;
    (c) to conduct interviews with my attending doctor and/or counselor.
II. I hereby authorize (*YOUR NAME*) to use these tapes and this information to teach student doctors and counselors about communication skills.
III. I understand that the information-gathering techniques described in Paragraphs I and II hold the potential to enhance doctors' or counselors' and patients' abilities to communicate with each other.
IV. I understand that my confidentiality will be protected by removing my name and all other personally identifying information from all teaching and research materials obtained by audiotaping, videotaping, and observing the interactions between me and my doctor and/or counselor.
V. I understand that (*YOUR NAME*) will answer any inquiries I may have at any time concerning the information-gathering techniques.
VI. I understand that my participation in the study is voluntary and that I may terminate it at any time with no risk to my doctor/counselor–patient relationship or to the quality of care I am receiving.

Subject's Signature: _____

Witness: _____

(Adapted from Burgess, 1986, p. 77. Reprinted with permission.)

death and dying; dependency, disability and disfigurement; sexual behaviour and orientation" (George, 1989, p. 69). AIDS is also challenging the medical profession to take on new roles as "social, cultural, and linguistic translators, [which roles] are vital to ensure accurate and motivational communication" (Gayle, 1989, p. 249).

Another major concern of those studying different types of medical discourse has been the power relationships obtaining between doctor (or counselor) and patient (e.g., Treichler, Frankel, Kramarae, Zoppi, & Beckman, 1984). However, Fisher and Todd (1986, p. 6) pointed out that the focus of much of the earlier research (up to the mid-1980s) was on the "politics of health care for women," rather than on "the actual discourse which expresses and maintains the doctor's authority." Since then, a great deal of the research has examined the discourse itself to identify "to what extent micro-level encounters between individuals reproduce macro-level structures of oppression" (Borges, 1986, p. 29).

This chapter reexamines previously published interview extracts from the different perspectives of the framework for discourse analysis, analyzing the contextual and language features of a variety of types of medical discourse. These reflect in differing degrees features of diagnostic and counseling discourses. The few studies specifically reporting on HIV/AIDS diagnosis and counseling provide an indication of possible future directions in research on medical discourse.

THE CONTEXT OF MEDICINE

Context is crucial in understanding the provision of medical care because two parallel strands of medicine operate simultaneously. In the first world, homeopaths and chiropractors work alongside formal medical professionals. Furthermore, even in the formal sector, counselors learn to communicate rather differently than doctors with their clients. Then, traditional healers in many developing countries are authorized to practice alongside the recently introduced Western-trained doctors working in newly built hospitals (Swantz, 1990, p. 12). Roscoe's (1980, p. 10) analysis may be too dichotomized, but it serves to highlight the fundamental difference in perspective: "There is the modern doctor on the one hand and the traditional healer on the other; the former knowing the disease but tending not to know the patient, the latter knowing his patient but not the disease. One deals in fine microscopic accuracy, the other in broad humane approximations. One is locked into a sharply defined world of science, the other manipulates metaphysics as well as the earthy vegetable world of nature." The two strands reveal differences in people's perceptions of the causes of disease, their perception of their place in the world in terms of their power as patients vis-à-vis doctors, and their interest in developing themselves as shown by their willingness and/or ability to take preventive measures to preserve their health and/or prolong their life, rather than waiting for illness that prompts them to seek a cure. The focus of this chapter is on these factors in the formal context of medical provision in the Western world.

Culture

Culturally, "[Western] medicine has become an institution of social control and . . . the health-care system helps promulgate the dominant ideologies of society" (Waitzkin, 1983, p. 138). Even in traditional societies, the health care system has probably served the function of social control. For example,

> the profession of *uganga* [traditional medicine] is a long-established and respected one in African traditional society. The *mganga* [singular, medicine man] is looked upon with respect, if not with a little awe and wonder, because of his ability to divine and to know the secret things in life. He is considered a strong and powerful man of the spirit, for his ability rests not only in his medicine but in his *baraka*, a word which means blessing but is often used in this sense as the *mganga's* gift of inner powers. (Swantz, 1990, p. 24)

This attempt to promulgate the dominant ideologies of society can be seen in the Western context, for example, in the negotiation of decisions to use oral contraceptives:

(121) Doctor: Well, are you having any other problems or things we need to direct our attention to today?

       Patient: Okay, there is another thing that has been weird. I don't know what's causing it. I've been getting these cramps in my legs. Once in a blue moon I'll get em, just out of the clear blue sky, and I always thought that on the pill there's a sort of relation, you need to know about that and smoking too, you know. But I was on the pill, I've only been on the pill for about five months.

... Now I am usually in perfect and never feel a cramp in my body whatsoever, but I was about 4 weeks ago, or something like that I was in N, and I got the strangest, it won't go away, it was all the way up along in here and in my leg and it lasted all day, hurt like anything. It wouldn't do like this. It felt really tight. I didn't know if it was my circulation or my muscle and then last week the same thing happened on this leg. But it wasn't near so bad. It didn't last as long and like I worry so I don't like, but that's all there was just that weird cramping sensation in my leg.

Doctor: I worry too, ah cramps, muscle cramps are a reason or a caution like in birth control pills. Uhm, it's, ah, one thing that makes doctors think that maybe it shouldn't be taking birth control pills.

Patient: Um hum, well that's why I'm here, to check into that.

Doctor: And the fact that you smoke and take birth control pills increases your risk of cardiovascular disease// (Patient: //Um hum, I know that.) about ten times and you're skirting several risk factors. ...

(Fisher & Todd, 1986, pp. 16–17)

Fisher and Todd (1986, p. 20) pointed out that, in this interview as in many others, the doctor seems to be blaming the patient rather than the pill. This parallels Aronsson and Rundstrom's comment, with reference to pediatric discourse, that "physical ailments are often interpreted in terms of moral judgments on life habits and so forth" (1989, p. 464). People with AIDS, more than in any other case, often hear such moral judgments and condemnation. The ideology held by the medical profession is theoretically one of service to society, and protection of individuals within the society, but, precisely because of this, in actual practice "its potential for exploitation is enormous" (Borges, 1986, p. 28).

The potential exploitation is seen in the patients' perception of their place in the world of sickness and the role of the doctor in that world. In Extract 121, the patient has come to the doctor, fairly soon after the onset of the symptoms, knowing they are something to be concerned about. The doctor sends her away with instructions to return if she does not stop taking the pill or stop smoking "within the next two periods" (Fisher & Todd, 1986, p. 18). However, he does not perceive part of his role as being to fully inform her of the seriousness of combining taking the pill with smoking. Heath (1992, pp. 241–242), however, claimed that patients more often than not do not seek opportunities to ask for more information on the nature and seriousness of their illnesses.[1] Nonetheless, the withholding of information is one of the ways in which the doctor reveals a patronizing attitude to patients, exploiting their ignorance. The provision of accurate information, and not withholding it, is one of the major areas that an AIDS counselor has to deal with, and as John Green (1989, p. 32) pointed out, "glossing over areas of difficulty in order to reassure patients and to avoid a long and technical discussion seldom works." He also gave an example of how he was able to give the requested information in one instance, without glossing over:

> (122) PAUL: Why is the HIV virus killed by washing-up liquid?
> COUNSELLOR: Well, the virus itself is wrapped in a sort of coat made of something called lipid. Really this is a very thin layer of fat. If this coat is damaged then the virus dies. Now, washing-up liquid breaks up fat. Do you ever roast a joint of meat?
> PAUL: Yes.
> COUNSELLOR: Then there's a lot of fat at the bottom of the tin?
> PAUL: Yes, sure.
> COUNSELLOR: And what do you do to clean it?
> PAUL: I put it in hot water with washing-up liquid and that takes the fat off.
> COUNSELLOR: That's right, and the same thing happens to the virus. You put it in washing-up liquid and the outside of the virus is broken up and it dies.
> (John Green, 1989, pp. 32–33)

A somewhat different problem is revealed in the exchanges of health visitors[2] making the first visit to first-time mothers (Heritage & Sefi, 1992). These mothers are very much aware that the health visitors are assessing their competence as mothers. This makes requesting and giving advice problematic. A mother's request for advice reveals her uncertainty or lack of knowledge about what to do in a

[1] The examples of discourse Heath included do not consistently provide contextual details such as age, sex, or ethnic background of the doctor and patient. This means that it is impossible to determine the extent to which the problem lies with the doctor, the patient, or contextual features that have a bearing on the power relationship between them.

[2] Heritage and Sefi (1992, p. 361) explained that health visitors are "fully trained nurses who work in association with general practitioners and community health centers. However, . . . [they] concentrate . . . on illness prevention, giving advice on health and social problems and case finding for other more specialized agencies."

given situation, and sets the health visitor up as the authority in any exchange. Many mothers resent the "surveillance and social control" implicit in the health visitors' visits and provision of unasked-for information. In this case, giving unasked-for information, rather than withholding information, can be seen as a kind of exploitation: It masks the "social control" function of health visitors.

Attitudes to territory are revealed in the common expectation that the patient will go to the doctor or counselor, either at the doctor's office or at a hospital. To take Britain as an example, there is currently a heated debate on whether the British G.P. (General Practitioner) should continue to make the traditional house calls, a service being increasingly abused by people whose only problem is, for example, a slight headache. First-time mothers prefer the health visitors to come to their homes, provided the visits are announced (Heritage & Sefi, 1992, p. 363).

Another possibility, which takes the problem out of the hands of the professionals, is increasingly available in the Western world: telephone hotlines, often operated by trained volunteers (e.g., Watson, 1986). Then there are the increasing number of voluntary support groups in the community for people with a particular medical condition, and their families, ranging from the different cancers to congenital conditions. Most recently, voluntary groups have been started for people with AIDS (e.g., Janet Green, 1989, p. 238). In a number of countries in Africa, home-based care projects have been started for people with AIDS (e.g., Zambia; see G. Williams, 1990). Communication is more likely to be open in such contexts.

Time, like territory, is a significant factor in the Western view of the world of medicine, and people's perception of their place in this world. Medical interest starts before birth, with the monitoring of the growth of the embryo to fetus within the mother's womb; a premature birth is something to be avoided if at all possible. Likewise, a premature death is feared, often more by relatives than by the patient. The following example shows how a young girl with leukemia handled the issue of "not having time," in particular in the future:

This girl was in the ambulatory section of the female medical ward and spent most of her days in the hospital walking up and down the corridors. . . . A new member of the nursing staff engaged her in conversation on the first day of a new admission, and, in the course of talking about those things which one talks with teenage girls about,

e.g., "do you have a boyfriend," "when do you want to get married?"
etc., the girl, who was said to be "very mature" in her attitude toward
her illness, interrupted the nurse with the announcement: "I'm going
to die in a few years and have learned not to think about such things."
(Sudnow, 1967, p. 70)

The former stigma of cancer—leading to a premature death if it is
not "caught" in time and aggressively treated—has now been over-
taken, if not replaced, by the greater fear of AIDS. A major time
factor in the AIDS epidemic, challenging beliefs about health and
sickness, is the delay between first infection with HIV and the onset
of persistent symptoms. Although there may be a period of acute
illness in the first 3 months following infection, there may then be
many years before the opportunistic infections associated with AIDS
itself actually appear. Patients may feel and look perfectly healthy
(John Green, 1989, p. 34). In this case, patients have to be confronted
with the need to understand that, even though they feel perfectly
healthy, they are living with a time bomb. In this connection, an
interesting metaphor is that AIDS is "the tip of the iceberg" (S. Smith
& A. Smith, 1990, p. 32), with the true dimensions of the problem,
HIV infection, remaining unseen.

With regard to medical discourse, prejudice can be seen in terms of
both ethnicity and behavior. Remember the challenge of AIDS to
doctors' attitudes toward certain sexual behaviors. With regard to
ethnicity, there was the case that came to light in Israel in late January
1996 of Ethiopian Jews' blood being discarded without being tested,
apparently because of the stereotype of Africans being more likely to
have AIDS. But long before the AIDS epidemic, prejudice was evident
in terms of race and/or other behaviors, as well as socioeconomic status.
Sudnow (1967, p. 104) named one type of prejudice: "The detection
of alcohol on the breath of a 'DOA' [Dead On Arrival] is nearly always
noticed by the examining physician, who announces to his fellow
workers that the person is drunk. This seems to constitute a feature he
regards as warranting less than strenuous effort to attempt revival." This
is similar to the "blame-the-victim" attitude in Extract 121. In the
following extract, however, it is difficult to establish whether the
prejudice is tied to ethnicity, religious beliefs, or sex of the patient. The
patient is a 24-year-old Mexican American woman, and the doctor is
"a third-year male Anglo resident of conservative religious persuasion"
(Burgess, 1986, p. 59). The patient hurt her leg when she fell off a

motorcycle, and wants to check that it is not broken, but at the same time asks where she can get an abortion cheaply, because she thinks she might be pregnant. The doctor says that hospital abortions are very expensive and he does not know where else she could go. Having confirmed that the leg is not broken, he continues:

(123) D = Doctor, P = Patient
D: Well, I'm real hesitant about medication.
P: Yeah.
D: You're not sure, even though, you know, you think you may want to have an abortion.
P: Definitely. I could make the mistake but it's not mine.
D: You may, it looks like uh, well the medication I want to use it's not recommended during pregnancy for treating nursing mothers or during pregnancy, tell you what to do. What kind of work do you do?
P: I'm a cook.
D: A cook. Uh, where do you work at?
P: I work at Hefty's Truck Plaza on Dixon Road. (names have been changed)
D: Uh huh. Are they pretty good to you?
P: Yeah, but they won't pay me (laughs).
D: They won't pay you.
P: Except peach pie.
D: Okay, I bet within another day or two you'll be able to get up and stand on it [the leg] without a whole lot of pain, and right now I would just use extra-strength Tylenol.
P: Okay.
(Adapted slightly from Burgess, 1986, p. 59. Reprinted with permission.)

The doctor is imposing on the patient his own views of abortion by withholding the preferred pain medication, rather than giving her the choice.

An important factor in the prejudice issue is the gender not only of the patient but also of the doctor. A study by Ainsworth-Vaughn (1992) suggests that female physicians manage discourse differently. They engage in almost four times as many reciprocal activities as male physicians in interaction with patients, indicating that they "do not regard the medical encounter as a 'power struggle' " (Ainsworth-Vaughn, 1992, p. 424).[3]

---

[3]The extracts of doctor–patient interviews with Ainsworth-Vaughn (1992) provided do not actually indicate the gender of doctor and patient—gender details only being given in quantitative tabular form.

Patients' perception of their place in the world is a factor in their willingness to take the initiative in self-development and self-preservation by taking responsibility for their own health. How women can be exploited by their doctors' withholding information was discussed earlier. Often, however, women will be given advice about something they already know and have told the doctor or health visitor (as seen in Extracts 121 and 124). In the first case, the patient used a hedge to soften the impact of her knowledge, suggesting that she was aware of her "status as ignorant" as a patient: "And I always thought that on the pill there's a sort of relation, you need to know about that and smoking too, you know." She actually said, "I know that," when the doctor started talking about the dangers of smoking when on the pill. In the second case, the mother (M) clearly does not need the information given by the health visitor (HV):

> [124] HV: Her eyes're okay.
> M: They ge— th— they get a bit weepy sometimes, but that's normal isn't it? And I swab th'm with wool with cotton wool.
> HV: Yes if they—if they: if you think they're pussie,
> M: Yeah.
> HV: then you must use boiled water with a
> M: Yeah I know.
> HV: little bit of salt in. One teaspoonful of salt to a pint of boiled water or half a teaspoon to half a pint. Okay?
> [Adapted slightly from Heritage & Sefi, 1992, p. 403]

These are indications that patients can treat themselves up to a point, and their "expertise" is needed for them to know when to seek professional medical help (cf. Heath, 1992, p. 236) and how to describe their medical symptoms, narrate their medical histories, and suggest potential causes of illness (Treichler et al., 1984, p. 64). But, the West has come to depend too much on "the expert" to give the final opinion. However, that attitude is changing. Some women took the initiative to counter this problem of sexual discrimination in the doctor's office by creating the book *Our Bodies, Ourselves* (Phillips & Rakusen, 1978). Clearly, in terms of health, women are beginning to take responsibility for their own self-development and self-preservation.

On the other hand, the formal medical sector often indicates a reluctance to treat patients who display too much knowledge, or will throw the diagnosis back onto such patients, as in the following case:

(125) Patient: I'm here because I'm just not feeling well. I uhm, I feel exhausted lately. I've been running around doing lots of things
entertaining and lots of social butterfly stuff and I'm just
exhausted. Everything hurts me. ... And uhm, going along with
it I just feel sort of nervous on and off. Loss of appetite at
times, frequent urination, oh, tired. I and uhm, oh. Occasionally
I get this very itchy feeling on my skin when I take my clothes
off. Whether that's due to some kind of nerves or not, I don't
know. And even last week I felt I was hyperventilating a little
bit, which uh, /stopped after/ a few minutes, but I felt that
I was doing.

Doctor: /you know enou——/ You know enough about that I take it,
you've done that before.

Patient: I'm not really terribly depressed or anything, I'm just sort of
tired and uptight about things, irritable a little bit.

Doctor: You have a pretty good insight, huh? Haven't you?

Patient: Well,

Doctor: Hmm?

Patient: Insight into what?

Doctor: Your story that you give me almost gives the answer with it,
doesn't it?

(Borges, 1986, p. 46. Reprinted with permission.)

Thus, a patient who is interested in looking after her own health is often
put down by a medical professional. Fortunately, at least some medical
professionals are aware of their own shortcomings. Kassler (1985, p.
121), for example, pointed to the frequent professional neglect of such
important health concerns as nutrition and preventive medicine.

Possibly the medical profession fears the loss of the typical power
relationship between doctor and patient when the patient takes an
interest in preventive medicine. Regardless of the reason, the power
relationship is evident in any doctor–patient interview, whether the
patient is a man or a woman. In most of the previous extracts, the
patient was a woman, but in the following case, the patient (P) is a
man who seems to be equally powerless to get the doctor (Dr) to
reconsider his colleague's assessment:

(126) Dr: Slip (.) slip your things: on now::.
(0.5)

Dr: 'hhhh I'm sure: Doctor: McKay's: right (.) I'm sure that these
headaches:: yer gettin are::er associated with a bit of arthritis::,
(0.5) in yerer:: (0.7) in yer neck (.) really:h (.) more than your (.)
spine::. (.) erm:. 'thh I mean more than your lower spine it's the in
your neck th[at's causin the::

P: [°It is]

```
P:    It [seems to be he:re:: anywa[y:.
Dr:      the problem.                    That's correct
      (0.2)
Dr:   Yes mhhh
      (3.2)
P:    That I could understood (.) because it (.) it's the headaches: was
      the thing that's: got me, (0.4) (More (....) than anything else) (1.2)
      > °More than the devil in hell< because they were gettin more or
      (.) less (.) permanent yer know:: (1.2) They were coming even when
      I was never pain in the back of me neck. (28.00)
Dr:   'hhhhhhh Right well I'll tell what we'll do Mister Tarrett (.) I'll give
      you ...
```
(Heath, 1992, pp. 253–254)

The patient emphasizes the fact that his symptoms have been getting worse, yet the doctor pays no attention at all to the possible need for a reassessment of his condition. This shows how the language of self-preservation is used, often not very successfully, in the doctor's or counselor's office.

Discourse Participants

As is the case with other discourses, the tendency is to assume that the situational contexts of medical discourse are relatively simple. Yet there is almost always more than one producer, and frequently more than one interpreter. The sources from which doctors gather information about the patient can include referral letters, lab reports on tests, previous visits, second opinions, and so on. Although patients will, for the most part, feel that the doctor they have an appointment with at that particular time is the source of all the information, it is rare that the doctor relies on the current information alone. A good example of the variety of sources is the following:

```
(127) D:    The events of the past year, I guess the most significant probably
            relates to your hysterectomy.
            /And the decisions on that, now,/ uh, what went on? I didn't
      P:    /which never took place, right./
      D:    hear from Dr. ____, uh, I know you had the class three Pap and
            he had /cauterized it and/
      P:    /and then, he had/cauterized it, and then came back (word) to
            normal and it was repeated 3 months later; normal, and now I've
            been repeating it every 6 months regularly.
      D:    Uh huh, OK.
```

P: And it's been normal. And he said that so far it looks good, so he has changed his mind—

D: —Fine—

P: —about (word) hysterectomy, as long as the Pap smear comes back normal.

D: Okay, all right, Now, you called about a week ago and mentioned that you had some vaginal discharge. Did you contact him then?

P: Yes I did, and he did some very extensive tests, and the only thing that they're showing is uh, a yeast infection, which I've had /over the years, yes/

D: /fifteen years (?), uh huh/ And he treated that?

P: And he's treating it now, yeah-

D: treating, and no (word) problem.

P: Right.

(Borges, 1986, pp. 36–37. Reprinted with permission.)

In this case, the sources include the current doctor, another doctor who performed the cauterization following the first Pap smear, and the laboratory technicians who took the repeated Pap smears and the laboratory tests. Added to that, most doctors keep up with current medical research as reported in major journals, and are sent samples of new medications from numerous pharmaceutical firms. Occasionally, a doctor will use an institutional "we," as the doctor in Extract 121 does in his opening utterance. Not only are such complexities typical of medical discourse, but they provide the doctor with numerous opportunities for monitoring and staging of the discourse, as in the following example, which refers as well to written material:

(128) Dr. B: Obviously you withdrew very much. (.) recently. (.) in your flat. (0.7)

Ms. K: Hu! That's private business. There is nothing to talk about!.=
=Withdrew.=I can do what I want. (0.8)

Dr. B: Well here [it says you had yourself -

Ms. K: Saying such things.=

Dr. B: Here it says you had yourself barricaded and (.) you we[re-

Ms. K: Pardon? (.)

Dr. B: You had simply disappeared in your flat and had no longer shown up, and uh (1.5)

Dr. B: [and were-

Ms. K: I can do what I want, that's really ridiculous what ( )

(Bergmann, 1992, pp. 152–153)

In this case, the doctor clearly perceives a violation of assumed normality and monitors the response of the patient to his reading of

her file. It is likely that he is staging by selecting what he reads out, and it is possible that he is not merely repeating the exact words in the report but choosing to refer to her actions as "withdrawal" and "barricading." She protests, perhaps too loudly, to these references and thus possibly reinforces the abnormality of her behaviors in the mind of the doctor.

Now consider the interpreters of medical discourse. Doctors may look at their patients as passive recipients of the diagnosis. Heath (1992, p. 241) commented, for example, on the "remarkable passivity" of patients at this stage of the medical interview. However, remember, with John Green (1989, pp. 29–30), that when the patient sits in silence, and nothing appears to be happening, "the patient is thinking over the information, often his mind is racing."

In certain types of medical discourse, there will be more than one interpreter of the doctor's or counselor's information. Pediatric discourse is an obvious case, where at least one parent will be present. But this situation poses an interesting problem in that often the parent is not only the interpreter but reinforces the doctor's diagnosis and prescription, as in the following example:

(129) Dr = Doctor, M = Mother, C = Child
    Dr: (*pause*) but then it's best to avoid cats or what do you say?
    M: uhm:
    Dr: What do you generally do in such cases?
    M: No, we don't have any cats so that's no, it's only in case he meets one outdoors somewhere. . . .
    Dr: You do avoid them (*to child*)
    C: Yes
    Dr: So you are uhm are not one of those who always has to pat every dog
    C: No:
    Dr: Well, that's fine
    C: Some of them, some: of them, I can pat
    Dr: WHAT?!
    C: Some of them I can pat
    Dr: Well, but that's really not so smart
    M: You shouldn't do that, you know
    C: No
    M: You SHOULD NOT do that
    (Adapted slightly from Aronsson & Rundstrom, 1989, p. 489)

A case where others may need to be helped to interpret bad news is that of people with cancer or AIDS, whose family or friends may need to be informed. Not only do they need information, but they frequently need as much counseling as the patient, counseling that helps them come to terms with the relative's or friend's condition (George, 1989; Kübler-Ross, 1981). Counselors spend a great deal of time listening. Here is one example:

(130) C = Counselor, P = Patient (John), W = Wife (Liza), B = Baby
    C: Can I just ask you what are your greatest concerns, Liz.
    P: [Liza
    C: [Liza: I can't get it
    W: (coughing)
    C: Liza about at this moment in time can you say aloud. (3.0)
    W: Erm, the uncertainty . . .
    C: mmh. (1.5)
    W: obviously, and (3.0) trying to get John to cope with it and lead as normal a life as possible? I'd I don't see I don't really see any feasible realistic alternative.
    C: mmh
    W: than both to carry on as as normal.
    C: mmh. (1.6)
    B: giuu.
    W: and what would happen to me?
    C: mmh
    W: and the children (2.1) if he did develop something?
    C: mmh
    (Adapted slightly from Peräkylä, 1993, p. 294)

Listening is essential to help the patient and significant others voice their fears. Until these fears have been voiced, it is impossible for counselors and their clients to begin to identify solutions to problems. According to Mishler (1984, pp. 182–183), "Listening is a necessary condition of the joint construction of meanings, but it is not sufficient. . . . [The] physician [who] ties his questions and comments to the patient's accounts . . . shows that he has not only listened, but that he has heard. He refers explicitly to what she has said." But a physician who listens is likely to be viewed as "exceptional and deviant" (Treichler et al., 1984, p. 63). Many are not willing to acknowledge that their patients may have crucial prior knowledge relevant to the diagnosis:

(131) Patient: And my mother, and my mother tends to be anemic.
      Doctor: Don't choose a diagnosis out of the blue. Buy a medical book and get a real nice diagnosis.
      (Borges, 1986, p. 48)

This is a later extract from the same medical interview as in Example 125, and the doctor remains equally arrogant and impolite.

Swantz (1990, p. 24) pointed out, in an interesting contrast with the previous Western doctor that "it is when we come to the *mganga–patient* relationship that we are touching an area where Western 'scientific' medical practitioners would have a few points to learn from the traditional *mganga*. It is perhaps because of these personal relationships that the *waganga* [plural, medicine men] are still so popular today and have a reputation for reasonable success." Certainly, the traditional *mganga* can be expected to show a great deal more politeness than the doctor in the following exchange, which is again part of the same interview as Examples 125 and 131:

(132) Doctor: Would you like something called meprobamate? . . .
      Patient: I don't know what it is.
      Doctor: Fine, I'll call the pharmacy and [inaudible]. And you can mix
                 that with aspirin. That's perfectly fine.
      (Borges, 1986, p. 47)

Fortunately, the patient must have been educated enough to persist, as the doctor does answer her rephrased question as follows:

(133) Patient: And what, how does it work?
      Doctor: It's /a tranquilizer/
      (Borges, 1986, p. 47)

In fact, in order to achieve desired results, patients may have to learn to take greater control of the interview, as Fig. 4.1 suggests.

Setting

Coming now to the setting, assume that all doctor–patient or counselor–client interviews except the health visitor–mother exchange in Example 124 took place in an office of some kind. Nowadays, counselors' offices may be somewhat more comfortable than in the past, and usually more so than doctors' offices. It was noted earlier, however, in connection with culture, that mothers generally prefer to be visited in their homes provided they know in advance. Otherwise, maybe Westerners have come to prefer the impersonality of most such offices. In this connection, though, it is worth noting Swantz's (1990, pp. 23–24) observation about the setting of most medicine men's offices in Tanzania:

FIG. 4.1. It is sometimes to the patient's advantage to take control
of the medical discourse. Reprinted with permission.

Apart from electric lights in some offices, no trend toward modern-
ization can be observed in the medicine man's facilities. The positive
side of this is that the clients feel immediately at home with the
mganga. There is none of the strangeness that they encounter when
going to the hospital or clinic. . . . The facilities needed to begin the
work of *uganga* are very simple: a rented room in which to meet
people, a mat, a stool, a stove and the knowledge of the profession.

Time is a pervasive problem in all doctor–patient encounters. In
the following extract, an AIDS counselor is questioning a patient (a
hemophiliac, whose brother, Christian, has the same problem) about
the timing of surgery:

(134) C = Counselor, P = Patient
     C: Now last time you came to the orthopedic clinic you wanted to
            have your knee done. What d'you feel about that now? Because
            that means being in hospital for weeks.
     P: Yeah I know. I don't know, I just don't know what to do. I mean if
            Christian's out I mean er I ju— I just don't know. To be honest I
            really don't know. And things are getting a bit complicated with—
            because he— he s— he seems to me to be getting much worse.

> Especially er er—medically anyway. And you know it's very hard to
> know what to do.
> C: If Christian died in the next few months ... I'm not saying he's
>   going to but if he did, how would that change your life?
> (Adapted slightly from Peräkylä, 1993, pp. 299–300)

Even in simpler cases, time is revealed to be a major concern of
both patients and doctors. Remember the doctor's instructions in
Extract 121 that the patient monitor the situation over the next couple
of months. Heritage and Sefi (1992) gave numerous examples showing a similar concern that the first-time mother has about when to
start activities with her infant, or how often, as in the following
example:

> (135) M = Mother, HV = Health Visitor
> M: I haven't bathed her yet. Is once a week enough?
> HV: Well, babies do sweat a lot. So I would recommend giving her a
>   bath every day.
> (Adapted from Heritage & Sefi, 1992, p. 393)

In Examples 134 and 135, changes in both tense and aspect mark
contrasts between past and present. In Extract 134, there is the
difference between last time and this time, in relation to the patient's
decision about when to have the operation on his knee, marked by the
shift from past to present and future, and from punctual to progressive.
In Extract 135, the shift is from perfective to habitual aspect.

Channel

It has already been mentioned how, even in the oral medical interview, written documents may be cited. Nevertheless, speaking is
what characterizes interviews between doctors and their patients. The
channel in all the previous extracts is clearly speaking. To show the
role of the spoken channel in one typical interview, refer back to
Extracts 132 and 133, which continue as Example 136:

> (136) Doctor: Would you like something called meprobamate? ...
> Patient: I don't know what it is.
> Doctor: Fine, I'll call the pharmacy and [inaudible]. And you can mix
>   that with aspirin. That's perfectly fine.
> Patient: And what, how does it work?
> Doctor: It's /a tranquilizer/

> Patient: /And what does it/
> Doctor: It's a tranquilizer.
> Patient: Is it, does it work quickly, or does it over a long period of time?
> Doctor: I don't know.
> Patient: Uhm.
> Doctor: What I mean by that is your reaction to it.
> Patient: In other words?
> Doctor: Can't predict. Each person is different. You use it four times a day. If you don't need it you use it once a day.
> Patient: Okay.
> (Borges, 1986, pp. 47–48. Reprinted with permission.)

By permitting interaction, spoken conversation enables adjustments in the power balance to be made. In the previous example, the patient, in the context of an oral exchange, is in a better position to put pressure on the doctor to justify each of his answers to her questions. She has thus managed to reduce slightly his power over her, although she does ultimately accept his prescription.

However, if patients do not have access to their own medical files, doctors may again be in a position to exert great power over the patients as a result of their access to the patients' (written) files before, after, and throughout any medical interview. For example, the doctor is referring to a written medical report in Extract 128, to which the patient is powerless to reply in other than generalizations such as "I can do what I want."

If writing is called for, it is the doctor who writes, not the patient; and that is the case in all the aforementioned cases of writing. Even in the counseling context, when John Green (1989, p. 47) mentioned how helpful it can be to write down the options available to the client in post-HIV-test counseling, it is the counselor who is advised to write out these options in front of the client. Only when the counselor gets patients to draw so as to encourage them to communicate both conscious and unconscious information, do patients actually put pen (or pencil) to paper (Furth, in Kübler-Ross, 1981, p. 68).

Participant–Text Relations

Participants in a doctor–patient interview (and in virtually all medical discourse) refer constantly to an enormous intertext surrounding the conversation at hand. Records of previous interviews, case histories, reports from other doctors, laboratory reports, and prescription guidelines are only a few of the most common texts consulted during a typical medical interview. As expected then, almost all the aforementioned extracts place themselves in a series, as do many medical encounters. Patients may have chronic ailments requiring repeated visits to the same doctor or counselor, as does Paul in Example 122 and John in Example 130. They may be referred from a general practitioner to a specialist, as was Mr. Tarrett in Extract 126, or from one specialist to another, as appears to be the case in Extract 128. Or between one visit and another, a set of laboratory tests may have been done that require follow-up, as is clear in Example 127. All these possibilities and more suggest the nature of such series. The only exchange that does not appear to be entirely coherent is Extract 128, although in Extract 136 the doctor initially produces a non sequitur after the patient's "I don't know what it is," when he answers, "Fine." However, the exchange does then recover its coherence.

Purpose and Intent

The purposes of the discourses being examined range from diagnosis of specific ailments, through treatment of the same, to counseling about how to live with an uncertain future. Fisher and Todd (1986, p. 4) added to these purposes that of persuasion to use a specific treatment. The diagnosis reveals a basis in fact, as in Example 126, although the doctor in this case seems unwilling to reassess the patient's condition, in other words, his own original diagnosis. The treatment may be subject to a certain amount of speculation, as is evident in Extract 136 when the doctor states that he cannot predict how the patient will react to the drug he is prescribing. Counseling may tend toward the imagination, encouraging patients and/or their relatives and friends to look to future possibilities without them, as in Examples 130 and 134.

Topic

Strictly speaking in a medical interview, it should be the patient who establishes the topic of discussion. Together with the doctor, the patient might generally be expected to move from the general to the particular, as in Example 127, where the discussion moves from the hysterectomy (the whole) to the Pap smear and cauterization (com-

> **Practice 58:**
> Analyze the cultural, intertextual, situational, and relational context of a selected page from Encounter A in Borges (1986, pp. 36–45). Compare your findings with your own transcript obtained for Practice 57.

ponents). Again in Extract 127, the move from "including" (vaginal discharge) to "included" (yeast infection) can be identified. However, a doctor–patient interview does not always proceed as smoothly. The extent to which the doctor or counselor listens to the patient or client is evident from the topic transitions between sections of the medical interview. Mishler examined topic switching in medical interviews and found that frequently the physician disrupts the patients' account, asking questions that ignore their "lifeworld contexts of meaning" (1984, p. 121). Ainsworth-Vaughn (1992) identified four kinds of topic changes on a continuum from symmetrical to completely asymmetrical behavior: reciprocal activities, links, minimal links, and sudden topic changes. Extract 127 gives an extended example of a reciprocal activity; Extract 123 gives two examples of a minimal link (the doctor's "tell you what to do" and "Okay"); and the end of Extract 126 gives an example of sudden topic change, preceded by a long silence. These different strategies for topic transition reflect different patterns of power in the doctor–patient relationship. The smoother the topic transition, the greater the balance of power, and the more abrupt the topic transition, the less powerful the patient.

The next section examines the language of medical discourse, which provides a picture of the ways in which doctor or counselor and patient negotiate their understanding of health and sickness.

THE LANGUAGE OF MEDICINE

Research into medical discourse has examined a wide variety of aspects of the language. Mishler (1984) was particularly concerned with the negotiation of meaning between physician and patient. This negotiation is frequently achieved by specific questioning techniques, such as the use of hypothetical questions and tag questions by both counselor and client or doctor and patient. Such techniques are particularly significant in counseling discourse. Politeness and coherence, giving and receiving advice, and persuasion are features of both clinical and counseling discourse. Several analyses of medical discourses have included some kind of conversational analysis. It is important also to note the nonverbal behaviors of both doctor and patient that accompany these different situations, and to take cultural differences into consideration while doing so.

Conjunction and Clause Relations

First consider an analysis of the ways in which clauses in medical discourse are typically conjoined to create a universe of discourse. Peräkylä (1993) reported on how counselors help AIDS patients talk about their "possible world" and "alternative reality" (p. 292). What the counselor and client do together is effectively negotiate their universe of discourse. Extracts 130 and 134 both show how the counselor elicits from the client or family member their perception of the reality. There is a concern on the part of counselors not to assume that their meanings are shared with their clients but to help the clients elaborate their own meanings, a point revealed more clearly in the following example:

(137) (P = Patient; C1, C2 = Counselors)

P: Can you ... what are the main uhm symptom ... what actually does pneumonia ... do to you? Once it's within your system.

C2: It gives you a cough,

P: Yeah.

C2: breathlessness (3.5)

C1: Are these things you've thought about before or not really? (2.0)

P: Uhm (0.2) Sorry what d'you mean ... what like the ...

C1: All these this discussion we're having about ... Symptoms and things. (0.4)

P: Yeah I had (0.2) I have thought about them, as I said I thought before more

C1: Mm

P: so that (0.2) err (1.0) that I am

C1: Mm

P: thinking more about them more now because (0.6) I'm a little bit more settled in this work ... job. And if it's you sort of

C1: Right

P: so now I've got more time I will be actually taking a leave so

C1: sSay ... (0.2) we can't say and you can't say,

P: Yeah

C1: but say you did begin to get ill or say you got so ill that you couldn't kind of (0.2) make decisions for yourself ... who would (0.4) you have to make them for you (0.3) ...

(Adapted slightly from Peräkylä, 1993, pp. 298–299)

THE DISCOURSE OF MEDICINE

Clearly, the client feels free enough to request the counselor to elaborate on what he means by "Are these things you've thought about before?", as well as to elaborate for the counselor his own meanings.

The following example from pediatric discourse shows the doctor negotiating with the parent the meaning of the child's medical problem in a similar way, prompting the parent with questions as did the counselor in Extract 137:

(138) Dr = Doctor, Mo = Mother
Mo: ... from what I was told in the beginning and you told me too, he will outgrow this as he goes along.
Dr: Well. Yeah. It's not exactly—
Mo: more or less
Dr: important what I said.
Mo: Yeah
Dr: What— what do you think, I mean do you think Barry will outgrow his problems?
Mo: Well! I think so, in way- I hope so! in ways. Because you know ...
Dr: What do you think is wrong with him.
Mo: Well, he's hyperactive child.
Dr: Mmhmm
Mo: so, the definition they said when a baby's born the brain is developed to that certain point, now with hyperactive child, that brai—the brain hasn't developed, to that certain point ...
Dr: So ... you suspect there's something wrong with Barry's brain then?
Mo: Well, um uhm, not really, I would say learning difficulties. You know, like uh he wasn't grasping. ... (So that's) how I thought something was
Dr: So that's why we—
Mo: wrong there.
Dr: right. and you know, we we agree with you, you know, we—ih—cer— to the certain degree. We feel that
Mo: Is he gonna be all right. heh huh
Dr: We—we feel that Billy [sic] is hyperactive.
Mo: Yeah.=
Dr: =y'know, and he has had trouble for a long time.
Mo: Yeah.
Dr: But we don't see this as something that's just gonna pass.
Mo: Yeah, well I know that.
(Adapted slightly from Maynard, 1992, pp. 345–346)

Extract 138 is a good example of negotiation of a socially unacceptable meaning: brain damage. The doctor works to "co-implicate" the parent in the diagnosis, helping the mother in this way to come to terms with a diagnosis that does not bode well for the future. The parent states her view of the problem, which the doctor then restates to represent a more accurate medical diagnosis. This linguistic strategy is a form of paraphrase. The doctor has translated from the "voice of the lifeworld" into the "voice of medicine" and back into the "voice of the lifeworld" (Mishler, 1984, p. 162).

Examples 137 and 138 are fairly smooth conversations with those involved taking turns without interruptions, only the encouraging words and vocalizations like "right," "yeah," and "mhm." In the counseling context, where the counselor is deliberately trying to get the client to speak, as in Examples 130, 134, and 137, it is not a question of the counselor insisting on a particular decision or course of action or treatment to be taken, so there cannot be either an expected answer or an unexpected answer. However, in the clinical context, the doctor is not always found to be so flexible, as seen in several previous examples. In both Extracts 125 and 131, for example, the doctor expresses his disapproval of the patient's self-diagnosis. In Example 136, the same doctor is clearly put out by the dispreferred questioning of his prescription.

Thus, although the recipient's assessment of the diagnosis and treatment is considered a part of the structure of a medical interview, not all doctors welcome it, and not all conversational analysts specify it. Byrne and Long (1976, in Heath, 1992, p. 237), for example, identify six phases of consultations: "I, relating to the patient; II, discovering the reason for attendance; III, conducting a verbal or physical examination or both; IV, consideration of the patient's condition; V, detailing treatment or further investigation; and VI, terminating." But within Phase IV, Heath (1992, p. 241) identified three further steps, which parallel Maynard's (1992, p. 333) three turns: "(1) clinician's opinion-query, or perspective-display invitation; (2) recipient's reply or assessment; (3) clinician's report and assessment." Heritage and Sefi (1992, p. 379), on the other hand, identified a five-step series in which one or two steps may be omitted in certain health visitor (HV)–mother (M) exchanges:

Step 1:   HV: initial inquiry.
Step 2:   M: problem-indicative response.
Step 3:   HV: focusing inquiry into the problem.
Step 4:   M: responsive detailing.
Step 5:   HV: advice giving.

They found that one variation is for Steps 2 and 4 to be combined, omitting Step 3, and a second is for Steps 3 and 4 to be omitted (pp. 381–382). A third more drastic variation is for Step 2 to become a "no problem" response, after which Steps 3 and 4 are again omitted, but in Step 5 the health visitor nonetheless issues the unnecessary advice. In all three analyses, presequences are identifiable, in Heath's case in Byrne and Long's Phase I, relating to the patient, in Maynard's case in the clinician's opinion-query or perspective-display invitation, and in Heritage and Sefi's case in the health visitor's initial inquiry.

Linguistic Features

The previous analysis points to a significant difference between the linguistic features of clinical and counseling discourses. Counseling discourse, on the one hand, is likely to tend toward Biber's (1988) Dimension 1, involved production, with private verbs such as "think" and "feel" and WH questions. On the other hand, clinical discourse appears likely to be high on Biber's Dimension 4, overt expression of persuasion, with, for example, necessity modals.

A number of researchers have looked at the linguistic features of medical discourse independently of Biber. Both Mishler (1984) and Treichler et al. (1984), for example, are concerned with how the type of questions physicians ask their patients may or may not elicit from the patients sufficient background information on the progression of the illness and its impact on their lives. Treichler et al. (1984, pp. 73–76) reported on the discrepancies between the medical student's interview with the patient and the physician's. The physician gets extensive detail on the medical history of the patient, but the medical student picks up on the indirect meaning of the patient by exploring:

(139) You said you had lots of sad problems. Is the [loss of social security payments] the major one? Is there anything else?
(Treichler et al., 1984, p. 74)

The student waits 3 seconds for the patient to respond that he is confused, and then, after prompting him to elaborate, waits a further 7 seconds for the patient to mention anger. He further encourages him, to be given the following information, which the physician has never heard:

(140) Patient: I have killed before and I could do it again—easy.
      Student: Uh huh.
      Patient: And I know that the court won't hold this against me cause
                  I got a mental case—brain damage [moving hands; slumps].
      Student: I see.
      (Treichler et al., 1984, p. 75)

The student explores not only psychological problems but also medical ones, finding out that the patient sees a psychiatrist regularly, and takes a powerful antipsychotic drug, which he feels may have led to the stomach problems that brought him to the doctor in the first place. Thus, it is that the student finds out about the real world of the patient.

The hypothetical question is one of the linguistic devices Peräkylä (1993) identified as useful for prompting and cueing persons with AIDS to formulate their own decisions. This is evident in Extract 134, when the counselor asks, "If Christian died in the next few months . . . I'm not saying he's going to but if he did, how would that change your life?" and again in Extract 137 when the counselor asks, "Say you did begin to get ill or say you got so ill that you couldn't kind of make decisions for yourself, who would you have to make them for you?" The linguistic tense (past) diverges from the metalinguistic tense (hypothetical future). This achieves a kind of hedging, putting distance between counselors and the truth of the statement, and protecting them from the full force of the client's interpretation. In this way, counselors make it difficult for the client to refuse to cooperate in discussing the hypothetical future. Furthermore, the hypothetical questions are based on comments or hints, however vague, that patients have already made, making it even more difficult for them to refuse cooperation. The future orientation of these hypothetical questions is not dissimilar to the future orientation of advice given by health visitors to first-time mothers (Heritage & Sefi, 1992, p. 368).

The tag question, like the hypothetical question, achieves a kind of hedging. A number of studies have shown the tag question to serve a deferential function (e.g., Lakoff, 1975). However, in a study of psychotherapeutic discourse of a male psychiatrist with a female patient, Winefield, Chandler, and Bassett (1989) found that the pragmatic intent of the patient's tag questions changed over the course of treatment, as the patient developed her self-esteem. They coded both the grammatical form and the pragmatic intent of the patient's tag questions as *disclosure, edification, question, interpretation, reflection, advisement, acknowledgment,* and *confirmation,* and combined the eight categories into interpersonal role dimensions: *pre-sumptuousness—unassumingness, directiveness—acquiescence,* and *attentiveness—informativeness.* The therapist noticed that initially he had to resist the temptation to talk too much (cf. John Green, 1989, p. 30), so that the patient would "explore her own thoughts and feelings further" (Winefield et al., 1989, p. 84). The patient's tags at this stage followed statements of public fact or conventional wisdom:

(141) P = Patient, T = Therapist
P: (referring to her son leaving school and looking for work): ... it's
      a crucial point of time in his life, isn't it.
T: Yes (pause) and an important point of time in your life.
(Winefield et al., 1989, p. 82)

Later on, the patient became more assertive, a shift marked by increased use of tag questions, the majority of which referred to the patient's own inner experiences and conclusions.

(142) P: ... but I believe that, if his loyalty goes to her and not to me well
            I really haven't done a very good job, have I.
T: Do you see it very much as a kind of competition?
(Winefield et al., 1989, p. 83)

Now it is the therapist who is hedging as well, with "a kind of competition."

In pediatric discourse, the doctor may ask questions, such as "what do you say?" and "What do you generally do in such cases?" in Extract 129, so as to avoid undermining parental authority, while at the same time maintaining his own authority as the medical expert. In the following example, however, the doctor negotiates the advice he is giving the mother, and the treatment he is suggesting, rather more indirectly, partly by using modals that suggest a hypothetical outcome:

(143) M: ... [retells what happened to C after his sister got home after
            visiting a farm]
Dr: then it ought to be furry animals or hay
M: mhm
Dr: (pause) something—we'll make a test on him even
M: yes
Dr: if it does not show, what's most important is what you notice
       yourself, if you notice
M: yes, precisely
Dr: that it's grass and hay and furry animals, then do keep him—

M: but not all dogs
Dr: no:, no there might be a difference
M: there might be, yes
Dr: yeah: there might be a difference, there might be a difference
     between long and short-haired
M: well yes
Dr: but the risk is, I guess, one can say so to say never have a dog
M: no:
(Aronsson & Rundstrom, 1989, p. 490)

The doctor encourages the parent to formulate her own decisions by prompting and cueing but not by confronting.

Literal and Nonliteral Meaning

This points to the ways in which doctors and patients, counselors and clients avoid being too blunt about particular diagnoses. Extract 138 showed how the doctor helped the parent move from an acceptable diagnosis of "hyperactive" to an unacceptable diagnosis of "brain-damaged." Another way of dealing with unacceptable diagnoses is to use euphemisms, metaphors, and other nonliteral meanings. For example, in some African countries, AIDS is referred to as "government disease." But this is really an avoidance strategy, enabling the relatives, and even the person with AIDS, to avoid confronting the facts of the disease. By contrast, metaphors can be useful for the doctor or counselor who is dealing with helping patients understand the reality of their future. Sontag's (1989) *AIDS and its metaphors* is probably the best-known examination of the metaphors used to describe illness. Sontag likened the virus causing AIDS by disarming the immune system to a military invasion. S. Smith and A. Smith (1990), whose metaphor of AIDS as the "tip of the iceberg" was already mentioned, also described HIV infection with such military metaphors, marked by underlining: "The destruction of the T4 cells, the body's primary immune soldier cells, ultimately proves devastating to the individual. Normally, the T4 cells are mobilized whenever any infectious threat to the body occurs" (p. 34). Another extended metaphor is Usher's (1992), which compares the breaking down of the immune system in people with AIDS with the environmental degradation of Thailand's ecosystem.

Inference, Implicature, and Presupposition

A number of speech acts are characteristic of medical discourse. These include "diagnose," "advise," "persuade," "warn," and some others. For example, when the doctor diagnosed the child as "brain-damaged" in Extract 138, in effect the diagnosis made the child so. All diagnoses operate in the same way. This can be disturbing in cases of misdiagnosis, because it may be difficult to get a reassessment (as seen in Example 126). A particularly dangerous misdiagnosis can be telling individuals they are HIV-positive, when in fact people can occasionally test false-positive. A similar speech act to diagnosis occurs upon the death of a patient: "for the physician to announce that a person is dead makes it so" (Sudnow, 1967, p. 132).

Advice-giving seems to be an area of medical discourse that may reveal the flouting of the Cooperative Principle. In their study of health visitors' exchanges with first-time mothers, Heritage and Sefi (1992, p. 377) found that the vast majority of advice-giving was initiated by the health visitor. Such advice was received in one of three basic ways: marked acknowledgment, unmarked acknowledgment, and assertions of knowledge or competence. In the first case, the advice was accepted as fulfilling the Cooperative Principle. In the second case, the advice was not actually rejected, but was probably unnecessary, thus flouting the maxim of quantity. In the third case, the advice was resisted as totally unnecessary, with the mother asserting that she already knew what she was being told, revealing that the health visitor was flouting the whole Cooperative Principle. An example of this is given in Extract 124. In none of these cases did the health visitor encourage the mother to negotiate the meaning of the advice. The closest to the negotiation of meaning between mother and health visitor was on the few occasions when the mother requested advice, as in Example 135, generally asking for "confirmation of a proposed course of action" (p. 371).

Another area of medical discourse in which the Cooperative Principle is flouted is persuasion to take a course of treatment. Fisher and Todd (1986, p. 8), for example, identified three interrelated strategies of persuasion to use a particular form of contraception: "the selective use of science, the selective presentation of information, and the selective use of authority." These strategies most noticeably flout the maxim of quantity, but also each of the other maxims. These strategies are at work in Extract 121. The doctor is selective in his use of science by discussing only the use of the contraceptive pill; in his presentation of information by not informing the patient of the serious consequences of smoking and taking the pill; and in his use of his authority by withholding information on alternative contraceptive devices, such as the IUD or the diaphragm. Here again, although outward appearances suggest that the doctor and patient negotiate the decision, ultimately "it is the doctor who has the authority to persuade" (p. 12). A similar acceptance of doctors' authority is seen in their routine willingness to characterize a patient's death as painless in response to a relative's question, even when the relative actually knew the death was painful (Sudnow, 1967, p. 146). This is a clear flouting of the maxim of quality.

Nonverbal Meaning

Heath (1986) conducted the most thorough analysis to date of the relation between nonverbal and verbal behaviors in the doctor–patient interview. He related the nonverbal behaviors to the phases in the doctor–patient series of exchanges described earlier. For example, a silence after the Phase IV diagnosis is characteristic. At this point, some nonverbal behaviors may serve to discourage the patient from responding, as, for example, if the doctor writes in the medical record (Treichler et al., 1984, pp. 69–72). Even if the patient does respond, ignoring the discouragement, as happened in Extract 126, the fact that the doctor spent his time writing out the prescription during this response (Heath, 1992, p. 254) clearly indicates that the doctor had no intention of encouraging the patient's opinion. Other nonverbal behaviors, on the other hand, encourage the patient to respond, as, for example, if the doctor shifts his gaze toward the patient. Treichler et al. (1984, p. 67) specifically mentioned that when the patient "initiates sustained eye contact with the physician . . . [his] answers become longer." If, however, the doctor combines the presentation of the diagnosis with that of the treatment without the intervening silence, which is a cue for the patient to respond to the diagnosis, then he employs an intonation and pace that signals that the utterance is incomplete. If the patient then wishes to respond, it is usually to the treatment, not the diagnosis (Heath, 1992, pp. 242–243).

Practice 59:
Analyze a selected feature of the language of your own transcript. You might, for example, wish to focus on what makes the interview cohesive and coherent, or on the speech acts, or on features of paralinguistic and nonlinguistic behavior of the doctor or counselor and patient.

In counseling, the nonverbal behaviors may be somewhat different, being more geared to discussion of problems than straight information giving. It is extremely important for a counselor not to show nonverbally any shock or discomfort at the revelations of a client. Treichler et al. (1984, p. 75) referred to the "considerable *sangfrois* [*sic*]" with which the medical student received the information that the patient was capable of killing. John Green (1989, p. 30) mentioned the discomfort counselors often experience with patients who start crying immediately after hearing the results of an HIV test. In this context, Green revealed that putting a hand on the patient's shoulder can help, although he acknowledged the problem of "the taboos against touching in Western medicine" (p. 31).

Kübler-Ross (1981, p. 43) also mentioned the role of touch (e.g., holding the hand of a loved one) in helping patients who are dying get over the grief at their own imminent death. She distinguished between nonverbal and verbal symbolic language. She pointed out that younger children who are coming to terms with their illness often use nonverbal symbolic means such as drawings or toys, as well as "acting out" (p. 19). She gave the example of a 13-year-old boy who was waiting for a kidney transplant. This boy's pretend shooting of girls in the ward, all of whom had good kidneys, was symbolic of his wanting someone to die soon so that he could get the chance to live by being given a cadaver kidney (pp. 19–20).

This brief survey of the context and language of medicine has touched on a wide range of issues, the core of which is how the doctor and patient, or counselor and client, jointly negotiate the meanings of health and sickness, death and dying.

CONCLUSION: SOME REMAINING QUESTIONS

The analysis of medical discourse has hinted at a number of possible future directions for communication in medicine. First, there might be a coming together of the clinical, problem-oriented approach and the relationship-centered approach, particularly in the treatment of people with AIDS. In such a merger, hopefully the skills of the traditional healer and the modern doctor would be balanced, if not in an individual, at least in such a way that both types of skills would be available to every patient. The microscopic accuracy could be complemented by the broad humane approximations, the sharply defined world of science by the metaphysical world of nature. Already in some innovative approaches to cancer treatment, the patient and a team of specialists (e.g., an oncologist, surgeon, radiologist, nutritionist, etc.) cooperate in developing the best treatment (see, e.g., D. Frahm & A. Frahm, 1992). Furthermore, some interesting experiments are under way in Africa. In Bulawayo, Zimbabwe, for example, an Integrated Clinic was established in 1981 to house traditional healers and Western-trained medical doctors under one roof, following the Traditional Medical Practitioners Act. Barbara Sibanda, the director of the clinic, revealed that the main aim is to give people a choice of treatment, and the number of cross-referrals is encouraging (Mmensa, 1995). And to parallel the innovation in the medical field, in the field of medical discourse analysis, some research has drawn on a team of specialists in medicine, conversational analysis, linguistics, sociolinguistics, and health education (Treichler et al., 1984, p. 65).

One of the areas where change is probably most needed is in teaching patient–medical professional communication skills to doctors and nurses in training. Such skills include delivering diagnostic information and explaining the proposed treatment in a way patients can understand, and allowing patients time to absorb the given information and explanation, even if their reaction causes the doctor or counselor to feel distinctly uncomfortable. The need for the professional to tell patients the facts about their case has already been discussed, but the professional needs specific guidance in how to present the facts in a clear, digestible way, "which attempts to integrate psychosocial information within a biomedical framework" (Treichler et al., 1984, p. 73).

For the purposes of discourse analysis, future research needs to pay much greater attention to the cultural and situational contexts of medical discourse than has generally been the case hitherto. Researchers have tended to concentrate on the relational context and/or the purely linguistic features, but in order to help medical professionals improve their communication skills, a complete analysis of medical and counseling discourses is necessary from both the contextual and linguistic perspectives.

As the saying goes, "Prevention is better than cure," and yet the medical profession generally seems to promote reliance on treatment, if not cure, rather than prevention. Maybe preventive medicine is one of the areas that could experience a major change over the coming decade. A move in this direction is already being made in the Third World. A number of countries have attempted to introduce the primary health care concept, with village-based health workers (see, e.g., Schmidt & Kerr, 1987), as a way of increasing the accessibility of health care to villagers who might otherwise have to walk up to 10 miles to the nearest dispensary, and thus cutting the delay before people seek help. However, it is not just a question of the distance, but the unwillingness of the Western-trained clinical officer to communicate with the poor villager that is often a more significant factor than distance in the reluctance of mothers to take their sick children to the dispensary or, especially, the hospital. It is crucial that in their Western-style training medical professionals in the Third World do not forget their cultural background such that they become unable to communicate with the people who most need their help.

Despite the first steps being taken in the provision of primary health care, the 1993 World Development Report of the World Bank made it clear that much more needs to be done:

> Decisive for the improvement of the health of the population as a whole are not the achievements of heart surgeons, but immunizations, regular check-ups in schools, information on family planning, care of women during pregnancy, and programmes to reduce tobacco and alcohol consumption. . . . Reforms make it necessary that additional state expenditure in the sphere of health be transferred from the specialist staff, specialist equipment and establishments at the top of the system to the "base of the pyramid," to the easily accessible health care provided in community and health centres. (Quoted by Adelmann, 1993, pp. 22–23)

A particularly important aspect of preventive medicine in the world today is the prevention of HIV infection. A major preventive tool is the education of girls, particularly an education that empowers them to take control of their lives by teaching them the necessary communication skills to protect themselves (de Selincourt, 1994). With such education, girls (in particular) and boys will begin to be able to negotiate their own health care, making their own meaning of their existence.

It will be interesting to see if the primary health care concept ever takes root in the West, encouraging the general population to take much greater control over their own health and preventive medicine. In this connection, it will be particularly interesting to note the eventual outcome of the various attempts at reform of the U.S. health care system, and the nature of this reform. Will it include passing on to the general population a much greater role in preventive health, encouraging them to negotiate their own care and make their own meaning of their existence, as it is hoped will happen in the developing world, or will it persist in the medicalization of health as a way of maintaining the status quo?

5

THE DISCOURSE
OF LAW

Law has, since ancient times, been recognized as an inherently rhetorical activity. It requires skills in both written and spoken language, even though historically, disputes were often settled "first by feud, and later by combat or ordeal," to be replaced by "words instead of weapons" even later (James, 1971, p. 84). The language of the law was of interest to both philosophers of language and lawyers themselves, who focused for the most part on syntax and word meanings in written documents, recognizing that "words are of central importance for the lawyer because they are, in a very particular way, the tools of his trade" (G. L. Williams, 1945a, p. 71). At the same time, lawyers recognized the need for a good command of the spoken language, "so as to put [the] client's case clearly and strongly before the judge" (Denning, 1955, p. 52), as well as to educate the general public about the law and how to use it (e.g., Dahl, 1987; Tsanga, 1990).

In the 1960s, lawyers (e.g., Hart, 1961) made extensive use of Austin's (1962) legal philosophical work on speech acts. Unfortunately, their analyses tended to naively postulate "an unmediated relation of individual utterance to formal system" (Goodrich, 1984a, p. 186). Subsequently, lawyers analyzed in depth "the technique of persuasion" (Napley, 1983), among other functions. More recently, some lawyers have sought to move away from the more purely philosophical approaches to the language of the law to consideration of both the semantics and the discourse structure (Mertz, 1992). Meanwhile, lawyers continue to write on the problems brought about

265

by the need to use language in all their work. They frequently return to discussion of such language issues as legal counseling (Heller, 1994), "hearsay" (Rein, 1994), "the right to silence" (Greer, 1990), and the use of the dictionary to assist in interpretation of legal documents (Looking it up, 1994). However, according to Goodrich (1984a, p. 173, emphasis added), "lawyers and legal theorists . . . have asserted deductive models of law application in which language is the neutral instrument of purposes peculiar to the internal development of legal regulation and legal discipline. What has been consistently excluded from the ambit of legal studies is the possibility of analysing law as a *specific stratification or 'register'* of an actually existent language system."

Fortunately, sociologists have begun to examine contextual features and discourse analysts have introduced new ways of analyzing legal discourse in greater linguistic detail. One of the major areas of interest of the former is "feminist jurisprudence" (e.g., Cheater, 1990; Dahl, 1987; Marcus et al., 1985). The latter ways involve a number of different approaches. One makes use of advances in phonetics, phonology, and prosody to assist in speaker identification (e.g., Baldwin & French, 1990). Another focuses on conversational analysis to compare the structure and meaning of recorded conversations (e.g., Shuy, 1986). In both these cases, forensic linguists, as "expert witnesses," have been able to show that slight linguistic differences can lead to different legal outcomes. Others (e.g., Conley & O'Barr, 1990) have concentrated on analyzing the relative power of different speech styles.

Thus, it is clear that discourse analysts may approach legal discourse from a variety of different perspectives. Contextually, they can consider the significance of differences in ideology, ethnicity, gender, social class, and so on between lawyer and client, which might lead to rather important differences in power relationships (e.g., Berk-Seligson, 1990; Merry, 1990; Wodak-Engel, 1984). Linguistically, their interests range from analyzing the congruence of the universe of discourse of lawyer and client through word meanings and meaning relations, pragmatic meanings, and structure of court discourse, to elements of nonverbal communication and their significance in the analysis of both evidence and examination of witnesses in court (e.g., Atkinson & Drew, 1979; Baldwin & French, 1990).

This chapter refers to some data, a "Last Will" drawn up in the United States. It also examines the issue of inheritance in other societies. In addition, it reexamines previously published court and

> **Practice 60:**
> Try to obtain a copy of a written legal document of particular interest to you, such as a will, a contract, or correspondence between a lawyer and client, and also a court transcript of a case (possibly one in published sources, such as Atkinson & Drew, 1979, pp. 107–110; or Wodak-Engel, 1984, pp. 98–100). Use these materials while reading this chapter in order to gain experience in identifying the context and language of law.

interview extracts, for an understanding of the features of oral, as opposed to written, legal discourse. At the same time, frequent reference is made to analyses by lawyers of key issues in the use of language in a variety of legal contexts. Thus, a wide range of types of legal language data is covered, remembering, with Atkinson and Drew (1979, p. 2), that "studies of the law in action should extend far beyond the courtroom walls."

THE CONTEXT OF LAW

Although this chapter focuses on the American legal system in the case of the contractual document being analyzed, frequent reference is made to legal issues currently facing other legal systems. The comparisons highlight the impact of context on legal discourse. Within each system, there is an additional division, between legislative and common or customary law, which further clarifies the significance of context for legal discourse. Of the discourses considered in this book, law stands out because "the most obvious feature of legal discourse is its production within specific, highly restricted, institutional settings" (Goodrich, 1984a, p. 187).

Culture

Ideally, the legal system of any country should serve as a cultural leveler, bringing justice to all, whether rich or poor, male or female, from the ethnic majority or an ethnic minority, from whatever religious background or none, and so on. However, according to James (1971, p. 209), "a nation that professes freedom and equality and justice as a basic concept is shaken when it is forcefully pointed out that we can be unjust, and that some Americans are more free and more equal than others." This points clearly to the perennial problem of the definition of law and how it relates to justice: "How does law differ from and how is it related to orders backed by threats? How does legal obligation differ from, and how is it related to, moral obligation? What are rules and to what extent is law an affair of rules?" (Hart, 1961, p. 13). It becomes evident how each of these questions relates to the data in the following extracts from the will:

(144)   II.
                          Rules of Construction
... "Heirs" shall be determined by the existing laws of the State of Washington controlling intestate succession. ...

(145)   IV.
                        Executor Administration
... Upon admission of my Will to probate, my Executor may manage and settle my estate with unrestricted non-intervention powers. (Authors' data)

Extract 144, from paragraph II, reveals a legal obligation, whereas Extract 145, from paragraph IV, reveals a moral obligation.

The same distinction applies elsewhere too. In many African countries, people are having to reevaluate the traditional laws of property inheritance. Under the traditional legal system operating in many southern African countries, for example, "property is inherited by the husband's relatives rather than the widow. In the (more prevalent) matrilineal systems of Zambia the property is inherited by the husband's uncles or nephews on his mother's side of his family; in patrilineal systems property is inherited by the deceased husband's brothers, or otherwise their sons. It may be noted that both the matrilineal and patrilineal systems are patriarchal in that property always passes into the hands of men" (Longwe & Clarke, 1990, p. 181).

Longwe and Clarke referred to the "corruption of traditional practice," which is happening all over southern Africa. As the following extract, criticizing Malawi's Wills and Inheritance Act, indicates, many people do not pay any attention to the justice of either the legal or the moral obligations:

2. Failure of the Act to protect the wife and children of the deceased from rampaging relatives of a dead man.

It has been noted that, in practice, as soon as a husband dies the relatives of the man descend on his home and forcibly help themselves to any of his assets on the pretext that they are his rightful heirs. By the time the provisions of the Act have [been] applied to the estate, substantial diversion of property will have occurred to the detriment of the widow and her children. These customary heirs, after the plunder, will rarely be seen thereafter to provide for the needs of the bereaved widow and children.
(National Commission on Women in Development [1993]. *Women and the law in Malawi.* Lilongwe: NCWID, p. 60)

A further complication is that "these beneficiaries of death want the widow as well. In northern Malawi the practice is called *kuhara,* in central and southern Malawi it is known as *chokolo,* where a brother to the deceased assumes the role of husband" (Mwanza, P. [1995]. *"Where dying is costly." The [Malawi] Nation,* 14 September, p. 11)

Both cases, the data presented here and southern Africa, point to the ways in which legal systems can define people's place in the world and consequently their perception of the world. Take, for example, the first paragraph of the will:

(146)   I.
                            Identification of Family
My only marriage was to [husband's name] who is now deceased. I have never had any children. The term "children" as used herein refers to all children born to or legally adopted by my spouse or me.
(Authors' data)

This identifies the author of the will as a woman, whose place in the world is defined in relation to her deceased husband and their children. It is not possible, however, to specify her resultant perception of the world, something that can be done in the case of southern Africa. The widow of a Malawian colleague who had made a will was fortunate. If her husband had died intestate, her place in the world would have been effectively established as "nonexistent" after the death of her husband. Others who are just property to be passed on to a brother-in-law are not so fortunate. For example, one woman took her own life and that of her child after her husband's death and his relatives' insistence on taking all the property ("Bangwe woman torches herself, son to death," *[Malawi] Daily Times,* 22 February

1996, p. 3). Such a situation would obviously have an impact on a woman's perception of her world.

Turning to the case of criminal law, the Judicial Studies Board (England) in its Report for 1987–1991 (quoted in Hood, 1992, p. 192) stated that "any court that exhibited prejudice against a defendant from an ethnic minority would be failing in its basic duty to treat all defendants before it equally." However, in an extensive survey of sentencing patterns in West Midlands (England) Crown Courts, Hood (1992, p. 203) found that "there were significant race differences in the way that sentences were distributed along the scale from imprisonment to discharge and in the alternatives to custody which were considered appropriate. Controlling for those variables which best explained severity of sentence, blacks were placed higher up the scale than were whites." The main factor contributing to this differential sentencing appears to have been that Blacks far more frequently pleaded not guilty (as do lower class defendants; Wodak-Engel, 1984, p. 95), a factor that could relate to a misunderstanding of the legal terminology. Blacks were consequently "more liable on conviction to receive longer custodial sentences" (Hood, 1992, p. 179). It may be further related to a nonverbal factor, judges' perception of a "different, less deferential, demeanour in court" (Hood, 1992, pp. 188–189). A similar example of differential sentencing in the United States is found in James (1971, p. 143).

Related to prejudice connected with ethnicity is that associated with social class, which may depend to a great extent on educational factors, but also on language. The people who write wills, all over the world, are for the most part members of the urban middle class, who have reached a high level of education, necessitating the ability to communicate in English, whereas the urban lower classes and the rural farmers, whose only language is a nonstandard dialect or a vernacular, die intestate. In an attempt to level social class differences on death, legal advisors to counselors who visit people with AIDS in Malawi's Home-Based Care Projects have drawn up a simple will in the vernacular, which the counselors merely have to fill in on the agreement of the patient. The latter may then sign, if able to, or confirm with a fingerprint.

In the data presented here it is possible to identify someone with enough property, that is a member of the middle class, to warrant specifying how that property should be distributed on her death. Although she will not have actually drafted the will in the words that appear, she will have been able to confirm that the wording represented her intent. Similarly, Merry (1990) in the United States and Wodak-Engel (1984) in Austria found that, in the courtroom, "defendants not socialized in [the implicit] norms of language use are discriminated against, and only [middle class] defendants succeed, as a rule, in good image management before the judge" (Wodak-Engel, 1984, p. 97). Lower class defendants typically start off in court attempting to speak in a formal speech style, and then switch into dialect, which may increase the hostility of the judge toward them. And lower class defendants who are women may have a "doubly negative status role" (Wodak-Engel, 1984, p. 96). The judge in one case openly revealed his prejudices: "This is a woman; they cannot drive anyway" (p. 93).

This brings up the questions of sex and discourse in the law. Traditionally, lawyers were male and clients were male or female. This fact is reflected in legal texts and articles (Kurzon, 1989). For example, in Heller's (1994) article on legal counseling, the client is consistently referred to as "she" and the lawyer as "he." The former designation was perhaps understandable in the context of the article. It discussed Zoe Baird's violation of the federal Immigration Reform and Control Act of 1986, which came to light after Clinton nominated her to be U.S. attorney general, and how Baird could have been given better legal counsel. But, given the fact that Baird herself is a lawyer, why use the latter designation, "he" = "lawyer"?

In the case of the data, interestingly, specific reference is made to the interchangeability of meanings of pronouns:

(147)   II.
                              Rules of Construction
            Unless some other meaning and intent are apparent from the context,
            the plural shall include the singular and vice versa, *and masculine, feminine*
            and neuter words shall be used interchangeably. . . .
            (Authors' data, emphasis added)

In addition to sexist language in legal texts, there is the question of gender and legal discourse. Dunlap (Marcus et al., 1985, pp. 13–14) identified four clusters of legal activity concerning feminist issues: "physical health," "money," "violence empowerment," and "creativity." Of particular interest, with the focus on contractual law, is the second cluster, which involves matters of "equal pay, comparable worth, property, benefits of employment, ownership, and control of the material means to equal opportunity." MacKinnon (Marcus et al., 1985, pp. 21–24) pointed out how people determine what constitutes "equal" and "comparable" according to a standard of masculinity, instead of searching for a new standard. She then referred to the time when women and children were considered "male property," a situation that is clearly still the case among most ethnic groups in southern Africa. Smart and Sevenhuijsen (1989) examined in greater depth the relation between child custody laws and the politics of gender in a number of countries (from North America to Australia)—a hot issue particularly in the United States. Boyd (1989, p. 153) specifically talked of "the potential of law as an arena of struggle for women." She summarized changes in family law in Canada resulting from attempts to eliminate gender-specific legislation as follows: "The legal system has moved . . . to an approach which attempts to apply gender neutral principles of equality to fathers and mothers in child custody cases. In so doing, the legal system fails to take account of the different positions of women and men within and outside the family, positions which are characterized by unequal power relations" (Boyd, 1989, pp. 152–153). In each case, the approach depends on a particular definition of the role of the woman in the family and in the society, a definition that may these days be couched in the language of equality. The language further reflects the ideologies of the society, a fact that is glaring in the case of Ireland, where "the status accorded to 'The Family' under the constitution reflects the strength of Catholic ideology and has had direct effects on the development and interpretation of statutory and case law on custody" (MacDevitt, 1989, p. 192).

What is particularly significant in terms of ideology, though, is the differences between men's and women's perceptions of the role of the law in society. Whereas men overwhelmingly (95%) focus on justice, women for the most part (60%) are concerned with caring (Gilligan, in Marcus et al., 1985, p. 48). Menkel-Meadow (Marcus et al., 1985, p. 53) considered the implications for the legal system: "Many of our conceptions of what the legal system ought to be and ought to do were derived exclusively from male practitioners and male scholars. The law may thus represent an embodiment of . . . the male voice." However, there are male voices that point to the faulty ideologies that prefer treating the individual to treating the conditions that gave rise to the crime, that choose punishment over rehabilitation (e.g., James, 1971, chaps. 10–11).

Ideologically, the document being analyzed here represents a legal system in which individuals own property. This system is radically different from that of many traditional African communities, "Traditional African rights strongly reflect the lifestyle, the nature of social relations, in short the entire civilization of traditional societies. Such rights are above all communal. Individuals possess rights and obligations only as members of a group, with which they entertain a mutually complementary relationship. These rights are shaped by oral tradition and religious empiricism" (Nsirimovu, 1994, p. 2).

The view expressed appears similar to that of lower class American plaintiffs: They "do not think in terms of specific doctrines or rules but instead think in terms of fundamental rights of property" (Merry, 1990, p. 38). In this respect, it is worth noting G. L. Williams' (1945b, p. 179) comments on the meanings of "ownership" and related terms: " 'Ownership' has two distinct senses, called by Salmond 'corporeal' and 'incorporeal'—i.e., ownership of things and ownership of rights; and the word 'estate' should be similarly differentiated, for it bears a different meaning when we speak of an estate in land from its meaning when we speak of an estate in a right." It would seem that Western legal systems focus on ownership of things. G. L. Williams (1945c, p. 293), for example, analyzed the English law that "ownership is lost when the marks of ownership are lost," showing that if an individual B modifies a thing obtained from an individual A, in the honest belief that B owns it, and A subsequently reclaims it, but it is now unrecognizable as the original object, B now owns it.

This clearly leads to the question of territory and discourse, as they relate to property and concepts of ownership. The expression, "An Englishman's home is his castle" gives us a picture of the Western focus on individual ownership of things, which therefore may be willed to relatives on the death of the owner. And that property is very clearly defined by law. The data, for example, specify the following:

(148)   III.
                              Disposition of Estate
        I give all of my estate, both real and personal, wheresoever situated, in
        equal shares to my deceased brother's children [nephew's name] cur-
        rently of Vancouver, Canada, and [niece's name] currently of Seattle,
        Washington. . . .
        (Authors' data)

By contrast, as already mentioned, most Africans continue to think of land and property as belonging to the community in which they are located, and therefore expect it to revert to the community on death. Furthermore, the widow is unlikely to be protected even if the husband did leave a written will: "firstly leaving a will is very uncommon in Zambia, and secondly it is not respected under customary law and is likely to mean in practice that the widow has an entitlement under statutory law which has already been distributed, and which is irretrievable" (Longwe & Clarke, 1990, p. 182). Thus, the African widow's position would in no way compare with that of the widow whose will is being analyzed here. The African widow in all likelihood would have no property at all to bequeath to her children.

Time also relates in interesting ways to legal discourse. In the context of the data, an aspect of time in contracts is the specification of the time at which the will comes into force. This specification comes immediately after the details of the estate given in Extract 148:

> (149)   III.
> Disposition of Estate
> ... if they survive me by ninety (90) days. If [niece] does not survive me by 90 days, her share shall go to her daughter [grandniece's name]. If [nephew] does not survive me by 90 days, his share shall go to [niece], or, if [niece] does not survive me by 90 days, to [grandniece].
> (Authors' data)

In criminal or political cases, in Western democratic societies there is recognition of the need to set time limits to arrest without charge, detention without trial, and so on (Harris & Spark, 1993, p. 90). Refusal to observe time limits is one cause of human rights violations in nondemocratic societies.

Discourse Participants

Extracts 144 to 146 and 148 indicate some of the producers and interpreters involved in legal discourses. Extract 146 specifies the author of the will, called the testator in legal language, although the producer is clearly the lawyer who drafted it, often relying on insti-tutionalized formulaic expressions. Extract 144 indicates the involve-ment of the state of Washington, through whoever drafted the laws regarding intestate succession, as another author, and the "Heirs" as interpreters. Extract 145 refers to the executor, who is another inter-preter. In Extract 148, although the beneficiaries are clearly interested parties to the interpretation of the will, strictly speaking they are not directly interpreters, rather overhearers, the primary interpreter being the executor named in Extract 145. In Africa, the elders would be considered producers, at least of customary law, and the community would be at least overhearers, if not interpreters.

In many countries there are legal aid societies, which employ lawyers and a variety of paralegal professionals to help lay people interpret the law. In the United Kingdom, for example, volunteers who work for the Citizens' Advice Bureaux are able to advise people who to contact to assist in their interpretation of a wide variety of laws, ranging from those dealing with consumer protection to those covering intestate death. Similar organizations have a more specific focus, such as Zimbabwe's Consumer Council (Tsanga, 1990, p. 166).

The situation in court cases is somewhat more complex. Here is just one example, in which the Counsel (C) cross-examines a senior Royal Ulster Constabulary police officer (W) about events during disturbances in Belfast, Northern Ireland, in 1969 (Atkinson & Drew, 1979, p. 107):

> [150] C: [reading from the police station log book] Then we have at 01.34
>   hours "Crowd coming down Conway Street from Shankill Road."
>   W: Yes.
>   C: Then at 01.36 hours "Crowd on Donegall Road from Sandy Row."
>   W: Yes.
>   C: And again immediately below that "Threat to burn Chapel at
>   Ardoyne" and "Also man injured in Butler Street." . . .

There is clear reference to the police station log book, of which the Witness was the producer for the entries referred to. He has to confirm Counsel's interpretation, so that he becomes the interpreter of Counsel's comments, and Counsel is both producer and interpreter at the same time.

In other cases, the number of "players" in a court case may be far greater, including alibis and "hearsay" evidence (e.g., Guest, 1985; Rein, 1994) as well as other witnesses. Philips (1986, p. 228) listed all the people involved as "players" in a civil trial: judge, witness, clerk, court reporter, defendant, defendant's lawyer, plaintiff, plaintiff's lawyer. James (1971, p. 174) noted that in big cities where large law firms operate, one team of lawyers may be responsible for preparing a case, and may then hand it over to the " 'persuaders'— lawyers who know how to be convincing with a jury or can skillfully handle a judge." James also devoted a whole chapter to "The Courtroom Team" (chap. 7), "the clerks, bailiffs, court reporters, and . . . the court administrators" (p. 165). This brings up the complex issue of producer–interpreter relationships.

Producer–Interpreter Relationships

The discussion so far has hinted at the nature of the power relationship between legal professionals and lay people. Within the legal profession there is an interesting array of power relationships between lawyers of different types, between lawyers and judges, and between these and the police. In the data and in the drafting of contracts in general (such as wills), it can be inferred that lawyers seek to negotiate meaning with their clients. In fact, Miles (1983, p. 3) specifically stated that "it is the responsibility of the [lawyer] preparing the will to ensure that it accurately expresses the testator's wishes. This can only be done by taking full instructions from the client himself (and not, e.g. from the bank manager introducing his customer as a client) and giving guidance and advice on a number of matters."

Clients generally have to trust that their lawyers' use of specialized language truly reflects their own intentions, as for example in the following extract from the data:

(151)   III.
                                Disposition of Estate

        . . .
        E. The trustee in exercising the discretion granted to it in making
        payments to [grandniece] hereunder may take into consideration the
        reasonable use of all resources, if any, which may then be known to
        the trustee to be available to or for the use of [grandniece]. The trustee,
        in its discretion, may request and rely upon a signed statement, from
        [grandniece] or from her parent or guardian, in form satisfactory to the
        trustee, as to such resources, and may, in its discretion, suspend such
        discretionary benefits from the trust for such beneficiary during any
        period in which such a statement is not furnished after the trustee's
        request therefor.
        (Authors' data)

This specialized use of language is considered in the next section but it is, of course, a major source of the lawyer's power, and an unscrupulous lawyer could easily abuse it.

In court cases, however, there is a much greater potential for legal professionals' abuse of power. Starting with the police, James (1971) pointed out that "the power society gives police is huge" (p. 151) and that "to enforce the law, policemen may break the law" (p. 189), in restricted ways. Greer (1990, p. 726), in considering the "right to silence," warned that "police officers acting in good faith are likely to see themselves as being capable of skillfully manoeuvring a guilty offender into giving the game away." The danger, as Greer cautioned, is that the police may inadvertently "trick an innocent suspect into compromising his position by making remarks which are open to misrepresentation at trial" (p. 726). Pattenden (1991, pp. 322–324) considered three ways in which the power of the police might be controlled for the protection of suspects before the trial: having an independent person present at the interview, such as a lawyer; banning "oppressive" interrogation; and tape-recording "all interviews in police stations for serious offences" (p. 324). However, she went on to point out that in each of these provisions there are serious loopholes, such that suspects may be protected in theory but not so much in practice (pp. 327–329). On trial protection, she quoted *Deane J. Carr v. R.* (1988) 165 C.L.R. 314 at p. 338 (Pattenden, 1991, pp. 329–330), showing the differential power relationship between police and defendants in a British courtroom: "The police witnesses are likely to be practised in giving evidence. The accused is not. The police will enter the witness box with the respectability of officialdom. The accused will enter it from the dock. The police evidence of an alleged . . . confession is likely to appear to some jurors as being safe to act upon to an extent which those with greater experience of the administration of criminal law would know to be unwarranted."

On the other hand, Atkinson and Drew (1979, chap. 5) clearly showed how witnesses may design answers "to include accounts and other defence components through which [they] can gain some control over the production of such objects as denials, defences, explanation, etc." so that they are less likely to be ascribed blame (p. 184). However, do not forget that in their case, the witness was a senior police officer, practiced in the art of giving evidence (as mentioned with reference to Extract 150).

Furthermore, although some lawyers may want to keep lay people informed, others prefer to keep them in the dark (James, 1971, pp. 197–198). Heller (1994) discussed the implications of four different models of legal counseling for lawyers keeping their clients informed, or not, and thus sharing, or not, the power of knowledge. In the positivist model, "the lawyer will not hesitate to manipulate the law in ways that frustrate the law's goals or run counter to his personal morals" (p. 2508). This type of lawyer is comparable with Conley and O'Barr's (1990, p. 87) "lawmaker" judge. The purposivist model believes that "law is meant to advance a common agenda, as well as to preserve order" (Heller, 1994, p. 2509). This description parallels that of Conley and O'Barr's (1990, p. 85) "strict adherent to the law." The discretionary model is closer to the purposivist than to the positivist, but holds that "the lawyer should not be constrained by the categorical nature of those approaches" (Heller, 1994, p. 2511). This type seems to correspond to Conley and O'Barr's (1990, p. 96) "authoritative decisionmaker," which emphasizes the lawyer's "personal responsibility" (i.e., power). Finally, as a way of insuring that the lawyer allows the client the right to decide what legal action to take, Heller (1994, p. 2514) described the full-picture model as fulfilling three objectives: "(i) describing the rule and the likely consequences of its violation, while communicating that violation of a legal rule is morally problematic in a society governed by law; (ii) describing the rule's purposes; and (iii) describing the practical problems the rule poses." In other words, the full-picture lawyer "considers his [or her] client to be entitled to the information that he [or she] possesses" (p. 2515). Neither of Conley and O'Barr's remaining two types of judge compared with the full-picture lawyer. The "mediator" seeks justice "primarily through the manipulation of procedure" (1990, p. 90). And the "proceduralist" is concerned with "maintaining procedural regularity" (1990, p. 101).

It can be dangerous if lawyers manipulate juries by not keeping them fully informed (James, 1971, p. 198). Menkel-Meadow (in Marcus et al., 1985, pp. 56–57) discussed how lawyers are trained "in the ethic of persuasion and argument and intimidation of the decisionmaker (especially if the decisionmaker is a jury of lay people as opposed to a judge)," although James (1971, p. 243) purported that judges may be susceptible to intimidation and manipulation, especially by local lawyers, who prefer a one-judge court where they can "set the judge up on a pedestal" and use this personal relationship to their advantage over outside lawyers (James, 1971, p. 149). Nonetheless, it remains true that trial judges have an enormous amount of power, which they may use to "separate a person from his [her] family, destroy his [her] good name and reputation . . . wreck his [her] career, and in fact . . .

deprive a person ultimately of life itself" (James, 1971, p. 157). Menkel-Meadow, however, described how a female judge moved out of this mode into a more relational approach, and "would ask [the jury] to examine their own views and values and sense of the facts in a way she thought attempted to appreciate their reality as well as her own" (Marcus et al., 1985, p. 57).

In this respect, it is worth considering the need for "a proper balance between the right of the public to be kept informed [the First Amendment] and the right of the individual to a fair and impartial trial [the Sixth Amendment]" (James, 1971, p. 223). The case of O. J. Simpson, the American football player accused of murdering his ex-wife and a friend in June 1994, points to a serious problem when the news media become obsessed with a criminal case. Sharkey (1994, p. 23) recorded that Simpson's defense attorney, Robert Shapiro, in an article entitled "Using the Media to Your Advantage," claimed that "an attorney's ability to influence the press may be as important as the ability to influence judges and juries in cases involving celebrities or other public figures." The American press has a code of ethics that is not unlike the British (Harris & Spark, 1993, p. 117), although "the law of contempt has its own nuances [and] there seems to be wide latitude for reporting and commenting before American trials" (p. 113). But in a number of instances in this case, journalists overstepped the mark, basing stories on rumors, "speculating that Simpson must be guilty," being willing "to be manipulated by prosecution or defense attorneys if it meant being first with a story," and "paying potential witnesses for their stories, thereby compromising their testimony" (Sharkey, 1994, p. 23). Sharkey quoted Quentin Kopp (Independent state senator) as saying that the "publicity frenzies" surrounding the Simpson case led to a "perversion of justice." In no way can the meaning of the case be negotiated between the client and the lawyer, and justice can no longer be either done or seen to be done.

Setting

Ignoring the time factor, as already seen in connection with culture, can lead to gross miscarriages of justice. In the case of the data, it is important for a will to be dated, such that all previous wills are rendered invalid. This necessity is evident in the opening paragraph of the will and the closing statement:

(152) I, [Name], of [address], Seattle, King County, Washington, declare this
to be my Last Will. I revoke all Wills and Codicils previously made by
me. ...
I have signed this Will the [date], at Seattle, Washington. [signature]
(Authors' data)

Of particular importance in the case of the signing of wills is
whether the signatory is "of sound mind" at the time of signing. This
aspect of time is particularly important if the beneficiaries subsequently wish to challenge the validity of the will and to revert to
a previous will that had been revoked (cf. Miles, 1983, p. 2).

In criminal cases, one serious way in which the police can abuse
their power and tamper with defendants' statements is to mislead
"the court about the contemporaneity of their records" (Pattenden,
1991, p. 317).[1] It is worth remembering that Counsel in Extract 150
referred to the precise timing of the sequence of events in the Belfast
disturbances, realizing the necessity for precision in such matters. In
the O.J. Simpson case, too, timing was a crucial element.

Place can be equally significant, in certain contexts. In the context
of definition of borders, jerrymandering—adjusting constituency
boundaries in order to manipulate the number of voters likely to vote
for your party—is a clear instance of abuse of the law related to
place. In the data, the significance of place is marked by the reference
to the deceased's estate, "wheresoever situated," mentioned earlier
in connection with the relation between territory and discourse and
repeated here:

(148)   III.
                          Disposition of Estate
        I give all of my estate, both real and personal, wheresoever situated, in
        equal shares to my deceased brother's children [nephew's name] cur-
        rently of Vancouver, Canada, and [niece's name] currently of Seattle,
        Washington. ...
        (Authors' data)

---

[1]This is precisely what happened in the case of the Guildford Four, who were
convicted in England in 1975, based on "confessions," and released only in 1989,
"when it was discovered that police officers had tampered with [the confessions]"
(Pattenden, 1991, p. 317). They had been accused of "causing explosions in two
Guildford pubs in which seven people died" (Pattenden, 1991, p. 317). They were
all Irish, and suspected of being members of the Irish Republican Army (IRA).

In a trial setting, James (1971) hinted at the possible impact of the courtroom itself in a number of places. For example, he stated that one judge he observed "operates in a huge cavern of a room. . . . You are immediately aware of and awed by the magnitude and majesty of the law" (p. 56). Philips (1986) showed the importance of spatial positioning and alignment in courts, particularly in marking status differences. Defendants who can afford a lawyer go before the bench with the lawyer at their side, "and they are not questioned about their financial solvency." By contrast, those defendants who cannot afford a lawyer go before the bench "with no one to their left," and are asked "if they want one appointed" (Philips, 1986, p. 231).

Another aspect of the setting, in court proceedings at least, is the judge's use of the gown—and, in Britain, the wig—which by setting them apart further reinforces the power of legal professionals over lay people.

Channel

Obviously, different cases require different combinations of oral + nonverbal + written language. In this case, the data are written, signed, and dated. Prior to the writing of the will, there must have been lengthy discussions between the lawyer and the woman, but these are not reflected in the written document. Miles (1983, p. 3) specifically stated that "almost invariably, obtaining the client's instructions for the preparation of a will involves an interview with the client—even if the client has set out his wishes in apparently clear terms in a letter to his [lawyer]."

In southern Africa, "customary law recognised the right of a person to leave property by oral will, but 'the distribution may be altered and the property distributed in a manner which the elders think right in the circumstances'" (Longwe & Clarke, 1990, fn. 5, p. 182; quoting Law Development Commission. [1976]. *Working paper on customary law of succession*, Lusaka: Government Printers, p. 1. Emphasis added). An oral will clearly cannot be signed and dated. The date will be remembered only as an approximation. But as already mentioned, even a written will does not always guarantee the widow her rights of inheritance in southern Africa.

Also noted earlier was the possible impact of nonverbal behaviors of defendants on judge and/or jury in court. In the courtroom, evidence may be oral (e.g., from witnesses), oral–written down–oral (e.g., confessions written down by the police after interrogation and signed by the suspect, referred to by the lawyers in court), and written down–oral (e.g., police statements, which may also be referred to in court), as in Extract 150.

There is another aspect of the relation between speaking and writing in legal discourse. Censorship has not been mentioned as a legal means for controlling what is written. Bowman and Woolf (1994, p. 6) pointed out that there are two facets to the relation between writing and power: "power over texts and power exercised by means of their use." They explained the first facet as follows: "In its most fundamental manifestation, this may mean that an elite or restricted group determines both the status of particular kinds of texts and also which people or bodies may use them to legitimise their behaviour. . . . Power can be wielded by changing either the way texts are written (both the scripts and formats employed), or the language they are written in" (pp. 6–7).

Bowman and Woolf went on to discuss how "power over texts allows power to be exercised *through* texts," distinguishing between "the use of texts to legitimise deeds and spoken words" and "the uses to which writing may be put in law, bureaucracy," and so on. What is particularly important in the consideration of the validity of unwritten versus written laws and contracts is that "what the text says may . . . not be the whole, or even the primary, point if most people could either not see the writing or could not read it anyway" (Bowman & Woolf, 1994, p. 8). This point is significant for a discussion of legal literacy in southern Africa and of the manipulation of witnesses in court, especially those of different socioeconomic or ethnic backgrounds who, even if literate, may not be able to fully understand a written legal text.

Participant–Text Relations

Intertextually, legal discourse provides some interesting examples in institutional settings. Lawyers depend extensively on legal precedents. First, Leith (1991, p. 205) mentioned the lawyer's need to refer to "legislation, case decisions, secondary reports, guidance from various government representatives offices, etc." Such legal precedents include, in this case, "the existing laws of the State of Washington controlling intestate succession," as indicated in Extract 144. The data contain other examples of intertextual reference that place the document within a set related to the drawing up of this particular Will. Extract 152 clearly refers to the set of wills previously drawn up by the producer of this will: "I revoke all Wills and Codicils previously made by me." In addition, there is indirect reference to a series of similar wills of other people, in the following extract:

[153]   III.
                                Executor Administration
        ... My estate shall be settled in the manner herein provided, and *letters*
        testamentary shall not be required except to admit my Will to probate
        and to file *the inventory required by law.*
        [Authors' data, emphasis added]

"Letters testamentary" and "the inventory required by law" refer to legal precedents in the drawing up and administration of any and all previous wills.

Miles (1983) referred to three types of immediate intertext of wills, in addition to the laws laid down to cover these types. There is, first, the grant of probate or letters of administration "necessary to establish the right to recover or receive any part of the deceased's estate in the United Kingdom" (p. 15). Second, there is the oath for executors, which "contains the evidence required to establish the executors' title to the grant" (p. 22). The third category of intertext is Inland Revenue [federal taxation] Account Forms (pp. 25–42).

In a society still very much impacted by oral tradition, legal precedents will still be established largely by oral means, and therefore with much less attention to distinctions that are only possible in written precedents. Rwezaura (1990, p. 9), for example, reported that in Tanzania:

It was clear that although the lower courts were part of the same judicial department and belonged to the same hierarchy, they had different legal backgrounds and working habits. The Resident Magistrate's Courts and the High Court were staffed by professional lawyers and were influenced largely by English legal ideas and procedures. The Primary Court magistrates, on the other hand, seemed to be having their feet deep in the African customary law, were sensitive to local public opinion, and were much less concerned about fine legal distinctions.

Purpose and Intent

Clearly, the will being analyzed here is based on fact and intended to transfer information. The assumption is that the author of the text actually owned the property that she was bequeathing to her relatives. Furthermore, it was assumed that she would actually predecease her heirs. The only hint of speculation is contained in the provisions for inheritance in the event that her nephew and/or niece die before her.

Consider the following moves within the legal subgenre of wills:

1. Establishing the identity of the author
2. Stating the rules for interpretation of the will.
3. Presenting the conditions for disposal of the estate:
   (a) Specific legacies
   (b) Pecuniary legacies
   (c) Trust
      (i)   Investment
      (ii) Maintenance
      (iii) Advancement
      (iv) Appropriation
      (v)   Insurance
4. Appointing the Executor(s) and Trustee(s) of the will.
5. Specifying the date and place, and signing the will.

The data present the previous order, whereas Miles' sample will (1983, pp. 11–13) places Move 4 together with 1.

Bhatia (1993, pp. 121, 124–127) identified four moves as typical of law cases, another subgenre. Consider these excerpts from the case he presented to illustrate each move:

1. Identifying the case	*Roles v. Nathan Court of Appeal.* (1963) 1 W.I.R. 1117; 107 S.J. 680; Court of Appeal. (1963) 2 ALL E.R. 908
2. Establishing facts of the case	The Manchester Assembly Rooms, owned and occupied by the defendant, were heated by an old coke-burning boiler which smoked badly. Two chimney sweeps were

called in to clean it, but it was no better after they had done so. An expert, Collingwood, was called, saw that the boiler-room was dangerous through fumes and succeeded, though only by force, in removing the sweeps from it. He said that the sweep-hole and inspection chamber should be sealed before the boiler was lit and the sweeps undertook to do that. On Friday evening, the defendant's son-in-law, Mr Corney, went to the boiler-room and found the sweeps working there with the fire on. They had not finished sealing off the apertures, and were to return the next day with more cement. On Saturday morning they were found there dead, the fire still burning brightly.

3. Arguing the case
   (a) Giving history
       of the case

Elwes J. gave judgment for the widows of the sweeps, but the Court of Appeal allowed the defendant's appeal, Pearson L. J. dissenting.

LORD DENNING M.R.: . . . The judge found Mr Corney guilty of negligence. . . . The occupier now appeals and says that it is not a case of negligence and contributory negligence, but that, on the true application of the Occupiers' Liability Act 1957, the occupier was not liable at all.

   (b) Presenting
       arguments

This is the first time we have had to consider that Act. . . .

"The common duty of care," the Act says, "is a duty to take such care as in all the circumstances of the case is reasonable to see that the visitor"—note the visitor, not the premises—"will be reasonably safe in using the premises for the purposes for which he is invited or permitted by the occupier to be there." . . .

The householder can reasonably expect the sweep to take care of himself so far as any dangers from the flues are concerned. These chimney sweeps ought to have known that there might be dangerous fumes about and ought to have taken steps to guard against them. . . .

(c) Deriving *ratio decidendi*

When a householder calls in a specialist to deal with a defective installation on his premises, he can reasonably expect the specialist to appreciate and guard against the dangers arising from the defect. The householder is not bound to watch over him to see that he comes to no harm. I would hold, therefore, that the occupier here was under no duty of care to these sweeps, at any rate in regard to the dangers which caused their deaths. . . .

4. Pronouncing judgment

I would, therefore, be in favour of allowing this appeal and enter judgment for the defendants.

Topic

The topic of the data is stated in the title of the document:

(154) LAST WILL OF [NAME]

This is a specialized topic, intended for surviving family members who would seek the specialist assistance of a lawyer. The subtopics are likewise clearly marked by section titles:

(155) I.   Identification of Family
II. Rules of Construction
III. Disposition of Estate
IV. Executor Administration

These subtitles reveal a progression of information from general to ever more particular.

Practice 61:
Choose one aspect of the context—either cultural, intertextual, situational, or relational—that particularly interests you, and compare the written and oral texts you identified for Practice 60 on this aspect.

The next section covers the language of the law, but do not forget that "a legal system which relies so heavily on out-of-date clothing, strange wigs and highly formalistic procedures is extremely likely, as well, to use other—more linguistic, or ideological—techniques to add to its seeming power" (Leith, 1991, p. 207).

THE LANGUAGE OF LAW

Lawyers certainly seem, to the average lay person, to wield great power by their use of aspects of language very specific to the law. James (1971, p. 181) pointed out that "we rely heavily on the words of witnesses— often more heavily than on evidence like measured skid marks, the extent of damage, position of the cars after impact, and mathematical calculations." The aspects of legal language examined range from the use of archaic expressions, definition, and extreme precision, through the use of conversational analysis as evidence, to unusual structures. Lawyers also make use of nonliteral meanings and "hearsay" evidence in court, even if not in contracts. Consideration of nonverbal meaning entails, among other things, discussion of the "right to silence" of witnesses, and again linguists can be called in to give expert evidence based on comparisons of taped conversations.

Coreference

The importance of producers and interpreters "speaking the same language" is underlined by the Legal Literacy Project in Zimbabwe. For example, Tsanga (1990, p. 175) reported:

If asked whether they have heard of the *Legal Age of Majority Act*, people in the rural areas react with a blank expression. The language is alien, the words totally unfamiliar. On the other hand, if asked whether they have heard about the law which says that a father cannot claim seduction damages they immediately liven up with hostility. The language, with an example from daily life, is perfectly understood.

And yet, it had never occurred to us to translate the phrase "Legal Age of Majority."

Prior to the rewording of the pamphlets outlining the new laws in Zimbabwe, people at the grassroots did not share the same universe of discourse as the paralegal workers trying to promote legal literacy. Subsequently, they did.

A striking feature of legal language is the careful use of coreference, or the opposite, extreme use of repetition, to avoid any danger of ambiguity. This is evident, for example, in Extracts 146, 148, 149, and 152 and is repeated here in the original order to highlight the use or nonuse of coreference:

> (156) I, [Name], of [address], Seattle, King County, Washington, declare this to be my Last Will. I revoke all Wills and Codicils previously made by me. . . .
>
> I.
> Identification of Family
> My only marriage was to [husband's name] who is now deceased. I have never had any children. The term "children" as used herein refers to all children born to or legally adopted by my spouse or me. . . .
>
> III.
> Disposition of Estate
> I give all of my estate, both real and personal, wheresoever situated, in equal shares to my deceased brother's children [nephew's name] currently of Vancouver, Canada, and [niece's name] currently of Seattle, Washington, if they survive me by ninety (90) days. If [niece] does not survive me by 90 days, her share shall go to her daughter [grandniece's name]. If [nephew] does not survive me by 90 days, his share shall go to [niece], or, if [niece] does not survive me by 90 days, to [grandniece]. . . .
> I have signed this Will the [date], at Seattle, Washington. [signature] (Authors' data)

Notice in particular the use of the demonstrative coreference term "this" as a deictic pointing to the contract within which the term is used, both at the beginning and at the end of the will. Furthermore, notice the repetition of "children" in Section I and of the names of the nephew and niece in Section III. This extreme care is needed because, once the author is deceased, there will be no way of checking that the interpretation of her Executor matches her original intentions.

The following extract, shown earlier in chapter 2, Practice 45, shows how reference and coreference is very carefully handled in court cases as well:

```
(157) Lawyer:   Can you identify these?
      Witness:  They are the pictures I took.
      Lawyer:   And what are they of?
      Witness:  A 3-year-old child.
      Lawyer:   And what was the child's name?
      Witness:  R____ M____.
      Lawyer:   And when were they taken?
      Witness:  The evening of September nineteenth, uh ...
      Lawyer:   1981?
      Witness:  Yes.
      (Nofsinger, 1983, p. 254)
```

In normal conversation, of course, the participants would not have to be quite so specific about what they were referring to, but in court, even if the lawyer and witness know what they are referring to, they have to use coreference rather than reference for the benefit of the jury, who do not know the details.

Although the desire to eliminate ambiguity is present in every court case, "prompting witnesses to provide unambiguous accounts is often like 'nailing jelly to the wall': a lawyer may gain the preferred response momentarily, but then it slips away into ambiguous territory" (Beach, 1985, p. 14). The problem is one of the "tensions between factual and perceived past." Whereas the lawyer wants "facts," the witness tries to reconstruct truthfully, some considerable time afterward, an event that could well have been "fraught with vagueness and ambiguity" (Beach, 1985, p. 13) even at the time. Furthermore, the witness may be perfectly justified in claiming "I don't remember" a specific detail as a way of indicating that the detail is unimportant or insignificant, so that "now, here in court [*coding time*], the witness is able to exhibit [*linguistic time*] her having taken no account of such matters at the time [*metalinguistic time*]" (Drew, 1992, p. 483). This points to the complexity of the relation between linguistic time, metalinguistic time, coding time, and receiving time in the courtroom, which Beach (1985, p. 12) suggested when referring to the "temporal density of the past."

Words and Lexical Units

An even more striking feature of legal discourse is the use of archaic expressions. Goodrich (1984a, p. 173) referred to the law's control "by means of an archaic, obscure, professionalised and impenetrable

FIG. 5.1. "For the purpose of this part of the schedule a person over pensionable age, not being an insured person, shall be treated as an employed person if he would be an insured person were he under pensionable age and would be an employed person were he an insured person" (U.S. National Insurance Bill, 1959). (Most of us have difficulty understanding legal texts.) Reprinted with permission.

language." This is certainly the case in Fig. 5.1. James (1971, p. 253) is equally critical, specifying several problem areas, all of which are identifiable in the data:

[158]   III.
                          Disposition of Estate
        A. The purpose of the trust shall be to provide for the *reasonable* maintenance, support, health and education of [grandniece]. The trustee shall make such *disbursements* from income or principle as the trustee shall determine to be appropriate in the trustee's sole discretion. (Authors' data, emphasis added)

The word "disbursements" is a word of French origin. The word "reasonable" is a "weasel word." In Extract 148, the expression "all of my estate, both real and personal" appears to be "designed to perplex laymen" (James, 1971, p. 253). However, it is important to comment on the apparently much greater insistence on perpetuating archaisms in the United Kingdom than in the United States, as is shown by the opening statement of this sample will (Miles, 1983, p. 11), which can be compared with Extract 152 for archaisms:

> (159) I IVAN WILLMADE of 1 Cherry Close Barset Barsetshire Computer Salesman hereby revoke all wills and testamentary dispositions at any time heretofore made by me and declare this to be my last will.

In the context of a courtroom, by contrast, Atkinson and Drew (1979, chap. 3) showed how the use of an archaic expression, "Be upstanding in Court for Her Majesty's Coroner," rather than perplexing lay people, may actually serve the triple purpose of "recognizing it as the first to be oriented to by everyone present" (pp. 91–95), of "accomplishing silence" (pp. 95–101), and of "consolidating shared attentiveness" (pp. 101–104).

Notice the almost complete absence of punctuation in Extract 159 from the British sample will, whereas in the American will punctuation is maintained, as seen in previous extracts and again in Example 160. Megarry (1959, p. 29) pointed out problems arising from punctuation and the use of "or" in earlier British legislation. In later acts, such as the Lease Under Housing Act 1985, not only is there no punctuation except a semicolon after a subsection, but none of the subsections ends with "or" or "and." At the same time, the extreme precision required in the drafting of statutes and contracts is evident in the apparently excessive redundancy caused by repetition of words that to the lay person may be synonyms, as in the following example from American data:

> (160)   III.
> Executor Administration
> ... My Executor shall have the power to *sell, convey, and encumber* the *real or personal* property of my estate, whether required in the ordinary course of probate or not, without an order of the probate court for that purpose, and without any notice or confirmation of sale, and no *application, notice, order, confirmation or authority whatsoever*, shall be *necessary or required* of any *court or officer* for my Executor to *do or perform* any *act or thing*, or execute any *conveyance, bill of sale, mortgage, satisfaction of mortgage, or any other instrument* in connection with the *management or disposition* of my estate.
> (Authors' data, emphasis added)

Such redundancy might seem to flout Grice's Cooperative Principle, especially the maxim of quantity, except for the counterbalanced need to eliminate all ambiguity.

This brings up the joint question of definition and extreme precision. Already, in 1945, G. L. Williams (1945c, p. 303) was claiming that "less attention should be paid to dictionary meanings and more to legislative policy." Almost 50 years later, the *Harvard Law Review* (Looking it up, 1994, p. 1437) continues to express concern that "the Court has come to rely on dictionaries to an unprecedented degree." The *Review* goes on to point out that "dictionaries are not ideal tools; they provide a range of definitions that bear an imperfect relationship to context and meaning. . . . Traditionally, the Court employed dictionaries to refresh the Justices' memory about the meaning of words, or to provide potential meanings from which the Court would select based on statutory purpose, legislative intent, common sense, or some other contextual argument" (pp. 1438–1439). What is happening now is that legal professionals are becoming overdependent on the dictionary for interpretation of statutes. A particular danger is the lack of relation between the date of publication (and revision) of the dictionary and the date of enactment of the statute. Given that meanings of words change over time, this could be crucial. Other flaws include "the imperfect relationship of dictionaries to statutory context" (p. 1449), the fact that "dictionary definitions may even run directly contrary to contextual ordinary meaning" (p. 1450), the danger of arriving at "strange or inconsistent decisions" when courts depend too much on dictionaries (p. 1451), and "the tendency to assign words to overly simplistic categories" (p. 1451). *A Dictionary of Modern Legal Usage*, by Bryan Garner (reviewed by Baker, 1988), may go some way toward addressing some of these dangers, particularly in naming the differences between legal and lay language and improving legal writing. But the *Review* elaborates two major differences between the needs of the courts and the purposes of dictionary editors:

First, courts must definitively resolve every case that comes before them. All judicial decisions invoke the coercive power of the state, whether or not the boundaries of statutory categories are readily identifiable. In contrast, dictionary editors have the luxury of listing many possible definitions without privileging any of them. Second, lexicographers seek to enumerate all possible general categories to which a word can belong, whereas courts must establish the relationship of words to specific situations. Both distinctions suggest that the tentative conclusions of dictionary editors cannot simply be transmuted into the authoritative findings of judges. (Looking it up, p. 1452)

Thus it is that in drawing up contracts, definitions are usually given at the very beginning. With reference to a contract, G. L. Williams (1945b, p. 184) specified that "to be valid [it] must be 'certain in its terms.' " So, for example, from the data, there are the Rules of Construction explaining the terms of the will:

(161)   II.
                                   Rules of Construction
        Unless some other meaning and intent are apparent from the context,
        the plural shall include the singular and vice versa, and masculine,
        feminine and neuter words shall be used interchangeably. "Heirs" shall
        be determined by the existing laws of the State of Washington control-
        ling intestate succession.
        (Authors' data)

It is the work of the draftsperson to insure that no ambiguous words are used in an ambiguous context. As G. L. Williams (1945b, p. 181) pointed out, "If . . . the draftsman of a statute uses a word . . . without defining it, it cannot be said that he [or she] is properly discharging the duty of his [or her] office."

On the other hand, even judges can be imprecise in court. Goodrich (1984a, pp. 192–200) analyzed a case that, in part, resulted from the vagueness of the Transport (London) Act 1969, and was appealed in the British House of Lords. He showed how the Law Lords failed to consider the "discursive context" of a key word in the appeal—"economic" (p. 199)—and thus "wholly excluded from consideration precisely those economic concepts and analyses which could have thrown some light upon the decision they were reviewing" (p. 200).

Conjunction and Clause Relations

A feature of legal discourse that makes it more difficult to understand is "the predominant use of backgrounding in judicial opinions" (Vargas, 1984, p. 9). Vargas (1984) explained the problem:

The language of legal professionals becomes harder to understand not just because they develop a specialized vocabulary or syntax. . . . Rather, it just so happens that to talk about categories (rather than individuals), relationships or states of being (rather than past actions) of those categories, and nonindividuated objects (rather than individuated objects) requires the linguistic components that signal backgrounding, and backgrounding . . . is harder to follow than backgrounding and foregrounding interspersed. (p. 10)

She went on to show how legal discourse that is highly transitive (with some foregrounding) is easier to understand than that which is not, describing in detail the components of transitivity. Most significant in this study is the finding that the more transitive the presentation of the case, the more likely compensation will be granted in "takings law" (p. 25). This fact is of great significance in terms of contracts and disputes between individuals and companies, for example, where "someone's home is razed to build a freeway" (p. 24). It was also significant in the Legal Literacy Project in Zimbabwe, referred to earlier in discussing the universe of discourse. The nominalizations typical of legal language (as discussed later) made their pamphlet on the Legal Age of Majority Act less balanced in transitivity, and it was only when the pamphlet was revised to include more foregrounding and higher transitivity that the intended audience was able to appreciate its meaning (Tsanga, 1990).

Turning now to conversation structure in legal discourse, Atkinson and Drew (1979) considered in depth the implications of the preallocation of turns for the witness in a court:

We can observe . . . that the production of such actions as accusations, justification, denials, challenges, etc., is achieved through the specific *design* and the *sequential placement* of the turns in which they are done, and that participants may monitor each other's talk for the production of such actions, such that, for instance if a witness recognises that a question has the purpose of challenging his evidence, he may design his answer as a sequentially relevant next action, as a rebuttal. (Atkinson & Drew, 1979, p. 76)

Thus it is that presequences (pp. 141–148) are significant, interpreted by witnesses as serving, for example, to preface blamings. By defending themselves before a projected blaming, they can "attempt to *minimise* the chances of having their accounts etc. rejected by the counsel" (p. 184). However, for the accusers, the preferred pair following an accusation is rejection not acceptance, although of course if accusation is followed by admission, then acceptance is the preferred pair. This structure could well point to a difference between lower class and middle class defendants' presentation of their cases.

By contrast, Atkinson (1992, p. 203) pointed to a very specific difference between Small Claims Courts and other courts: the arbitrator's acceptance of nonminimal or elaborative responses, which provides an examination structure as follows:

1. *Arbitrator* [PROJECTION OF MINIMAL RESPONSE]
2. *Litigant* [NONMINIMAL RESPONSE]
3. [PAUSE]
4. *Arbitrator* [RECEIPT]
5. [PAUSE]
6. [QUESTION]

This structure is exemplified in Atkinson's (1992, p. 203) Example 3:

(162) 1. Arbitrator: They'd be black leather with a cross front?
2. Defendant: Yes, cross front (1.0) of soft leather as Mister (NAME) asked me to.
3. (1.2)
4. Arbitrator: Yes.
5. (0.4)
6. and the heel (0.8) is as for an ordinary shoe?

This type of conversational exchange marks the arbitrator as not hostile, which is totally unlike the judge's or attorney's rejection of elaborate responses and pursuit of minimal responses, as exemplified elsewhere (cf. Drew, 1992).

A somewhat different use of conversational analysis is as "expert" evidence. Shuy (1986) described a case in which his evidence was used to confirm the innocence of two people who had been accused of corruption. Shuy first analyzed the structure of a "Proposal Conversation" (1986, p. 237), which can be summarized as follows:

1st Party	2nd Party
1. greetings	greetings
2. establish problem	respond to problem
3. present offer	consider offer, make conditions

4. recheck conditions, control, details	recheck conditions, control, details
5. complete contract offer	check conditions of offer, accept/reject offer
6. extend business relationship	extend business relationship
7. closing	closing

He then gave the data, pointing out that there is "no agreement on a deal, no handshake, no binding contract, . . . no extension phase" (p. 241), in other words, no Stage 5 or 6. It is significant that one of the most important features of agreement on a contract in the West is the handshake. Remember this when reading the next chapter.

Linguistic Features

Looking at Biber's (1988) dimensions of linguistic features, written legal discourse is clearly high on informational production (Dimension 1), high on nonnarrative concerns (Dimension 2), and extremely high on explicit reference (Dimension 3). These features of legal register arise from the attempt to be clear, precise, all-inclusive, and unambiguous. Bhatia identified five syntactic features of legislative sentences: sentence length, nominal character, complex prepositional phrases, binomial and multinomial expressions (1993, pp. 105–110), and syntactic discontinuities (1984). Extract 160 illustrates the first four of these features. For example, it consists of 102 words. It is nominal in character, containing long noun phrases such as "the power to sell, convey, and encumber." It contains complex prepositional phrases like "in the ordinary course of" and "in connection with." And the numerous binomial and multinomial expressions are already italicized, to emphasize the extreme redundancy necessary to avoid ambiguity. With respect to syntactic discontinuities, Bhatia (1984) identified three constituents that are "rendered discontinuous by embedded qualificational insertions in legislative writing" (p. 90): verb groups, binomial sequences, and nominal groups. An instance of a verb group discontinuity (italicized) is found here:

(163)   III.
                          Disposition of Estate
        C. If at any time the total principle amount remaining in the trust is
        $5,000 or less, the trustee *may*, in its sole discretion, *distribute* all

remaining principle and income to [grandniece].
(Authors' data)

The register in the previous extract, as in all the other extracts quoted from the will, is very clearly formal, with no contractions and no colloquialisms at all. The technical legal vocabulary associated with legal discourse, particularly in the case of a will, has already been noted. The formality in the written register highlights the difficulties of a lower class defendant in court, who is unable to maintain a formal speech style under the stress of examination. Wodak-Engel's (1984) comparison of middle class and lower class defendants in a Vienna courtroom hearing cases dealing with serious automobile accidents reveals "the differential power and prestige of speech varieties that are linked to social class" (p. 90). Even though the transcripts are given in translation (pp. 98–100), the middle class defendant's ability to maintain a formal style is obvious, whereas the lower class defendant is "unable to draw on her verbal resources to defend herself" (p. 96) when faced with the hostility of the judge. (The attitude of the judge was mentioned earlier in connection with prejudice.) By comparison, Atkinson (1992, p. 210) reported that "the [less formal] way Small Claims Court arbitrators display neutrality may make for a much less intimidating atmosphere than in other types of court."

Thus, in oral legal discourse, there are likely to be some differences in linguistic features. For example, it is in the interests of defence and prosecution lawyers to use techniques of persuasion (Biber's Dimension 4) in examining and cross-examining witnesses, a point that is touched on again in discussing nonverbal meaning with reference to the "right to silence." Furthermore, both parties in the court are likely to use online informational elaboration (Dimension 6), even while differences may remain between middle-class and lower class defendants' success in elaborating.

Nonliteral Meaning

Now consider nonliteral meaning, which G. L. Williams called "ulterior meanings" (1945d, p. 400) and related to nonverbal behaviors (p. 401). He later considered figures of speech (1946), in the context of the emotive functions of words, pointing out that using "emotive language in the presentation of facts may prevent the hearer or reader from examining the alleged facts critically" (p. 389). In this connection, he discussed legal euphemisms (pp. 392–394), insults (p. 394), the use of words as a stimulus to action (pp. 394–395), and the uncertainty brought about by the use of emotive words such as "right" and "duty," in the application of legal rules.

Turning to another form of nonliteral meaning, there are some fascinating metaphors describing the relationship of legal professionals to their clients. James (1971, p. 37) described a minor court magistrate in this way: "Day by day he dispenses justice like an Army mess sergeant dishing out boiled potatoes and meat loaf." Elsewhere, he described the law as a game (p. 86), similar to the analogy of a "drama" drawn by Atkinson and Drew (1979, pp. 11, 13) in their discussion of recent sociological studies of the law. James (1971, p. 93) pictured the prosecutor as the navigator of a ship. None of these descriptions suggests a serious attempt at the lawyers' negotiation of meaning with their clients in court cases.

Inferences

This observation is confirmed when key aspects of speech acts are examined. Considering first the felicity conditions, van den Hoven examined the legal argument as an illocutionary act complex, the most specific general descriptive model of the conditions of which is:

> *propositional content condition*: the constellation of statements S1, S2 (. . . , Sn) consists of assertives in which propositions are expressed;
> *essential condition* (for pro-argumentation): advancing the constellation of statements S1, S2 (. . . , Sn) counts as an attempt by speaker S to justify him holding opinion [+O] to listener L's satisfaction;
> *preparatory conditions (for pro-argumentation)*:
> (1) S believes that L does not (in advance, completely, automatically) accept that S can hold [+O];
> (2) S believes that L will accept the propositions expressed in the statements S1, S2 (. . . , Sn);
> (3) S believes that L will accept the constellation of statements S1, S2 (. . . , Sn) as a justification of him holding [+O].
> *sincerity conditions (for pro-argumentation)*:
> (1) S believes that [+O] is acceptable;
> (2) S believes that the propositions expressed in the statements S1, S2 (. . . , Sn) are acceptable;
> (3) S believes that the constellation of statements S1, S2 (. . . , Sn)

constitutes an acceptable justification of him holding [+O].
(van den Hoven, 1988, pp. 41–42)

Van den Hoven specified that the sincerity conditions are the felicity conditions. Pattenden (1991) touched on the violation of felicity conditions in her consideration of the causes, risks, and frequency of false confessions and the safeguards needed against "police-invented confessions" (p. 327). Rein (1994, p. 441) likewise mentioned felicity conditions in his consideration of the scope of the hearsay rule: "The indirect employment of evidence of an assertion as evidence of its truth has two stages. The first stage is the inference from the fact that the assertion was made to the fact that the author believed that what he asserted was true. The second stage is the inference from the existence of that belief to its truth." Guest (1985, p. 391) clarified Rein's statement by giving an example of the presuppositions on which the admissibility of evidence under the hearsay rule depends. His example concerned a telephone call, where the presupposition, "I am talking to a person who is taking bets at an illegal gambling house," cannot be implied from the WORDS recorded in the telephone conversation, "Look Guv, put 10 quid on Nijinski in the two-thirty at Newmarket." The presupposition can, however, be implied from the FACT of "the speaker's having made a telephone call to that address and his uttering those words" (p. 394). However, as Rein (1994, p. 435) pointed out, "there is no single relation of implication between an expression or action and the proposition 'implied.' " It could be argued that in cases where hearsay evidence is considered, the lawyers concerned are negotiating the meanings of the evidential statements. However, these meanings are being negotiated not with their clients but with the judge.

Aspects of the Cooperative Principle and the maxims of relation, quality, quantity, and manner have been discussed, but Munday (1994) specifically considered the matter of relevance of a defendant's previous bad character to his trustworthiness as a witness under cross-examination. A concern with the maxim of quality can be identified when he mentioned (p. 315) that "to treat previous unsuccessful pleas of not guilty as proven cases of perjury is a hazardous exercise." Yet, it is not uncommon for witnesses to swear to tell the truth, the whole truth, and nothing but the truth, "so help me, God," in the full knowledge that they are committing perjury (James, 1971, chap. 13), and in some cases actually encouraged by their lawyers, thus deliberately flouting the maxim. Munday (1994, p. 325) quoted Karl Llewellyn's comments on the famous case of Sacco and Vanzetti, which should remind the legal profession of the need to observe the Cooperative Principle: "Angel or devil, a man has a claim to a fair trial of his guilt. Angel or devil, he has a claim to a fair trial, not of his general social desirability, but of his guilt of the specific offense charged against him. Such is the letter of our law. Such is also our law's spirit." This issue was equally significant in the case of O. J. Simpson.

Libel, slander, and defamation provide other instances of speech acts that could be considered to flout one or more of Grice's maxims. In the case of the data, there is a clear instance of three speech acts in Extract 152, repeated here for convenience:

> (152) I, [Name], of [address], Seattle, King County, Washington, declare this to be my Last Will. I revoke all Wills and Codicils previously made by me. . . .
> I have signed this Will the [date], at Seattle, Washington. [signature]
> (Authors' data)

The verbs "declare" and "revoke" are clearly declaratives. But so is "give" in Extract 148. Another example is "appoint" in the following extract:

> (164)   III.
>   Executor Administration
> I appoint [name of family friend] as Executor of my Will to serve without bond. If for any reason [family friend] is unable or unwilling to serve or to continue to serve, I appoint [niece] as Executrix of my Will to serve without bond.
> (Authors' data)

The aforementioned extract also contains a legal hedge, "If for any reason [family friend] is unable or unwilling . . . ."

The felicity conditions surrounding the writing of a will obviously include the requirement that the will be valid. Miles (1983, p. 2) identified three issues related to the validity of a will under English law:

1. The testator must have the necessary capacity. Normally, this means that he must be aged 18 or over, and must understand the nature of his act and its effects; the extent of his property; and any moral claims he ought to consider. . . .

2. The testator must have the necessary intention to make the will. This involves the intention not only to make a will but also the particular will he executes. He must, therefore, know and approve its contents. . . .

3. The formalities in the *Wills Act 1837* must be observed. There are two matters to be considered here:

    (a) *Section 9.* This section, in effect, requires that a will (to be valid under English Law) must normally be in writing; be signed by the testator (or by someone else in his presence and at his direction) and have such signature made or acknowledged in the presence of two or more witnesses present at the same time. The witnesses must then attest and sign the will (or acknowledge their signatures) in the testator's presence, though not necessarily of each other.
    . . .

    (b) *Section 15.* Witnesses must be competent to act as such.
    . . .

The laws of the state of Washington, referred to in Extract 144 in all likelihood contain similar clauses.

Nonverbal Meaning

The importance of punctuation, which is the equivalent of prosody in written language, has already been considered. This section examines the significance of nonverbal meaning in court cases. James (1971, p. 56) hinted at the role of prosody when he referred to a judge's voice as "strong enough to wilt the thorns on a desert cactus." In this connection, Walker (1986) discussed at length the problem of the absence of nonverbal information in so-called verbatim records, pointing out (p. 211) that "in a court situation, a question or an answer, for example, delivered rapidly in a high pitch and loud voice, punctuated by gasps, or tears, or laughter, can be shown in the record as consisting only of the words spoken, thus presenting only a partial representation of what actually went on at the time." Atkinson and Drew (1979, pp. 188–194) considered the problems of their database and ways of improving it, one of the most significant problems being the lack of tape recordings. They also considered the role of stress (pp. 198–209), lengthening of vowels, and pauses in achieving audibility and clarity. Pauses are especially helpful in enabling the witness to monitor "piece by piece" the segmented parts of the question, serving a similar purpose to punctuation in written text.

This brings up a discussion of the aforementioned "right to silence" of witnesses, an issue of great concern in Britain, because the Criminal Justice and Public Order Act 1994 abolished this right (Rosenberg, 1994). Greer (1990) already foresaw the introduction of the act, pointing out that silence is usually taken as "indicative of guilt" (p. 711). He gave an important list of 11 legitimate reasons why innocent people might be advised to remain silent in the face of police questioning:

> They may be in an emotional and highly suggestible state of mind. They may feel guilty when in fact they have not committed an offence. They may be ignorant of some vital fact which explains away otherwise suspicious circumstances. They may be confused and liable to make mistakes which could be interpreted as deliberate lies at the trial. They may forget important details which it would have been to their advantage to have remembered. They may use loose expressions unaware of the possible adverse interpretations which could be placed upon them at trial. They may not have heard or understood what the police interviewer said. They may be concerned that an early disclosure of their defence could be to their disadvantage. They may have already given an explanation in the police car on the way to the police station which was not believed and thus prove reluctant to repeat it in the formal interview. Their silence may be an attempt to protect others or a reluctance to admit to having done something discreditable but not illegal. Some suspects may not want to be tricked into giving information about others because this could result in being stigmatised as an informer with all the dangers which this label carries. (Greer, 1990, p. 727)

Greer also illustrated the dangers of inferring guilt from silence by comparison with responses to leading questions. In this example, the silence might be in response to a question that refers to a nonverbal communication inferred from clothing:

> Take the case of a youth wearing a heavily studded belt, who has been arrested in connection with an assault. Skilful police questioning can convert the belt from an item of clothing into an offensive weapon, eg "If you were involved in a fight would you use your belt?" The accused in these circumstances may be well advised to stay silent in order to avoid being drawn on to such potentially compromising ground. But with the right to silence gone greater risks of being convicted may arise than hitherto. (Greer, 1990, p. 728)

Guest (1985, p. 398), however, pointed out that "it should not be supposed that statements cannot be made by silence." He mentioned pointing and saluting as nonverbal alternatives to making verbal statements (p. 387). Harris and Spark (1993, p. 102) quoted a newspaper report on a court case in which the suspect's "refusal to answer police questions about the incident after his arrest was within his rights and should not be held against him" by the jury, which nonetheless convicted him.

Apart from the right to silence, mentioned earlier in connection with ethnicity and social class were the problems Black defendants may cause by their apparent lack of deference to the judge (Hood, 1992) and the hostility the judge may show to lower class defendants (Wodak-Engel, 1984); both of these problems contrast strikingly with the nonverbal behavior of a middle class defendant, who "succeeds in presenting himself as contrite, capable, and socially acceptable" (Wo-dak-Engel, 1984, p. 95). James (1971, p. 87), considering the problems facing any unpracticed witness, quoted Henry Taft at length:

> Counsel and court find it necessary through examination and instruc-tion to induce a witness to abandon for an hour or two his habitual method of thought and expression, and conform to the rigid ceremo-nialism of court procedures. It is not strange that frequently truthful witnesses are . . . misunderstood, that they nervously react in such a way as to create the impression that they are either evading or inten-tionally falsifying. It is interesting to account for some of the things that witnesses do under such circumstances. An honest witness testifies on direct examination. He answers questions promptly and candidly and makes a good impression. On cross-examination [by the other side's lawyer], his attitude changes. He suspects that traps are being laid for him. He hesitates; he ponders the answer to a simple question; he seems to "spar" for time by asking that questions be repeated; perhaps he protests that counsel is not fair; he may even appeal to the court for protection. Altogether the contrast with his attitude on direct examination is obvious; and he creates the impression that he is evading or withholding.

In this connection, Pattenden (1991, p. 332) discussed "expert analysis of confessions," mentioning how the polygraph (lie detector) "meas-ures involuntary physiological reactions characteristic of stress in the subject produced by carefully worded questions." However, unfor-tunately, the polygraph is not "an infallible predictor of the truth."

Practice 62:

Compare the use of technical legal terminology in your written legal document with the presence (or absence) of such technical terms in your chosen oral transcript. Analyze the impact of such technical terms on the lay interpreter in each case.

As Munday (1994, p. 307) pointed out, "applied psychologists seem largely agreed that gauging subjects' credibility is extremely difficult." Although some may believe that information gathered from facial expressions, body movements, voice, and verbal behavior, combined, is reliable, custodians of the law should remain cautious in their interpretation, acknowledging that "the connection, if any, between behavioural and psycho-physiological indications of deception remains a mystery" (Munday, 1994, p. 308). In this respect, it is worth noting Nolan's (1991, p. 491) "reservations about aspects of forensic phonetic practice in the area of speaker identification" in his review of Baldwin and French's (1990) work on forensic phonetics.

Clearly, although a great deal of research has already been done by both lawyers and linguists, there is still scope for an enormous range of studies showing the interrelation between language and law.

CONCLUSION: SOME REMAINING QUESTIONS

This brief survey of legal discourse has touched on a broad range of issues, from the definition of law through gender issues to the nature of legal language. The discussion has hinted at some of the questions that lawyers are likely to have to face up to in the coming decade. A major question is whether there will be a shift in the definition of law from justice to compassion, from punishment to rehabilitation, or at least a balance between the two extremes. Although Britain and the United States are both trying to clamp down on crime from the perspective of punishment, it seems that many countries in southern Africa are focusing on legal literacy education.

Related questions are: Will more attention be paid to a "female voice" in the legal profession? Will more attention be paid to an "ethnic voice" in the legal profession? Will more women and/or members of ethnic minorities become legal professionals? Will male professionals become more sensitive to female perspectives on the law? Will white professionals become more sensitive to Black perspectives, and vice versa? President Clinton has tried to bring more women and Blacks into his administration. Will the same trend continue under future presidencies? Will it be replicated in other legal systems?

A further question is whether legal professionals will seek to clarify the relation between theory and practice (Dunlap, in Marcus et al., 1985, p. 17). Will any attempt be made to make law school courses more practical? Will the professors be able to continue operating in isolation from the professionals who work on a daily basis with the practical issues? Or will they seek to interact more regularly to make the theory they teach more relevant to the practice in the field? And will both the theoreticians and practitioners accept change, or even actively promote it? Or will they continue to resist change, especially that suggested by lay people, regardless of the potential for such change to improve the implementation of the law in a way that is both just and compassionate?

Again related to the question of the definition of law is the question of whether policy makers will consider "the relative merits of different types of court" (Atkinson, 1992, p. 211). That is, will the legal systems of the world become more flexible, allowing less formality in the structure of the proceedings, such that people may feel less intimidated if and when they do come into conflict with the law? And will they develop "training programs in arbitration techniques" (Atkinson, 1992, p. 211)? The development of such a training program would be of particular interest to discourse analysts, who could give useful input.

This brings up the nature of legal language. James (1971) suggested two areas of concern. First, he suggested that lawyers need to take courses in writing and public speaking so that they "become more articulate as a group" (p. 252). Woolever (1987) highlighted many more specific skills that lawyers need to become better able to "think like lawyers." These include critical thinking skills and considering the audience. In this respect, a pertinent question might concern the provisions law schools are making for teaching their students effective legal writing skills. At the same time, James (1971) suggested the need to improve the "language of the law," as seen earlier in the discussion of the use of archaic expressions. "Easification" is a method proposed by Bhatia (1993) to do just that. One of its techniques would be to create a parallel text, easier than the original for the lay person to read, yet making frequent cross-references to the original with added explanations and definitions. Such a technique would retain the extreme precision of the original texts, while at the same time making them accessible to the general public. The Legal Literacy Project in Zimbabwe (Tsanga, 1990) has adopted other helpful and hopeful ways of increasing legal literacy in the country, among both the literate and the illiterate. Until now, however, little has been done to "easify" legal texts, and one wonders if such a reevaluation will ever happen on a large scale.

In this connection, will the search for precision in identification reach the point of Nolan's (1991, p. 486) question: "Are voices, in principle, like fingers?" Nolan mentioned (p. 484) the formation in 1989 of the International Association for Forensic Phonetics, which might help legal professionals find the answer to whether, as Baldwin and French (1990, p. 126) believed, there will one day be available a "voiceprint" as reliable as the "fingerprint."

Meanwhile, will computers be more widely used in the legal profession? In the early 1970s, James (1971, p. 108) was pointing to the future when he mentioned the use of computers "to keep track of cases and to assemble dockets, as well as to keep track of verdicts and prisoners." However, James may have been too optimistic in stating that "systems to look up the law for judges and lawyers are being perfected," because 20 years later, while "we can use data retrieval techniques, a variety of presentations of annotating informa-tion and case synopsis to give a wider context to the general rules of law (p. 213) . . . the problem is how to classify the [case] which is presented to the judge (or lawyer for that matter) so that the relevant rule can be particularised (p. 212)" (Leith, 1991). In other words, the computer cannot work through the philosophical and psychological positions of the participants in a particular legal problem. Ultimately, it is the judge who has to make the decision, on the basis of consultation of relevant precedents and consideration of current cir-cumstances. The computer can only assist in administrative matters. However, Leith gave warning that it is already making a difference in the way lawyers practice the law (1991, p. 51).

Perhaps those of you who choose to enter the legal profession will be instrumental in finding answers to the previous questions, and go some way toward providing a "precise analysis of the social, political and ideological values existent throughout the syntactic and discursive processes of the law" (Goodrich, 1984b, p. 534), which Goodrich claimed has not yet been achieved.

6

THE DISCOURSE
OF NEWS MEDIA

⌡News media provide discourse analysts with a rich source of texts, and at the same time provide students with access to a prominent and pervasive use of language in context. ⌊An analysis of news media can be used to see how differently text interacts with context and with language in a genre that radically alters certain components and introduces others that are absent in many other genres, perhaps the most notably different features being found in the roles of producer(s) and interpreter(s). Indeed, as the context and language of news media texts are examined, the differences between news media discourse and the discourses of education, medicine, law, and literature become evident. Although media discourse preserves some similarities with the discourse of advertising, here again there are some differences, largely because the main function of advertising is to persuade and that of news discourse is to inform (Whale, 1977).

In order to illustrate the significant features of news media discourse, a transcript of a British Broadcasting Corporation (BBC) television news item broadcast on 1 September 1993 (about the expectation of a peace settlement in the Middle East) and five different reports (of the actual signing of the Middle East Peace Accord on 13 September 1993) appearing in British newspapers (*The Guardian, The Independent, The Daily Telegraph, Daily Mail,* and *Daily Express*) are used as a point of reference. Where necessary for purposes of illustration, a passing reference is made to news discourse from and/or about other parts of the world. Contextual features are examined first, starting with the cultural context of news reporting, moving on to a

307

consideration of the power relations among and between producers and interpreters, setting, spoken versus written news, participant–text relations, purpose and intent, and ending with topic. The discussion then turns to the language of media discourse, considering how the register of news reporting is achieved through a variety of types of cohesion, a particular set of linguistic features, and the manipulation of both verbal and nonverbal meaning.

First, however, consider definitions of the two key terms, *media* and *news*. Strictly speaking, a medium (singular) is the means by which a communication is achieved, so in the sense of channel, air is a medium (for radio waves, etc.). Or, as Inglis (1990, p. 3) put it, a medium is "what transforms experience into knowledge." The more recent meaning, which is usually referred to in the plural, media, is that they "provide the signs which give meaning to the events of everyday life" (Inglis, 1990, p. 3). The media now include a range of technological innovations, from telephones, photographs, and such like in the 19th century to fax, e-mail, and laser printing in the late 20th century (Enzensberger, 1970, pp. 13–14; Inglis, 1990, p. 111).

News is, by definition, new. In fact, B. Anderson (1983, p. 39) called the newspaper a "one-day bestseller." The moment after some new information is broadcast, that information ceases to be news, unless some person has not yet heard it. News is a "commodity everyone wants, which gets old and goes bad immediately. . . . [N]o one buys yesterday's news" (Inglis, 1990, p. 117). As G. Mitchell (1994, p. M2) put it: "There is a huge demand for news that's 24 hours a day and into it must be fed something on a daily basis. If something doesn't exist to be fed in, then it must be made up. And the reality is that much of the commentary, analysis, criticism is highly speculative, often false, usually tinged with sensationalism. . . . Increasingly in America what is news is defined by what is or is not controversial. If it's not controversial, it's not news." However, the fact that people in more remote areas of the world do not have immediate access to media—because of illiteracy or lack of such facilities as a radio—means they can still receive "news" that is old, many days, weeks, or even months later, and is therefore no longer news by any other standards.

This leads to something of a paradox in this chapter. It is analyzing, as instances of news discourse, news that is actually outdated, although the choice of topic has already had, and will no doubt continue to have, longer term implications and repercussions resulting in aspects remain-

---

Practice 63:

Collect current newspaper reports and record television and/or radio news broadcasts on the same topic for analysis while reading this chapter, possibly a follow-up on the Middle East Peace Accord. Transcribe the recorded news broadcasts, noting accurately and in as much detail as you can the intonation and, in the case of television, nonverbal features. Refer to your own materials alongside the materials discussed here, to check if you can identify the feature(s) being discussed at each stage.

---

ing in the news. But, unfortunately, it is not possible to show ways of looking immediately and simultaneously at all aspects, or even at only a very restricted aspect of the discourse of the news media, in a text of this sort. This book can only show what typifies news discourse and indicate how to analyze the news retrospectively.

THE CONTEXT OF NEWS MEDIA REPORTS

This chapter has already hinted at variations in production and reception of news media in different parts of the world, when defining the meaning of "news." It is probable that the news media differ most significantly from other types of discourse in specific features of their context.

Culture

There is a very real sense in which the advent of news media has acted as a cultural leveler, in that the news media play a role in determining literate people's perception of their view of the world and their place in the world, regardless of whether they are based in First-, Second-, or Third-World countries: "Almost 80 percent of the total news flow emanates from West-based major transnational agencies. One-fifth of the total of the foreign correspondents of the western agencies are based in the developing nations where four-fifths of the world's population lives. No wonder that the western agencies devote only 20 to 30 percent of news coverage to developing countries" (Pattanayak, 1985, p. 401). Thus, in developing countries, literate people's perception of their view of the world or place in the world is leveled by the input received from the (mostly Western) media. In some ways, this is even truer of Second-world countries like North Korea, whose communist government has, like the former Soviet Union (Thom, 1989), worked consistently at "thought control" through severe restrictions on access to the media (Short, 1994). Then, of course, the news media have played a role in people's attempts at self-development and self-preservation, although those from the Third World may agree with Pattanayak (1985, p. 400) that the use of English in the mass media "threatens to homogenize cultures, obliterate languages and reduce people into a mass," rather than helping them to develop and preserve themselves, their languages, and their cultures.

Possibly one of the main reasons for the threatened homogenization of cultures is that the international media are dominated by a capitalist ideology. News is big business. However, there are cases of news media "for the people, of the people, and by the people," in different parts of the world, perhaps most notably in the former apartheid South Africa (Tomaselli & Louw, 1991). Take the case of *Grassroots*, for example: It "started as an experimental project in community publishing in Cape Town [South Africa] in early 1980, rejected the conventional Western values attached to newspapers and journalism . . . [providing] a unique conduit for a community inadequately served by the mass media" (Johnson, 1991, p. 191).

An examination of the example news reports shows that, culturally, both the television news of 1 September 1993 and the headlines of the news reports on the Middle East Peace Accord of 14 September 1993 reveal aspects of view of the world, place in the world, self-development and self-preservation of all the participants, including the reporters themselves. In other words, cultural considerations in news discourse involve not only the content of the reports themselves, but also the positions taken by the reporters. First, consider the introductory words of the television newscaster:

(165) It's the first step towards a peace agreement negotiated in secret between Israel and the PLO. It would start with mutual recognition, lead on to autonomy for the Palestinians in the Gaza Strip and Jericho, then to an overall Middle East settlement.

newscaster sitting at desk in front of wall with "BBC" written on map of Europe and North Africa

Underlying this report segment is the cultural content itself: The Jews and Palestinians acknowledged that they needed to revise their view of the world and place in the world in order for them to peacefully coexist. The element of self-preservation is seen in the PLO's insistence that the full PLO executive ratify the statement before it was made public, and again in Shimon Peres' visit to the European Community to request financial aid for Palestinian autonomy. It is highlighted by the interviews with Jewish settlers in Jericho, for example:

(166) I don't believe that er police er Arab police will er will be able to ... to control er Jews. It's not er ... I don't understand it and I don't believe it.

caption: AVI GORDON
Jewish Settler
(*seen against background of field*)

Next, it is the job of the news media to interpret cultural matters for local understanding. The map of Europe and North Africa referred to in Example 165, is no doubt useful as an aid in this interpretation. Also, there may be an unintended or unnoticed cultural bias on the part of the reporters themselves. It is significant, for example, in connection with Example 166, that no Palestinians were interviewed, which reveals something about the author's (reporter's) position in the text with regard to the material being presented (Said, 1978, p. 20). Specifically, immediately prior to the interviews, the camera showed the marketplace in Jericho, which the reporter, Justin Webb, merely described as "sleepy."

View of the world, place in the world, self-development, and self-preservation can likewise be seen in the one photograph of the two former enemies shaking hands in front of the U.S. president, which accompanied every one of the newspaper headlines. Here are three examples:

(167) *The Daily Telegraph*

Signed and sealed with a handshake

(168) *The Independent*

The destiny of two peoples captured by a handshake as White House provides a perfect stage

(169) *Daily Express*

THE HAND OF PEACE

Particularly significant in these news reports is, of course, the aspect of self-preservation. Here, on the same stage, were two men who had been bitter enemies. As *The Daily Mail* put it:

> (170) With [the handshake], Israel and its sworn enemy the Palestine Liberation Organization set the course for peace in the Middle East.

It is significant that President Clinton apparently had to encourage Rabin to take Arafat's proffered hand. One wonders about the differential cultural significance of the handshake to Arabs, Jews, and Westerners.

But these descriptions do not really reflect a focus on the *language* of self-preservation. In that respect, far more significant are the actual words of the different actors in the drama, many of which are quoted in connection with producer–interpreter and participant–text relations. It was significant, for example, that Mr. Rabin spoke in English, whereas Mr. Arafat spoke in Arabic, with his words being translated— although in one sense both actors were at an equal disadvantage in being outside their home territories. At one point, Mr. Peres switched to Hebrew, "in the day's most emotionally charged moment" (*The Guardian*). It was also significant that, as reported in *The Guardian*, President Clinton tried to bring together the three worlds by using the three languages of the main actors, Hebrew, Arabic, and English, when he said, "Shalom, salaam, peace."

Whereas Mr. Peres' switch to Hebrew was probably purely for emotional reasons, Mr. Arafat's decision to speak only in Arabic was possibly a way of stressing his ethnicity. An additional way in which he stressed his ethnicity was in his dress, which simultaneously advertised his ideology: "Would he wear a suit, or in a gesture to his hardline PLO foes, appear in battle fatigues? In the event, he compromised" (*The Independent*). "Mr Arafat wore a green military tunic with epaulettes, a black and white head-dress and matching cravat" (*The Daily Telegraph*).

Discourse Participants

In terms of the discourse participants, the news media provide interesting problems for the discourse analyst, who might hope for a single producer, a single interpreter, and a single source, something that rarely happens in the case of news media. Given the presence of multiple inputs, both producers and source texts, as well as mass audiences, the complementary issues of power relations and participants' knowledge are extremely complex.

Journalists select from numerous sources the information they present in many different versions of the same story, and, in the case of these texts, all hit the front pages of their respective newspapers. This selection of sources hints at the extremely complex nature of participant relations in the news media, and leads to a fascinating, usually unanswerable, question: To what extent is the person whose name appears in the byline as the "author" of the report the one truly responsible for the final product? A great many people are involved in news production. Bell (1991, p. 39) tabulated the many roles in producing news language, naming the Principals (proprietor, managers, editorial executives), the Author (the journalist), the Editor (including overseers, copy editors, interpreters), and the Animator (including transmitters and technicians). Weaver (1994, p. 73) discussed how, increasingly, "it is the editor, not the reporter, who is the key figure in modern journalism. It is the editor, not the reporter or even the newsmaker, who is the true villain of the culture-of-lying story in which the very definition of news leads journalists and officials to fabricate events and stories." Tarutz (1992, chap. 4), on the other hand, talked about "The Editor as Team Player," and how editors can define their role by (p. 45): ensuring quality, reducing costs (quality is free; rework is expensive), improving efficiency and productivity, performing a unique function on a team, and working with other team members. Regardless of which view is taken, Tarutz' or Weaver's, such multiple authorship can lead to problems of accountability (Clayman, 1992, p. 164). However, in a totalitarian regime such as pre-1993 Malawi, journalists try to avoid the danger of accountability by printing bylines only for the most harmless of news items, preferring to name a news agency or use a catchall title like "Staff Reporter" or "Our Correspondent," rather than risk detention without trial for "misreporting" an event (S. Chimombo & M. Chimombo, 1996, chap. 5).

Those other than the author responsible for producing the final product appearing in a newspaper often remain invisible. But, in broadcast news, some of these individuals are visible and/or audible. Consider first the case of broadcast news. A number of "players" were represented: the newscaster, who was seen and heard on and off throughout the news item; Michael Macmillan, the BBC's Middle East correspondent, who was heard but was not seen as he talked about Yasser Arafat, PLO Chairman, and the PLO executive's discussions in Tunis; Arafat, who was seen, filmed in Morocco, speaking animatedly in Arabic, but his words were not audible, nor was any attempt made to translate them; Shimon Peres, Israeli foreign minister, was first seen as Michael Macmillan described his visit to the European Community in Brussels, and then was heard at a press conference; Sari Nusseiba, PLO spokesperson, was seen and heard talking about support for Arafat in the occupied territories; Martin Bell, another correspondent, was interviewed, live in Tunis, by the newscaster; Justin Webb, another reporter, was heard, but was not seen, commenting on the Palestinians in Jericho, and then interviewing Avi Gordon, Shimon Cohen, and Pierre Hamel, all Jewish settlers on the edge of Jericho. Thus, in just one short broadcast news item, there were 10 people who participated in the production, as animators (the newscaster, correspondents, and reporter) and authors (those we see and hear contributing their beliefs and opinions).

Similarly, in the newspaper reports, the bylines named the reporters, simultaneously naming the place. For example:

(171) RUPERT CORNWALL in Washington
(*The Independent*)

(172) By Stephen Robinson in Washington
(*The Daily Telegraph*)

It has already been noted that the reporters quoted liberally from the main actors in the drama of signing the Accord: Clinton, Arafat, Rabin, Peres, so that at least some of the authors are heard, alongside the animators (the reporters themselves and their editors).

Producer-Interpreter Relationships

Before turning to the interpreters of news media, it is necessary to examine the producer's relationship to the text and to the interpreter(s), as revealed in the various ways in which producers may manipulate the situation. However, this is an ambiguous situation, because in the case of news media the manipulations of the main actors in the actual drama being reported on, or alternatively the manipulations of the reporters themselves, can be interpreted. Clearly, the focus should be on the latter, but the former are revealed in the impact on the reporters.

In the examples, monitoring and manipulation are seen in the variety of ways that the two leaders were referred to, ironically in some cases by two different reporters on the front page of the same paper. For example, reporting for *The Daily Telegraph*, Stephen Robinson referred to "Mr Yasser Arafat, PLO chairman" and "Mr Yitzhak Rabin, the Israeli prime minister," and his colleague Maurice Weaver referred to "the Palestinian rebel" and "Israel's Prime Minister." The *Daily Mail* reporter referred to the "Israeli premier" and the "mastermind of a long terrorist war against Israel." Each of these techniques is, of course, designed to have different impacts on the readers.

Another form of manipulation is seen in the way the different reporters chose to refer to the nonverbal language of the two leaders, playing either up or down the enthusiasm of the one and the reluctance of the other. *The Guardian*, for example, referred to "the merest flicker of hesitation and a nudge from Mr. Clinton" in Mr. Rabin, when Mr. Arafat offered his hand. On the other hand, *Daily Mail* stated that Mr. Arafat was "beaming" while Mr. Rabin, "consumed by years of hatred, needed gentle persuasion."

Staging, achieved by deliberate choice of words, is characteristic of news discourse and is revealed in numerous examples. Staging was further achieved in the written reports by the universal phenomenon of news headlines being in various sizes of letters, examples of which were reproduced in Extracts 167, 168, and 169. In the broadcast, it was aided by intonation and stress, which is considered further in the discussion of the language of news media. Obviously, though, there are plenty of Israelis who still view Arafat and the PLO as terrorists, and see the Accord as a violation of assumed normality.

Turning now to the interpreters of news media, Britain's Independent Broadcasting Authority (IBA) carried out a survey in 1987, which found that 65% of people in the United Kingdom get their news from the television, 25% from newspapers, and 10% from the radio. Hulteng (1985) commented, however, that in the United States, despite the apparent availability of large numbers of television and radio channels and newspapers, few people actually have free access to the various channels, and most U.S. cities have only one daily newspaper, and minimal access to local radio. But, as Bell (1991, p. 86) put it, "Audience members can be anywhere that technology, physical conditions and social custom permit." Whereas constraints in the United States may be financial, in North Korea they are political. The communist government has maintained such strict control that radios are only tunable to North Korean radio, and North Korea is unequaled in lack of access to "unauthorized ideas" (Short, 1994).

The production process was necessarily viewed from the perspective of a variety of roles, and the layering of roles in media audiences must likewise be considered. Bell (1991, p. 92) named the following roles for media audiences: "the target audience who is addressed, the auditors who are expected but not targeted, the overhearers who are not expected to be present in the audience, and the eavesdroppers who are expected to be absent from the audience." Bell was, however, quick to point out that these roles are on a "finely graded continuum" (p. 93), with only the two extremes being clearcut, unlike the situation in face-to-face communication. Although media communicators (newscaster or reporters in this case) may have some idea of the ideal audience for any particular communication, they cannot pinpoint anyone of whom they can say definitely, "I addressed that person." In some sense this is the heart of both the power and the powerlessness of a media audience.

Whale (1977, p. 84) confirmed the power of a media audience:

> It is readers who determine the character of newspapers. The *Sun* illustrates the point in its simplest and saddest form. Until 1964 the *Daily Herald*, and between 1964 and 1969 the broadsheet *Sun*, had struggled to interest working people principally through their intellect. The paper had declined inexorably. Murdoch [the Australian newspaper owner who bought the *Sun*] gave up the attempt and went for the baser instincts. Sales soared. It was an owner's decision, certainly; but it would have meant nothing without the enthusiastic ratification of the readers.

A recent assessment of the power relationship between media producers and their audience refers to the O.J. Simpson case, well-known former American football player, arrested in June 1994 on suspicion of murder and subsequently acquitted after a long trial. It hints, like Whale, at the power of media audiences to control what the producers provide: "Once O.J. Simpson was under lock and key, the press found itself in a quandary: How would it keep the most exciting murder case in years alive without looking as if it were pandering to its insatiable, irresponsible, hopelessly vulgar audience?" (Rich, 1994, p. 21).

Yet, media audiences remain powerless in the sense that "they can no more communicate among themselves than they can reach back to the media sender" (Bell, 1991, p. 86), except in the relatively rare cases of live phone-ins, or community-based newspapers. Then they can at least communicate with the media sender. As Inglis (1990, p. 134) put it, "We can shout at the television, no doubt, or throw the newspaper across the room, but audience or spectator, solitary members of a huge crowd, are our principal public roles."

All this may change within the next decade with the advent of new interactive technologies, which could well give the audiences much greater control over coverage (Dennis, quoted in Sharkey, 1994, p. 26). Ultimately, all that can be said in an attempt to define the audiences of the news broadcast and news reports analyzed in this chapter is that, as already mentioned, two-thirds of the British public gets its news from television, and one quarter gets the news from newspapers. A clearer picture of the kind of listener/reader of the different television channels/newspapers is obtained from a study of media language described later.

Setting

News discourse is characterized by multiple and/or rapidly changing textual and metatextual settings. Clearly, the textual setting of the majority of the written reports in the examples was the South Lawn of the White House in Washington, DC, although some papers had additional reports from the Middle East, such as one in *The Guardian* from Jericho. A complex evolving context is seen in a number of reports, with the focus in most accounts moving from the general to the ever more specific. For example, in *The Daily Telegraph*, the focus moved from "Israel and the Palestine Liberation Organisation" to the "White House" to Arafat and Rabin, to their handshake, the garden, and the table where the signing took place.

The difference between the textual and metatextual settings is more easily observed in the television news broadcast of 1 September 1993: The textual setting moved for different segments of the report, whereas the metatextual setting remained the BBC headquarters in

London for the newscaster, but could be anywhere for other people interviewed. So, for example, the newscaster in London reported on the peace delegations waiting in Washington, DC, while viewers saw film footage of Washington, DC:

(173) In Washington, then, the Israeli and Palestinian peace delegations await the announcement that their respective governments officially recognize one another.

film footage of Washington, DC, limousines pulling up, delegates getting out, going into building

Here the textual setting was Washington, DC, but the metatextual setting for Sari Nusseiba (in Extract 174) could have been anywhere, given the fact that a background picture of palms does not necessarily mean that Nusseiba himself was in the Middle East. He could have been in the BBC studios in London:

(174) I think, in spite of the opposition, er, Arafat will be able ... to garner as much support as as er is needed. And in the occupied territories itself, I think people will very soon realise, I think there's already recognition on the part of most people, that this is far better than the er framework within which we were negotiating only last week.

caption: SARI NUSSEIBA
                 PLO Spokesman
[standing against background of palms, no gestures]

Channel

The channel of the newspaper reports is writing, but newspapers are nonetheless interspersed with photographs or other graphics (such as cartoons). The televised news is a combination of spoken and written, with a variety of graphics, such as video segments, photographs, and maps, accompanying the words of the newscaster, for example:

(175) The success of the plans for limited Palestinian autonomy also depends heavily on how the Israeli government handles the reaction of tens of thousands of Israeli settlers who've made their homes in the Gaza Strip and the West Bank.

map of Israel with Gaza Strip and West Bank labeled

> Under the draft accord, the town of Jericho would be the first in the West Bank to be placed under Palestinian administration. *close-up of map shows Jericho in relation to Jerusalem.*

Furthermore, news broadcasts are frequently accompanied by signing for deaf viewers.

Participant–Text Relations

One of the most striking characteristics of news discourse is the enormous intertext that comes with it. Even the smallest, seemingly most insignificant news item relates to items on the same topic in all other newspapers appearing around the world on the same day. Furthermore, it relates to current news broadcasts and news discussion programs. But, in addition, it draws on an ever-growing history of reports tracing the topic from the moment when it first appeared as news. All of these texts, in turn, relate to other texts, some far afield from news discourse, which define, explain, or give added meaning to information reported in the news.

There were, for example, fascinating intertextual allusions in the reports being analyzed. Only a small selection of the intertextual references appearing in the various articles is given here. First, the newspaper headlines in many cases are summaries or extracts from words actually spoken the previous day. Both *The Independent* and *The Daily Telegraph* quoted Yitzhak Rabin, "Enough of blood and tears," the former in a headline and the latter within the text. *The Guardian's* use of President Clinton's words, "Shalom, salaam, peace," was mentioned in connection with the cultural context, discussed earlier.

Then in the lead of *The Guardian's* front-page report, there is one allusion to the Christian Bible, if not the Torah and the Koran:

(176) With faith, hope and ... charity, Yitzhak Rabin of Israel and Yasser Arafat of the PLO shook hands on a joint accord at the White House yesterday. . . .

Later in the same report, Mr. Peres, Israeli foreign minister, is quoted as having switched to Hebrew to say:

(177) Let's say together in the language of our Bible: "Peace to him that is far off and to him that is near, sayeth the Lord. And I will hear."

A somewhat different allusion was made in reference to those who witnessed the signing of the Accord: "a Who's Who of the American establishment." Then *The Independent* contained an interesting cross-cultural reference to the crossing of the Rubicon:

> (178) Maybe a half-circling of Bill Clinton's arm was needed to pull [Rabin] across the Rubicon of history.

A reference to crossing the Jordan might have been more appropriate! The other aspect of participant–text relations, the study of the relation between production and interpretation, again proves fascinating. In the case of production, the televised news reveals examples of online production contrasted with segments that must have been edited and/or scripted. The following is a typical sample of online production:

> (179) These are the meetings that really matter now, of the PLO leadership. Er, the responsibility for this is going to be shared as widely as possible because it's a huge step they're taking. Er ... and I understand that the difficulty is to find the form of words of recognition so / ... / it could take today and there's another meeting tomorrow. It er it could drag on a bit.

This is in sharp contrast with the newscaster's smooth reading of the opening sentences of the news item:

> (180) The Central Committee of Fatah, the leading group within the Palestine Liberation Organization, is meeting in Tunis tonight to approve an announcement that it will renounce terrorism and acknowledge Israel's right to exist.

Such distinctions are not found in the newspapers. However, the producers of newspapers are aware of the circumstances of interpretation of many of their readers. They are careful to select the most significant stories to put on the front page. They are aware that many readers flip through the papers, glancing at the headlines, prior to settling down to read those items of particular interest. The interpreters, of course, determine how much time they will devote to reading any item, aided by the prominence of different headlines but also by their own background knowledge, and so on. Few readers buy more than two newspapers on any one weekday, the vast majority contenting themselves with the one that most appeals to them.

Purpose and Intent

The purpose of the news discourse being examined was to provide information on the current political situation in the Middle East. Bell (1991, p. 171, cf. van Dijk, 1988, pp. 49–59) outlined the model structure of news texts, which is applied to the text of the *Daily Express*'s report as an example:

(181) ABSTRACT	HEADLINE	THE HAND OF PEACE
		Deal at long last as Israel and the PLO sign historic accord.
	LEAD	THE world's most bitter enemies shake hands across a life-long gulf of hatred.
ATTRIBUTION	SOURCE	From PETER HITCHENS (journalist's
	PLACE	byline) at the White House
	TIME	yesterday (specified in Episode 1 of story)
STORY	EPISODE 1 (includes Attribution, Actors, Setting, Action, Follow-up, Commentary, Background)	This was the historic moment yesterday when Palestinian leader Yasser Arafat and Israeli Premier Yitzhak Rabin grasped tentatively at peace. President Bill Clinton smiled encouragingly at the two men on the White House lawns as they swallowed hard and touched for the first time. It was a gesture many feared would never happen. Arafat made few concessions for the occasion, wearing his military uniform and scarf draped in the shape of the Palestine he wants back. ...

This structure makes indirect reference to each of the situational elements already discussed: participants, setting, and so forth. In relation to factuality, the facts are given in the headline and lead, but both these and the story serve to illustrate how news articles combine description with speculation and/or imagination. If individuals distance themselves from the knowledge of the complexities of the peace process since the signing of the peace accord, they realize that at that particular point in time, the reporter had no way of knowing with any kind of certainty that the moment would prove historic. A certain amount of imagination also crept in, revealed in the choice of descriptive words suggesting opinion as much as fact, such as "tentatively," "they swallowed hard," and "scarf draped in the shape of the Palestine he wants back." Of course, newspapers adopt a style geared to the preferences of their readers, as already discussed, so the text may have persuaded its readers that there were grounds for optimism, at the same time as transferring information on the peace accord.

The genre of news reporting is also clearly exemplified in Example 181. No literate person would fail to recognize the structure of Extract 181 as a news report, and most would be able to recognize it even without visual help—large lettered headlines in bold face in telegram form, lead in bold face, and so on. Even broadcast news has a somewhat similar structure, although the headline is more often a complete grammatical sentence. The moves in newspaper reports have already been identified by Bell (1991): (a) headline, (b) lead, (c) source, (d) place, (e) time, and (f) episodes. Of these, only (a), (b), and (f) are obligatory. *Daily Mail*, for example, did not name (c), mentioned (d) in the middle of the episodes, and at no point, even within the episodes, specified (e). In the news broadcast, the moves are (a), (b), (d), (e), and (f) for the main segment, but (c) was announced when the newscaster hands over to other producers. The first four of these moves are found in Example 180, the opening sentence of the newscaster, after his greeting, "Good evening."

Topic

Remember van Dijk's observation (1988, p. 75), that the topics of news discourse are typically politics, war, society, violence, disaster, sports, arts, and human interest. The topic of the example texts is clearly politics, and specifically Middle East politics. The fact that all newspapers put it on the front page indicates its significance for all readers. This is typical of a newspaper in a democratic country, and contrasts vividly with the topic coverage of newspapers in nondemocratic countries. For example, in a detailed analysis of differences between topic coverage and specificity of Malawian newspapers in 1985, when Malawi had been under a one-party dictatorship for 21 years, and 1995, when it had been a multiparty democracy for 1½ years, S. Chimombo and M. Chimombo (1996, chap. 5) found major differences. Within the general topic of politics, for example, only 8 of 21 items (38%) reported on local politics in the 1985 issues examined, 8 of 21 reported on African politics, and 5 of 21 (24%) reported on world politics. In stark contrast, in the 1995 issues of the same newspaper, 25 of 33 items (76%) reported on local politics. Even more significant is the selection of particular items covering world politics. In 1985, the major political events on the international scene at the time when the two issues came out (in the first 2 weeks of November) were an international summit on arms control and the Middle East peace process, but the Malawi newspapers chose not to mention either, choosing instead to report on Palestinians stoning Israelis in the West Bank town of Bethlehem. On the other hand, the major political events on the international scene at the time the two 1995 issues came out (again in the first 2 weeks of November), the execution of Nigerian Ogoni Rights activist, Ken Saro-wiwa, and the assassination of Israeli premier Yitzhak Rabin, were both reported.

The topic is not necessarily contained in full in the headline, or even in the "subheadline"; in fact, a hint at the topic is more likely to be contained in the lead. Examples of leads are seen in Examples 176 and 181, and in the following:

> (182) As the world looked on yesterday Israel and the Palestine Liberation Organization called for an end to decades of bloodshed in the Middle East by signing a peace accord at a sombre ceremony lacking flags and anthems in the White House garden.
> (*The Daily Telegraph*)

The aforementioned leads had approximately the same level of specificity of the topic: They mentioned the Middle East and, in one way or another, peace. They also, in one sense, thematized the handshake by having the same photograph accompany their reports. However, in the following lead, the topic was specified differently:

> (183) It was the most hesitant of handshakes. And one of the most historic. With it, Israel and its sworn enemy the Palestine Liberation Organization set the course for peace in the Middle East.
> (*Daily Mail*)

"It" is clearly identified as "the handshake," which is confirmed by the headline immediately before it, "Handshake for history." "The handshake" is thematized by the use of the coreference tie "it," in the process of extraposition, which is discussed further in the section on news media language. The thematization is continued in the following sentence by a further coreference tie, "This."

As informational discourse, the news broadcast and reports all identified the topic early on and then provided supporting details, while reiterating the topic in varied ways. However, there was also a certain amount of narration, with a sequence of time adverbials, which modified the structure somewhat from pure information. *The Guardian* provided one example of a narrative segment (emphasis added):

> (184) With faith, hope and a careworn charity, Yitzhak Rabin of Israel and Yasser Arafat of the PLO shook hands on a joint accord at the White House yesterday and rolled the dice of history in what President Bill Clinton called "a bold gamble for peace."
> *As the Declaration of Principles was signed* at a sunlit South Lawn ceremony, Mr Arafat, dressed in chequered keffiyeh and a military uniform, offered his hand to Mr Rabin—the symbolic gesture of reconciliation for which a watching world was waiting.
> *After the merest flicker of hesitation and a nudge from Mr Clinton,* Mr Rabin acquiesced in the handshake, making eye contact for the first time with a man who for most of his life, and that of most Israelis, he has considered a mortal enemy.

However, as is typical of news discourse, the time adverbials may not actually be signaling a topic shift as in normal narrative discourse. Often paragraphs in news reports are merely one sentence long.

In news broadcasts, on the other hand, topic shifts clearly marked by paratones would be expected. For broadcast reports calling on input from a variety of people, like the example broadcast, the newscaster will end each person's contribution with a statement such as the following, which, as expected, ended with a significant drop in pitch and a longish pause:

> (185) Martin Bell, thanks very much.

Topic and topic structure in news discourse clearly differentiate this type of discourse from nearly all others. Restricted to a predictable set of topic areas, the topic structuring, according to van Dijk (1988), follows a top-down pattern in which summary precedes episodes, and in which all essential general information is given before specifics and details.

This analysis of the contextual elements of this discourse, in particular, has shown how the interaction between producer and interpreter is necessarily different from their interaction in other genres.

Practice 64:
If possible, obtain two newspaper reports of the same event from two different countries (one from your own country and one from another country, e.g., on an international event like the Olympic Games), and analyze carefully all the features of context that make the two reports similar and/or different.

The discussion also has identified the predictable elements of the context that give rise to the genre of news media discourse.

THE LANGUAGE OF NEWS MEDIA REPORTS

The danger with analyzing the language of the news media is that the sheer quantity of words written every day on just one topic is overwhelming. So, the focus here is only on language features that differentiate news media discourse from other kinds of discourse. As already mentioned, a clearer picture of the expected reader/listener emerges from a study of the distinctive language of the media. With respect to newspapers, as Whale (1977, p. 78) pointed out, "All newspapers demand a measure of literacy in their readers. Popular papers keep the demand as gentle as they can: they deal in short words, short sentences, few paragraphs of more than a single sentence, few articles of more than a few paragraphs, and a great many pictures."

Reference and Coreference

The headlines of newspaper reports contain a wealth of data for the discourse analyst whose initial focus is on the language. Often written in a telegraphic style, headlines frequently contain not only the expected elements of reference and coreference typical of all discourse, but also significant uses of exophora and deixis. Concerning coreference in news discourse, it has been found, for example, that "quality" newspapers are at least six times more likely to preserve the determiners "the" and "a" than the "popular" tabloids (Bell, 1991, p. 108).

Patterns of coreference and deixis in news headlines clearly depend on the way such headlines structure information. With regard to topic, whereas the headlines of both radio and televison news broadcasts are frequently presented separately from the actual reports, in newspapers the headlines provide a summary or identification of the main idea immediately above the full report. First consider the language of the headlined information in the five newspaper reports of the signing of the Middle East Peace Accord on 13 September 1993. In just the few words of the headlines, there are examples of exophora, deixis, reference, significant word meanings and meaning relations, literal and nonliteral meanings, and even nonverbal meanings. Further examples are found in the news broadcast as well, although the focus there is specifically on nonverbal meanings—that being the category that most distinguishes written from oral news reports.

In the news broadcast, the place deictic references are immediately recoverable from the context of accompanying pictures, as for example in the following comment, where the correspondent, Michael Macmillan, is heard but not seen (emphasis added):

> (186) Yasser Arafat, pictured here *in Morocco* . . .
>
> *film footage of Arafat with PLO Executive seated at table, with microphones in front of Arafat*

Because of the nature of the news, time deictic references are also frequent, both in oral and written news reports. Just two examples, the first from the broadcast and the second from a newspaper, will suffice (emphasis added):

> (187) I think there's already recognition on the part of most people, that this is far better than the er framework within which we were negotiating only *last week*.

> (188) This was the historic moment *yesterday* when Palestinian leader Yasser Arafat and Israeli Premier Yitzhak Rabin grasped tentatively at peace. (*Daily Express*)

In both cases, the italicized words are only interpretable from the context of the day on which the broadcast was viewed or the newspaper was bought. Furthermore, in Example 187, tense and aspect are combined in "were negotiating" to describe a process that took some time in the past, but "now," at the time of coding, is different. The linguistic tense of the other verbs is present simple, and they are metalinguistically tenseless. In both Examples 187 and 188, obviously the receiving time was when the viewers first watched the news and the readers first read their respective newspapers. Notice also the first word of Example 188, which is an example of discourse deixis.

Words and Lexical Units

It was noted earlier, in connection with staging and the violation of assumed normality, how one of a set of words can be deliberately chosen. Such words can be significant for their connotative, social, or affective meanings, to emphasize a bias in newspaper reporting. In particular, Yasser Arafat was described in many different ways, indicating the possible social and/or affective meanings, quite apart from the simple connotative meanings, the producer attached to him, for example:

> [189] [a] ... a man who for most of his [Rabin's] life, and that of most Israelis,
> he has considered a mortal enemy.
> (*The Guardian*)
> [b] ... mastermind of a long terrorist war against Israel.
> (*Daily Mail*)

Ironically, elsewhere similar words were used to describe Yitzhak Rabin, emphasizing just how important attention to social and affective meanings, especially, is for staging:

> [190] Mr Yasser Arafat, PLO chairman, thrust his hand towards his bitter
> enemy, Mr Yitzhak Rabin, the Israeli prime minister and military mas-
> termind of the 1967 war.
> (*The Daily Telegraph*)

Coming now to meaning relations, a quick survey of lexical cohesion shows extensive use of both reiteration and collocation between the

TABLE 6.1
Sample Lexical Chains Showing Density of Collocation

In Sentence 1		In Sentence 2
Yitzhak Rabin of Israel	→	Mr Rabin
Yasser Arafat of the PLO	→	Mr Arafat, dressed in chequered *keffiyeh* and a military uniform
the White House	→	South Lawn
President Bill Clinton		
shook hands	→	offered his hand
		the symbolic gesture of reconciliation
on a joint accord	→	the Declaration of Principles
rolled the dice of history		
a bold gamble for peace		

headlines and the full reports of each newspaper. In this case, one of the most striking points is the lexical cohesion not just within each report but from report to report across newspapers. All reports, either in the headlines or later, made reference to the handshake, the newly found peace, and the former war. Taking just the first two sentences of *The Guardian's* report, Table 6.1 gives several lexical chains showing the density of both reiteration and collocation, presented earlier. These collocations are clear examples of paraphrases. The collocations were followed through meaningfully even in nonliteral expressions, as the last expression in Table 6.1 shows. Metaphor is a prominent feature in news discourse. One of the examples in *The Daily Telegraph* specifically mentions the use of metaphors by the various players:

[191] ... the need for "high bridges to span deep chasms" (Mr Peres), a "journey ahead beset by dangers" (Mr Abbas) and of peoples "caught in a well of hatred of their own making" (Mr Clinton again).

Conjunction and Clause Relations

Although patterns of conjunction and clause relations are not distinctive in news discourse, transitivity is a major issue. Thom (1989) found that state-controlled newspapers—such as those of the former Soviet Union, whose language, Newspeak, she studied closely—deal in vagueness, repetition, and a preference for passives and certain other features, which are all ways of distancing authors from responsibility, and also of controlling the thought patterns of their readers. Wang (1993) found similar features in the Chinese Communist party newspaper—*Renmin Ribao* (People's Daily)—report on the 1991 failed Soviet coup, which contrasted significantly with *The New York Times* report of the same event. Such features have also been found in the newspapers of noncommunist totalitarian states, such as Malawi until 1993 (S. Chimombo & M. Chimombo, 1996).

Both *The Independent* and *Daily Mail* chose to thematize the handshake on the Middle East Peace Accord by using the strategy of extraposition for their first lead sentence:

[192] IT WAS the moment when disbelief, finally, was suspended.

[193] IT was the most hesitant of handshakes.

However, in keeping with the prevalent patterns of democratic news discourse, neither revealed any serious tendencies toward Newspeak, with the former containing only four finite passive verbs, and the latter none. Nonetheless, both passives and nominalizations were quite common in the broadcast. Example 165 is typical of this usage.

Linguistic Features

Coming to the linguistic features identified by Biber (1988) as common in press reportage, this genre has a high negative score on Dimension 1, meaning that it has a high degree of informational content. This is reflected in the fact that the number of nouns, attributive adjectives, place adverbials, WHIZ deletions (removal of "which," "who," and so on followed by a form of the verb "be"), and agentless passives, among other features, is significantly higher than in "involved" production. The nominalizations and passives were already mentioned in connection with transitivity, but taking participial WHIZ deletions as just one example, in the 245-word *Daily Mail* front-page report there were six such deletions:

[194] This was the moment no one had dared hope for, [which had been] orchestrated for a worldwide TV audience by President Clinton on the South Lawn of the White House. At his right hand was Israeli premier Yitzhak Rabin, 71, [who had been] a former general in the 1967 Six Day War when Israel grabbed the occupied territories, [which were] including Gaza and the West Bank, from the Arabs. ... Once bitter enemies, they were risking their political lives on an agreement [which was] giving Palestinians self-rule in the Gaza Strip and the West Bank town of Jericho in return for official recognition of the Jewish state. ... Arafat, [who was] beaming, stretched his palm forward. Rabin, [who was] consumed by years of hatred, needed gentle persuasion from the President to take Arafat's hand and give the briefest of shakes. ...

In *The Independent* there were 14 such deletions in 764 words, a similar proportion. By contrast, in the broadcast news, there were only 7 such deletions in over 1,000 words, in keeping with Biber's findings for online production, rather than planned and scripted text.

Of course, within the press reportage genre, the reports being analyzed fall under the subgenre of political press reportage. If written and spoken texts of a different subgenre of press reportage have been selected, then try comparing some of the features across the two subgenres, political and personal. To do so, choose to follow Biber's dimensions, or alternatively van Dijk's (1988) analysis, given in chapters 1 and 2.

Nonliteral Meaning

Another characteristic feature of news discourse is nonliteral meanings, including a high frequency of idioms, as well as metaphors (as
already noted). Although idioms are often associated with casual
discourse and especially spontaneous conversation, Henry and Roseberry (1995) showed that they also occur with significant frequency
in certain kinds of informative texts as well. Supporting this view in
the case of news discourse is the frequent complaint that students of
language often find newspapers among the most difficult texts to read
in a second language, in spite of the fact that the vocabulary and
grammar alone present no unusual difficulties, and the demands on
the reader's knowledge are no greater than those made by newspapers
in the first language. The example texts have already illustrated a
couple of examples of nonliteral meaning, which are repeated here:

(178) Maybe a half-circling of Bill Clinton's arm was needed to pull [Rabin]
      across the Rubicon of history.
      (The Independent)

(191) ... the need for "high bridges to span deep chasms" (Mr Peres), a
      "journey ahead beset by dangers" (Mr Abbas) and of peoples "caught
      in a well of hatred of their own making" (Mr Clinton again).
      (The Daily Telegraph)

Strictly speaking, Extract 191 is not an example of nonliteral meaning
in news discourse, because the newspaper is merely quoting the
words of people present at the White House. This is, however,
common practice in news discourse. On the other hand, Example
178 contains one of a number of idioms appearing in the various
reports. The television broadcast likewise contains a few idiomatic
expressions, such as the following, in the newscaster's exchange with
the BBC's correspondent, Martin Bell:

(195) This is obviously the meeting that matters but if it's a form of words
      that that can't be sold er in the occupied territories, then it's obviously
      worthless anyway.

And a few sentences later is another expression:

(196) I think they're casting a much warier eye on ... on Palestinians else-
      where because they themselves don't want to be left out in the cold here.

As is to be expected, most of the examples of nonliteral expressions came from spoken discourse, which is closer to conversation than straight reporting.

Inference

The most noticeable trigger of inferences in news discourse, and one that sets it apart from many other kinds of discourse, is hedges. Hedges are frequent in both written and oral news reports, although *The New York Times* would claim that "presenting both sides of the issue is not hedging but the essence of responsible journalism" (Hulteng, 1985, p. 15). Like journalists writing for newspapers, newscasters "systematically refrain from aligning with or against the opinions they report" (Clayman, 1992, p. 174). Nonetheless, here are a few, of many, examples of hedges using the variety of modal verbs available in English:

(197) The PLO system *appears* to be delaying ...
      (BBC)

(198) [The peace agreement] *would* start with mutual recognition ...
      (BBC)

(199) Rabin *seemed* to avoid [Arafat's] eyes ...
      (*Daily Express*)

(200) The agreement ... *may or may not* signify a lasting peace ...
      (*The Independent*)

And, even if the business of news reporters is in theory facts (despite the cynicism of Weaver and Mitchell, quoted earlier), reporters color their item with a personal interpretation, as can be seen from the variety of ways in which Rabin's reluctance to take Arafat's hand was described:

(201) Rabin ... needed gentle persuasion from the President ...
      (*Daily Mail*)

(202) After the merest flicker of hesitation and a nudge from Mr Clinton, Mr Rabin acquiesced in the handshake ...
      (*The Guardian*)

Nonverbal Meaning

The pragmatic features tie in with the last aspect of the language of news media to be considered: prosody and nonverbal language. Even some written reports attempted to give readers a feel for the tone of the ceremony. Mr. Arafat gave "an unemotional speech" in Arabic, (*The Independent*), and Mr. Peres switched to Hebrew "in an emotionally charged moment" (*The Guardian*). But far more evident in the written reports are the references to body language and facial expressions, quite apart from the already mentioned picture of the famous handshake. Take, for example, *The Daily Telegraph*'s description of Mr. Rabin as "stony faced throughout." The response of the audience was "a spontaneous roar" (*The Daily Telegraph*). According to the *Daily Mail*, "The 3,000 crowd of diplomats and politicians cheered, some with tears in their eyes."

Obviously, in the written reports, none of the hesitations are reproduced that are found in the unscripted, interview segments of the news broadcast. Here is just one extract from the news broadcast (parts already seen elsewhere) revealing the expected accompaniment of hesitations, repetitions, and gestures in an unscripted interview:

(203) MARTIN BELL:

These are the meetings that really matter now, of the PLO leadership.	*no gestures or facial expressions*
Er, the responsibility for this is going to be shared as widely as possible because it's a huge step they're taking. Er ... and I understand that the difficulty is to find the form of words of recognition so / ... / it could take today and there's another meeting tomorrow. It er it could drag on a bit.	/ ... / *breathes in sharply*
NEWSCASTER:	*Close-up of newscaster*
So /er/ have you got any feel for how long it could go on and whether it is	/er/ *shakes head*
/ ... / **this** particular group who will actually produce the announcement of recognition?	/ ... / *stress plus circular gesture, camera takes in both speakers*
MARTIN BELL:	*Close-up of Bell*
We think they will they will produce the form of words.	

> The announcement itself could er
> could come in some in some other
> forum.
> This is obviously the meeting that
> matters but if it's a form of words
> that that /CAN'T/ be /SOLD/ er   /stress/ /stress/
> in the occupied territories, then it's
> obviously worthless anyway.

Whether scripted or unscripted, the newscast reveals all the elements of intonation discussed earlier. For example, in Extract 203, prominence is given to the word "this," which indicates a clue to the informativeness of the exchange. This prominence is accompanied with an interactive gesture, a circular motion emphasizing "this" as opposed to any other group. In the same example, there are instances of high, mid, and low key as well as high, mid, and low termination. The hesitations and repetitions contrast with the probably scripted sections that open the report, as seen in comparing Examples 179 and 180 in connection with participant–text relations. Example 204 indicates the facial expression of the newscaster:

(204) NEWSCASTER:
> Good /evening/. The Central Committee   /smiles /
> of Fatah ...

Of course, he could not actually see the home audience to whom he is smiling: Some might actually be shouting at him, as Inglis (1990, p. 134) suggested. But most people would not be too happy to see a blank, staring face in a newscaster. On the other hand, each of the other people seen live, being interviewed, also revealed a variety of expressions, from one that could be interpreted as expectancy on the face of the PLO Spokesperson, Sari Nusseiba, to one that could be interpreted as fear on the face of one or more of the Jewish settlers interviewed.

Practice 65:
Select an interview segment of your television news broadcast and attempt to identify the meanings of the facial expressions and gaze behaviors of the interviewer and interviewee. You will need to play through the segment several times. Determine whether the meanings are identifiable independent of the words or only in conjunction with them.

It should be clear from the previous analysis of the language of the news media, that the more aware people are of the register, the better able they are to accept or reject a report as unbiased. However, this analysis leaves a number of questions.

CONCLUSION: SOME REMAINING QUESTIONS

This necessarily brief survey of the discourse of news media has been unable to do more than hint at such interesting questions as the future of newspapers and broadcasting. Given the pace at which new technologies are being introduced, for example, it is not unrealistic to expect that soon there will be greater potential for interaction between the producers and interpreters of the news media (already happening on some local radio stations), lessening the disjunction of time and place (Bell, 1991, p. 85). Again, it is possible that local people will be used as correspondents to counteract the imbalance noted by Pattanayak (1985), such that local news of international import is reported more frequently by locals rather than by foreign correspondents and there is less emphasis on news from Europe and North America to the virtual exclusion of coverage of the Third World. Already, the BBC World Service (radio) makes use of many such people for its regional services, such as the Africa Service, and also has specific news bulletins for these areas. Similar programs of regional interest are broadcast on the Voice of America.

A second question concerns the nature of the audiences of the mass media, and the power they have to control the output of the media they devour. Are they really going to become more and more "insatiable, irresponsible, [and] vulgar" as Rich (1994, p. 21) suggested? Or, are they going to continue to hold the media to account for breaches of ethics (Hulteng, 1985)? Or, are they simply going to carry on as before, with some following Rich's description and others fitting Hulteng's better?

A related question is whether communities might become more active in producing their own genuinely democratic outlets for news, along the lines of the alternative press in apartheid South Africa (Tomaselli & Louw, 1991). The case of *Grassroots* is particularly enlightening in this respect:

> *Grassroots* is run by an executive which is answerable to the general body (which meets every 5 weeks) whose members are in turn an-

swerable to their democratically-elected organisations. The . . . news-letter is produced in a 5-week cycle . . . [that] starts just 2 days after the previous issue is published. . . . [T]he first news-gathering meeting . . . "gives birth" to the new . . . issue of *Grassroots*. All workers and community organisations are invited to send representatives. At this meeting a list of stories for the coming issue is discussed and approved. Certain members are given the task of putting together certain stories. . . . Running parallel with the work of the news-gathering committee is the Advice committee . . . a committee of experts who put together articles on health, law, worker's rights and so on. Once the news-gathering committee has finished its work, the process of bringing out an issue of *Grassroots* is taken over by the Production committee. . . . On printing day about 50 representatives of youth, civic, worker and other bodies come together to (collate and fold the paper) . . . the full-time distribution official together with a small group of volunteers deliver the paper to all our distributors. They sell the paper from door-to-door . . . using it as an opportunity to renew contacts with their members and make contacts with potential members. (*Grassroots*, 3(2), p. 8; quoted by Johnson, 1991, pp. 194–195)

Might it be possible for other communities to initiate such demo-cratically run media? What about the enormous amount of time and energy that needs to be invested in such a project? Increasing access to desk-top publishing has made the process of preparing camera-ready copy much shorter, but how many disenfranchised communi-ties in poor countries would have such access?

Another interesting question, which parallels the one asked in connection with literature in the next chapter, is: What effect will changes in media preferences have on newspapers as more people spend ever more time in front of television sets? Already, according to Bagnall (1993, p. 1),

The language of journalism is nearer the spoken word than business language is on the one hand, or academic language on the other. In fact it is closer to the spoken word than it ever was in the past.

Television and radio have made this happen. People are so used to getting their news from a live announcer, and their views from live interviewees, that they expect something like the same language from their newspapers and their periodicals.

And, as recently as 1987, three quarters of Britain's population preferred to get its news from the television and radio, thus suggesting that if newspapers are to survive at all, then their main role might well, in future, move even further from providing news to a greater focus on entertainment. Even now, because television and radio can get the current, up-to-the-minute news out to listeners and viewers more quickly than newspapers, it might be claimed that newspapers are no longer providing genuine news, in the sense that it is already at least 12 hours old by the time the newspapers reach the newsstands.

Finally, what effects will the new interactive technologies have on the news business? The relative powerfulness and/or powerlessness of media audiences have already been discussed. Dennis (quoted by Sharkey, 1994, p. 26), claimed that the public's fascination with the trial of O.J. Simpson foreshadows "all kinds of potential changes in news decision making" as a result of the "primitive beginnings of interactivity." He added that interactive technology could make the public's voice (in Sharkey's words) "so strong that instead of asking people what they think about a program that they are watching today, the news executives might be more interested in asking the public what events it would like to see tomorrow."

These questions will probably be answered within the next decade. If newspapers do change their role toward more entertainment, it will be interesting to see whether and how television and radio increase their provision of news. Already, with satellite television, CNN is providing virtually round-the-clock, round-the-world news programs, interspersed with commentary and documentary. Regardless of what happens, it is sure that, as humans, people will adapt to the changes.

7

THE DISCOURSE
OF LITERATURE

Part II concludes by providing a description of literary discourse to aid in its analysis. First, a definition of literature is provided. Then the context and language of literature are examined. The focus will be primarily on literature of Europe and the Americas with most examples being drawn from literatures written in English, because a cross-cultural analysis of literature would be a major undertaking in itself. However, the principles applied here to literature in English or in English translation can be equally well applied to literature in other languages if sufficient cultural information is available.

The term *literature* in its most general sense is synonymous with "written discourse." In its more restricted sense, it is commonly taken to mean "written discourse that has enduring value." Even more specifically, the term is usually applied to enduring written works that are primarily narrative or descriptive and therefore exhibit the typical features of such discourse, as identified by Biber (1988). This excludes philosophies, histories, biographies, anthropological studies, and other similar writings that are typically informative or argumentative.

In nonliterate societies, the meaning of "literature" is often extended to include "oral literature"—strictly speaking an oxymoron referring to works that would have appeared as written literature if a writing system had been available. Without written records, there is no way to ascertain dates of origin, variants, or indications that a work accurately reflects the historical culture that produced it or is in any sense culturally prophetic, as people have come to expect of the most highly valued examples of literature, the so-called classics. For the purpose of analyzing the discourse of "literature," therefore, oral literature is disregarded. However, bear in mind that some works that originated as oral literature were later set down in writing. A few of these, such as the Arthurian epics, have taken their place alongside the literary classics.

The discourse of literature, as defined here, is therefore a written form of culturally sensitive, primarily narrative and/or descriptive discourse. It reflects and gives meaning to the values of the sociocultural group of which the producer is a member. To achieve this purpose, it typically uses language in novel or unusual ways, thus often inventing new semantic, pragmatic, and even occasionally syntactic meanings and meaning constellations. Other genres such as the written history, the philosophical treatise, and the advertisement, for example, may demonstrate equal linguistic sophistication and cultural sensitivity; and some advertisements have contributed as much to linguistic experimentation and to reinvented constellations of meaning as have some of the most highly regarded poems. However, these genres are predominantly informative or argumentative; and their purposes, as seen elsewhere in this book, are significantly different from that of "literature," which aims to give pleasure through personal and cultural recognition and discovery.

Traditionally, a literary text is thought to be an example of either poetry or prose. "Poetry" is characterized as seeming to the interpreter to have enough of "meter" (i.e., a rhythmical pattern of stressed and unstressed syllables) and/or of "rhyme" (i.e., repetition of stressed vowels and consonants at the ends of words) to be perceived as something different from prose, which an interpreter would judge as being largely devoid of these characteristics. Some modern poetry has neither of these qualities, however, and claims its status as poetry on the basis of other features. On the other hand, some prose passages may seem to some interpreters to be even more poetic than some poems. The ultimate judge is the interpreter.

Literature, together with all the other written and spoken genres examined in this book, is part of the social and cultural use of language. As such, it is a small but significant branch of the ethnography of language, which in turn is but one of the fields of study comprising sociolinguistics. Within a comprehensive social semiotics, literature would take its place beside the other arts, all of which have the purpose of depicting, describing, and giving meaning to the personal and social values of groups.

THE CONTEXT OF LITERATURE

Perhaps more than any other discourse, literature is regarded as an expression of the context of the writer who produced it. Writers may write not only about contexts in which they have grown up but also about contexts in which they have spent some time (Forster's *A Passage to India* comes to mind). Writers may even write about contexts of which they have only an outsider's view, as does the South African writer, Andre Brink, whose novels take the reader into the world of the black African as well as into his own white African background. However, writers who write about a context with which they are totally unfamiliar are unlikely to be successful—except, of course, science fiction writers. But, even the science fiction writer needs to be familiar with the context of science to write successfully.

Culture

Perhaps more than any other discourse, literature is regarded as an expression of the culture that produced it. Literature is a powerful tool for gaining insight into other contemporary cultures as well as into historical cultures that no longer exist. Reading literature as cross-cultural discourse, however, often leads to predictable difficulties of interpretation. Just as cross-cultural communication breakdowns can occur in the discourses of daily life, so too can they occur in literature. For this reason, when individuals study the literature of a particular culture or age, they also study the social history that produced it. For example, little would be gained from reading the classic literature of Japan or China without a thorough understanding of the Japanese or Chinese cultures of the period. The same problem exists even in the literatures of closely related cultures and in contemporary literature. Consider two examples, both from modern South American authors.

In Gabriel García Márquez' short story "The Saint,"[1] a man travels from his South American homeland to Italy, bearing the body of his young daughter who had died at age 7. When, 11 years later, a construction project necessitates that the body be disinterred, it was found that the body had not decomposed. The villagers viewed this as a miracle and arranged to send the father and the corpse to Italy in the hope that this evidence of the girl's assumed sainthood might be

---

[1] In *Strange Pilgrams* (1993). London: Penguin, pp. 26–53.

brought before the Pope. Culturally, the actions described in this story probably suggest piety and devotion to the culture represented by the author. To other cultures, however, the same behavior might seem macabre and even demented, especially when it is revealed that the father is still seeking a Papal audience 22 years after his arrival in Rome.

As a second example, consider the following (translated) quotation from Mario Vargas Llosa's novel *The War of the End of the World*, in which the uniquely red-headed Gall commits adultery with Rufino's wife, Jurema. While Rufino searches for them, friends of Rufino find them and cut off Gall's hair to take back with them as proof of identity. Later, Gall asks Jurema,

(205) "Why didn't you convince the *capangas* to take my head away with them instead of just my hair? Why are you with me? You don't believe in the things that I believe in."

"The person who must kill you is Rufino," Jurema whispered, with no hatred in her voice, as though she were explaining something very simple. "By killing you, I would have done a worse thing to him than you did."

(Vargas Llosa, M. [1981]. *The War of the End of the World*. New York: Farrar, Straus & Giroux, p. 227)

Here, what might appear to be simple justice to the members of one culture, could seem an act of barbarism to the members of another.

Another important way in which culture influences literature is the growth of literature in dominant languages that have been transplanted to other cultures where other languages already existed. Today literatures are arising throughout the Third World in the languages of the former colonial rulers. In Africa alone, major literatures in English, French, and Portuguese, among others, have begun to take their place alongside the older home-grown literatures. What is significant about these literatures is that they do not attempt to imitate linguistic or cultural norms handed down from the older literatures, but rather they invent new standards that reflect the cultural values of the societies in which they arise. A writer such as Chinua Achebe in Nigeria, for example, successfully captures not only the cultural values of Nigerian society, but also the special flavor of Nigerian English, as in the following example:

(206) Later in the Proprietor's Lodge I said to the Minister: "You must have spent a fortune today."

He smiled at the glass of cold beer in his hand and said:

"You call this spend? You never see something, my brother. I no de keep anini for myself, na so so troway. If some person come to you and say "I wan' make you Minister" make you run like blazes comot. Na true word I tell you. To God who made me." He showed the tip of his tongue to the sky to confirm the oath. "Minister de sweet for eye but too much katakata de for inside. Believe me yours sincerely."
[Achebe, C. [1975]. *A Man of the People*. London: Heinemann, pp. 14–15]

Turning from the culture to the more immediate situational elements of literary context, the focus is primarily on the writer, setting, characterization, action, and plot of a story. The last three of these grow out of the writer's need to structure and present a topic. First, however, examine the participants in literary discourse.

Discourse Participants

For literature, as defined here, the discourse participants include one or more writers, typically a large intended readership, and possibly overhearers. There is rarely an institutionalized author, although it is quite common for a writer or writers to use a false name, or pseudonym, to maintain anonymity. A famous example of this is Mark Twain, whose real name was Samuel Clemens. An equally significant example is George Eliot, who did not, for reasons related to her religiously orthodox background and to the era in which she lived, want to be known by her real name, Mary Ann Evans.

An additional participant, the narrator, may occasionally act as an intermediary between producer and interpreters. A parent who reads or recites a bedtime story to a child is acting as a narrator, for example. And in drama, actors fulfill the function of intermediaries by performing the roles and actions of a literary text. In effect, they "bring it to life." Similarly, in the case of oral literature in its original context, the narrator or story teller is effectively the intermediary, but also the author, because each oral performance is in a sense an original one.

Producer–Interpreter Relationships

The most common kind of narrator is a kind of persona, or *alter ego*, of the author. This type of narrator appears when the writer is projected into the literary work as the one who tells the story. This narrator is usually a fictionalized creation of the writer and takes a form that defines the relationship between the writer as producer and the reader as interpreter. Toolan (1994), drawing on Fowler (1986), described four possible positions of the narrator. First of all, a narrator may be a central part of the story, but limited to the role of a character, as are the various fictional narrators in Wilkie Collins' *The Woman in White*. This type of narrator is also found in autobiographies, such as Carter's *The Education of Little Tree*, as well as fictional autobiographies, such as Flagg's *Daisy Fay and the Miracle Man* and Courtenay's *The Power of One*. This narrative type is characterized by first-person narration: "I," references to the time of narration, modalities expressing personal judgments, descriptions of the narrator's thoughts and emotions, and a characteristic vocabulary, establishing the narrator as an individual. All of these characteristics appear in the following example from the opening of *Daisy Fay and the Miracle Man*:

> (207) Hello there ... my name is Daisy Fay Harper and I was 11 years old yesterday. My Grandmother Pettibone won the jackpot at the VFW bingo game and bought me a typewriter for my birthday. She wants me to practice typing so when I grow up, I can be a secretary, but my cat, Felix, who is pregnant, threw up on it and ruined it, which is OK with me. I don't know what is the matter with Grandma. I have told her a hundred times I want to be a tree surgeon or a blacksmith.
> (Flagg, F. [1981]. *Daisy Fay and the Miracle Man*. London: Vintage, p. 13)

If narrators are omniscient and unlimited, they provide a second narrator type. The omniscient narrator writes in the third person, uses the past tense, and stands almost godlike above the characters peering into their hearts and minds, as in the following (translated) excerpt from García Márquez' story "Maria dos Prazeres."

> (208) She walked into the lobby, dim in the oblique light from the street, and began to climb the first flight of stairs with trembling knees, choked by a fear she would have thought possible only at the moment of death.
> (García Márquez, G. [1993]. Maria dos Prazeres. In *Strange Pilgrims*. London: Penguin, p. 114)

A third type of narrator is detached from the action, limited in knowledge, and impersonal. Verb phrases are more prominent than noun phrases in this type of narration, with the result that action prevails over description. If adjectives are used at all, they tend to be basic and not "flowery." In extreme cases, this type of narrator can seem to disappear completely, giving the impression that readers are witnessing actors on a stage rather than a narrative text. The following excerpt from Hemingway's short story, "A Clean, Well-lighted Place," serves as an illustration:

(209) "He's drunk now," he said.
"He's drunk every night."
"What did he want to kill himself for?"
"How should I know?"
"How did he do it?"
"He hung himself with a rope."
"Who cut him down?"
"His niece."
"Why did they do it?"
"Fear for his soul."
"How much money has he got?"
"He's got plenty."
"He must be eighty years old."
"Anyway I should say he was eighty."
(Hemingway, E. [1938]. A Clean, Well-lighted Place. Quoted in Heilman, R. [1950]. *Modern Short Stories: A Critical Anthology* (pp. 387–388). Westport, CT: Greenwood Press.

Related to the position of the narrator are two further relational concerns: the position of the narratee (reader or listener) and the focalization of the narrative. The position of the narratee is usually transparent in literature. Rarely is a narratee mentioned in a literary text. Some exceptions to this include *Tom Jones* and a number of other English works primarily from the 19th century Romantic and Victorian periods, which mention the reader outright.

A more problematic concern is that of *focalization*. Focalization is concerned with whose perspective dominates the reader's view of the action and through whose words the reader hears the story. These do not always refer to the same person. Toolan gave as an example the early chapters of Dickens' *Great Expectations*. Here, the perspective is that of the child Pip. However, the words are those of the adult Pip, speaking with the experience and vocabulary of a grown man, as he recalls the thoughts and emotions of himself as a boy. A similar example is provided by the following excerpt from the opening pages of *The Power of One* in which the man Peekay recalls his childish emotions during a trip home through South Africa from boarding school:

(210) As we choofed along in the car, with me in the dicky seat open to the wind and the sunshine, I was no longer a *rooinek* and a *pisskop* but a great chief. We passed through African villages where squawking chickens, pumping their wings desperately, fled out of the way and yapping kaffir dogs, all ribs and snout and brindle markings, gave chase—although only after my speeding throne had safely passed. As a great chief, I was naturally above such common goings-on. Life was good. I can tell you for certain, life was very good.
(Courtenay, B. [1989]. *The Power of One*. New York: Ballantine, p. 8)

The relationship between the writer and the reader also can be defined through a writer's style. An entire study of stylistics has arisen that focuses almost exclusively on the language of literary texts. Although this chapter looks in some detail at literary language later, it is appropriate here to examine the individual stylistic characteristics of a given writer. Like all personal styles, a writer's style represents a set of choices aimed at uniquely identifying the speaker or writer as an individual. All elements of language may legitimately contribute to style: structure of sentences, choice of vocabulary, patterns of coreference; use of indirect and nonliteral constructions; use of prosody and paralanguage; and even the use of nonverbal language may contribute to a specific style. Story tellers in an oral narrative performance develop their own characteristic prosody, paralanguage, and nonverbal language. In written literature, of course, style is largely restricted to the verbal elements of communication. However, certain prosodic and paralinguistic features may be approximated by the use of specific punctuation and type faces. As an example of a personal writing style, consider the following passage from *Brideshead Revisited* by Evelyn Waugh:

(211) Something quite remote from anything the builders intended, has come out of their work, and out of the fierce little human tragedy in which I played; something none of us thought about at the time; a small red flame—a beaten-copper lamp of deplorable design relit before the beaten-copper doors of a tabernacle; the flame which the old knights saw from their tombs, which they saw put out; that flame burns again for other soldiers, far from home, farther, in heart, than Acre or Jerusalem. It could not have been lit but for the builders and the tragedians, and there I found it this morning, burning anew among the old stones.
(Waugh, E. [1945, 1983]. *Brideshead Revisited*. Harmondsworth: Penguin, p. 395)

Perhaps most noticeable about this passage is the author's unusual use of multiple clauses and the way in which commas are intended to indicate pauses rather than structures of language. This style is in sharp contrast to the terse, dramatic style of Hemingway, for example, as shown in Example 209. And, although both authors are speaking through narrators or characters, this fact in no way diminishes the significance of uniquely identifiable writing styles.

Merely transferring the writer's personal style to the style of the narrator does not in itself give rise to stylistic problems. But a more interesting use of style is to uniquely identify different characters within a literary text and thus also to differentiate them from the narrator. This is often accomplished by exaggerating the use of a certain word or phrase or a peculiar structure of sentences. As with the primary narrative style, this style may also involve paralinguistic and prosodic features, represented in punctuation and different type faces, as in the following extract, where the character's peculiar high-pitched voice is suggested by the use of capital letters:

> (212) "PUT ME DOWN!" he would say in a strangled, emphatic falsetto. "CUT IT OUT! I DON'T WANT TO DO THIS ANYMORE. ENOUGH IS ENOUGH. PUT ME DOWN! YOU ASSHOLES!"
> (Irving, J. [1990]. *A Prayer for Owen Meany.* London: Black Swan, p. 17)

Style may also include local or nonstandard dialects spoken by one or more characters, as in Achebe's *A Man of the People* and Forrest Carter's *The Education of Little Tree*, the source of the following example:

> (213) One time a woman stood up. She said the Lord had saved her from wicked ways. The man in the corner hollered, "Tell it all!"
> Her face turned red, and she said she had been fornicatin'. She said she was going to stop. She said it was not right. The man hollered, "Tell it all!" She said she had done some fornicatin' with Mr. Smith. There was a commotion while Mr. Smith disassociated hisself from the bench he was on and come walking down the aisle. He walked real fast and went out the church door. About that time two fellers on a back bench got up and eased out the door without hardly any commotion atall.
> (Carter, F. [1976]. *The Education of Little Tree.* Albuquerque: University of New Mexico Press, pp. 156–157)

In addition to nonstandard forms such as "hisself," "he . . . come walking," and "fellers" and unusual lexical phrases such as "disassociated . . . from the bench" and "eased out the door," certain pronunciations such as "fornicatin'" and "atall," collocations such as "wicked ways," and word choices such as "hollered" and "commotion" in the cotext mark this text as an example of localized or regional usage.

Foreign accents are also related to this phenomenon and are one of the most difficult stylistic devices to achieve. Not only must the writer be familiar with the supposed native language of the character, but a delicate balance must be achieved between too little and too much of an accent. Overdoing it can result in an unintentionally humorous effect.

Setting

To seem appropriate and acceptable to the interpreter, all elements of the context, as well as the language in which these are realized, must be believable. It is perhaps paradoxical that actual settings, plots, and so on are rarely believable any more than actual conversational dialogue as transcribed by a linguist seems realistic. Good writers are aware of this need to create believable, rather than real, settings. They may do this in various ways; one of the most famous devices is the Ancient Greek concept of the "three unities," which is commonly employed to define the settings of dramas. According to this concept, time, place, and action are held nearly constant throughout the drama. As a result, the action focuses on a single major event, a very short time period is portrayed, and the location is not greatly changed. A famous and powerfully effective example of this technique is provided by O'Neill's play *A Long Day's Journey into Night*, which takes place in one house during a single day and focuses on the effects that a mother's drug addiction has on herself and on her immediate family. In a corresponding real situation, the action would probably be drawn out over many months or even years. Whereas such a time frame could be depicted easily in a motion picture or novel, for instance, it would lose enormously in the kind of power and impact that the play, with its compression of action into time, is able to provide. Although attempts to violate the three unities in drama have usually met with failure, some notable exceptions exist. One of the most famous of these is Goethe's *Faust*, which spans nearly 2,000 years and moves from Heaven to medieval Germany and then back through time and across the continent to Ancient Greece.

Referring to Genette, Toolan (1988) noted that there are three aspects of time in narratives: *order*, which refers to the actual order of events as contrasted with the order in which they are presented; *duration*, which is concerned with the time required for an event to happen as opposed to the amount of text devoted to the event; and *frequency*, which refers to how often something happens in a story versus how often it is narrated in the text. An interesting example of order used as a structuring device in a literary text is the following passage from Nabokov's *Pnin*:

> (214) His sloppy socks were of scarlet wool with lilac lozenges; his conservative black Oxfords had cost him about as much as all the rest of his clothing (flamboyant goon tie included). Prior to the 1940s, during the staid European era of his life, he had always worn long underwear, its terminals tucked into the tops of neat silk socks, which were clocked, soberly coloured, and held up on his cotton-clad calves by garters. In those days, to reveal a glimpse of that white underwear by pulling up a trouser leg too high would have seemed to Pnin as indecent as showing himself to ladies minus collar and tie; for even when decayed Mme Roux, the concierge of the squalid apartment house in the 16th Arondissement of Paris where Pnin, after escaping from Leninized Russia and completing his college education in Prague, had spent 15 years—happened to come up for the rent while he was without his faux col, prim Pnin would cover his front stud with a chaste hand. All this underwent a change in the heady atmosphere of the New World. Nowadays, at 52, he was crazy about sunbathing, wore sport shirts and slacks, and when crossing his legs would carefully, deliberately, brazenly display a tremendous stretch of bare shin. Thus he might have appeared to a fellow passenger; but except for a soldier asleep at one end and two women absorbed in a baby at the other, Pnin had the carriage to himself.
> (Nabokov, *Pnin*, quoted in Toolan, 1994, pp. 50–51)

The narrative order here is (a) present, (b) prior to the 1940s, (c) escape from Russia, (d) education in Prague, (e) prior to the 1940s, (f) move to the New World, (g) present. However, the actual order of the events is clearly (c) escape from Russia, (d) education in Prague, (b) and (e) prior to the 1940s, (f) move to the New World, (a) and (g) present.

Flashbacks are a popular device in literature, but a less common use of the narrative order technique occurs when the author wishes to provide a glimpse into the future. In such a case, an event that has not yet happened in the narrative is presented together with present events, as in the following example, in which the future events mentioned out of sequence are underlined:

(215) "Speech is silver but silence is golden. Mary, are you listening? What was I saying?"

Mary Macgregor, lumpy, with merely two eyes, a nose and a mouth like a snowman, who was later famous for being stupid and always to blame and who, at the age of twenty-three, lost her life in a hotel fire, ventured, "Golden."

(From Spark, M. *The Prime of Miss Jean Brodie*; quoted in Toolan, 1994, p. 54)

This technique, combined with the stance of the omniscient narrator, can become a dominating force in a narrative. In Isabel Allende's novel *The House of the Spirits*, for instance, it is nothing less than an expression of one of the main themes of the work, namely, that time is an illusion and the universe is eternally repeating itself within one endless moment. The following example is typical of the many *flashforwards* that occur throughout that novel:

(216) When they found them, the little boy was on his back on the floor and Blanca was curled up with her head on the round belly of her new friend. Many years later, they would be found in the same position, and a whole lifetime would not be long enough for their atonement.

(Allende, I. [1982, 1993]. *The House of the Spirits*. New York: Bantam, p. 105)

A more difficult matter of time structuring involves duration. A story that took as long to narrate as the events it depicts would be tedious indeed. At the opposite extreme, compressing an entire lifetime of events into a few words of narrative can have a startling, even humorous effect. Nabokov used this effect to great advantage at the opening of *Laughter in the Dark* in order to focus the reader on the importance of detail in life:

(217) Once upon a time there lived in Berlin, Germany, a man called Albinus. He was rich, respectable, happy; one day he abandoned his wife for the sake of a youthful mistress; he loved, was not loved; and his life ended in disaster.

This is the whole story and we might have left it at that had there not been profit and pleasure in the telling, and although there is plenty

This is the whole story and we might have left it at that had there not been profit and pleasure in the telling, and although there is plenty of space on a gravestone to contain, bound in moss, the abridged version of a man's life, detail is always welcome.
(Nabokov, *Laughter in the Dark*, quoted in Toolan, 1994, p. 57)

Turning to frequency, note that in literature as in life events are often mentioned numerous times. Occasionally, as in Faulkner's *Absalom! Absalom!*, repetition is central to the narrative. In *Absalom! Absalom!*, the murder of Charles Bon by Henry Sutpen is told 39 times by different characters.

Channel and Medium

Although the channel of literature, by the definition given here, is invariably writing, various media are available for its transmission, as for the transmission of many other discourses. Television, the cinema, video, photographs, computer discs, print, speech, audiorecordings, theater, and so on are among the many media available to literature, as Fig. 7.1 suggests. These may often be mixed in different ways, producing innovative effects. Computers may generate slide shows or motion pictures, movies may contain still photographs or written or signed messages, theatrical performances may utilize music

FIG. 7.1. Different media can be used to convey literary works. Reprinted with permission.

or show drawings or posters, and so on. In addition, texts designed for one medium or channel may often be adapted for a different medium or channel. A common instance of this is showing dramas, musicals, films based on novels, recitations of poetry, and so on, on television. Most channels are recordable, and that fact enables the permanence, not only of literature itself, but often of recitations and performances of literary works as well.

Participant–Text Relations

Unlike the other major discourses discussed in Part II, the writers of literature seek primarily to evoke emotional responses from their readers. Characterization, story development, and even the careful use of language are powerful tools for influencing the reader to "suspend disbelief" and to accept what is presented in the narrative as a reality that may seem even more real than the world itself. Often a novel that is moving involves readers so deeply that they wish it would not end but continue on. Occasionally an author responds to such wishes by writing a sequel or a series of novels, continuing the characters, settings, and themes of the original book. Some novelists, such as Robertson Davies, write almost exclusively in series. The cinema, especially in recent times, has begun to provide motion picture series, such as the *Star Wars* series, and has even coined a new word related to series: "prequel," a subsequently produced text, but one that belongs in an earlier, rather than later, position in the series. In this way, an immediate intertext surrounding any single work in the series comes into being.

There are, however, many other kinds of intertexts of particular importance to literature. No other discourse reaches as far into time and across distance for its influences and borrowings. In any culture, the primary religious documents of the society provide what is probably the most powerful intertextual source for literature. In European literature generally, no source has had as profound an influence as the Bible. It is unlikely that any well-known example of European literature exists that has not been directly or indirectly influenced by biblical scripture. Even works by avowed atheists such as Brecht reflect a reactionary stance toward Judeo-Christian ethics. Literature may show its biblical basis merely by depicting a society in which Judeo-Christian values are observed. An example of this is Tolstoy's

Anna Karenina, in which the biblical sin of adultery overcomes a mother's love for her child and leads to suicide—a blatant rejection of Christian teaching. On another level, literature may borrow topics or stories from the Bible and recast them as modern parables. Mark Twain's novel *Puddin'head Wilson* provides an emotionally powerful example of this technique in its retelling of the story of the infant Moses and the Pharaoh's son, set among slaves and their owners in pre–Civil War America. Finally, a work of literature may focus directly on the Bible itself or on some part of it. Any number of books and movies have retold the story of Jesus and other biblical figures, and some, such as Umberto Eco's *The Name of the Rose*, present a mystery that can be solved only through an interpretation of scripture—in this case the Book of Revelation.

Other important sources of intertext providing a background for many literary works are other works by the same author, works by different authors but dealing with the same topics, works based directly on another work, works that incorporate parts of another work, and many nonfictional sources (e.g., histories, biographies, news reports). Because literature spans such a wealth of topics within a culture, almost any cultural artifact is likely to provide an intertext for some literary work. Occasionally, intertexts cross cultures too. The Nigerian author Chinua Achebe's first novel, *Things Fall Apart*, for example, takes its title from Yeats' poem, "The Second Coming," actually quoting the first four lines of the poem in an epigram. David Rubadiri, the Malawian poet, modeled his "Stanley Meets Mutesa" on T. S. Eliot's "The Journey of the Magi."

The second aspect of participant–text relations is the study of production and interpretation. This is of particular interest in literature because of the ambiguity of the dividing line between poetry and prose. For example, some modern poetry, as mentioned earlier, has neither meter nor rhyme, qualities expected in "classical" poetry, and the poet would claim its status as poetry on the basis of reinvented word meanings, unlikely collocations, frequent repetitions, and other kinds of semantic patterning, as in the following example from Walt Whitman's "Song of Myself":

(218) The spotted hawk swoops by and accuses me,
    he complains of my gab and my loitering.

I too am not a bit tamed, I too am untranslatable,
I sound my barbaric yawp over the roofs of the world.

The last scud of day holds back for me,
It flings my likeness after the rest and true as any on the shadow'd
wilds,
It coaxes me to the vapor and the dusk.

I depart as air, I shake my white locks at the runaway sun,
I effuse my flesh in eddies, and drift it in lacy jags.

I bequeath myself to the dirt to grow from the grass I love,
If you want me again look for me under your boot-soles.

You will hardly know who I am or what I mean,
But I shall be good health to you nevertheless,
And filter and fibre your blood.

Failing to fetch me at first keep encouraged,
Missing me one place search another,
I stop somewhere waiting for you.
(Whitman, W. [1986]. *The Complete Poems*, pp. 737–738, Harmondsworth, England: Penguin)

On the other hand, the following prose passage by Virginia Woolf may seem to some interpreters to be even more poetic than some poems:

> (219) What a lark! What a plunge! For so it had always seemed to her, when, with a little squeak of the hinges, which she could hear now, she had burst open the French windows and plunged at Bourton into the open air. How fresh, how calm, stiller than this of course, the air was in the early morning; like the flap of a wave; the kiss of a wave; chill and sharp and yet (for a girl of eighteen as she then was) solemn, feeling as she did, standing there at the open window, that something awful was about to happen.
> (From *Mrs. Dalloway*. Quoted in McNichol, S. [Ed.]. [1992]. *The Collected Novels of Virginia Woolf* [p. 35]. London: Macmillan.)

It is important to note here that only the interpreter can judge whether a literary text is poetry or prose. Indeed, many literary texts may be perceived by various interpreters as containing a mixture of poetry and prose. Furthermore, different interpreters may disagree about whether a specific literary text is primarily poetry or prose.

Purpose and Intent

The primary purpose of literature, as mentioned earlier, is to give pleasure through personal and cultural recognition and discovery. Literature can do this in different ways, however, and these ways define its various genres. To take one example, tragic drama is a genre. Its purpose (following the Ancient Greeks who invented it) is to evoke catharsis in a physically present audience by means of a fatalistic story based on a tragic flaw in the character of a mighty individual. The flaw results, often against the character's wishes, in a horrible and undeserved death, perhaps of someone beloved by the tragic protagonist. An example is Sophocles' *Antigone*, in which the king's own daughter is put to death for violating a blasphemous law decreed by her father in a fit of anger, stubbornness, and pride. To achieve its purpose, tragedy moves traditionally through five acts, each having its own part in the total purpose. At its conclusion, the audience is intended to feel chastened, humbled, emotionally cleansed, and refreshed.

Other relatively pure literary genres include dramatic comedy, novella, sonnet, reggae, fable, situation comedy, and epic. Many literary genres, however, are not "pure," but seem to be a mixture of two or more pure genres. The most famous is the novel, which may be a collection of novellas tied together by topic and characters (like Andric's *The Bridge on the Drina* or Wilder's *The Bridge of San Luis Rey*); a single novella-like plot developed into a longer and more complex work by the addition of characters and subplots (like Craven's *I Heard the Owl Call My Name*); an extended drama written in prose form (like the novels of Hemingway); a very long poem written as prose (like Broch's *The Death of Virgil*); a series of letters or testimonials, possibly by multiple narrators (like the novels of Wilkie Collins); a fictionalized history (like Dickens' *A Tale of Two Cities*); a nonfictional history written as narrative (like Keneally's *Schindler's List*); and many others.

The Ancient Greeks recognized three primary modes of literature: dramatic (characters talk), epic (narrator and characters talk), and lyric (only narrator talks). These are merely different kinds of narration. Although the Greeks maintained that these different kinds of narration should not be mixed in any literary text, very few modern works of literature are completely free of such mixing. Even drama can be effectively presented in epic mode, as shown, among others, by .Brecht in *The Caucasian Chalk Circle* and by Wilder in *Our Town*, where the drama is "told" by a narrator as actors alternately take over the action and then fade out again as the narrator reappears. Indeed, many innovative modern writers, by experimenting with ways of mixing modes and genre, have developed interesting new mixed genres and subgenres capable of fulfilling purposes beyond the reach of the traditional pure genres. Among the most popular of these hybrid-mode genres in modern times are the musical stage play (combining lyric, music, and drama) and the motion picture (combining narrative, epic, and drama).

Because of their complexity and the nature of their purpose, literary genres can rarely be described as a series of moves. There are acts in a play and chapters in a novel, and it is often possible to describe drama as a progression from rising action, to a dramatic turning point, and then to a decline and resolution. However, these are very general descriptions of the parts of the genre and often do not characterize a particular example of the genre. After all, there are novels without chapters, and dramas without action or turning points.

One notable attempt to isolate the moves of narrative was undertaken by the Russian formalist Vladimir Propp (1968), who defined 31 moves of a typical narrative, although many of these are optional. Propp arrived at his conclusions after analyzing hundreds of Russian folktales, and subsequent studies have shown that his scheme applies equally well to other folktales of Europe. The opening move, according to Propp, requires a member of a family to leave home. As the story progresses, later moves introduce a villain, a transformation of the hero, combat, rescue, and so on. The story ends with marriage and the attainment of power. The scheme breaks down, however, when applied to more formal or experimental types of narrative, such as novels or lyric poems, and it does not work well with the narratives of many non-European cultures. Nevertheless, it seems clear that some typical moves are at work in stories, and these bear resemblance to the move structure that characterizes genres.

Topic

One of the most important elements of the situational context of literature is topic. The great topics of literature are those with continuing relevance to a culture that focus on such concepts as love, conflict, nature, religion, death, human relationships, the social order, and so on. Topic is not heavily thematized in narrative or descriptive discourse. Therefore, the process of extracting the topic from the discourse is sometimes a laborious one, requiring a great deal of frame knowledge, a thorough familiarity with cultural and intertextual contexts, and a very close and careful reading of the text. Literature,

---

Practice 66:
Select one of your favorite works of literature. Analyze the cultural and situational contexts of the work in relation to the information given earlier. What contextual elements contribute to your enjoyment and appreciation of the work?

---

unlike informative prose, is capable of allowing a topic to develop gradually. This gives the illusion that the topic is more enduring or more basic than the text. Topic seems to embrace literary texts, whereas informative texts seem to embrace topics. Great literature can give the impression that in touching on a certain topic, it has revealed a part of a greater truth.

THE LANGUAGE OF LITERATURE

The language of literature has undoubtedly been the subject of many more studies than has any other register. The remainder of this chapter touches on some of the more striking features of the literary register. In the process it attempts to indicate the most significant differences between this register and the others examined in the previous chapters.

Reference and Coreference

Tying the various contexts of literature to literary language is the concept of the universe of discourse. Literature as defined here can operate within a greater variety of universes of discourse than can any other register of discourse. Aside from depictions of an everyday world familiar to the reader within a specific culture, literature may depict foreign cultures, other historical periods, nonexistent times and places (fantasy), futuristic societies, and unknown worlds (science fiction). Furthermore, mixtures of these worlds may be created by the writer. For example, P. D. James has created what might be termed a bioethical fiction in her futuristic novel *The Children of Men*, in which some unspecified human misalignment with ethical values results in apparent divine retribution on a universal scale. Such universes of discourse require unusual and complex systems of deixis, reference, and coreference for their portrayal, because the named referents are not only invisible to the interpreter but may not even exist in the universe as people know it. Thus, when James, in *The Children of Men*, refers to the "Warden of England," the interpreter must construct a concept of a person and office that do not exist and never have existed, the closest analogy being the historical Cromwell. Even in novels set in real places and times that may to some extent be familiar to the interpreter, literary deixis presents a problem that clearly differentiates it from the deixis of current situational contexts. In the displaced contexts of literature, deixis takes on an added dimension, giving it one meaning to the characters and another to the interpreter. Consider the following example:

> (220) "This way," Reouf murmured again and led him through the narrow tortuous streets of Scutari's Turkish quarter. . . .
> (Wheatley, D. [n.d.]. *The Eunuch of Stamboul.* London: Hutchinson, p. 69)

For the fictional character accompanying Reouf, "this way" is made clear by reference to the immediate surroundings. For the interpreter, however, a fictional universe of discourse, perhaps based on real experience, must be conceived of before the deictic can have meaning. Sometimes, the interpreter is assisted in delineating the fictional universe by the provision of fictional maps by the author, as in Sigrid Undset's trilogy, *Kristin Lavransdattar.*

Together with its unique approach to deixis, literature has its own characteristic pattern of achieving coreference. Lexical cohesion and personal reference are used in literature with significantly greater frequency than they are in conversation, for example, or in nonnarrative types of discourse. One of the reasons for this characteristic usage is the necessity, mentioned earlier, of making literary dialogue sound real without being real. Another equally important reason, however, is the fact that literature cannot draw on deixis in the same way as situationally related texts. As a result, more reference and coreference ties are needed within the text.

Words and Lexical Units

An important characteristic of literature is its frequent use of unusual meaning relations. There is often ambiguity and contradiction, especially in poetry (as in Wordsworth's line, "The Child is Father of the Man"). Indeed, some writers have specialized in creating a new vocabulary and syntax for their writing. Such writers include poets such as e. e. cummings, novelists such as Burgess (*A Clockwork*

Orange) and, perhaps the most famous example, Joyce. The following example from Joyce's *Finnegan's Wake* (1939) is indicative of the author's love of word play and word creation:

> (221) Now, to compleat anglers, beloved bironthiarn and hushtokan hish-takatsch, join alpha pea and pull loose by dotties and, to be more sparematically logoical, eelpie and paleale by trunkles.
> (Joyce, J. [1939/1992]. *Finnegan's Wake*, p. 296. London: Paladin)

The traditional poem is a form that combines unusual word choices and collocations with sound patterning to achieve cohesion in various ways simultaneously. If, in addition, rules of grammar are violated and nonstandard morphological forms are used, then it is often possible to achieve the impression that language is being made to say more than it is normally thought capable of saying. Consider the following poem by e. e. cummings in which even the rules of English grammar are violated in order to contribute to the poem's cohesiveness:

> (222) love is more thicker than forget
> more thinner than recall
> more seldom than a wave is wet
> more frequent than to fail
>
> it is most mad and moonly
> and less it shall unbe
> than all the sea which only
> is deeper than the sea
>
> love is less always than to win
> less never than alive
> less bigger than the least begin
> less littler than forgive
>
> it is most sane and sunly
> and more it cannot die
> than all the sky which only
> is higher than the sky
>
> ("love is more thicker than forget")
> (Firmage, G. [Ed.] [1991]. *E. E. Cummings: Complete Poems 1904–1962*. New York: Liveright, p. 530)

Not only are words and morphologically deviant lexical units contrasted on meaning alone (thicker–thinner, seldom–frequent, mad–sane, moonly–sunly, etc.), but elements of English grammar are restructured to contribute to the effect. Consider only the first word of each line, and it becomes clear why forms such as "more thinner" occur in the poem: love-more-more-more; it-and-than-is; love-less-less-less; it-and-than-is. The initial words of the lines in Stanzas 2 and 4 are identical. In Stanzas 1 and 3, however, after the word "love" the following initial words contrast "more" with "less" three times. It becomes clear that repetition and antonymy are the primary semantic structuring devices in this poem, and that the structure is drawn with precision.

A further cohesive device, combining with the others in this poem and typical of many poems generally, is the use of nonverbal meanings such as rhymes to enhance the cohesive potential.

Substitution and Ellipsis

Interestingly, although substitution and ellipsis are fairly common in spontaneous conversation, they are used with much less frequency in literary dialogue, as the following example shows:

(223) "What did you see Baker do?"
   "He stooped down and picked up a brick, my Lord. Then he hurled it at the coach driver." Jebb gave us the facts with effective reluctance.
   "Did he hurl it hard?" And although I rumbled a warning "Don't lead, Mr Ballard!" the witness supplied the answer. "He hurled it with full force, my Lord."
   (Mortimer, J. [1990]. Rumpole and the Summer of Discontent. In *Rumpole à la Carte*. London: Penguin, p. 56)

In natural conversation the witness's last statement might be expected to be something like, "Yes, he did, my Lord. Very hard." The literary dialogue has much less ellipsis and substitution than, for example, the actual courtroom dialogue reported in Practice 45 (chap. 2), or even in a typical casual conversation such as in Example 33 in chapter 2. In this regard, notice how ineffectual the latter conversation would be if transposed verbatim into a literary text.

In poetry, ellipsis is indeed used, and with far greater frequency than in conversation or even literary dialogue, as might be expected. Ellipsis is an effective way to remove unneeded words and thus help to achieve the verbal economy that characterizes poetry. The Lawrence poem in Practice 33 (chap. 2) offers a striking example.

Conjunction and Clause Relations

Because of its use of narrative, literature uses temporal conjunction to a much greater extent than additive, adversative, or causal conjunction, which are more commonly found in informative or argumentative discourse. This phenomenon was examined in chapter 1 in connection with Example 16. Look back at that example to remember how time is typically structured in narrative discourse, including literature. Note that although a small amount of additive and causal conjunction also appears in that text, temporal conjunction predominates.

Another use of temporal conjunction in literature, and one that combines effectively with tense and aspect, is the technique of the *flashback*. The flashback is a device of time ordering, as already discussed. In flashbacks, the writer provides a glimpse into events that occurred prior to the current situation of the text. In the following example, the author narrates an event that is happening in the "now" of the story's situational context. She then shifts immediately to a flashback recalling an event of several years before. The only indicators of the flashback are a blank space between the lines, the shift in tense from present to past, and the use of temporal conjunction:

> (224) But as she stretches out on the bed under the open window, as she curls up and lays one hand under the pillow, she reaches out with the other and takes mine. Like a sick person or a child she means me to hold her hand while she sleeps.
>
> When we came back from Italy, Cosette and I, Bell had moved away from Admetus's house and disappeared. . . .
> (Rendell, R. [n.d.]. *The House of Stairs*. London: Penguin, p. 114)

Hypotactic clause relations, as expected, predominate in written narrative as they do in spoken narrative (see Halliday, 1989). Clauses typically depend on prior clauses for meaning. A type of clause connectivity results in which each succeeding clause in the same time order answers a question that could have been generated by the clause that precedes it (see Bruffee, 1980). This pattern of connectivity is illustrated clearly in Example 224. The first clause could result in the question, "What does she do next?" to which the second clause is the answer. The same relation exists between the second and third clause. The third clause could generate the question, "Why does she do this?", which is answered by the last clause in that time order. The time order then shifts to the flashback already discussed, and a new connectivity pattern begins. Note that in narrative clauses, linked as they often are by temporal conjunction, the question, "What does X do next?" is a typical linking question drawing two clauses together.

Linguistic Features

Biber (1988) identified many of the linguistic features of literature. "General fiction" has a high positive score on Biber's Dimension 2 (narrative vs. nonnarrative concerns), a significant negative score on both Dimension 3 (explicit vs. situation-dependent reference) and Dimension 5 (abstract vs. nonabstract information), and a high negative score on Dimension 6 (online informational elaboration). Thus, literature is expected to exhibit the kinds of language associated with narrative concerns, situation dependence, nonabstract information, and planned elaboration. The linguistic features associated with these scores include past-tense verbs, third-person pronouns, perfect aspect (e.g., "has seen," "had seen"), public (speech act) verbs (e.g., "say," "warn," and so on), clauses beginning with "-ing" words (e.g., "looking"), time and place adverbials and other adverbs, and much repetition of words. Because of the way linguistic features group on Biber's factors, the following features are expected to be infrequent in literary discourse: present tense, attributive adjectives, relative clauses, and passive voice.

An examination of almost any piece of literary prose will reveal a high density of the linguistic items listed here. But more importantly, as Biber showed, these features are factored together and do not appear in isolation in literary discourse. Consider the following typical narrative passage:

(225) I let him pull me up from the dark cavern of sleep, and I opened my eyes and looked up at him. He was already dressed, in his dark brown uniform with his name—Tom—written in white letters across his breast pocket. I smelled bacon and eggs, and the radio was playing softly in the kitchen. A pan rattled and glasses clinked; Mom was at work in her element as surely as a trout rides a current. "It's time," my father said, and he switched on the lamp beside my bed and left me squinting with the last images of a dream fading in my brain.

The sun wasn't up yet. It was mid-March, and a chill wind blew through the trees beyond my window. I could feel the wind by putting my hand against the glass. Mom, realizing that I was awake when my dad went in for his cup of coffee, turned the radio up a little louder to catch the weather report. Spring had sprung a couple of days before, but this year winter had sharp teeth and nails and he clung to the south like a white cat. We hadn't had snow, we never had snow, but the wind was chill and it blew hard from the lungs of the Pole.

"Heavy sweater!" Mom called. "Hear?"

"I hear!" I answered back . . .

(McCammon, R. [1991]. *Boy's Life*. New York: Penguin, p. 7)

The following linguistic features, listed previously and identifying the text as narrative, occur in this segment:

past tense	let, opened, looked, was, etc.
third-person pronouns	he, his, her, it
perfect aspect	had sprung
public verbs	said, called, answered
-ing clauses	squinting with the last images, putting my hand against the glass, realizing that I was awake
time/place adverbials	up from the dark cavern, already, in the kitchen, in her element, beside my bed, in my brain, yet, mid-March, through the trees, beyond my window, against the glass, a couple of days before, this year, to the south, never, from the lungs of the Pole
other adverbs	softly, surely, little, hard
word repetition	blew, chill, dark, glass(es), hear, Mom, radio, snow, white, wind

The following features, as predicted, either do not occur here or are infrequent: phrasal coordination, attributive adjectives, relative clauses, and passive voice.

This pattern of linguistic features, so indicative of narrative texts, is not common in other discourses such as news reporting, academic writing, or spontaneous conversation, for example. A quick glance at some of the other examples of discourse in Part II of this book lends support to this fact.

Literal and Nonliteral Meaning

An earlier section looked at some examples of figures of speech as used in literature. In fact, literature depends heavily on figures of speech and makes extensive use of metaphor and simile in particular. Sometimes, an entire work of literature may be metaphorical, as for instance Frost's poem "The Silken Tent," in which the tent, as it is described through a series of metaphors, is ultimately revealed as a woman.

When all the characters and actions of a literary work symbolize general truths and have moral implications, the work is known as an allegory. The *American Heritage Dictionary* defines allegory as a "literary, dramatic, or pictorial device in which characters and events stand for abstract ideas, principles, or forces, so that the literal sense has or suggests a parallel, deeper symbolic sense." A famous example is Melville's *Moby Dick*, an allegory of mankind's destructive quest for the unobtainable. Like all allegories, *Moby Dick* is heavily symbolic. In other words, people and things are at once what they appear to be and symbols of something greater. Virtually every character and object in the work symbolizes someone or something from the Bible. Interpreting such symbols requires inferences, based often on a knowledge of the relevant biblical intertext. To take one example, in *Moby Dick*, Captain Ahab's ship at one point comes across another ship that is retracing its course, searching for its captain and some others who apparently have been lost overboard. The name of this searching ship is the "Rachel," symbolizing the biblical Rachel, who wandered far and wide searching for her children.

Nonverbal Meaning

Finally, consider the use of nonverbal language in literature. Nonverbal meaning in literature is conveyed in two main ways: as sound patterns such as intonations and rhymes, and as nonverbal language, such as descriptions of gestures and expressions. As indicated earlier, lexical repetition and repetition of sound patterns can be used to enhance the cohesive potential of a poem. There are three main kinds of sound repetition in poems. If the repeated sound comes at the beginnings of words, then it is called *alliteration*. Repetition of sounds in the middle of words is *assonance*. And, when the repetition is at the end of words, it is called *rhyme*. All of these appear in the following lines from Poe's "Lenore":

> (226) Ah, broken is the golden bowl!—the spirit flown forever!
> Let the bell toll!—A saintly soul floats on the Stygian river:—
> And, Guy De Vere, hast *thou* no tear?—weep now or never more!
> See! on yon drear and rigid bier low lies thy love, Lenore!
> (Poe, E. "Lenore"; quoted in Durant & Fabb, 1990, p. 131)

Here alliteration is represented by the sets "broken . . . bowl," "flown . . . forever," "saintly . . . soul . . . Stygian," "now . . . never," "low . . . lies . . . love . . . Lenore." End rhyme is provided by "forever . . . river" and "more . . . Lenore." Assonances include "broken . . . golden . . . bowl . . . flown," and "lies thy." A somewhat unusual feature of this poem is the internal rhyme, involving "toll . . . soul" in line 2, "Vere . . . tear" in line 3, and "drear . . . bier" in line 4. Note that there is a further linkage between the internal rhymes of lines 3 and 4.

Together with rhyme, poetry may use complex systems of meter, or stress patterns, to achieve cohesiveness. The most common stress patterns are iambic (unstressed—stressed: "There wás a mán of Thés-saly . . ."), trochaic (stressed—unstressed: "Máry hád a líttle lámb . . ."), anapestic (unstressed—unstressed—stressed: "In a cóign of a cliff between lówland and híghland . . ." [Swinburne]), and dactylic (stressed—unstressed—unstressed: "Híckory, díckory, dóck . . ."). A limerick, for example, is a genre that uses anapestic meter and consists of five lines. Lines 1, 2, and 5 have three tone units whereas lines 3 and 4 have only two each. It is this pattern of meter and tone units that identifies the following famous example as a limerick, even though it is one of the few that do not have rhymes. (It uses an interesting scheme of synonyms instead.)

> (227)   There once was a man of St. Bees
> Who was stung in the arm by a wasp.
> When asked, "Does it hurt?"
> He replied, "No it doesn't;
> It's a good job it wasn't a hornet!"

Obviously, in genres such as drama, nonverbal language and paralanguage are prominent. Lady Macbeth's sleepwalking scene would be unimaginable without the intonations and gestures that depict a sleepwalking person who is going insane. Even nondramatic literature, such as poetry, can be enlivened by the use of effective paralanguage and body language. In both of these examples, however, the success or failure of the performance rests largely with the performer. All a writer can do is to indicate appropriate nonverbal behavior in the stage directions. Hundreds of actors can attempt to follow these directions, but audiences learn to appreciate the few great actors who can bring these directions to life and make them work effectively. Consider, for example, Olivier in his various Shakespearian roles, or Maggie Smith in the film version of *The Prime of Miss Jean Brodie*.

In written prose, nonverbal language is a much more difficult phenomenon to use effectively because of the absence of trained actors. Intonations, gestures, silences, kinesics, and facial expressions must be described for the reader. Writers therefore are faced with an almost insoluble problem. They must avoid writing something like, "Jones seemed to be on the verge of a nervous breakdown," because such an observation interposes the narrator between the character and the reader. The reader, faced with the same evidence, may draw a different conclusion. At the same time, writers must avoid being overly descriptive. Such a technique would slow down the reading and at the same time give it a clinical effect, which, in the wrong situational context, could seem unintentionally humorous, as in the following extract:

> (228) He reddened, clenched his jaw, and his mouth began to twitch. I watched his shoulders stiffen, then slump. Suddenly he looked helpless, a kid playing dress up in the executive suite.
> (Kellerman, J. [1987]. *Over the Edge*. New York: NAL Penguin, p. 135)

The greatest writers of enduring literature use a much more subtle approach, whereby a single gesture or glance can evoke in the reader an entire constellation of the most powerful emotions. Observe how García Márquez, in the final paragraph of his biographical novel *The General in His Labyrinth* (1989), shows Simón Bolívar's final acceptance of his own impending death, which is indicated through a single glance revealing the truth, and a single gesture of resignation, with arms crossed over his chest:

> (229) He examined the room with the clairvoyance of his last days, and for the first time he saw the truth: the final borrowed bed, the pitiful dressing table whose clouded, patient mirror would not reflect his image

---

Practice 67:
Using the work of literature that you selected for Practice 66, analyze its most striking linguistic and nonverbal meanings. What linguistic elements contribute most to your enjoyment and appreciation of the work?

---

again, the chipped porcelain washbasin with the water and towel and soap meant for other hands, the heartless speed of the octagonal clock racing toward the ineluctable appointment at 7 minutes past one on his final afternoon of December 17. Then he crossed his arms over his chest and began to listen to the radiant voices of the slaves singing the 6 o'clock *Salve* in the mills, and through the window he saw the diamond of Venus in the sky that was dying forever, the eternal snows, the new vine whose yellow bellflowers he would not see bloom on the following Saturday in the house closed in mourning, the final brilliance of life that would never, throughout all eternity, be repeated again. (London: Penguin (1989), pp. 267–268)

CONCLUSION: SOME REMAINING QUESTIONS

This chapter brings up some hard questions about literature. These questions are in need of answers and will probably be resolved in one way or another in the near future. And the answers will come from intelligent and informed individuals who must find ways of living and coping in a society whose cultural values are in a state of flux.

First, will literature continue to play the important social and cultural role that it has maintained over the last century or so, as more and more people achieved literacy and were able to acquire books? Is a close reading of literature the most efficient way (as is often claimed) to come to grips with the social, cultural, and political trends of the age; or can this kind of education be achieved more effectively through other, more direct, methods? Does it make sense for writers in emerging nations, in which a majority of people cannot read a European language (if they can read at all) to write their books in French or English, for example, but to address their writing culturally to a local audience, as is frequently done by such writers? Is it possible that literatures in the New Englishes are arising just at a time when fewer and fewer people are interested in reading literature at all, much less literature that can be read only with difficulty by people who are not fluent in the New English dialects? What effect will changes in media preferences have on literature as more and more people spend ever-increasing periods of time in front of television sets and videos? How will changes in leisure-time activities affect the acceptance of literature or determine what kinds of literature will be read? In a fast-paced urban and industrialized society, who will have time to read, when will reading take place, and what kinds of materials will be read? Will the changing roles of women in society have an effect on the market for literature? Will the emphasis on literature in the schools change in response to greater socioeconomic pressures on students to be fit for useful employment on leaving school? Is it reasonable to expect the study of literature to provide students with useful literacy skills required in business or the labor force?

Most people will live through a time when social and cultural changes will provide answers to many of these questions and perhaps redefine the role of art in general. If literature does continue to lose value in modern societies, as many expect, it will be interesting to see what kinds of cultural artifacts step in to fill the gap and to help protect the culture as a whole from the danger of losing identity and social cohesiveness. Throughout the centuries, cultures have proved to be remarkably adaptive and resilient organizations. Undoubtedly, as long as people care deeply about the importance of human communication, our culture will continue to survive and grow.

Conclusion to Part II:
The Power of Discourse

Hopefully, as this part has cultivated skills to analyze the variety of discourses examined, it has also developed and empowered readers as informed interpreters. It has analyzed the characteristics of context and language of five different kinds of discourse to determine the features of appropriateness of each genre and grammaticality of each register. Readers should have developed a sounder understanding of the diagram (shown again here) linking process to product and acceptability to appropriateness and grammaticality. It is easier to understand why it is that some texts seem more acceptable than others do within a particular kind of discourse.

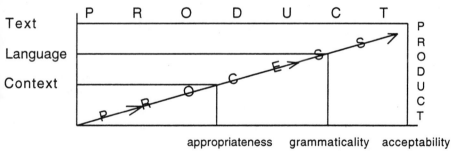

appropriateness   grammaticality   acceptability

Each of the chapters provided the opportunity to examine how the different samples of discourse varieties were "context acceptable," reflecting the basic values of the culture in which they were produced, without violating these values. Each pointed to how differences in the type and roles of discourse participants, leading to often strikingly different relationships between producer(s) and interpreter(s), were reflected in significant differences between the genres examined.

Take, for example, the difference between teachers asking a question to which they know the answer to confirm that students also know it and a doctor questioning a patient to glean important information about a health problem prior to diagnosing and prescribing. Also considered was the impact of different settings on genres and sub-genres, such as the court of law as compared with the classroom. Attention was drawn to the fact that differences in channel may lead to significant variations between subgenres, noticeable, for instance, in the differences between broadcast and print media. It was pointed out that there is great variation in intertext and the other processes of production and interpretation between, for example, the discourse of literature and that of medicine. Also discussed was the significance of purpose in determining differences between the genres examined, such as the purpose of news reporting and the purpose of education. Finally, the overriding significance of topic in determining genre was realized. Remember that no text is ever devoid of context.

These chapters also examined the ways in which each discourse variety was "language acceptable." They considered how reference and coreference are used in different ways in different discourses, such as law and literature. It was shown how subtle differences in the use of words and lexical units distinguish the language of the news media from that of medicine. The discussions pointed out variations in the use of substitution and ellipsis. Also pointed out was how conjunction and clause relations, in particular transitivity, can be used to convey significantly different messages in different contexts. Attention was drawn to the different combinations of linguistic features that lead to significant differences between the registers of, for example, the classroom and wills. The use of nonliteral meanings and implicature to differentiate between, for example, education and literature, was also examined. And, finally, the significance of nonverbal meaning in distinguishing the registers of a variety of subgenres (e.g., the medical interview and cross-examination in a court of law) was revealed.

Thus, the discussion moved from a consideration of appropriate context, *genre*, to an examination of grammatical language, *register*, in order to make understood the overall acceptability of each discourse variety. A product was examined in order to come to a deeper understanding of the process by which that product had been created. In examining the discourse of education, the majority of examples was drawn from a single mathematics lesson. The discussion of the discourse of news media drew on newspaper and broadcast reports on one significant event: the Middle East Peace Accord. The discussion of the discourse of law focused on a Last Will and Testament. Even in the chapters on the discourses of medicine and literature—although examples were taken from many different sources—the examples were still products, not the actual processes. Maybe there was some frustration at the irony of having to analyze products such as these that were fixed, unchanging, and unique, in order to come to grips with the process.

However, with the knowledge purveyed in this book, it should be possible to at least begin analyzing discourses as they are in process—which is further empowering. With practice, readers should find that they are able to think on their feet and respond appropriately in a wide range of encounters in which, previously, they might only have been able to think of the appropriate rejoinder some time after. Confronted with highly persuasive advertisements, they will no longer be taken in so easily. In the classroom, whether as teacher or student, they will become more sensitive to the language of manipulation that for many teachers has become second nature. In the doctor's office, they will be more willing to demand information to which they are entitled, such as the doctor's reasons for a particular diagnosis or the side effects of a drug being prescribed. In reading the newspapers and watching or listening to broadcast news, they will beware of taking everything they read or hear at face value, and realize that journalists very often manipulate the news, consciously or unconsciously. In their encounters with lawyers, they will be able to break through the screen of legal language to achieve a greater understanding of their rights. And in reading novels, short stories, or poetry, or watching plays, they will come to a deeper appreciation of the author's skill.

Even more importantly, it is hoped that everything learned in this book will be applied to the wide variety of genres and registers that have not been examined in any kind of depth here. If readers follow through the process of discourse—from the genre, context acceptability, to the register, language acceptability, to the product of discourse, the text, as outlined in these pages—they will be able to make their own discourses powerful and be a powerful interpreter of others' discourses.

NOTES TO
PART I

CHAPTER 1

The arrangement of chapter 1 is based on Biber (1994), and particularly on his classification scheme for the situation of a genre or register. The Guidelines for Analysis at the end of each section are also based largely on Biber's scheme.

Culture

The structuring of culture in this section is based on Hall (1959/1973), who divides culture into 10 "isolates," which have been subsumed into four. The terms *context of culture* and *context of situation* were coined by the cultural anthropologist Malinowski in 1923. The Ngoni example is reported by Hymes (1989, p. 446). The information from Wierzbicka (1991) is found expecially on pp. 69 and 83. The role-plays from Gumperz and Roberts (1980) are on p. 17, and much of the information on British-Asian cross-cultural miscommunication comes from their work. The Nuer example is from Evans-Pritchard (1948), reported in Wardhaugh (1986, p. 259). Information on Javanese is from Geertz (1960), reported in Wardhaugh (1986, p. 268). Fowler (1985) provided the information on what kinds of words are likely to carry power. The two excerpts from the Thatcher interview are quoted in Fairclough (1989, pp. 174–175). The information on the Nuer and time is reported in Taylor (1980, p. 86). Much of the information on prejudice in discourse is based on van Dijk (1984, esp. pp. 37, 70, 136). Much of the information on speaking about women is based on Wardhaugh (1986, pp. 303–307), and the section on the speech of women is based on Poynton (1989, pp. 69–74) and Coates (1986, pp. 96–118).

Discourse Participants

Information in this section is derived in part from Hymes (1972), Lewis (1972), Brown and Yule (1983), Halliday (Halliday & Hasan, 1989), and Biber (1994).

Producer–Interpreter Relationships

The information on monitoring is based on van Dijk (1977) and Brown and Yule (1983, pp. 58ff.). Some of the information on staging and thematizing is from Brown and Yule (1983). The three types of style discussed here are from van Dijk (1988, pp. 73–74), who included several others as well. These others are not included under style because they are viewed as elements of register. The concept of "frame" is from Minsky (1975). Schank and Abelson (1977) developed the parallel concept of "script." "Scenario" is from Sanford and Garrod (1981). A number of investigators, including Tannen (1980) and R. Anderson et al. (1977), have advanced the concept of "schema." Parts of the discussion of these concepts have been based on the discussion provided by Brown and Yule (1983, pp. 238–250). "Spreading activation" is based on de Beaugrande and Dressler (1981, pp. 88–89), who derived the concept from Collins and Loftus (1975). The information on politeness draws largely on Goffman (1956) and Lakoff (1973).

Setting

Information in this section is derived in part from Hymes (1972), Lewis (1972), Brown and Yule (1983), Halliday (Halliday & Hasan, 1989), and Biber (1994). Much of the information about displaced contexts is from Brown and Yule (1983, pp. 50–58).

Channel

Information in this section is derived in part from Biber (1994).

Participant–Text Relations

The Dunkirk anecdote at the beginning of this section is from Will, G.: Education of the moment. *Washington Post*, 6 May 1984. The three kinds of text are based on Stoddard (1991, pp. 9–12), who also supplied much of the impetus for the ensuing discussion of texture.

Purpose and Intent

Some of the information relevant to genre comes from Swales (1981), Bhatia (1993), Leckie-Tarry (1993), and Hasan (Halliday & Hasan, 1989). Although Swales subsequently modified his position somewhat (cf. Swales, 1990, p. 141), his original description of report introductions has been used for pedagogical reasons.

Topic

Van Dijk (1977, 1988) provided the method of extracting the topic structure, as demonstrated in the section on topic. Also, this section has relied to some extent on Halliday (1989) to differentiate between topic structures in some written and oral texts. Brown (1977), as reported in Brown and Yule (1983, pp. 100–106), is the source of information about paratones, representing topic shifts in oral texts. Some of the ideas on how topic information is structured in texts derives from Bruffee's (1980) classic work on rhetorical structuring in exposition and argumentation. Bruffee's work on common discourse patterns and the relation of clause complexes as information structures remains unsurpassed.

CHAPTER 2

Reference and Coreference

Within the section on reference, the exchange given for the universe of discourse is taken from Brown and Yule (1983, p. 93) and the description of exophora is based on Levinson (1983), Halliday and

Hasan (1976, pp. 18, 33), and M. Chimombo (1986, pp. 13–14). The discussion of deixis is based on Levinson (1983, chap. 2), Halliday and Hasan (1976), and M. Chimombo (1986, chap. 4). The information on coreference is based on Halliday and Hasan (1976, chap. 2), Hill (1979), and M. Chimombo (1986, chap. 4).

Words and Lexical Units

The section on word meanings is based on Leech (1981), Fairclough (1989), and Hurford and Heasley (1983). Within the section on meaning relations, the discussion of Lexical Cohesion is based in part on Halliday and Hasan (1976, chap. 6), Hill (1979), and M. Chimombo (1986, chap. 7). Van Dijk's concept of "lexical stylistics" is discussed in van Dijk (1988, pp. 81–82).

Substitution and Ellipsis

This section is based in part on Halliday and Hasan (1976), Hill (1979), and M. Chimombo (1986).

Conjunction and Clause Relations

The information on conjunction is based in part on Halliday and Hasan (1976), Hill (1979), and M. Chimombo (1986). The section on transitivity is based in part on Tsunoda (1994) and Fowler (1991). Within the section on structure of conversational discourse, the information on turn-taking is drawn in part from Sachs (MS); Sachs et al. (1974), quoted in G. Green (1989, p. 151); and Coulthard (1985, pp. 64–69). The information on adjacency pairs is based in part on Sachs (MS); Coulthard (1985, pp. 69, 70–71); Pomerantz (1978, 1984); Atkinson and Drew (1979); and Levinson (1983, pp. 306–307, 334–335). The table of preferred and dispreferred parts is from Levinson (1983, p. 336). In the section on presequences, some information is drawn from Levinson (1983, pp. 345–356, 363).

Linguistic Features

This section is based largely on Biber (1988). Some of the information on register is drawn from Halliday (Halliday & Hasan, 1989), especially chapter 3. The register specifications were derived from van

Dijk (1988, pp. 71–82) for news discourse, and Bhatia (1993, pp. 105–113) for legal discourse.

Literal and Nonliteral Meaning

The information on idioms depends in part on Nattinger and DeCarrico (1992).

Implicature, Presupposition, and Inference

The section on speech acts depends largely on work by Austin (1962) and Searle (1969, 1976), with passing reference to Hurford and Heasley (1983, p. 259) on direct and indirect illocutions. The section on macrospeech acts relies heavily on van Dijk (1977, pp. 215, 243, 246; van Dijk, 1981, pp. 220, 236ff.). The section on lexical phrases is based largely on Nattinger and DeCarrico (1992). Grice (1975, 1978) provided the basis for conversational implicature. The section on activity types is based on Levinson (1992).

Nonverbal Meaning

This section is in part based on Dittman (1972) as adapted in Druckman et al. (1982, p. 24), although Stubbs did mention in passing the cohesive potential of prosody, paralanguage, and gestures (1983, p. 19). It is also based to some extent on Feyereisen and de Lannoy (1991). The comments introducing prosody and paralanguage are based on Coulthard (1985, chap. 5) and Druckman et al. (1982, pp. 43–44). The information on elements of intonation is based on Brazil (1973, 1975, 1978, 1985a, 1985b) and Coulthard (1985, pp. 100–119; 1992a, pp. 35–49). The contributions by Coulthard are descriptions and elucidations of Brazil's work. The information on silences and other paralinguistic signals is based on Coulthard (1985, chap. 5), Duncan (1972, 1974, and Duncan & Fiske, 1979, all cited in Druckman et al., 1982, pp. 47–50), Edmondson (1981), Fanselow (1987), and Stubbs (1983, p. 22). The information on facial expressions and visual behavior depends on Druckman et al. (1982, pp. 52–64, 73–84). The section on gestures draws on Druckman et al. (1982, pp. 64–73); Feyereisen and de Lannoy (1991); Bavelas et al. (1992); McNeill (1985, pp. 351–352), whom Bavelas et al. cite; and Levy and McNeill (1992).

ANSWERS TO SELECTED PRACTICES IN CHAPTERS 1 AND 2

These Answers to Selected Practices in chapters 1 and 2 are merely suggestions on how to approach the analyses. In many cases, there will be other equally valid answers. Furthermore, often only partial answers are given, pointing you in the right direction but leaving it up to you to complete the answer.

Practice 1

(i) Putting stress on the word "please" sounds rudely insistent, somewhat like "I've told you repeatedly. Didn't you hear me the first time?"

(ii) Falling intonation in most standard varieties of English, including American, expresses impatience or anger.

(iii) The Nambiquara regard a request for information as meaningful only if the purpose of the request is made plain.

Practice 6

The text teaches that the environment is perceived as something to be exploited for capital gain. A capitalist ideology pervades it. Consider how the text would read from an environmentalist point of view.

Practice 7

"Our" refers to the source. The source could include not only the person who wrote the words for the advertisement, but also the illustrator of the advertisement, the editor of *Newsweek*, in which the advertisement appeared, plus the sales manager of the company placing the advertisement.

"Your" refers to the target. The target is the interpreter, reader of the advertisement, who will in this case also be a reader of *Newsweek*. A more specific target would be someone interested in keeping fit.

Practice 8

There are several instances of monitoring here. Take the last one only, "And YOU forgot!"

(a) The principle of analogy has been violated. Students are expected not to forget important instructions given by the teacher.
(b) The monitoring reinforces this principle and with it, the power differential that allows teachers to make such demands on their students.
(c) Try acting out the teacher's role to discover appropriate intonation, gestures, and so on.

Practice 9

(a) Staging here depends largely on a selective reporting of information. Text (i) gives much more information about acts that might have motivated Reagan's actions. Text (ii) pays more attention to innocent victims of the American bombing raid.
(b) In (i) the "we group" is more strongly aligned with the Americans, whereas in (ii) it is more strongly aligned with the Tripoli victims.
(c) Just one example is that the term "mad dog" is applied to Gadaffi in (i), but to Reagan in (ii).

Practice 12

In retelling this story, many people report that the men had gone fishing rather than seal hunting. Sometimes, more modern phrasing replaces the more traditional phrasing of the story. For example, one respondent said that the one man who returned home did so "on the ground of family ties." Some change specific terms to more general ones, such as "war cry" to "yell," and so on. All such changes represent schemata at work.

Practice 16

(a) Just as the phonology of a spoken language describes sounds in terms of the places and manners of articulation that are needed to produce them (e.g., "t"—unvoiced dental plosive), so in a sign language such as ASL, the sign is comprised of elements of the four articulatory parameters: shape of hand, orientation of hand, location, and movement. An interesting difference between the phonologies of spoken and signed languages is the fact that in spoken languages, the sounds must be produced one at a time in a linear order, whereas in a sign language, the articulatory parameters work simultaneously to produce a sign. The morphology and syntax of signed languages work in a manner similar to those of their verbal counterparts.

Practice 17

(a) Most of the factual information referred to in the article appears to have been based directly on Buchanan's speech.

(b) Such expressions as "drawing a hard line between right and wrong," "These Republicans have seen the enemy and it's not them," "charismatic instrument," and so on, indicate a mild ridicule of the Republican viewpoint as expressed by Buchanan and reveal an anti-Republican or anti-Buchanan bias in the news article. In particular, the news writer's manipulation of the term "cross-dressers" indicates bias. In the article, it is used with its usual meaning of "transvestism" or "wearing the clothes of a person of the opposite sex." Buchanan, however, used the term figuratively as a loaded pun, casting doubt on the Democrats' morals without actually accusing them of anything.

(c) Virtually all the key terms in the article require knowledge of an extensive intertext, especially if one is to understand the meaning of these issues in the context of modern American society. In addition, terms such as "holy war" require a knowledge of intertexts referring to recent events in the Middle East or events in the Middle Ages involving crusaders. The expression "These Republicans have seen the enemy, and it's not them" is a take-off on the cartoon character Pogo's famous line, "We have seen the enemy, and it is us."

Practice 21

(a) The obligatory moves seem to be identification, location, description, and facilities/activities.
(b) The moves appear in approximately the same order in which they were introduced.

Practice 22

The moves are indicated with brackets and identified to the left of the text. A move that splits another move is indented. Joined moves are indicated with + between the move names:

I	{Vancouver}
L	{49 13N 123 06W}
E	{A city and port}
L	{in W Canada, in British Columbia on Burrard Inlet and the Fraser River delta.}
H(la)	{Established in 1862}
D(la)	{on a beautiful site}
L	{at the S end of the Coast Mountains,}
D(pr)	{it has developed a rich tourist industry.}
R+E+D(pr)	{Vancouver is Canada's largest Pacific port and railhead.}
D(pr)	{With a large airport, it is a center for international trade and warehousing. It is the commercial and industrial center of British Columbia, important especially for its timber, paper, and associated industries. Other industries include food processing, ship repairing, and fishing.}

D(ln)   {Vancouver has two universities and a thriving cultural life.}

(PP)   {Population (1986): 431 147.}

The L (location) move is split by an E (explanation) move and by the following block of moves to which it is joined. The other moves in this joined block are an H(la) (history of landscape) move and a D(la) (description of landscape) move. The long D(pr) (description of economy) move may appear at first glance to be split by an R (raison d'être) move, but in fact this is not the case. Bearing in mind that strategies themselves are rarely split, we can see that what is actually happening here is that the R move is joining with the D(pr) move, because it contributes to the information about the economy of the city. It is also functioning as the completion of the defective E move at the beginning of the first sentence of the text. An E move in this genre almost always defines the city uniquely, but here that is accomplished only in the second part of the E move.

This rather complex pattern of joined and split moves is more typical of short texts in this genre than of long ones. It is necessitated by the producer's attempt to fit as much information into the short text as possible.

Practice 23

This is a partial advertisement. We know this in part because a personal letter genre would have many more early moves dedicated to exchanging personal and/or intimate information, such as requests to provide information about one's personal well being, one's family, and so on. For more on this text, see Halliday and Hasan (1989, pp. 115–116).

Practice 24

Example 20 thematizes "burns" prominently because it is an information-giving text. Such texts normally thematize their topics. This is not the case with conversations, such as Example 19, in which topics can shift frequently and in which information structuring cannot be planned.

Practice 29

(a) Deictics: your, you. Coreference includes ellipsis, as in "[Imagine one that is] more economical." Additional cohesive links are provided by "one" and the demonstrative "that." There is also a great deal of mystifying comparative reference here: "more economical, more efficient," etc. See chapter 2 for more information on these different kinds of cohesion.

(b) In order to be in a position to manage the discourse that produced this text, the interpreter-target needs to be able to ask "more economical than what?", and so on. Note also the unusual use of "cares for." The semantic meaning of this verb usually does not extend to inanimate actors. By using this expression, the advertiser is trying to invest this machine with a kind of human persona, capable of emotion.

Practice 33

Personal coreference: man . . . he, and so on; clausal ellipsis: Why [must he have a job of some sort]?; clausal substitution: But you said so [that he made chairs]; lexical chain: (chairs—cabinet maker—carpenter—joiner). The pattern of coreference here is typical of conversation, which is what the poem tries to imitate.

Practice 34

Connectedness with the question is lacking. No attempt is made to tie the "answer" to the original question. Texts with similar patterns of unity and connectedness are often produced by young children, and there is a good example of this in Example 44.

Practice 39

"Come through for you," "in a big way," "burn bridges behind you"—these are fixed expressions and are therefore more like Example 71. "Aiming towards," is somewhat variable. Instead of "towards," one could use "at" or "to," for example. This expression is thus more like Example 72. Such lexical phrase frames as "because of ___," "in respect of ___," and "it could be important [not] to ___" are much more open. Not only can large numbers of different words fit the blanks, but even some of the stated words can be replaced by others, though usually with the effect of changing the meaning. The last of these, for example, has such variants as "it might be important," "it can be crucial," and "it could be essential." This type of lexical phrase is sometimes called a sentence builder. It is more like Example 73.

Practice 41

(a) Directive.

(b) Illocutionary force: request; indirect.

(c) Perlocutionary act: he sits beside her.

(d) Felicity conditions: She wants him to sit beside her; he is capable of doing so; he may wish to do so; he believes her to be sincere; and so on.

(e) The wording of this sentence is very effective in establishing the somewhat assertive personality of the character. At the same time, it prevents her from sounding bossy, as she would have if she had used a command.

Practice 43

(a) Nonconventional.

(b) The felicity conditions make it a request.

(c) Different felicity conditions might make it a warning, advice, and so on.

Practice 44

(b) The doctor violates the maxim of quantity in his last turn. This suggests unease with what he is saying. It may be an attempt to convince himself as well as the patient that he is capable of the operation.

Practice 45

Without taking the activity type into consideration, the witness's contributions would seem to violate the maxim of quantity by failing to respond fully to the lawyer's requests for information. The quality maxim is also violated along with sincerity conditions on the speech acts insofar as information is being given that is already known to all participants in the discourse. Only when the activity type (trial at law) is taken into consideration do these apparent pragmatic short-comings disappear. In the context of a trial, the verbal behavior of the lawyer and witness can be understood as part of a standard procedure to introduce factual information into the court record.

Practice 48

The GARDENER is standing in the driveway (Answer to Question (a)).
The gardener is standing in the DRIVEWAY (Answer to Question (b)).

REFERENCES

Adelmann, K. (1993). Millions of human lives could be saved. *Afrika*, *34*(9–10), 22–23.

Ainsworth-Vaughn, N. (1992). Topic transitions in physician–patient interviews: Power, gender, and discourse change. *Language in Society*, *21*, 409–426.

Anderson, B. (1983). *Imagined communities.* New York: Verso.

Anderson, R., Reynolds, R., Schallert, D., & Goetz, E. (1977). Frameworks for comprehending discourse. *American Educational Research Journal*, *14*, 367–381.

Aronsson, K., & Rundstrom, B. (1989). Cats, dogs, and sweets in the clinical negotiation of reality: On politeness and coherence in pediatric discourse. *Language in Society*, *18*, 483–504.

Atkinson, J., & Drew, P. (1979). *Order in court.* London: Macmillan.

Atkinson, J. (1992). Displaying neutrality: Formal aspects of informal court proceedings. In P. Drew & J. Heritage (Eds.), *Talk at work* (pp. 199–211). Cambridge, England: Cambridge University Press.

Austin, J. (1962). *How to do things with words.* Oxford, England: Clarendon.

Bagnall, N. (1993). *Newspaper language.* Oxford, England: Focal Press.

Baker, P. V. (1988). Review of *A dictionary of modern legal usage*, by Bryan A. Garner. *Law Quarterly Review*, *104*, 641–642.

Bakhtin, M. (1981). Discourse in the novel. In M. Holquist (Ed.), *The dialogic imagination.* Austin: University of Texas Press. (Original work published 1934–1935)

Baldwin, J., & French, P. (1990). *Forensic phonetics.* London: Pinter.

Barley, N. (1983). *The innocent anthropologist: Notes from a mud hut.* Harmondsworth, England: Penguin.

Barnes, D., Britton, J., Rosen, H., & the L.A.T.E. (1971). *Language, the learner and the school* (2nd ed.). Harmondsworth, England: Penguin.

Bartlett, F. (1932). *Remembering.* Cambridge, England: Cambridge University Press.

Baum, A. (1990). *Procession: Stories from a Polish past.* Toronto: Childe Thursday.

383

Bavelas, J. B., Chovil, N., Lawrie, D. A., & Wade, A. (1992). Interactive gestures. *Discourse Processes, 15*(4), 469–489.

Beach, W. (1983). Background understandings and the situated accomplishment of conversational telling-expansions. In R. Craig & K. Tracy (Eds.), *Conversational coherence: Form, structure, and strategy* (pp. 196–221). Beverly Hills, CA: Sage.

Beach, W. (1985). Temporal density in courtroom interaction: Constraints on the recovery of past events in legal discourse. *Communication Monographs, 52,* 1–18.

Becker, J. (1975). The phrasal lexicon. In R. Schank & B. Nash-Webber (Eds.), *Theoretical issues in natural language processing* (pp. 70–73). Boston: Bolt, Beranek & Newman.

Bell, A. (1991). *The language of news media.* Oxford, England: Basil Blackwell.

Bellack, A., Bliebard, H., Hyman, R., & Smith, F. (1966). *The language of the classroom.* New York: Teacher's College Press.

Bereiter, C., & Engelmann, S. (1966). *Teaching disadvantaged children in the preschool.* Englewood Cliffs, NJ: Prentice-Hall.

Bergmann, J. (1992). Veiled morality: Notes on discretion in psychiatry. In P. Drew & J. Heritage (Eds.), *Talk at work* (pp. 137–162). Cambridge, England: Cambridge University Press.

Berk-Seligson, S. (1990). *The bilingual courtroom: Court interpreters in the judicial process.* Chicago: University of Chicago Press.

Bernstein, B. (1972). A critique of the concept of compensatory education. In C. Cazden, V. John, & D. Hymes (Eds.), *Functions of language in the classroom* (pp. 135–151). New York: Teacher's College Press.

Bhatia, V. (1984). Syntactic discontinuity in legislative writing and its implications for academic legal purposes. In A. Pugh & J. Ulijn (Eds.), *Reading for professional purposes: Studies and practices in native and foreign languages* (pp. 90–96). London: Heinemann.

Bhatia, V. (1993). *Analysing genre: Language use in professional settings.* London: Longman.

Biber, D. (1988). *Variation across speech and writing.* Cambridge, England: Cambridge University Press.

Biber, D. (1994). An analytical framework for register studies. In D. Biber & E. Finegan (Eds.), *Sociolinguistic perspectives on register* (pp. 31–56). Oxford, England: Oxford University Press.

Biber, D., & Finegan, E. (1989). Styles of stance in English: Lexical and grammatical marking of evidentiality and affect. *Text, 9*(1), 93–124.

Borges, S. (1986). A feminist critique of scientific ideology: An analysis of two doctor–patient encounters. In S. Fisher & A. Todd (Eds.), *Discourse and institutional authority: Medicine, education, and law* (pp. 26–48). Norwood, NJ: Ablex.

Bowman, A. K., & Woolf, G. (1994). Literacy and power in the ancient world. In A. K. Bowman & G. Woolf (Eds.), *Literacy and power in the ancient world* (pp. 1–16). Cambridge, England: Cambridge University Press.

Boyd, S. (1989). From gender specificity to gender neutrality? Ideologies in Canadian child custody law. In C. Smart & S. Sevenhuijsen (Eds.), *Child custody and the politics of gender* (pp. 126–157). London: Routledge & Kegan Paul.

Brazil, D. (1973). *Intonation.* Working Papers in Discourse Analysis No. 2. Mimeo. Birmingham: English Language Research.

Brazil, D. (1975). *Discourse intonation.* Discourse Analysis Monographs No. 1. Birmingham: English Language Research.

Brazil, D. (1978). *Discourse intonation.* Unpublished doctoral dissertation, University of Birmingham.

Brazil, D. (1985a). *The communicative value of intonation.* Birmingham, England: English Language Research.

Brazil, D. (1985b). Phonology: Intonation in discourse. In T. van Dijk (Ed.), *Handbook of discourse analysis* (Vol. 2, pp. 57–75). London: Academic Press.

Brown, G. (1977). *Listening to spoken English.* London: Longman.

Brown, G., & Yule, G. (1983). *Discourse analysis.* Cambridge, England: Cambridge University Press.

Brown, P., & Levinson, S. (1987). *Politeness: Some universals in language usage.* Cambridge, England: Cambridge University Press.

Brown, R., & Gilman, A. (1989). Politeness theory and Shakespeare's four major tragedies. *Language in Society, 18*(2), 159–212.

Bruffee, K. (1980). *A short course in writing.* Boston: Little, Brown.

Burgess, M. (1986). An empirically grounded approach to ethical analysis and social change. In S. Fisher & A. Todd (Eds.), *Discourse and institutional authority: Medicine, education, and law* (pp. 49–77). Norwood, NJ: Ablex.

Byers, P., & Byers, H. (1972). Nonverbal communication and the education of children. In C. Cazden, V. John, & D. Hymes (Eds.), *Functions of language in the classroom* (pp. 3–31). New York: Teacher's College Press.

Byrne, P. S., & Long, B. E. D. (1976). *Doctors talking to patients: A study of the verbal behaviours of doctors in the consultation.* London: HMSO.

Cazden, C., John, V., & Hymes, D. (Eds.). (1972). *Functions of language in the classroom.* New York: Teacher's College Press.

Chafe, W. (1994). *Discourse, consciousness, and time.* Chicago: University of Chicago Press.

Cheater, A. (1990). Investigating women's legal rights and social entitlements: Some suggestions from social anthropology. In *Perspectives on Research Methodology: Women and Law in Southern Africa Research Project* (pp. 79–90). Working paper no. 2. Harare: Women and Law in Southern Africa Research Project.

Chimombo, M. (1986). *Workbook in discourse analysis.* Mimeo. Zomba: Department of English, Chancellor College, University of Malawi.

Chimombo, S., & Chimombo, M. (1996). *The culture of democracy: Language, literature, the arts, and politics in Malawi, 1992–1994.* Zomba, Malawi: WASI Publications.

Clayman, S. (1992). Footing in the achievement of neutrality: The case of news interview discourse. In P. Drew & J. Heritage (Eds.), *Talk at work* (pp. 163–198). Cambridge, England: Cambridge University Press.

Coates, J. (1986). *Women, men and language.* London: Longman.

Collins, A., & Loftus, E. (1975). A spreading-activation theory of semantic processing. *Psychological Review, 82,* 407–428.

Conley, J. M., & O'Barr, W. M. (1990). *Rules versus relationships: The ethnography of legal discourse.* Chicago: University of Chicago Press.

Coulthard, M. (1985). *An introduction to discourse analysis* (2nd ed.). London: Longman.

Coulthard, M. (Ed.). (1992a). *Advances in spoken discourse analysis*. London: Routledge & Kegan Paul.

Coulthard, M. (1992b). Forensic discourse analysis. In M. Coulthard (Ed.), *Advances in spoken discourse analysis* (pp. 242–258). London: Routledge & Kegan Paul.

Coulthard, M. (Ed.). (1994). *Advances in written text analysis*. London: Routledge & Kegan Paul.

Coupland, N., Giles, H., & Wiemann, J. (Eds.). (1991). *Miscommunication and problematic talk*. Newbury Park, CA: Sage.

Craig, R., & Tracy, K. (Eds.). (1983). *Conversational coherence: Form, structure, and strategy*. Beverly Hills, CA: Sage.

Dahl, T. (1987). *Women's law: An introduction to feminist jurisprudence*. Oslo: Norwegian University Press.

de Beaugrande, R., & Dressler, W. (1981). *Introduction to text linguistics*. London: Longman.

de Selincourt, K. (1994). The family way. *WorldAIDS, 36,* 6–10.

Denning, A. (1955). *The road to justice*. London: Stevens.

Dittmann, A. T. (1972). *Interpersonal messages of emotion*. New York: Springer.

Drew, P. (1992). Contested evidence in courtroom cross-examination: The case of a trial for rape. In P. Drew & J. Heritage (Eds.), *Talk at work* (pp. 470–520). Cambridge, England: Cambridge University Press.

Drew, P., & Heritage, J. (Eds.). (1992). *Talk at work*. Cambridge, England: Cambridge University Press.

Druckman, D., Rozelle, R. M., & Baxter, J. C. (1982). *Nonverbal communication: Survey, theory, and research*. Beverly Hills, CA: Sage.

Duncan, S. D., Jr. (1972). Some signals and rules for taking speaking turns in conversations. *Journal of Personality and Social Psychology, 23,* 283–292.

Duncan, S. D., Jr. (1974). On the structure of speaker–auditor interaction during speaking turns. *Language in Society, 2,* 161–180.

Duncan, S. D., Jr., & Fiske, D. W. (1979). Dynamic patterning in conversation. *American Scientist, 67,* 90–98.

Durant, A., & Fabb, N. (1990). *Literary studies in action*. London: Routledge & Kegan Paul.

Edmondson, W. (1981). *Spoken discourse: A model for analysis*. Harlow: Longman.

Edwards, A., & Furlong, V. (1978). *The language of teaching: Meaning in classroom interaction*. London: Heinemann.

Ekman, P., & Friesen, W. V. (1975). *Unmasking the face: A guide to recognising emotions from facial clues*. Englewood Cliffs, NJ: Prentice-Hall.

Enzensberger, H. (1970). The consciousness industry: Constituents of a theory of media. *New Left Review, 64*(November–December).

Evans-Pritchard, E. (1948). Nuer modes of address. *Uganda Journal, 12,* 166–171.

Fairclough, N. (1989). *Language and power*. London: Longman.

Fanselow, J. (1987). *Breaking rules: Generating and exploring alternatives in language teaching*. London: Longman.

Feyereisen, P., & de Lannoy, J-D. (1991). *Gestures and speech: Psychological investigations*. Cambridge, England: Cambridge University Press.

Fisher, S., & Todd, A. (1986). Friendly persuasion: Negotiating decisions to use oral contraceptives. In S. Fisher & A. Todd (Eds.), *Discourse and institutional authority: Medicine, education, and law* (pp. 3–25). Norwood, NJ: Ablex.

Fowler, R. (1985). Power. In T. van Dijk (Ed.), *Handbook of discourse analysis* (Vol. 4, pp. 61–82). London: Academic Press.

Fowler, R. (1986). *Linguistic criticism*. Oxford, England: Oxford University Press.

Fowler, R. (1991). *Language in the news*. London: Routledge & Kegan Paul.

Fox, B. (1987). *Discourse structure and anaphora: Written and conversational English*. Cambridge, England: Cambridge University Press.

Frahm, D., & Frahm, A. (1992). *A cancer battle plan*. Colorado Springs, CO: Pinon Press.

Fraser, B. (1990). Perspectives on politeness. *Journal of Pragmatics, 14*, 219–236.

Fraser, B., & Nolen, W. (1981). The association of deference with linguistic form. *International Journal of the Sociology of Language, 27*, 93–109.

Garratt, G., Baxter, J., & Rozelle, R. (1981). Training university police in Black-American nonverbal behaviors. An application to police-community relations. *Journal of Social Psycology, 113*, 217–229.

Gattegno, C. (1972). *Teaching foreign languages in schools the silent way*. New York: Educational Solutions.

Gayle, J. (1989). The effect of terminology on public consciousness related to the HIV epidemic. *AIDS Education and Prevention, 1*(3), 247–250.

Geertz, C. (1960). *The religion of Java*. Glencoe, IL: The Free Press.

George, H. (1989). Counselling people with AIDS, their lovers, friends and relations. In J. Green & A. McCreaner (Eds.), *Counselling in HIV infection and AIDS* (pp. 69–87). Oxford, England: Blackwell.

Goffman, E. (1956). *The presentation of self in everyday life*. Edinburgh, Scotland: University of Edinburgh Press.

Goodrich, P. (1984a). Law and language: An historical and critical introduction. *Journal of Law and Society, 11*(2), 173–206.

Goodrich, P. (1984b). The role of linguistics in legal analysis. *Modern Law Review, 47*(5), 523–534.

Green, G. (1989). *Pragmatics and natural language understanding*. Hillsdale, NJ: Lawrence Erlbaum Associates.

Green, Janet. (1989). The role of voluntary groups in the community. In J. Green & A. McCreaner (Eds.), *Counselling in HIV infection and AIDS* (pp. 238–247). Oxford, England: Blackwell.

Green, John. (1989). Post-test counselling. In J. Green & A. McCreaner (Eds.), *Counselling in HIV infection and AIDS* (pp. 28–68). Oxford, England: Blackwell.

Greer, S. (1990). The right to silence: A review of the current debate. *Modern Law Review, 53*(6), 709–730.

Grice, H. P. (1975). Logic and conversation. In P. Cole & J. Morgan (Eds.), *Syntax and semantics: Vol. 3. Speech acts* (pp. 41–48). New York: Academic Press.

Grice, H. P. (1978). Further notes on logic and conversation. In P. Cole (Ed.), *Syntax and semantics: Vol. 9. Pragmatics* (pp. 113–127). New York: Academic Press.

Griffin, P., & Mehan, H. (1981). Sense and ritual in classroom discourse. In F. Coulmas (Ed.), *Conversational routine: Explorations in standardized communication situations and prepatterned speech* (pp. 187–213). The Hague: Mouton.

Guest, S. (1985). The scope of the hearsay rule. *Law Quarterly Review, 101,* 385–404.

Gumperz, J. (1982). *Discourse strategies.* Cambridge, England: Cambridge University Press.

Gumperz, J., & Roberts, C. (1980). *Developing awareness skills for interethnic communication.* Singapore: SEAMEO Regional Language Centre.

Hall, E. (1959). *The silent language.* Garden City, NY: Doubleday.

Halliday, M. (1985). *An introduction to functional grammar.* Baltimore: Edward Arnold.

Halliday, M. (1989). *Spoken and written language.* Oxford, England: Oxford University Press.

Halliday, M., & Hasan, R. (1976). *Cohesion in English.* London: Longman.

Halliday, M., & Hasan, R. (1989). *Language, context, and text: Aspects of language in a social-semiotic perspective* (2nd ed.). Oxford, England: Oxford University Press.

Harris, G., & Spark, D. (1993). *Practical newspaper reporting* (2nd ed.). Oxford, England: Focal Press.

Hart, H. L. A. (1961). *The concept of law.* London: Oxford University Press.

Hatch, E. (1992). *Discourse and language education.* Cambridge, England: Cambridge University Press.

Heath, C. (1986). *Body movement and speech in medical interaction.* Cambridge, England: Cambridge University Press.

Heath, C. (1992). The delivery and reception of diagnosis in the general-practice consultation. In P. Drew & J. Heritage (Eds.), *Talk at work* (pp. 235–267). Cambridge, England: Cambridge University Press.

Heckman, P. (1987). Understanding school culture. In J. Goodlad (Ed.), *The ecology of school renewal* (pp. 63–78). Chicago: University of Chicago Press, for the National Society for the Study of Education.

Heller, J. G. (1994). Legal counseling in the administrative state: How to let the client decide. *Yale Law Journal, 103,* 2503–2530.

Henry, A., & Roseberry, R. (1995). *Strategies for selecting EAP vocabulary.* Paper presented at ESP '95 Seminar, Johor Bahru, Malaysia.

Henry, A., & Roseberry, R. (1996). A corpus-based investigation of the language and linguistic patterns of one genre and the implications for language teaching. *Research in the Teaching of English, 30*(4), 472–489.

Henry, A., & Roseberry, R. (in press-a). An evaluation of a genre-based teaching approach. *TESOL Quarterly.*

Henry, A., & Roseberry, R. (in press-b). *Read! Write! Succeed!*

Heritage, J., & Sefi, S. (1992). Dilemmas of advice: Aspects of the delivery and reception of advice in interactions between health visitors and first-time mothers. In P. Drew & J. Heritage (Eds.), *Talk at work* (pp. 359–417). Cambridge, England: Cambridge University Press.

Hertweck, A. (1986). The language of attribution: Constructing rationales for educational placement. In S. Fisher & A. Todd (Eds.), *Discourse and institutional authority: Medicine, eduation, law* (pp. 164–186). Norwood, NJ: Ablex.

Hill, C. (1979). Class notes for course *Applied Linguistics and the Language Teacher.* Teachers College, Columbia University, New York.

Hills, P. (1979). *Teaching and learning as a communication process.* London: Croom Helm.

Hoey, M. (1991). *Patterns of lexis in text.* Oxford, England: Oxford University Press.

Hood, R., with Cordovil, G. (1992). *Race and sentencing.* Oxford, England: Clarendon.

Hornby, P. (1974). Surface structure and presupposition. *Journal of Verbal Learning and Verbal Behavior, 13,* 530–538.

Hulteng, J. (1985). *The messenger's motives: Ethical problems of the news media* (2nd ed.). Englewood Cliffs, NJ: Prentice-Hall.

Hurford, J., & Heasley, B. (1983). *Semantics: A coursebook.* Cambridge, England: Cambridge University Press.

Hyde, K. (1993). *Gender streaming as a strategy for improving girls' academic performance: Evidence from Malawi.* Zomba: University of Malawi Centre for Social Research.

Hymes, D. (1972). Models of the interaction of language and social life. In J. Gumperz & D. Hymes (Eds.), *Directions in sociolinguistics: The ethnography of communication* (pp. 35–71). New York: Holt, Rinehart & Winston.

Hymes, D. (1989). Ways of speaking. In R. Bauman & J. Sherzer (Eds.), *Explorations in the ethnography of speaking* (2nd ed., pp. 433–451). Cambridge, England: Cambridge University Press.

Inglis, F. (1990). *Media theory.* Oxford, England: Blackwell.

Jackson, P. (1968). *Life in classrooms.* New York: Holt, Rinehart & Winston.

James, H. (1971). *Crisis in the courts* (rev. ed.). New York: David McKay.

Johnson, S. (1991). Resistance in print I: Grassroots and alternative publishing, 1980–1984. In K. Tomaselli & P. E. Louw (Eds.), *The alternative press in South Africa* (pp. 191–206). Bellville, South Africa: Anthropos.

Kassler, W. (1985). Testimony: Nutrition education in the undergraduate medical curriculum. *National Academy of Sciences,* 1 January, p. 121.

Kochman, T. (1972). Black American speech events and a language program for the classroom. In C. Cazden, V. John, & D. Hymes (Eds.), *Functions of language in the classroom* (pp. 211–261). New York: Teacher's College Press.

Kress, G. (1985). Ideological structures in discourse. In T. van Dijk (Ed.), *Handbook of discourse analysis* (Vol. 4, pp. 27–42). London: Academic Press.

Kress, G. (1989). *Linguistic processes in sociocultural practice.* Oxford, England: Oxford University Press.

Kübler-Ross, E. (1981). *Living with death and dying.* New York: Macmillan.

Kurzon, D. (1989). Sexist and nonsexist language in legal texts: The state of the art. *International Journal of the Sociology of Language, 80,* 99–113.

Labov, W. (1972). *Language in the inner city.* Philadelphia: University of Pennsylvania Press.

Lakoff, R. (1973). The logic of politeness: Minding your p's and q's. *Proceedings of the Ninth Regional Meeting of the Chicago Linguistics Society* (pp. 292–305). Chicago: University of Chicago Press.

Lakoff, R. (1975). *Language and women's place.* New York: Harper & Row.

Leckie-Tarry, H. (1993). The specification of a text: Register, genre, and language teaching. In M. Ghadessy (Ed.), *Register analysis: Theory and practice* (pp. 26–42). London: Pinter.

Leech, G. (1981). *Semantics* (2nd ed.). Harmondsworth, England: Penguin.

Leith, P. (1991). *The computerised lawyer: A guide to the use of computers in the legal profession.* London: Springer-Verlag.

Levinson, S. (1983). *Pragmatics.* Cambridge, England: Cambridge University Press.

Levinson, S. (1992). Activity types and language. In P. Drew & J. Heritage (Eds.), *Talk at work* (pp. 66–100). Cambridge, England: Cambridge University Press.

Levy, E. T., & McNeill, D. (1992). Speech, gesture, and discourse. *Discourse Processes, 15*(3), 277–301.

Lewis, D. (1972). General semantics. In D. Davidson & G. Harmon (Eds.), *Semantics of natural language* (pp. 169–218). Dordrecht: Reidel.

Longwe, S., & Clarke, R. (1990). Research strategies for promoting law reform: Lessons from changing the law on inheritance in Zambia. *Perspectives on Research Methodology: Women and Law in Southern Africa Research Project* (pp. 180–204). Working paper no. 2. Harare: Women and Law in Southern Africa Research Project.

Looking it up: Dictionaries and statutory interpretation. (1994). *Harvard Law Review, 107*(6), 1437–1453.

Love, A. M., & Roderick, J. A. (1971). Teacher nonverbal communication: The development and field testing of an awareness unit. *Theory into Practice, 10*(4, October), 295–299.

MacDevitt, D. (1989). The custody of children in the Republic of Ireland. In C. Smart & S. Sevenhuijsen (Eds.), *Child custody and the politics of gender* (pp. 190–216). London: Routledge & Kegan Paul.

Malinowski, B. (1923). The problem of meaning in primitive languages. In C. Ogden & I. Richards (Eds.), *The meaning of meaning* (Supplement I). London: Routledge & Kegan Paul.

Marcus, I., & Spiegelman, P. J. (moderators), DuBois, E. C., Dunlap, M. C., Gilligan, C. J., MacKinnon, C. A., & Menkel-Meadow, C. J. (conversants). (1985). The 1984 James McCormick Mitchell Lecture: Feminist discourse, moral values, and the law—A conversation. *Buffalo Law Review, 34*, 11–87.

Martin, J. R. (1993). Literacy in science: Learning to handle text as technology. In M. Halliday & J. R. Martin (Eds.), *Writing science: Literacy and discursive power* (pp. 166–202). London: Falmer Press.

Maynard, D. (1992). On clinicians co-implicating recipients' perspective in the delivery of diagnostic news. In P. Drew & J. Heritage (Eds.), *Talk at work* (pp. 331–358). Cambridge, England: Cambridge University Press.

McCarthy, M. (1994). It, this and that. In M. Coulthard (Ed.), *Advances in written text analysis* (pp. 266–275). London: Routledge & Kegan Paul.

McConnell-Ginet, S. (1978). Intonation in a man's world. *Signs: Journal of Women in Culture and Society, 3*, 541–559.

McDermott, R., & Tylbor, H. (1986). On the necessity of collusion in conversation. In S. Fisher & A. Todd (Eds.), *Discourse and institutional authority: Medicine, education, and law* (pp. 123–139). Norwood, NJ: Ablex.

McHoul, A. (1986). Writing, sexism, and schooling: A discourse-analytic investigation of some recent documents on sexism and education in Queensland. In S. Fisher & A. Todd (Eds.), *Discourse and institutional authority: Medicine, education, and law* (pp. 187–202). Norwood, NJ: Ablex.

McNeill, D. (1985). So you think gestures are nonverbal? *Psychological Bulletin*, *92*, 350–371.

Megarry, R. E. (1959). Copulatives and punctuation in statutes. *Law Quarterly Review*, *75*, 29–32.

Mehan, H. (1986). The role of language and the language of role in institutional decision-making. In S. Fisher & A. Todd (Eds.), *Discourse and institutional authority: Medicine, education, and law* (pp. 140–163). Norwood, NJ: Ablex.

Merritt, M. (1976). On questions following questions (in service encounters). *Language in Society*, *5*(3), 315–357.

Merry, S. E. (1990). *Getting justice and getting even: Legal consciousness among working class Americans*. Chicago: University of Chicago Press.

Mertz, E. (1992). Review essay: Language, law and social meanings: Linguistic/anthropological contributions to the study of law. *Law and Society Review*, *26*(2), 413–445.

Michaels, S., & Collins, J. (1984). Oral discourse styles, classroom interaction and the acquisition of literacy. In D. Tannen (Ed.), *Coherence in spoken and written discourse* (pp. 219–244). Norwood, NJ: Ablex.

Miles, G. (1983). Succession. In C. Blake & G. Huddy (Eds.), *Introduction to legal practice* (Vol. 2, pp. 1–57). London: Sweet & Maxwell.

Minsky, M. (1975). A framework for representing knowledge. In P. Winston (Ed.), *The psychology of computer vision* (pp. 211–277). New York: McGraw-Hill.

Mishler, E. (1984). *The discourse of medicine*. Norwood, NJ: Ablex.

Mitchell, C. (1995, June). *That's funny, you don't look like a teacher*. Department of Curriculum and Teaching Studies Seminar, University of Malawi, Zomba.

Mitchell, G. (1994). The media may devour democracy. *Los Angeles Times*, Sunday 13 March, pp. M2, M6.

Mmensa, K. (1995). Focus on Africa. Interview with Dr. Barbara Sibanda on the BBC World Service at 17.05 GMT, 4 June.

Moon, R. (1994). The analysis of fixed expressions in text. In M. Coulthard (Ed.), *Advances in written text analysis* (pp. 117–135). London: Routledge & Kegan Paul.

Munday, R. (1994). The paradox of cross-examination to credit—simply too close for comfort. *Cambridge Law Journal*, *53*(2), 303–325.

Napley, D. (1983). *The technique of persuasion* (3rd ed.). London: Sweet & Maxwell.

Nattinger, J., & DeCarrico, J. (1992). *Lexical phrases and language teaching*. Oxford, England: Oxford University Press.

Neill, S. (1991). *Classroom nonverbal communication*. London: Routledge.

Nofsinger, R. (1983). Tactical coherence in courtroom conversation. In R. Craig & K. Tracy (Eds.), *Conversational coherence: Form, structure, and strategy* (pp. 243–258). Beverly Hills, CA: Sage.

Nolan, F. (1991). Forensic phonetics. (A review of John Baldwin and Peter French, *Forensic phonetics*. London: Pinter, 1990.) *Journal of Linguistics*, *27*(2, September), 483–493.

Nsirimovu, A. (1994). *Human rights education techniques in schools: Building attitudes and skills*. Port Harcourt, Nigeria: Institute of Human Rights and Humanitarian Law.

Pattanayak, D. (1985). Diversity in communication and languages: Predicament of a multilingual nation state. India, a case study. In N. Wolfson & J. Manes (Eds.), *Language of inequality* (pp. 399–407). Berlin: Mouton.

Pattenden, R. (1991). Should confessions be corroborated? *Law Quarterly Review*, *107*, 317–339.

Peräkylä, A. (1993). Invoking a hostile world: Discussing the patient's future in AIDS counselling. *Text*, *13*(2), 291–316.

Philips, S. (1972). Participant structures and communicative competence: Warm Springs children in community and classroom. In C. Cazden, V. John, & D. Hymes (Eds.), *Functions of language in the classroom* (pp. 370–394). New York: Teacher's College Press.

Philips, S. U. (1986). Some functions of spatial positioning and alignment in the organization of courtroom discourse. In S. Fisher & A. Todd (Eds.), *Discourse and institutional authority: Medicine, education, and law* (pp. 223–233). Norwood, NJ: Ablex.

Phillips, A., & Rakusen, J. (1978). *Our bodies ourselves: A health book by and for women*. London: Penguin.

Pierce, B. (1989). Toward a pedagogy of possibility in the teaching of English internationally: People's English in South Africa. *TESOL Quarterly*, *23*(3), 401–420.

Pomerantz, A. (1978). Compliment responses: Notes on the co-operation of multiple constraints. In J. Schenkein (Ed.), *Studies in the organization of conversational interaction* (pp. 79–112). New York: Academic Press.

Pomerantz, A. (1984). Agreeing and disagreeing with assessments: Some features of preferred/dispreferred turn shapes. In J. Atkinson & H. Heritage (Eds.), *Structures of social action* (pp. 57–101). Cambridge, England: Cambridge University Press.

Postman, N., & Weingartner, C. (1971). *Teaching as a subversive activity*. Harmondsworth, England: Penguin.

Poynton, C. (1989). *Language and gender: Making the difference*. Oxford, England: Oxford University Press

Propp, V. (1968). *The morphology of the folktale*. Austin: University of Texas Press. (Original work published 1928)

Rein, A. (1994). The scope of hearsay. *Law Quarterly Review*, *110*, 431–447.

Renkema, J. (1993). *Discourse studies: An introductory textbook*. Amsterdam: John Benjamins.

Rich, F. (1994). Waking up to one more media hangover. *Daily News*, Thursday 30 June, p. 21

Robinson, J. (1982). *An evaluation of health visiting*. London: Council for the Education and Training of Health Visitors.

Roscoe, A. (1980). Myth, modernism, and medicine. *Medical Quarterly* [Journal of the Medical Association of Malawi], No. 4, 6–11.

Roseberry, R. (1995). A texture index: Measuring texture in discourse. *International Journal of Applied Linguistics*, *5*(2), 205–223.

Rosenberg, J. (1994). The world today. Report for the BBC World Service at 06:15 GMT, 4 October, on the [British] Criminal Justice and Public Order Act, 1994.

Rosenthal, R. (1976). *Experimenter effects in behavioral research* (enlarged ed.). New York: Irvington.

Rosenthal, R., & Jacobson, L. (1968). *Pygmalion in the classroom*. New York: Holt, Rinehart & Winston.

Rwezaura, B. A. (1990). Researching on the law of the family in Tanzania: Some reflections on method, theory and the limits of law as a tool for social change. *Perspectives on Research Methodology: Women and Law in Southern Africa Research Project* (pp. 1–23). Working paper no. 2. Harare: Women and Law in Southern Africa Research Project.

Sachs, H. (MS). Aspects of the sequential organization of conversation. Mimeo.

Sachs, H., Schegloff, E., & Jefferson, G. (1974). A simplest systematics for the organization of turn-taking in conversation. *Language, 50,* 676–735.

Said, E. (1978). *Orientalism.* London: Routledge & Kegan Paul.

Sanders, T., Spooren, W., & Noordman, L. (1992). Toward a taxonomy of coherence relations. *Discourse Processes, 15*(1), 1–35.

Sanford, A., & Garrod, S. (1981). *Understanding written language.* Chichester, England: Wiley.

Schank, R., & Abelson, R. (1977). *Scripts, plans, goals and understanding.* Hillsdale, NJ: Lawrence Erlbaum Associates.

Scheffler, I. (1960). *The language of education.* Springfield, IL: Thomas.

Schlegloff, E. (1972). Notes on a conversational practice: Formulating place. In D. Sudnow (Ed.), *Studies in social interaction* (pp. 75–119). New York: The Free Press.

Schegloff, E. (1979). Identification and recognition in telephone conversation openings. In G. Psathas (Ed.), *Everyday language: Studies in ethnomethodology* (pp. 23–78). New York: Irvington.

Schmidt, H., & Kerr, D. (1987). Motivation for primary health care in Machinga district. *Medical Quarterly* [Journal of the Medical Association of Malawi], *4*(1), 17–21.

Scollon, R., & Scollon, S. (1995). *Intercultural communication: A discourse approach.* Oxford, England: Blackwell.

Searle, J. (1969). *Speech acts.* Cambridge, England: Cambridge University Press.

Searle, J. (1975). Indirect speech acts. In P. Cole & J. Morgan (Eds.), *Syntax and semantics, Vol. 3. Speech acts.* New York: Academic Press.

Searle, J. (1976). The classification of illocutionary acts. *Language in Society, 5*(1), 1–24.

Sharkey, J. (1994, September). Judgment calls. *American Journalism Review,* 18–27.

Short, P. (1994). Report for BBC World Service News at 05:00 hours GMT, 19 July, on The burial of the North Korean Leader, Kim Il-sung, in Pyongyang.

Shuy, R. W. (1986). Some linguistic contributions to a criminal court case. In S. Fisher & A. Todd (Eds.), *Discourse and institutional authority: Medicine, education, and law* (pp. 234–249). Norwood, NJ: Ablex.

Silberman, C. (1973). *Crisis in the classroom: The remaking of American education.* London: Wildwood House.

Simon, A., & Boyer, E. (Eds.). (1970). *Mirrors for behavior: An anthology of classroom observation instruments* (II). Philadelphia: Research for Better Schools Inc.

Sinclair, A. (1976). *The sociolinguistic significance of the form of requests used in service encounters.* Unpublished Diploma dissertation, University of Cambridge.

Sinclair, J., & Coulthard, R. (1975). *Towards an analysis of discourse: The English used by teachers and pupils.* Oxford, England: Oxford University Press.

Smart, C., & Sevenhuijsen, S. (Eds.). (1989). *Child custody and the politics of gender.* London: Routledge & Kegan Paul.

Smith, S., & Smith A. (1990). *Christians in the age of AIDS.* Wheaton, IL: Victor Books.

Söderbergh, R. (1992). *Word, sentence and text.* Paper presented at the Institut Européen pour le Développement des Potentialités de Tous les Enfants.

Sontag, S. (1989). *AIDS and its metaphors.* New York: Farrar, Strauss & Giroux.

Stevick, E. (1974). The riddle of the right method. *English Teaching Forum, 12*(2), 1–5.

Stevick, E. (1980). *Teaching languages: A way and ways.* Rowley, MA: Newbury House.

Stoddard, S. (1991). *Text and texture: Patterns of cohesion.* Norwood, NJ: Ablex.

Stubbs, M. (1976). *Language, schools and classrooms.* London: Methuen.

Stubbs, M. (1983). *Discourse analysis: The sociolinguistic analysis of natural language.* Oxford, England: Basil Blackwell.

Sudnow, D. (1967). *Passing on: The social organization of dying.* Englewood Cliffs, NJ: Prentice-Hall.

Swales, J. (1981). *Aspects of article introductions.* Aston ESP Research Report No. 1, Language Studies Unit, University of Aston. Birmingham: University of Aston.

Swales, J. (1990). *Genre analysis: English in academic and research settings.* Cambridge, England: Cambridge University Press.

Swantz, L. (1990). *The medicine man among the Zaramo of Dar es Salaam.* Uppsala and Dar es Salaam: Scandinavian Institute of African Studies with Dar es Salaam University Press.

Sykes, M. (1985). Discrimination in discourse. In T. van Dijk (Ed.), *Handbook of discourse analysis* (Vol. 4, pp. 83–101). London: Academic Press.

Tannen, D. (1980). A comparative analysis of oral narrative strategies: Athenian Greek and American English. In W. Chafe (Ed.), *The pear stories: Cognitive, cultural and linguistic aspects of narrative production* (pp. 51–87). Norwood, NJ: Ablex.

Tannen, D. (1985). Cross-cultural communication. In T. van Dijk (Ed.), *Handbook of discourse analysis* (Vol. 4, pp. 203–215). London: Academic Press.

Tarutz, J. (1992). *Technical editing: The practical guide for editors and writers.* Reading, MA: Addison-Wesley.

Taylor, R. (1980). *Cultural ways* (3rd ed.). Boston: Allyn & Bacon.

Thom, F. (1989). *Newspeak: The language of Soviet communism.* London: Claridge Press.

Tomaselli, K., & Louw, P. E. (Eds.). (1991). *The alternative press in South Africa.* Bellville, South Africa: Anthropos.

Toolan, M. (1988). *Narrative: A critical introduction.* London: Routledge.

Toolan, M. (1994). Narrative: Linguistic and structural theories. In R. Asher & J. Simpson (Eds.), *The encyclopedia of language and linguistics* (Vol. 5, pp. 2679–2696). Oxford, England: Pergamon.

Torode, B. (1977). Interrupting intersubjectivity. In P. Woods & M. Hammerley (Eds.), *School experience* (pp. 109–128). London: Croom Helm.

Treichler, P. A., Frankel, R. M., Kramarae, C., Zoppi, K., & Beckman, H. B. (1984). Problems and *problems*: Power relationships in a medical encounter. In C. Kramarae, M. Schulz, & W. O'Barr (Eds.), *Language and power* (pp. 62–88). Beverly Hills, CA: Sage.

Tsanga, A. S. (1990). "Action research in Zimbabwe: Two case studies." *Perspectives on Research Methodology: Women and Law in Southern Africa Research Project* (pp. 164–179). Working paper no. 2. Harare: Women and Law in Southern Africa Research Project.

Tsui, A. B. M. (1989). Beyond the adjacency pair. *Language in Society, 18,* 545–564.

Tsunoda, T. (1994). Transitivity. In R. Asher & J. Simpson (Eds.), *The encyclopedia of language and linguistics* (Vol. 9, pp. 4670–4677). Oxford, England: Pergamon.

Tyler, A. (1992). Discourse structure and specification of relationships: A cross-linguistic analysis. *Text, 12*(1), 1–18.

United Nations. (1983). *Basic facts about the United Nations.* New York: United Nations Department of Public Information.

Usher, A. (1992). After the forest: AIDS as ecological collapse in Thailand. *Development Dialogue, 1–2,* 12–49.

van den Hoven, P. J. (1988). Legal argumentation as an illocutionary act complex: A critical analysis. *International Journal for the Semiotics of Law, 1*(1), 29–45.

van Dijk, T. (1977). *Text and context.* London: Longman.

van Dijk, T. (1984). *Prejudice in discourse.* Amsterdam: John Benjamins.

van Dijk, T. (Ed.). (1985). Handbook of discourse analysis (4 vols.). London: Academic Press.

van Dijk, T. (1988). *News as discourse.* Hillsdale, NJ: Lawrence Erlbaum Associates.

Vargas, D. M. (1984). Two types of legal discourse: Transitivity in American appellate opinions and casebooks. *Text, 4*(1–3), 9–30.

Vickers, K. M., Tipler, M. J., & van Hiele, H. L. (1993). *National Curriculum Mathematics Level 6.* Chiddingstone Causeway, Kent: Canterbury Educational Ltd.

Virtanen, T. (1992). Issues of text typology: Narrative—a "basic" type of text? *Text, 12*(2), 293–310.

Waitzkin, H. (1983). *The second sickness: Contradictions of capitalist health care.* New York: The Free Press.

Walker, A. G. (1986). The verbatim record: The myth and the reality. In S. Fisher & A. Todd (Eds.), *Discourse and institutional authority: Medicine, education, and law* (pp. 205–222). Norwood, NJ: Ablex.

Wang, S. (1993). The *New York Times'* and *Renmin Ribao's* news coverage of the 1991 Soviet coup: A case study of international news discourse. *Text, 13*(4), 559–598.

Wardhaugh, R. (1986). *An introduction to sociolinguistics.* Oxford, England: Blackwell.

Watson, D. (1986). Doing the organization's work: An examination of aspects of the operation of a crisis intervention center. In S. Fisher & A. Todd (Eds.),

Discourse and institutional authority: Medicine, education, and law (pp. 91–120). Norwood, NJ: Ablex.

Weaver, P. (1994, Summer). Editocracy. *Forbes MediaCritic, 72–81.*

West, C., & Zimmerman, D. (1985). Gender, language, and discourse. In T. van Dijk (Ed.), *Handbook of discourse analysis* (Vol. 4, pp. 103–124). London: Academic Press.

Whale, J. (1977). *The politics of the media.* London: Fontana/Collins.

Wierzbicka, A. (1991). *Cross-cultural pragmatics: The semantics of human interaction.* Berlin: Mouton de Gruyter.

Wilkins, D. (1976). *Notional syllabuses.* London: Oxford University Press.

Williams, G. (1990). *From fear to hope: AIDS care and prevention at Chikankata Hospital, Zambia.* London: ActionAid.

Williams, G. L. (1945a). Language and the law—I. *Law Quarterly Review, 61,* 71–86.

Williams, G. L. (1945b). Language and the law—II. *Law Quarterly Review, 61,* 179–195.

Williams, G. L. (1945c). Language and the law—III. *Law Quarterly Review, 61,* 293–303.

Williams, G. L. (1945d). Language and the law—IV. *Law Quarterly Review, 61,* 384–406.

Williams, G. L. (1946). Language and the law—V. *Law Quarterly Review, 62,* 387–406.

Williams, R. (1976). *Keywords: A vocabulary of culture and society.* London: Fontana/Croom Helm.

Winefield, H, Chandler, M., & Bassett, D. (1989). Tag questions and powerfulness: Quantitative and qualitative analyses of a course of psychotherapy. *Language in Society, 18,* 77–86.

Winter, E. (1994). Clause relations as information structure: Two basic text structures in English. In M. Coulthard (Ed.), *Advances in written text analysis* (pp. 46–68). London: Routledge & Kegan Paul.

Wodak-Engel, R. (1984). Determination of guilt: Discourse in the courtroom. In C. Kramarae, M. Schulz, & W. O'Barr (Eds.), *Language and power* (pp. 89–100). Beverly Hills, CA: Sage.

Wong, J. (1984). *Using conversational analysis to evaluate telephone conversations in ESL textbooks.* Master's thesis, Applied Linguistics, University of California, Los Angeles.

Woolever, K. R. (1987, March). *Critical thinking and legal discourse.* Paper presented at the 38th Annual Meeting of the Conference on College Composition and Communication, Atlanta, GA. (ERIC Document Reproduction Service No. ED280083)

Yule, G. (1985). *The study of language.* Cambridge, England: Cambridge University Press.

AUTHOR INDEX*

*Note. Page numbers in italics refer to annotated references in the Suggested Readings at the end of each section of chapters 1 and 2.

397

SUBJECT INDEX WITH GLOSSES[*]

A

ACCEPTABILITY: The degree to which a TEXT appears to the INTER-PRETER to have COHERENCE, as well as being grammatically and contextually appropriate, 3–4, *91*, 102–103, 153, 195–196, 367–369
See also APPROPRIATENESS, CONTEXT, GRAMMATICALITY

ACTIVATED FEATURES OF DISCOURSE: Features of DISCOURSE, and especially CONTEXT, that must be recalled by INTERPRETERS from their own knowledge store in order to comprehend a TEXT, 47
See also SPREADING ACTIVATION

ACTIVITY TYPE: An alternate term for the SITUATIONAL CONTEXT, stressing the PURPOSE and the event of the DISCOURSE, 174–176

Address
pronouns of, 10
terms of, 10
See also HONORIFICS, POLITENESS

ADDRESSEE: The person(s) to whom a TEXT is directed. Other INTER-PRETERS besides the ADDRESSEE may be OVERHEARERS and TARGETS, 32–33

AD HOC STYLE: STYLE that is characterized by a particular circum-stance, usually an emotional reaction to an event, 41

ADJACENCY PAIR: In conversation, a turn that consists of two related

---

[*]Note. Definitions are provided for words and phrases appearing in capital letters. Within entries, capitalized words refer to items that are defined elsewhere in the Index. Page numbers in italics refer to Practice exercises on the subject.

utterances, a *first pair part* and a *second pair part*, each spoken by
a different person, 139–141
preferred and dispreferred parts, 139–140
See also INSERTION SEQUENCE, SPEECH ACT

AFFECT: Feeling or emotion, 50
and CONVERSATION STRUCTURE, 142–143
and FACIAL EXPRESSIONS, 183
lexical and grammatical marking of, 148–149
and PARALANGUAGE, 181
in producer–interpreter relationship, 48–50
in speech, 8
and TOPIC, 93
See also POLITENESS

AFFECTIVE MEANING: An ASSOCIATIVE MEANING of a word reflected
in the PRODUCER'S attitude toward the communication,
116–117
and NONVERBAL LANGUAGE, 116, 183
See also AFFECT

AGENT: The subject or initiator of a PROCESS, 120
and FUNCTIONAL TRANSITIVITY, 134–137

ANALOGY, principle of: A principle stating that things will behave
according to people's expectations, based on their experience of
the behavior of similar things, 36

ANAPHORA: In ANAPHORIC COREFERENCE, the NODE precedes the
COHESIVE ELEMENT, 111
gestural, 184
See also ENDOPHORA

APPROPRIATENESS: The degree to which a TEXT conforms to social
norms of behavior that apply to DISCOURSE, 3–4, 5–6, 77,
102–103, 195–196
and INTERPRETER's judgement of TEXT, 74–75
and territory, 26
and time, 26

ARTICULATORY PARAMETERS: The units from which the signs of a
SIGN LANGUAGE are constructed. In American Sign Language, for

example, these consist of shape of the hand, orientation of the hand, location relative to the body, and movement, 63–65

ASPECT: Type of action, for example, progressiveness, as shown mainly through inflections of the verb. For example, "I was singing" as opposed to "I sang." 109–110
See also Time DEIXIS, TENSE

Assertiveness training, 52–53

ASSOCIATIVE MEANING: Meaning of a word based on any or all of the following: CONNOTATIVE, SOCIAL, AFFECTIVE, REFLECTED, and/or COLLOCATIVE MEANING, 116

ASSUMED NORMALITY: A condition that holds only so long as all elements of the SITUATIONAL CONTEXT conform to people's understanding, based on experience, of the world and how it behaves, 36
in the discourse of medicine, 243–244
See also Principle of ANALOGY, Principle of LOCAL INTERPRETATION

B

BODY LANGUAGE: Communication by means of movements of the body, including GESTURES, 184, 186–187
when MONITORING, 36
and STYLE, 40
See also CHANNEL

C

CATAPHORA: In CATAPHORIC COREFERENCE, the NODE follows the COHESIVE ELEMENT, 111
See also ANAPHORA, ENDOPHORA

CHANNEL: Way of communicating, written, oral, NONVERBAL, SIGNed, or any combination of these, 25–27, 61–66, 71
and COOPERATIVE PRINCIPLE, 172
in the discourse of
education, 210–212
law, 281–282
literature, 349–350

E

ELLIPSIS: Omission, from a noun phrase, verb phrase, or clause, of words appearing previously in a text, i.e., SUBSTITUTION by nothing, 127–129, *128*
in the discourse of
    education, 220–222
    literature, 358
guidelines for analyzing, 129
sample analysis, 129–130
suggested reading, 130

EMBEDDING: The containment of one clause within another, 133
of INSERTION SEQUENCES, 140–141
in written discourse, 144

EMBLEMS: GESTURES that substitute for words, 185

ENDOPHORA: The condition that exists when REFERRING EXPRES-SIONS refer both within the text and to the real world, 111
See also ANAPHORA, CATAPHORA, EXOPHORA

ENTAILMENT: A condition that exists when the truth of one PROPOSI-TION requires another PROPOSITION to be true, 123–124
contrasted with PRESUPPOSITION, 160–161
See also HYPONOM

Ethnicity and discourse, 6

Evidentiality, *see* Stance

Evolving contexts, 57, *58*
and CHANNEL, 63

EXOPHORA: Reference from a word or phrase within a TEXT to an entity in the SITUATIONAL CONTEXT surrounding the TEXT, usually by means of DEIXIS, 106
and clause structure, 133
and LEXICAL COHESION, 121
See also ENDOPHORA

EXPRESSIVE: Type of SPEECH ACT consisting of a statement expressing emotion, 163

EXTRAPOSITION: A grammatical structure similar to the passive voice that has the form "it + [linking verb] + ... + clause" (e.g. "it was in the course of ... that"; "it became necessary to ..."). Like passives, EXTRAPOSITIONS appear to distance the producer from the truth of the stated proposition, 136–137, *138*

F

FACE: The projected personal image of a DISCOURSE PARTICIPANT, 48
and PRESEQUENCES, 142–143

FACE THREATENING ACT: An act, including an act of DISCOURSE, that causes TARGETS to feel that their projected personal image has been threatened. The level of tolerance of such acts may vary from culture to culture, 48, 50
See also POLITENESS, POLITENESS PRINCIPLE

FACIAL EXPRESSION: Communication of information, emotion, and so forth, by means of facial features, 7
when MONITORING, 36
in news discourse, 333
See also NONVERBAL LANGUAGE, SIGN LANGUAGE

Factuality
attitudes to
fact, 77–78
imagination, 77–78
speculation, 77–78
See also PURPOSE

FELICITY CONDITIONS: Types of inferences. For example, to be successful, a request to close a door requires that the door is open, that the ADDRESSEE is capable of closing it, and so forth, 162, *165*, *175*
and ACTIVITY TYPE, 175
in the discourse of
education, 174, 175
law, 175
See also SPEECH ACT

FIGURE OF SPEECH: Expression that means something different from what the words contained in it suggest, 155–158, 170
See also METAPHOR, METONYMY, OVERSTATEMENT, SARCASM, SIMILE

FRAME: A type of PARTICIPANTS' KNOWLEDGE consisting of slots and fillers and providing a means of structuring concepts in memory; analogous to SCRIPTS, 43–44, *45*, 46, 62–63
and MACROPROPOSITIONS, 93–94
and LEXICAL COHESION, 121

FUNCTIONAL TRANSITIVITY: The degree to which a verb (the PROCESS) carries its meaning to a direct object (the PATIENT), 134–137
in the discourse of
law, 293–294
news media, 135–136, *138*, 328–329
See also AGENT, NOMINALIZATION

G

Gaze behavior, see VISUAL BEHAVIOR

Gender, 20–23
in the discourse of
law, 271–272
medicine, 238–239

GENRE: A DISCOURSE format designed to accommodate a specific PURPOSE through a series of MOVES. Thus "Letter of Application" is a GENRE whose PURPOSE is to represent a candidate as wanting and being qualified for a specific job. Among the moves typically contained in such a letter are "offering candidature," "promoting the candidate," "referring to an advertisement," and so on. The GENRE is represented as a form of DISCOURSE that derives its APPROPRIATENESS from the SITUATIONAL and CULTURAL CONTEXTS, 4, 6, 37, 78–85, 102–103, 138, 143–144, 367–369
Biber's definition of, 146n
and clause structure, 133
LINGUISTIC FEATURES of, 145–153
and NONLITERAL MEANING, 158
and TOPIC, 86–87

IDEOLOGY: Belief system of a culture, revealed in attitudes to time and territory, among other things, 6, 11–12, 23, *24*, 37–38
and breakdown of grammar, 137
in the discourse of
education, 201–202
law, 272–273
medicine, 234–235
news media, 310
and STAGING, 38
and WORD MEANINGS, 115–117, *118*
See also POWER RELATIONSHIP

IDIOM: A nonvariable LEXICAL PHRASE having NONLITERAL MEAN-ING, 121, 156–158

ILLOCUTIONARY ACT: The act performed by the SPEECH ACT itself, e.g., promise, request, 162–163
See also LOCUTIONARY ACT, PERLOCUTIONARY ACT

ILLOCUTIONARY FORCE: The force of the ILLOCUTIONARY ACT, 163–166, *165*
of LEXICAL PHRASES, 167
See also SPEECH ACT

ILLUSTRATOR: A type of GESTURE that accompanies and contributes to the flow of conversation. These consist of INTERACTIVE GES-TURES and TOPIC GESTURES, 185–186

IMPLICATURE: Inferences derived from TEXT, including CONVEN-TIONAL IMPLICATURE and CONVERSATIONAL IMPLICATURE, 159–176
in the discourse of
education, 225–227
medicine, 259–260
guidelines for analyzing, 176
sample analysis of, 176
suggested reading on, 177
See also COOPERATIVE PRINCIPLE

INDIRECT ILLOCUTION: An ILLOCUTION having a NONLITERAL MEANING, 164–168, *168*
See also MACROSPEECH ACT, SPEECH ACT

INTERTEXT: A part of the SITUATIONAL CONTEXT that draws from other TEXTS of a kind similar to the TEXT under scrutiny to provide additional information, often needed in the interpretation of that TEXT. Includes texts in series, sequels, and prequels, 68–71, 74
in the discourse of
advertising, 71
education, 212–213
law, 282–283
literature, 71, 350–351
medicine, 249–250
news media, 70, 319–320
religion, 68
and GENRE, 81, 83
in reading acquisition, 69

INTONATION: The combined voice features of pitch, pitch movement, loudness, and length, 178–181, *179*
and STAGING, 62
See also CHANNEL, PROSODY

K

KEY: Relative pitch, 178, 179–180
and nonverbal meanings, *180*
See also INTONATION, PROSODY

L

Language, 3–4, 102–192, 367–369
in the discourse of
education, 217–230
law, 287–304
literature, 355–365
medicine, 251–261
news media, 325–334
grammar
of discourse, 3, 104, 145, 149–150
and SPEECH ACTS, 164
of sentence, 3, 104, 145–149, 150
of power

sample analysis of, 158–159
suggested reading on, 159
See also FIGURE OF SPEECH, METAPHOR, METONYMY, OVER-
STATEMENT, SARCASM, SIMILE

Nonverbal communication, see NONVERBAL LANGUAGE

NONVERBAL LANGUAGE: The nonlinguistic elements of DISCOURSE,
related to the five senses, that contribute to the meaning of a TEXT.
These include, among others, FACIAL EXPRESSIONS, VISUAL
BEHAVIOR, BODY LANGUAGE, and GESTURES, 40, 177–188
in ACTIVITY TYPES, 175
in the discourse of
education, 227–229
law, 301–304
literature, 187–188, 362–365
medicine, 260–261
news media, 332–333
guidelines for analyzing, 188–189
of the PRODUCER, 35
sample analysis of, 189–190
and STYLE, 40
suggested reading on, 190
See also PARALANGUAGE, PROSODY, SEMIOTIC COMMUNICA-
TOR, STYLE

NORMAL ORDERING: The tendency of certain kinds of elements to
appear before others in a GENRE. An aspect of TEXTURE, 89–91,
97
in descriptive texts, 97
in the discourse of
education, 91
literature, 90

Normality, see ASSUMED NORMALITY

O

OLD INFORMATION: Information that is restated from earlier in a TEXT,
specifically from the previous clause, 88, 88, 94–95
in the discourse of medicine, 88
and TONE, 179

SIMILE: A FIGURE OF SPEECH in which a comparison is made between two dissimilar things, using "like" or "as," 155

SITUATIONAL CONTEXT: A part of the total CONTEXT that includes those elements of the real world, including time and PLACE, from which a TEXT draws meaning and to which a TEXT is relevant. PRODUCERS and INTERPRETERS may change textual meaning and RELEVANCE by manipulating the elements of the situation in various ways, 3–4, 5–6
and ACTIVITY TYPE, 174–176
and COOPERATIVE PRINCIPLE, 171–172
and EXOPHORA, 106
See also CULTURAL CONTEXT

SOCIAL MEANING: An ASSOCIATIVE MEANING of a word reflected in stylistic choices and in historical usage, 116–117
See also AFFECTIVE MEANING, STYLE

SOLIDARITY: Unity of purpose and interest in a group. Marked linguistically in different ways by different languages, e.g., by pronoun distinctions, 6, 9–13
and stance, 149
See also GROUP STYLE, POWER RELATIONSHIP

SOURCE: Person(s), authorities, institutions, and so on, who are responsible for the content of a TEXT and from whom the concepts behind the TEXT emanate. The SOURCE may or may not be the PRODUCER, 31–32

SPECIFICITY: An impressionistic judgement on the part of the INTERPRETER as to how far a specific clause or short segment of COTEXT is removed from actual examples, anecdotes, statistical information, facts, and so on. At the opposite (general) end of the specificity scale are clauses, for example, that refer to the TOPIC but without providing quantifiable information of any kind. Different GENRES exhibit different patterns of SPECIFICITY, 73, 99–100

Speech
    attitudes to, 8
    and gender, 11, 22
        grammatical features of
            hedges, 20, 163–164
            intonation, 21

T

Tag questions, *see* Discourse markers and Speech and gender, grammatical features of

TARGET: The person(s) whom a TEXT PRODUCER has the INTENT to affect, also called the intended audience, 32–33
See also ADDRESSEE and OVERHEARER

TENSE: Indication of the time of an event or action relative to the moment of speaking, shown in the grammar of a language, usually in inflections of the verb. For example, "I see" as opposed to "I saw," 55–56, 109–110
See also ASPECT, Time DEIXIS

TERMINATION: Pitch with which a speaker begins a falling TONE or ends a rising TONE, 178–181, *181*
See also INTONATION, PROSODY

Territory, 6
    attitudes to, 23, 25–26
    in the discourse of
        education, 209–210
        law, 272–273
        literature, 56–57
        medicine, 237
    grammatical features of, 56
    See also CULTURAL CONTEXT, Evolving contexts, PLACE, SETTING, Time

TEXT: A coherent sequence of symbols, sounds, words, gestures, silences, or any combination of these, intended (but perhaps failing) to communicate information, including emotional states and attitudes. A TEXT may be spoken, written, SIGNed, mimed, or a combination of these. A TEXT consists of the PHYSICAL TEXT, the PRODUCER'S TEXT, and the INTERPRETER'S TEXT, ix, 3–4, 5–6, 34–35, 71–74, 102–104
See also COHERENCE, COTEXT, TEXTURE

TEXT TYPE: Categorization of TEXTS across GENRES on the basis of LINGUISTIC FEATURES rather than PURPOSE and MOVE structure, 148

TEXTUAL SETTING: The setting portrayed in the TEXT, 55–59
See also METATEXTUAL SETTING, SETTING

TEXTURE: The multidimensional mapping of all TEXT components. In particular, CONJUNCTION, CONJUNCTIVE REACH, CONNEC-TIVITY, SPECIFICITY, TOPIC, and TOPIC SHIFT are among the most important devices contributing to TEXTURE. A more mature or more experienced INTERPRETER may perceive a more complex TEXTURE than a less mature INTERPRETER, 72–74, 80, 91, 130–134
See also COHERENCE, COHESION, PARTICIPANTS' KNOWL-EDGE

Thematizing, see STAGING

THEME: The first or most prominent word or words in a phrase, clause, sentence, or longer TEXT, 88, *88*, 94–95
in a PROPOSITION, 122

Time, 6
 attitudes to, 23–26
 in the context of
  education, 200–201, 210
  law, 273
  literature, 346–349
  medicine, 237–238
 DEIXIS, 106, 109–110
 grammatical features of, 55–56
 See also CULTURAL CONTEXT, Evolving contexts, Narrative time, SETTING, Territory, TENSE

TOKEN: The part of the SIGN that is intended to stimulate a sense organ of the INTERPRETER, 103–105
See also ICON, SYMBOL

TONE: Rising or falling pitch, 178–179, *179*
in SIGN LANGUAGE, 66
See also INTONATION, PROSODY

Tone unit, see INTONATION, PROSODY, TONE

TOPIC: What a TEXT is about. The dominant MACROPROPOSITION of a TEXT, 68, 73, 86–100, 102–103, 141
and CONVERSATION STRUCTURE, 141–142